MINORITY DISCOURSES IN GERMANY SINCE 1990

SPEKTRUM: Publications of the German Studies Association
Series editor: David M. Luebke, University of Oregon

Published under the auspices of the German Studies Association, *Spektrum* offers current perspectives on culture, society, and political life in the German-speaking lands of central Europe—Austria, Switzerland, and the Federal Republic—from the late Middle Ages to the present day. Its titles and themes reflect the composition of the GSA and the work of its members within and across the disciplines to which they belong—literary criticism, history, cultural studies, political science, and anthropology.

Recent volumes:

Volume 23
Minority Discourses in Germany since 1990
Edited by Ela Gezen, Priscilla Layne, and Jonathan Skolnik

Volume 22
Beyond Posthumanism
The German Humanist Tradition and the Future of the Humanities
Alexander Mathäs

Volume 21
Feelings Materialized
Emotions, Bodies, and Things in Germany, 1500–1950
Edited by Derek Hillard, Heikki Lempa, and Russell Spinney

Volume 20
Names and Naming in Early Modern Germany
Edited by Marjorie Elizabeth Plummer and Joel F. Harrington

Volume 19
Views of Violence
Representing the Second World War in German and European Museums and Memorials
Edited by Jörg Echternkamp and Stephan Jaeger

Volume 18
Dreams of Germany
Musical Imaginaries from the Concert Hall to the Dance Floor
Edited by Neil Gregor and Thomas Irvine

Volume 17
Money in the German-Speaking Lands
Edited by Mary Lindemann and Jared Poley

Volume 16
Archeologies of Confession
Writing the German Reformation, 1517–2017
Edited by Carina L. Johnson, David M. Luebke, Marjorie E. Plummer, and Jesse Spohnholz

Volume 15
Ruptures in the Everyday
Views of Modern Germany from the Ground
Andrew Bergerson, Leonard Schmieding, et al.

Volume 14
Reluctant Skeptic
Siegfried Kracauer and the Crises of Weimar Culture
Harry T. Craver

For a full volume listing, please see the series page on our website:
http://berghahnbooks.com/series/spektrum

Minority Discourses in Germany since 1990

Edited by
ELA GEZEN,
PRISCILLA LAYNE,
and
JONATHAN SKOLNIK

First published in 2022 by
Berghahn Books
www.berghahnbooks.com

© 2022, 2026 Ela Gezen, Priscilla Layne, and Jonathan Skolnik
First paperback edition published in 2026

All rights reserved. Except for the quotation of short passages
for the purposes of criticism and review, no part of this book
may be reproduced in any form or by any means, electronic or
mechanical, including photocopying, recording, or any information
storage and retrieval system now known or to be invented,
without written permission of the publisher.

Library of Congress Cataloging-in-Publication Data

A C.I.P. cataloging record is available from the Library of Congress
Library of Congress Cataloging in Publication Control Number: 2022004818

British Library Cataloguing in Publication Data

A catalogue record for this book is available from the British Library

EU GPSR Authorized Representative

LOGOS EUROPE, 9 rue Nicolas Poussin, 17000, LA ROCHELLE, France
Email: Contact@logoseurope.eu

ISBN 978-1-80073-427-2 hardback
ISBN 978-1-83695-401-9 paperback
ISBN 978-1-80758-623-2 epub
ISBN 978-1-80073-428-9 web pdf

https://doi.org/10.3167/9781800734272

❦ CONTENTS ❧

List of Illustrations	vii
Introduction. Minority Discourses in Germany since 1990 *Ela Gezen, Priscilla Layne, and Jonathan Skolnik*	1
Chapter 1. Refugee—Migrant—Immigrant *Esther Dischereit*	39
Chapter 2. "Strange Stars" in Constellation: Özdamar, Lasker-Schüler, and the Archive *Kristin Dickinson*	54
Chapter 3. Jewish Tales from a Muslim Turkish Pen: Feridun Zaimoğlu and *Moses* in Oberammergau *Joshua Shelly*	78
Chapter 4. *Schwarz tragen*: Blackness, Performance, and the Utopian in Contemporary German Theater *Olivia Landry*	99
Chapter 5. German Comedians Combating Racist Stereotypes and Discrimination: Oliver Polak, Dave Davis, and Serdar Somuncu *Britta Kallin*	119
Chapter 6. Dialogue and Intersection in German Holocaust Memory Culture: Stumbling Blocks and the Memorial to the Murdered Jews of Europe *Nick Block*	152
Chapter 7. Young, Diverse, and Polyglot: Ilker Çatak and Amelia Umuhire Track the New Urban Sound of Europe *Berna Gueneli*	172
Chapter 8. Subjunctive Remembering; Contingent Resistance: Katja Petrowskaja's *Vielleicht Esther* *Maya Caspari*	196

Chapter 9. Posthumanism and Object-Oriented Ontology in
  Sharon Dodua Otoo's *Synchronicity* and "Herr Gröttrup
  setzt sich hin" 228
  Evan Torner

Chapter 10. Future Narrative as Contested Ground: Emine Sevgi
  Özdamar's "On the Train" and Michael Götting's *Contrapunctus* 247
  Leslie A. Adelson

Index 273

~: ILLUSTRATIONS :~

6.1. Plaque on ground in front of 141A Brunnenstraße commemorating the arrest of Gabriele M., who attempted to flee East Germany in 1989. © Nick Block. — 153

6.2. Plaque on ground in front of 50 Brunnenstraße commemorating the arrest, deportation, and murder of Walter Michaelis in 1943. © Nick Block. — 153

6.3. Daniel Haw's Jewish-inflected cartoon characters Moishe Hundesohn and Ruthi pull up one of the stumbling blocks in "Based on Wilhelm Busch" (2008). © Daniel Haw. — 157

6.4. Henryk Broder attends the fifth anniversary of the Memorial to the Murdered Jews of Europe dressed as one of the concrete stelae. © Zorro Medien. — 159

7.1. Contemplative Aslı (Sanem Öge) crosses the Bosporus on a Ferry in Istanbul in *Fidelity*. Press image, film still, *Fidelity*, Turkey, Germany, 2014. Photo source: Hamburg Media School. — 178

7.2. Contemplative Ayten (Nurgül Yeşilçay) traverses the Bosporus in *The Edge of Heaven*. Film poster. With kind permission of Pyramide Distribution. — 179

7.3. Babiche Papaya (Amanda Mukasonga) talks on the phone about her apartment hunt in Berlin. Screen capture, *Polyglot*, "The Bewerbungsgespräch" (2015). With kind permission of Amelia Umuhire. — 183

7.4. Amanda (Amanda Mukasonga) gets her hair done in Berlin. Screen capture, *Polyglot*, "Le Mal du Pays" (2015). With kind permission of Amelia Umuhire. — 185

Introduction
Minority Discourses in Germany since 1990

ELA GEZEN, PRISCILLA LAYNE, and JONATHAN SKOLNIK

Olga Grjasnowa's 2012 debut novel *Der Russe ist einer, der Birken liebt* (*All Russians Love Birch Trees*) depicts a diverse group of twentysomething friends in Frankfurt am Main.[1] In one conversation, Cem, a gay second-generation Turkish German man, confides in his best friend, Mascha, who, like Grjasnowa, is an immigrant to Germany from a mixed Russian/Jewish family. In school, Cem was subjected to the discriminatory message that higher education was too ambitious for someone like him, but he declares to Mascha that he intends to avenge himself by pursuing a PhD in cultural studies:

> But this little guy here won't screw up. He'll read and understand everything. All the classics of postcolonial studies, critical witness [sic] studies, racism theories, Fanon, Said, Terkessidis.[2]

"Whitness" is neither a typo nor a misprint. It is a slippage that suggests a conflation of critical whiteness studies with Holocaust studies and its emphasis on witnessing. Grjasnowa's novel invites us to consider how a diverse and complex German society compels us to rethink the conceptual models we use to analyze its culture. How do issues of racism, antisemitism and the shadow of the Holocaust, colonial legacies, class, migration, and politics, etc., inform institutional cultures and daily life for a new generation? Do cultural studies and critical race theory methodologies, especially as they have been developed in the Anglophone academy, illuminate analyses in the German-speaking context? Are there points of contact that nonetheless reveal a sometimes uneasy fit?[3]

In March 2017, the University of Massachusetts Amherst hosted a three-day conference, "Minorities and Minority Discourses in Germany since 1990: Intersections, Interventions, Interpolations," which included three keynote speakers, three artist presentations (including a reading by Olga Grjasnowa), along with fifteen papers presented by scholars from Austria, Canada, Germany, the United Kingdom, and across the United States. The goal of the conference was to explore intersections (and divergences) regarding cultural, political, and theoretical interventions by different minorities into German public and political discourse on issues of memory, racism, citizenship, immigration, and history. The rationale for this conference came from our experiences of a disconnect in the field of German studies between scholars who focus on different minoritized groups. Recent conferences of the German Studies Association have included seminars specifically for Black German studies, Turkish German studies, migration studies, and German Jewish studies, but there was no space to develop dialogue across these fields. Such cross-discipline communication seemed especially necessary to us, the conference organizers, since each of us teaches and researches texts that deal with multiple minoritized groups in Germany, in particular Turkish Germans, Black Germans, and Jews in Germany. And while we acknowledge that there are important and necessary differences between these groups' historical experiences and the conceptual paradigms with which they are discussed, it is still pertinent that these scholarly conversations do not happen in isolation from each other.

Indeed, recent cultural productions and longstanding historical conditions call for this kind of expanded scholarly dialogue. For example, literary texts by Turkish German authors like Zafer Şenocak, Emine Sevgi Özdamar, and Feridun Zaimoğlu highlight ways that German Jewish history impacts Turkish Germans' present-day experiences.[4] Many Black Germans also have a unique relationship to German Jewish history, as there are both Black Germans who were interned in concentration camps by the Nazis as well as Black Germans who are biologically related to Nazi perpetrators or Jewish victims.[5] And as a community that has been present in Germany, albeit in small numbers, since at least World War I, Black Germans undoubtedly have a particular perspective on how Germany's changing ethnic landscape has affected society and themselves in particular. German Jewish writing since 1990 has also explored iterations of Jewishness within a more diverse and complex German, European, and global context. If Grjasnowa's abovementioned novel holds up diaspora, migration, and cosmopolitan identities as positive, unifying ideals, then we might consider the provocative title of Maxim Biller's 1990 story "Harlem Holocaust" as a shorthand for the hazards of identities formed by trauma and a negative relation to self and other.[6] Finally, although our conference highlighted these three groups—Black Germans, Turkish Germans, and Jews in Germany, because these are the groups with which our own research intersected most— we also included papers that address how more recent arrivals of refugees, especially since 2015 (largely from Syria, Iraq, and Afghanistan), contribute to and transform these discussions. Thus, one aim of the conference was to explore the continued centrality of Holocaust memory for contemporary discussions of racism, xenophobia, and refugees in German society. For this volume, we have decided to focus the discussion to Black Germans, Turkish Germans, and Jews in Germany so as not to allow the project to become so broad that a cohesive thread is no longer possible to find. We realize that with this, there are other racialized populations in Germany that are not engaged with here, including Sinti and Roma, Vietnamese Germans and other Asian Germans, and Arab Germans. Future volumes will undoubtedly address these and other facets of the radically expanding diversity of today's Germany, and it is our hope that this volume will contribute to this dialogue.[7]

We have limited the papers to those addressing German society since 1990, because we recognize the fall of the Berlin Wall and German unification as a critical juncture in German identity, a point where it started being reframed. These events promised a new historical beginning, yet they also stirred deep discussions about contemporary Germany's relation to the genocidal Nazi past and about ideas of citizenship and belonging in a changing Europe. Migration to Germany (including instances undertaken by People of Color from around the world, as well as Jews and ethnic Germans from the former Soviet Union) demonstrated the economic and cultural vitality and attraction of a changing society, while a wave of murderous attacks on new migrants and Turkish Germans (resident in Germany for two generations) stoked fears. In "blues in schwarz weiss" (blues in black and white, 1990), Black German poet May Ayim writes that "a reunited germany celebrates itself in 1990, without its immigrants, refugees, jewish and black people."[8] In this poem Ayim forges a collective "we" out of immigrants, refugees, Jews, and Black people, united in their experience of exclusion, here in the context of German/German unification. Taking Ayim's poem as its departure, the chapters presented in this volume explore questions including: What are possible intersections (and divergences) between Black German, Turkish German, and German Jewish experiences and aesthetic interventions into German public and political discourses on memory, racism, citizenship, immigration, and history? How do collaborations—such as Esther Dischereit and DJ Ipek's multimedial bilingual performance of *Blumen für Otello* (Flowers for Otello, 2014), the anthologies *Talking Home* (1999) and *aus dem Inneren der Sprache* (from within language, 1995), the repertoire of the Ballhaus Naunynstraße, the rap songs by Advanced Chemistry, and projects of the transethnic activist network Kanak Attack—between artists from various backgrounds reveal, emphasize, and/or communicate similarities, differences, and overlap in their cultural, social, and political positioning?

Following our conference, we aimed to bring together in this edited volume scholars from various fields and disciplines working on minoritized groups in the German context to collaboratively examine conceptual overlap and methodological approaches pertinent to our research. Despite the ways in which their histories, discrimination, and strategies for resistance overlap, ethnic minorities in Germany are often discussed in isolation. Thus, this volume brings together scholars who seek a dialogue that will both investigate differences and similarities but most importantly consider what we as scholars can learn from each other to work toward an understanding of Germanness as plural, culturally diverse, and multilingual. Throughout German history, one can find numerous examples of minoritized groups who seek a dialogue with other groups. But we have chosen the focus of our edited volume to start in 1990, as a seminal moment in German history and a critical juncture when German identity started being reframed. At the same time, we would like to address the current situation in Germany. How have discourses on immigration, integration, and racism shifted, changed, and/or remained consistent in the context of the so-called "refugee crisis"?

One question that many of the contributions gathered here implicitly address is how German studies conceptualizes race as a category for thinking about marginalized communities, especially in view of the histories of colonialism, antisemitism, the Holocaust, and anti-Black racism both before and after 1945. Rita Chin and Heide Fehrenbach have argued powerfully that "race," rendered taboo through the refutation of National Socialism, nonetheless continues to exert a silent grip on the social imagination, as cultural difference is essentialized. Thus, for example, in their view Muslim identity can be seen as "racialized."[9]

Fatima El-Tayeb's critical interventions have also been influential, focusing on processes of marginalization and exclusion of minority and migrant communities. El-Tayeb calls attention to a cyclical process of perpetual othering, through which "Migrantisierte" (those made migrant), those born and raised in Germany but denied status of Germanness, are "externalized as un-German" and thus "eternal newcomers."[10] These processes of "Rassifizierung" (racialization) and "Migrantisierung" (migrantization) are tied to the "refusal of mainstream society to separate itself from the image of a white, Christian Germany" and linked to a "concept of history … in which an essentially-defined, white, Christian Europe always and forcibly remains the norm."[11] Our edited volume is further in conversation with recent *German Quarterly* fora: "Migration Studies" (2017) and "What Is Asian German Studies?" (2020).[12] In the former, Bala Venkat Mani calls to move beyond nationalism to understand connected pasts of exiles, migrants, and refugees.[13] David Gramling and Deniz Göktürk introduce a shift from the question of how Germany is in transit to how migration is framed.[14] Bettina Brandt inquires into possible intersections between Asian German studies and Black German studies through Yoko Tawada's work.[15] Johanna Schuster-Craig focuses on processes of exclusion as shared—albeit not identical—experiences by different minoritized groups, and Veronika Füchtner introduces the concept of a global German studies that would allow for the inclusion of different archives and enable new forms of collaborations, among other things.[16]

The appeal and practices of racialization—as outlined by El-Tayeb above—have a long history in Germany, exacerbated by decades of German politicians refusing to acknowledge immigration as a reality, in addition to politically motivated legal restrictions to asylum laws in the 1990s. And since 2013, racist views and anti-immigrant sentiment have found a new outlet in the populist political party the Alternative für Deutschland (AfD, Alternative for Germany). The AfD has had successful campaigns not only in eastern territories, where distrust of democracy is often linked to a feeling of being left behind by globalization in the new German states formerly belonging to the GDR, but also in prosperous western states like Baden-Württemberg. What has made the AfD a unique threat to a pluralist society is that unlike the Nationaldemokratische Partei Deutschlands (NPD, National Democratic Party of Germany), which was the source of the most extreme racist rhetoric in the 1990s and 2000s and which was embraced by violent groups like skinheads, the AfD attracts a more educated and middle-class following, raising concern that racist beliefs are not only moving closer to the center but are also viewed as a viable, defendable position. And it is not only the AfD's rhetoric, such as that found in offensive campaign posters, that have caused alarm among German critics. The AfD's populist appeal has also contributed to the racist violence that People of Color have faced in increasing numbers since reunification.

Two years ago, there were violent protests led by neo-Nazis that erupted in Chemnitz after two Afghani refugees were alleged to have stabbed Daniel Hillig. Although the media alleged that Hillig was a member of the right-wing hooligan scene, as it turns out he was a Black German "who himself had to suffer from years of right-wing violence and racism."[17] But by failing to report this fact and suggesting that Hillig was right-wing, the German media "played right into the hands of right-wing networks."[18] In response to these events the Initiative Schwarze Menschen in Deutschland (ISD, Initiative of Black People in Germany) published a press release online, noting how the violence recalled what had happened (and been silenced) during the early 1990s. The ISD warned how the dangerous rhetoric of "us" (white Germans) versus "those foreigners" created the circumstances for more violence.[19] Unfortunately, things have only escalated since then. In the past year alone, a recent wave of violence against racialized people in Germany leads one to believe that the popularity of the AfD could make life in Germany even more dangerous for People of Color.

According to the Mediendienst Integration, a free and independent service for journalists, racist criminal offenses increased by 20 percent in 2018 from the previous year, and hate crimes increased by 80 percent from 2016 to 2018.[20] There was an attempted shooting at a synagogue in Halle on 9 October 2019; however, the shooter was unable to enter the synagogue and attacked bystanders instead, killing two and wounding two others. In Hanau, on 20 February 2020, ten victims were shot and killed and five victims injured at two local hookah bars. The choice of the hookah bars and the racist manifesto left behind by the shooter were an indication that these attacks were motivated by Islamophobia. And there have been several individual anti-Black attacks, increasingly against schoolchildren. These recent incidents of violence have not only affected all of the minoritized groups we discuss in this volume but also migrant communities and German politicians who support refugees, such as Walter Lübcke, the district president of Kassel, who was assassinated in front of his house on 2 June 2019 by a right-wing extremist. Two days after the racist attacks in Hanau, the linguist Clara Herdeanu provided a critical commentary on the online platform MiGAZIN (which was founded in 2010 as a forum to *mitgestalten* (shape) discourses on integration and migration) by analyzing formulations used by various media outlets, social networks, and public figures in reference to these murders. The use of terms like *Shisha-Morde* (shisha-murders) and *fremdenfeindlich* (xenophobic), according to Herdeanu, not only trivialize these murders but also hide the racist motives behind them. In a *Deutschlandfunk* interview, the activist and journalist Kübra Gümüşay also noted the continued trivialization of racism in Germany, drawing connections to the NSU killings (referred to as "Döner Morde" [Döner kebab murders] until the discovery of the *Zwickauer Terrorzelle* [Zwickau terror cell]) which remain unsolved to this day.[21]

The Nationalsozialistischer Untergrund (NSU, National Socialist Underground) was perceived and presented as an isolated case instead of being recognized as part of a network and as a manifestation of right-wing violence, terror, and racist ideology, and thus as part of a structural German problem with a historic context, a process that Fatima El-Tayeb characterizes as racial amnesia. In response, with images of the perpetrators of the NSU murders dominating the media, Esther Dischereit collaborated with DJ Ipek on *Klagelieder* (*Lamentations*, 2013), a bilingual text-performance, intended to shift attention away from the perpetrators and to focus on the victims and their families, to publicly address and collectively mourn their loss.[22] In 2014 the *NSU-Komplex auflösen* initiative was founded to "fill a gap in the current public debate." In order to address the *Aufklärung(sverweigerung)* (refusal to investigate), they drafted an "indictment," charging everyone who "condoned, supported, and stood by the NSU,"[23] which was published in 2017. The collaboratively written indictment charges ninety individuals, including neo-Nazis, intelligence officials, police officers, journalists, extremism experts, state officials, and politicians linking past and present attacks and practices and thus demonstrating that right-wing violence and racist ideology are long-standing issues and not isolated incidents without context.

Today, one can observe a resurfacing of a rhetoric and such metaphors as "flood," "invasion," and "full boats"—not limited to Germany—that are connected to racist trends visible in campaigns and parliamentary debates in the context of German foreigner policy in the 1980s and the asylum policy of the 1990s. Furthermore, today's antiracist activism in Germany not only focuses on issues particular to German society but also builds on a decades-long tradition of activism in solidarity with political movements across the globe that can be traced back to antiracist and anti-imperialist protests in the 1960s.[24] A recent example of this were the aftershocks in Germany following the murder of African American George Floyd at the hands of Minneapolis police in May 2020. Floyd was murdered by a white policeman, Derek Chauvin, who kneeled on his neck for eight minutes, ignoring Floyd's cries that he couldn't breathe. In response, demonstrations broke out throughout Germany, from Munich to Berlin, where protesters held signs stating, "I Can't Breathe" and "Black Lives Matter." These demonstrations, attended by a diverse crowd of white Germans and BIPOC, were aimed not only at showing solidarity toward African Americans but also to draw attention to the problem of racial profiling in Germany, which commonly targets BIPOC, in particular refugees and immigrants.[25] As a result of media coverage in Germany and attention received from German politicians, summer 2020 was a landmark moment for addressing racism, anti-Blackness in particular, resulting in concrete actions like the Berlin government's decision to finally rename the offensive M-strasse (M*** Street)[26] to Anton W. Amo Street, a move that activists had long advocated.

While our focus here is on the post-unification period, there are longstanding intersectional collaborative efforts, particularly among artists and activists in Germany, even if the scholarship in Germanistik and German studies has not always reflected this dialogue. The Polynationaler Literatur- und Kunstverein (PoLiKunst, 1980–87) for example, foregrounded political solidarity and cultural resistance bringing together writers and workers from different backgrounds (including Franco Biondi, Rafik Schami, and Suleman Taufiq). The anthology *Entfernte Verbindungen* (Distant connections) was published in 1993 with the goal of "publishing a book about racism and antisemitism in the women's movement."[27] Its editors included several pioneers in the Black German movement like Ika Hügel-Marshall, May Ayim, and owner of the Orlanda Verlag, Dagmar Schultz, as well as Turkish German educator and social worker Gülşen Aktaş. In the volume's introduction, the editors note the fall of the wall as an important conjuncture not only for minorities in the German women's movement but also for coming to terms with Germany's colonial and Nazi past, as well as for situating themselves vis-à-vis contemporaneous international conflicts like the Gulf War. They express a desire to account for a variety of differences among women, whether based on "skin color, religion, class, cultural tradition, education, age, sexual orientation, illness and disabilities."[28] Furthermore, echoing Audre Lorde's push for intersectional feminism, they insist that if one ignores differences or if one can only think in broad categories like "immigrants, Black women, Jewish women, [and] white Christian women," this will only create insecurity and a latent distrust within the women's movement.²⁹ Keeping in the vein of women's activism, the anthology *AufBrüche* (Departures) also consists solely of female voices and is based on the 1997 conference "Marginale Brüche" (Marginal breaks), centering on "cultural productions by migrants, Black, and Jewish women," providing a space for "junior scholars" and artists who "will take up a new self-determined position in political and cultural discourses [conducted by others] about them."³⁰ In addition to contributions by its editors Peggy Piesche, Kader Konuk, and Cathy Gelbin, it featured essays by Yasemin Yildiz and Esther Dischereit, among others. While *Entfernte Verbindungen* and *AufBrüche* may have included some voices of queer, minoritarian women, the volume *Talking Home* (1999), edited by Olumide Popoola and Beldan Sezen, explicitly sought to highlight an understanding of queerness among BIPOC in Germany that went beyond sexuality. In their introduction, Popoola and Sezen define queerness as a characteristic of anyone who resists "bending themselves to accommodate the forces of prescribed social roles."³¹

More recent collaborations between racialized groups in Germany have made a point of not allowing the white German majority to play favorites, offering some groups more recognition than others. For example, in 2011, the edited volume *Manifest der Vielen: Deutschland erfindet sich neu* (Manifest of the many: Germany reimagines itself), appeared as a response to Thilo Sarrazin's best-selling book *Deutschland schafft sich ab* (Germany does away with itself, 2010), in which he claimed that increased immigration from Muslim countries causes the "decay" and "intellectual degeneration" of German society.³² Sarrazin further stated that Muslim immigrants, and in particular Turks and Arabs, are "threatening the cultural and civil balance" in Europe.³³ With contributions by journalists, writers, academics, and actors, including Ilija Trojanow, Naika Foroutan, Feridun Zaimoğlu, Hatice Akgün, and Navid Kermani, the *Manifest der Vielen* focused on their varied experiences in Germany, critically reflecting on notions of *Heimat* (home) and *Fremde* (the foreign), and their "Muslim- oder Nicht-Muslim-Sein" (being Muslim or non-Muslim) in the context of the Sarrazin debate. Sarrazin's book attempted to turn discussions about integration into a debate about "good" and "bad" immigrants. According to Sarrazin, Germany's multicultural society was plagued not by Germans who were racist but by specific immigrant groups who would not integrate. In "Gegenwartsbewältigung" (Overcoming the present), an essay in a different anthology, *Eure Heimat ist unser Albtraum* (Your homeland is our nightmare), the German Jewish author Max Czollek adds to this response to Sarrazin, asking why the burden of integration is always placed solely on the immigrant with no expectation that the white majority also needs to be accommodating.³⁴

Likewise, in *Undeutsch: Die Konstruktion des Anderen in der postmigrantischen Gesellschaft* (Ungerman: The construction of Otherness in the postmigrant society), Fatima El-Tayeb notes a failure on the part of white Germans to see themselves as the problem. Namely, perhaps it is not the case that specific groups like Turkish Germans have difficulty integrating, but more the case that mainstream society prefers those immigrants deemed closest to whiteness, and those immigrants whose presence can be instrumentalized to prove Germany is now good. While white Germans applauded themselves for their generosity toward recent Syrian refugees, they turned a blind eye to the persistence of racism toward Black Germans and People of Color; their support of Syrian refugees had effectively turned them into *good* Germans.[35] Czollek also scrutinizes the functionality of German Jews that allows white Germans to feel good about themselves—"where Jews live, there cannot be National Socialism."[36] In Czollek's view, the essentialist role German Jews are assigned in the German *Gedächtnistheater* (a term he borrows from Michal Bodemann, namely a role that is always already relational to the Holocaust) both ignores diversity among Jews in Germany *and* creates artificial divisions between Jews and other racialized groups: "The overwhelming majority of the Jewish population are also migrants. At the same time, Jews are never mentioned in the context of the current binary determining integrated vs parallel societies."[37] Czollek proposes the concepts of *Desintegration* (de-integration) and "radical diversity" (*radikale Diversität*) as an answer to this essentialism. Czollek's essay is included in an anthology, conceived as "a manifesto against Heimat—a *völkisch*, glorified concept, against which 14 German-speaking authors defend themselves."[38] It was published in 2019 to coincide with the first anniversary of the "Heimatministerium," formerly the German Ministry of Interior, and includes essays by Sasha Marianna Salzmann, Sharon Dodua Otoo, Deniz Utlu, and others.

In recent years we have witnessed the publication of a number of anthologies featuring works by writers from conflict zones, such as *Weg sein—hier sein* (Being away—being here, 2016) and *Das Herz verlässt keinen Ort, an dem es hängt* (The heart never leaves a place it is attached to, 2018), the first anthology of the state-funded project Weiter Schreiben. It was launched in 2017 and provides a platform for artistic creativity and continuity for writers in refuge. At the core of this project are writing partnerships, tandems, between established writers in Germany, such as Olga Grjasnowa, Saša Stanišić, Tanja Dückers, and recently arrived writers, such as Galal Alahmadi, Ramy Al-Asheq, and Lina Atfah.

Theater is another site where issues of migration, contemporary politics, Holocaust memory, and minority perspectives are explored. The Gorki Theater's Studio Я hosted the fourth PostHeimat (After Heimat) network meeting in March 2020. With a focus on exchange, different theater ensembles engage with audiences through discussion, performances, and artists' lectures over a period of four days. Their first meeting was held in 2018 at the Münchner Kammerspiele and focused on "questions of migration, representation, identity, and seeking refuge."[39] The question of "how . . . intersectional and more equitable forms of (transnational) cooperation [can] take place in the theatre and the arts" has been a central question for this network since its inception.[40] The Gorki Theater has adapted several of Olga Grjasnowa's novels for the stage, and the Gorki's in-house director Yael Ronen, an Israeli working in Germany, has also staged her own work. The Ballhaus Naunynstraße Theater in Berlin has also been a center for this kind of engagement. Founded in 1983 in Berlin-Kreuzberg, a neighborhood that has had a large population of Turkish inhabitants since the 1960s, the Ballhaus experienced a revival following unification with its so-called "postmigrant" productions led by Shermin Langhoff. Coined by Langhoff in 2006, *postmigrant theater* "stands for the successful promotion and institutionalization of cultural diversity and global cosmopolitanisation."[41] It has since focused on "cultural education," emphasized "diversity beyond origins," promoted "extended participation," and celebrated "Transkulturalität" (transculturality).[42] In an interview in 2011, Langhoff further stated that theater has to "promote diversity, individual perceptions and autarkic forms of expressions instead of subordination to hegemonic ideology."[43] Postmigrant theater put Turkish German artists on stage, and in the role of writer and director. It told the stories of those who may not have migrated themselves but whose lives had been affected by stories of migration. When Langhoff departed for the Gorki Theater in 2013, her position was taken over by a Black German of Brazilian descent, Wagner Carvalho, who has since led a variety of projects revolving around issues of special interest to the Black German community, including a spectrum covering everything from everyday discrimination to confronting Germany's colonial past. The Ballhaus Naunynstraße is an excellent example of the complicated nature of different racialized groups in Germany working together to change the narrative of the country. While postmigrant theater had previously been criticized as focusing primarily on Turkish German experiences, Carvalho's work at the Ballhaus has allowed for them to address topics like colonialism, anti-Black racism, and the problematic legacy of blackface in German theater. Olivia Landry's chapter in this volume focuses on the Black-centered performances that have taken place at the Ballhaus since this shift, which have expanded the possibilities of postmigrant theater. Landry finds that postmigrant theater shares the following with Black German theater: (1) focusing on histories that have been otherwise made invisible, (2) introducing new techniques to make the space of the theater less a space of cultural exclusion, and (3) depicting the struggle and demand for recognition within the predominantly white institution of German theater.

While the purpose of this volume is to think about the entanglements between different minoritized groups in Germany, we outline brief sketches in the following section, of each respective subdiscipline to offer context for anyone unfamiliar with them. Rather than a comprehensive overview, these histories briefly introduce approaches and discussions in each subdiscipline and reflect on exchanges and intersections between them. With this bigger picture in mind, it becomes clearer in what kinds of discussions our contributors are intervening and how they are expanding on what has come before.

Turkish German Studies

In the past thirty years the critical examination of "the cultural effects of Turkish migration" and "interventions into and beyond national archives of twentieth-century German culture"[44] has been at the core of and shaped Turkish German inquiry.[45] Scholars from a variety of disciplines have addressed questions pertaining to race, nation, ethnicity, religion, diaspora, gender, sexuality, and class and their intersections, with a particular focus on the postwar period: Leslie Adelson, Ayşe Çağlar, Tom Cheesman, Rita Chin, Deniz Göktürk, Randall Halle, Kader Konuk, Nilüfer Kuruyazıcı, Margaret Littler, Ruth Mandel, B. Venkat Mani, Moray McGowan, Jennifer Miller, Esra Özyürek, Azade Seyhan, Levent Soysal, Beverly Weber, Karin Yeşilada, Yasemin Yildiz, Gökçe Yurdakul, to name a few.[46]

A 2015 special issue of *Colloquia Germanica* titled "Turkish-German Texts and Contexts" examined the significance of the Turkish literary archive for Turkish German studies. This special issue emerged out of a panel series that took place at the German Studies Association conference in 2013, with the aim of exploring how Turkish German texts represent interactions of various cultural, national, ethnic, and political contexts. In his contribution to this special issue, David Gramling, while acknowledging the importance of Leslie Adelson's call to (re)situate Turkish German literature within German literature, culture, and history rather than placing it "between two worlds customarily reserved for these authors and their texts,"[47] points to scholars' inattention to "the Turkish national archive, the Ottoman imperial archive," but also "transnational materials that were always too precarious to make it into an archive of any sort."[48] In the same year, a German Studies Association seminar titled "Turkish-German Studies: Past, Present, and Future" brought together scholars from a variety of disciplines and institutions to assess and discuss the current state of scholarship in the interdisciplinary field of Turkish German studies while at the same time providing a forum to identify possible directions for the future—including an examination of Turkish contexts for our research.[49] Taking the Turkish archive into account alongside its German counterpart, seminar contributions and conversations focused on the mutual interaction between both archives (and their ensuing transformation in the process), foregrounding the multidirectionality of exchange.

Scholars have indeed increasingly turned to engage with the Turkish archive, expanding geographical, methodological, and temporal frameworks thus offering new insights into Turkish German exchanges, encounters, and intersections. Mert Bahadır Reisoğlu, for instance, has attended to Turkish literary criticism's importance for Emine Sevgi Özdamar's poetics, Ela Gezen has uncovered the central role of Brecht reception in Turkish theater and Turkish German literature, and Karin Yeşilada has illustrated the significance of Turkish literary traditions for Turkish German poetry. Randall Halle has analyzed the effect of Europeanization on Turkish cinema and its implications for Turkish German film. Kader Konuk has investigated the impact of German Jewish exiles on Turkey's humanist reform movement. Yasemin Yildiz has drawn upon the Turkish student movement in her analysis of translational practices, and Kristin Dickinson has explored a multilingual archive of German and Turkish translated texts. Deniz Göktürk has incorporated the Turkish visual archive into discourses on German unification, and Berna Gueneli has examined intertextual references to the Turkish film genre *Yeşilçam* in Fatih Akın's cinematic oeuvre.[50]

There have been longstanding points of intersection between Turkish German and German Jewish scholarship. This dialogue has been characterized by a continuous and increasing engagement—across a variety of disciplines—with links between Turkish and Jewish (hi)stories, positionalities, and texts through an examination of migrants as subjects of Holocaust memory, of "proximate narratives of Turks, Germans, and Jews," of Muslim and Jewish claims for religious accommodation, of Jewish exiles in Turkey, of shared histories of Jews, Muslims, and Christians in Europe, and of antisemitism and anti-Muslim racism.[51] Beyond scholarly inquiries that bring Turkish German and German Jewish studies into conversation, collaborative exchanges in academic conference settings that involve, among others, Turkish German, Black German, and German Jewish communities have explored questions of (non)citizenship and artistic practice, (post)migrant theater, radical diversity, refuge, diaspora, exile, and memory.

Black German Studies

The first time a significant Black German community came together was in the late nineteenth century, when young sons and a few daughters of royal families from German colonial territories in Africa were sent to Germany for education and job training. Cameroon sent the most people. At the time, Cameroon was one of the few German colonies in Africa, and it remained a so-called German protectorate from 1896 to 1918 when, following World War I, Germany lost its colonies to England and France as part of the Versailles Treaty. Prior to World War I, primarily Cameroonian youth sent to Germany were dispatched with the hope that they could be of service to the colonial administration, helping to negotiate between the Germans and the ethnic tribes. The German organizations that helped facilitate their travels wished to keep these young people isolated, fearing that if they were exposed to bigger cities, their moral and political views would be affected. A further worry was that if Africans were able to congregate, anti-colonial activity and sentiment could grow among them. Nevertheless, despite efforts to suppress the formation of a Black German community, African immigrants were able to maintain familial ties and congregate in spaces like missions. What also made it difficult to sustain a sense of community was the fact that these African immigrants usually had brief stays in Germany and were meant to return to their home country when their schooling and training had ended. However, with the loss of Germany's colonies in 1918, the hundreds of Africans who had come to work and study in Germany suddenly became stateless overnight. The first ever organization for Blacks in Germany, the Afrikanischer Hilfsverein (AH) (African Welfare Association), was formed to help these stateless individuals deal with bureaucracy, establish residency, and find work.[52]

In contrast to this first Black German movement, which was predominantly male, the second Black German movement grew out of the German feminist movement in the mid-1980s and was heavily influenced by the presence of African American feminist poet and activist Audre Lorde. In 1984, Lorde taught classes at the Free University in Berlin, in which several Black German women participated. Lorde encouraged these women to write their own narratives into German history, thus planting the seeds for the collaborative project *Farbe bekennen: Afrodeutsche Frauen auf den Spuren ihrer Geschichte* (1986; *Showing Our Colors*, 1992), which was coedited by May Ayim, Black German scholar Katharina Oguntoye, and white German feminist Dagmar Schultz, whose Orlanda Frauenverlag would publish several of Ayim's poetry volumes. *Farbe bekennen* has become the most foundational text for Black German studies, consisting of "poetry, autobiographical texts, interviews from Afro-German women ranging in age from sixteen to seventy, and [May] Ayim's master's thesis from the University of Regensburg."[53]

The publication of *Farbe bekennen* was followed by several historical studies written by Black Germans about Black German history, such as Katharina Oguntoye's *Eine afrodeutsche Geschichte* (An Afro-German history, 1997), which traces the experience of Black people in Germany from the German Empire (1871–1918) until the period following World War II, and Fatima El-Tayeb's *Schwarze Deutsche* (Black Germans, 2001) which focuses more closely on the years leading up to and including the Third Reich. Both Oguntoye's and El-Tayeb's books focus primarily on three important moments in Black German history. First is the period of German colonialism (1890–1918), during which Africans from German colonies traveled to Germany to study and work. The second moment is the period following World War I—the Weimar era

(1918–33)—when many of these individuals became stateless and remained in Germany attempting to establish a life there. What is also significant about the Weimar period is that following World War I, when there were French stationed in the Rhineland area as part of the Versailles Treaty, the French also deployed between twenty-five and forty thousand colonial soldiers from Africa and Asia in the area.[54] As a result of fraternization between local white German women and the colonial soldiers, it is estimated that between five and six hundred Black German children were born during this time.[55] The third moment is the Nazi dictatorship (1933–45), during which Hitler and the Nazis targeted Black Germans as "non-Aryans" and subjected them to discrimination, forced sterilization, internment, forced labor, and murder.

A fourth, important historical moment within Black German history is the postwar era of the late 1940s and 1950s, during which around four thousand Black German children were born to unions of white German women and African American soldiers stationed in the country. Yara-Collette Lemke Muniz de Faria's book *Zwischen Fürsorge und Ausgrenzung* (Between welfare and exclusion, 2002) tackles this fourth historical moment, examining how Black German children were racialized and discussed using terms reminiscent of Nazi racial science. These publications by Black Germans were soon followed by publications by historians within the American academy: Heide Fehrenbach's *Race after Hitler* (2004) and Tina Campt's *Other Germans* (2005), which both cover the period of the Third Reich and the postwar era. Like de Faria's book, Fehrenbach's focuses on the racialization and exclusion of Black German children born in the postwar era, while Campt's follows two Black Germans in particular—Fasia Jansen and Hans Hauck—from their youth during the 1930s and 1940s to their lives after the war. Campt argues that how Black Germans were treated under the Nazis was not uniform but rather dependent on their intersectionality. For example, while Fasia Jansen was banned from her dance profession and forced to work in a labor camp, Hauck may have been forcibly sterilized, but his maleness made him acceptable as a Wehrmacht soldier. Additionally, books like Maria Höhn's *GIs and Fräuleins* (2002) specifically focused on the policing of interracial relationships between African American GIs and white German women.

Since this initial focus on Nazi Germany and the postwar era, historians have broadened their scope, reaching as far back as the Middle Ages. The volume *Germany and the Black Diaspora, 1250–1914* (2016) edited by Mischa Honeck, Martin Klimke, and Anne Kuhlmann-Smirnov, offers an investigation of many different periods, showing that Germany's engagement with the Black diaspora did not begin with colonialism. Peter Martin's *Schwarze Teufel, Edle M***en* (Black devils, noble m***s, 2001) demonstrates that German ideas about Blackness have never been consistent, but while prejudices in the Middle Ages revolved around religion, they became associated with inferiority with the emergence of the transatlantic slave trade. *Slavery Hinterland* (2016), edited by Felix Brahm and Eve Rosenhaft, investigates Germany's often disputed ties with the transatlantic slave trade. Rosenhaft's research with Robbie Aitken in *Black Germany* (2015) has also contributed significant knowledge to our understanding of the first Black German movement.⁵⁶ Kira Thurman's book *Singing like Germans: Black Musicians in the Land of Bach, Beethoven, and Brahms* is an interdisciplinary approach combining Black German studies, history, and musicology that traces the history of Black classical musicians in modern German-speaking Europe. She argues that the presence of Black musicians performing the works of "great German masters" challenged audiences' understanding of national identity and who had the right to express it. And in *Mobilizing Black Germany*, Tiffany Florvil tells a history of the second Black German movement through the lens of international Black feminism and highlights the important role that queer Black women played.

In addition to these historical accounts, some scholars have also concerned themselves with Black German fiction, poetry, and drama. In 1995, Leroy Hopkins published "Speak, So I Might See You! Afro-German Literature," in which he proposed that more Afro-German literature could be integrated into German curriculum. In Michelle Wright's book *Becoming Black* (2004), she proposed May Ayim's dialogic poetry as a more inclusive, feminist understanding of Black identity than constructions of Black identity previously proposed by Black male thinkers across the diaspora. In *African Diasporas* (2006), Aija Poikane-Daumke compares Afro-German literature with common themes found in African American literature. Natasha A. Kelly's *afrokultur* (2016) analyzes Ayim's poetry against the thinking of W. E. B. Du Bois and Audre Lorde. Priscilla Layne's *White Rebels in Black* (2018) considers how white German fascination with Black popular culture has influenced an understanding of Blackness as other than German and made it difficult to conceive of a Blackness that is not contradictory to Germanness. By situating Sharon Dodua Otoo's fiction vis-à-vis global discussions around Afrofuturism, Evan Torner's essay in this volume continues the work of earlier scholars who have considered how Black German literature is always in conversation with other African diasporic traditions.

In addition to these monographs and essays, there have also been several recent dissertations addressing Black German literature and history. Felicita Jaima's dissertation "Adopting Diaspora" (2016) focuses on the relationship between Black Germans and African American servicewomen.⁵⁷ Rosemarie Peña's dissertation "The Rekinning: Portrayals of Postwar Black German Transnational Adoption" (2020) concerns the experience of Black German adoptees in the United States.⁵⁸ In terms of cultural studies, Jamele Watkins's "The Drama of Race: Contemporary Afro-German Theater" (2016) is the first definitive study of Black German theater, looking at both German influences (Brecht) and non-German influences (Paulo Freire's *Pedagogy of the Oppressed*) on Black German performances from the early 2000s that "draw together pieces of the diaspora to reflect their own Black German identities."[59] In "Black-Red-Gold in 'der bunten Republik': Constructions and Performances of Heimat/en in Post-Wende Afro-/Black German Cultural Productions" (2016), Vanessa Plumly looks at Black Germans' conceptions of the term *Heimat* in writing, theater, film and hip-hop. Plumly argues that Black Germans apply a decolonizing lens to the notion of *Heimat*, in order to create a space that is no longer exclusionary and tied explicitly to whiteness. Finally, in her work, Kevina King, whose dissertation is forthcoming, investigates Black German critique of whiteness.[60]

It is apparent from previous Black German scholarship that the global African diaspora, in particular African American culture, has often been a more important point of contact for Black Germans than other minoritized groups in Germany. This is likely because Black Germans and the rest of the Black diaspora are united by "shared narratives of experiences of racialized oppression" in the form of slavery, colonialism, and white supremacy.[61] Furthermore, Black Germans are uniquely affected by anti-Blackness, a global phenomenon found not only among the white German majority but also within other minoritized groups, which is why Black Germans might feel more drawn to the work of other Black diasporic artists and activists. Nevertheless, Black Germans *do* collaborate with other minoritized individuals. For example in volumes like *Eure Heimat ist Unser Albtraum* and the poetry collection *Haymatlos*, Black Germans are portrayed side by side with Turkish Germans, German Jews, and refugees, addressing the same issues of representation, racism, and integration. Black Germans have also actively worked along with other minoritized group in theater productions staged at the Ballhaus Naunynstraße Theater and the Gorki Theater. Leslie Adelson's chapter demonstrates the usefulness of placing Black Germans in dialogue with other racialized Germans, as she discusses how futurity is central to two texts by Emine Sevgi Özdamar and Michael Götting.

It is also important to note that the close relationship long shared by Black Germans and African Americans does not mean that Black Germans have not recently taken a more critical stance toward power imbalance between these two groups. Philipp Khabo Koepsell has written about the academy's tendency to overlook older examples of Black German writing and community, claiming in doing so that Audre Lorde's collaboration with Black Germans in the 1980s is the birth of Black German politics.[62] And Noah Sow has warned about the ways in which Black German voices can be silenced in the academy and in publishing, when African American scholars' work is privileged.[63] Sow's comments could be considered part of an ongoing discussion, in which Peggy Piesche is also prominent, about who can and should do Black German studies and what the ramifications are when more privileged scholars (white and Black Americans, for example) don't reflect on their positions vis-à-vis the discipline.[64] For example, a lot of the academic work in Black German studies is being done in North America and written in English. This reveals a structural imbalance between Black Germans and scholars in North America. In the United States and Canada, it is slowly becoming common practice to include Black German literature and history in both undergraduate and graduate programs. This creates a basis on which students can pursue Black German studies for MA and PhD theses. And often, the study of Black German history benefits from the existence of Black studies and African diaspora programs already present. In contrast, in Germany, Black Germans' call for establishing Black studies programs have yet to be answered.[65] Currently, if one wants to study a topic related to Blackness in Germany, one would either have to get a degree in North American studies or in African studies, an institutional design that clearly places Blackness outside of German Studies. Furthermore, scholars like Natasha A. Kelly, Emily Ngubia Kuria and Priscilla Layne have also written about the structural racism Black students in Germany grapple with as well as about the difficulties Black German scholars likely face in higher education, both in pursuing a PhD and in gaining employment.[66] Finally, another important thread that has emerged within Black German studies is the focus on futurity—imagining alternative futures and counterhistories and reflecting on what is necessary to secure a future for Black German life. The importance of futurity in the work of Black German prose and theater is explored in three chapters in this volume: those by Leslie Adelson, Evan Torner, and Olivia Landry.

German Jewish Studies

Since the Holocaust, German Jewish studies has focused on the tragedy and trauma of persecution and annihilation, which necessarily inflects any analysis of centuries of Jewish integration, modernization, and achievement in the German-speaking regions. Conceptually, the "assimilation" paradigm has dominated the field for the longest time, although, in recent decades, scholars have turned instead to "acculturation" or "dissimilation" as analytic frames.[67] Whether they focus on religion, ethnicity, political or social standing, or other elements in discussing Jewish positionality, most studies use a binary model of Jews as a minority with reference to a dominant non-Jewish German majority culture. Few studies also conceptualize Jews in relation to other minorities in Germany.[68] Some scholars have used a colonial or postcolonial framework to discuss Jewish experience in various contexts from the eighteenth century to the present;[69] however, social histories tend instead to approach modern German Jewish history through a cultural-economic lens of *embourgoisement* and integration.[70] Hans Mayer's influential 1975 study pioneered a comparative approach, examining literary representations of women, Jews, and gays as "outsiders" to the bourgeois enlightenment (which, in the wake of the Holocaust, Mayer understands as a failed project).[71] Since the 1980s, Sander Gilman's work has probably done the most to develop a cultural studies methodology that has put German Jewish studies in dialogue with critical race theory and sexuality studies, examining constructions of Jewishness in relation to perceptions of Blackness, disability, and other categories of perceived difference.[72]

By 1989, the Jewish community in West Germany numbered less than forty thousand and was aging and shrinking (the tiny community of Jews in the GDR even more so). The immigration to Germany of more than one hundred thousand Jews from the former Soviet Union since 1989 (plus a roughly equal number of non-Jewish family members), as well as the presence of a sizable number of Israelis and Jews from other countries living for extended periods in Germany, has created the third-largest and fastest-growing Jewish community in Europe, an exception to the Europe-wide trend of shrinking Jewish communities.[73] Scholars of German Jewish culture have posited a bifurcated Jewish response to German unification and an attendant yearning for "normalization": on the one hand, Dan Diner's concept of a "negative symbiosis" summarizes how the wounds of the Holocaust remain at the center of German/Jewish relations, functioning both as a permanent divide and a continuing bond; on the other hand, there is a new vibrant Jewish life that claims its rightful place as part of a dynamic and evolved German society.[74] The migration of Jews from the former Soviet Union to Germany as a destination of choice is sometimes cited as a sign of generational change, and some claim, as Y. Michal Bodemann does, that the Holocaust no longer occupies a central place in their worldview.[75] However, the literary and film works produced by a new generation of Jews in Germany, many of which focus on stories of Holocaust, survival, loss, and the impact of these on the self-understanding of later generations, contradicts such assertions.[76]

Whereas studies of contemporary German Jewish writing in the 1990s and 2000s raised the open questions of "rebirth" and "reemergence," celebrating a proliferation of new voices and exploring continuities with the German Jewish past and possibilities for new beginnings,[77] more recent studies have focused on the works of a third generation of post-Holocaust German Jewish writers, including many who came from the former Soviet Union as children and who have grown up in Germany.[78] The concerns of these writers reflect the complex positionality of Jewish writing in German as a literature of migration in a dynamic German, European, and world context. One the one hand, there are explorations of cosmopolitan identity and Holocaust memory in a global context.[79] There are related questions of place and space, especially in relation to history and politics (Israel, Germany, etc.).[80]

In films such as *Kaddisch für einen Freund* (dir. Leo Khasin, 2012) we find expressions of fear of a "new" antisemitism,[81] something that has only increased in the wake of the 2014 firebombing of a synagogue in Wuppertal (an event that shocked Jews in Germany not only because of the outrage that decades after November 1938 a synagogue would again be a target of an arson attack but also because the German courts declined to view this act as an antisemitic hate crime and merely as a political expression of anti-Israel sentiment)[82] and street attacks on visibly identifiable Jews.[83] These violent attacks on Jews and Jewish symbols, which have sadly become unsurprising occurrences in many European countries since 2000 but in Germany are a particularly disquieting countertheme to a narrative of a thriving renewal of Jewish life and an overcoming of the Nazi past, raise difficult questions of the relation of Jews in Germany to ethnic Germans and to other minoritized communities.[84] What does this say about the "racialization" paradigm of Chin and El-Tayeb? Can a historically conscious German studies productively engage with "whiteness" as an analytic framework in relation to German Jewish studies and the history of antisemitism?[85] Beyond race/racialization as an analytical frame for thinking about Jews and other minorities in contemporary Germany (one that perhaps accentuates divisions), we might also consider religion as a central category. For example, the mobilization against a 2012 German court injunction against circumcision (and related efforts across Europe, often with a far-right agenda, against halal and kosher meat preparation) encouraged deeper political alliances across communities, with Jews and Muslims finding common cause.[86]

The debate surrounding the postcolonial theorist Achille Mbembe, which dominated German feuilletons in April and May 2020, added new layers and complexities to discussions of racism, politics, antisemitism, Holocaust memory, and cultural theory.[87] The affair started with controversy over Mbembe's connection to the "BDS" boycott Israel movement (which a May 2019 Bundestag resolution, supported by all parties except the AfD and Die Linke, had denounced as antisemitic), but it quickly became conflated with questions of Holocaust relativization and the contribution of postcolonial thought to discussions of Germany's colonial and Nazi pasts, and to issues of racism, antisemitism, and Islamophobia in contemporary Germany.[88] One impact of this debate has been an increased politicization of scholarship.[89] Another impact is that the animated, if contentious, public interest in the Mbembe affair demonstrates the immediate relevance of the issues and approaches gathered in this volume.

Chapter Outline and Concluding Remarks

This volume could not include all papers and performances presented at the March 2017 Amherst conference (some were published elsewhere), but perspectives from these can illuminate aspects of the included contributions we introduce below. In particular, the contributions of Christine Achinger, Farid

Hafez, and Susannah Heschel to the conference, each of which explored issues of antisemitism and Islamophobia in comparative and historical context, brought to the discussion a conceptual framework that illuminates several of the chapters gathered here.[90] Holocaust memory is a third filter through which to consider minority discourse in contemporary German society. The work of Damani Partridge, who also contributed to our UMass Amherst conference, critiques the culture of Holocaust commemoration in Germany as a force that, in his view, obscures contemporary racism and even produces exclusions in the name of combating prejudice; by contrast, Michael Rothberg and Yasemin Yildiz highlight the grassroots initiative of diverse groups in Germany to engage with the Holocaust as a central historical trauma.[91] Both approaches develop from a set of questions positioned outside of the perspective of German Jewish studies. That is to say, they take up the meaning of Holocaust remembrance for non-Jewish minoritized groups and for a diverse German society generally, but not specifically from the perspective of Jews in Germany, a perspective of people who also make their lives in a changing German society and for whom the Holocaust is an inescapable subjective point of departure rather than something monumentally imposed or empathetically approached. Two chapters in this volume, by Joshua Shelly and Nick Block, offer a more comparative and dialogic approach, analyzing contemporary Jewish voices in Germany in conversation with dominant and minoritized groups in a more multifaceted society. Kristin Dickinson's chapter also explores a dialogue across groups, with an additional historical dimension, reading a Turkish German writer in relation to a German-Jewish exile from Nazi Germany.

In addition to scholarly contributions, this edited volume also includes an essay by Esther Dischereit, "Refugee—Migrant—Immigrant," the first publication of this text in English (translation by Peter Thompson).[92] Dischereit's essays, including "Refugee—Migrant—Immigrant," are understood as "interventions in political and moral issues of society, asking how democratic and solidary processes can move forward."[93] Dischereit first presented this essay as a lecture at the conference "Flight and Refuge: The European Crisis in Global Perspective" at the University of Virginia in April 2016.

Kristin Dickinson's contribution, "'Strange Stars' in Constellation: Özdamar, Lasker-Schüler, and the Archive," examines references to Else Lasker-Schüler's work in Emine Sevgi Özdamar's novel *Seltsame Sterne starren zur Erde* (2003). Özdamar's literary text, the third installment of her Berlin-Istanbul trilogy, creates, as Dickinson argues, a constellation of textual imaginaries across Berlin, Jerusalem, and Istanbul, calling for a planetary perspective on both the East-West divide and various archival frameworks that condition it. Her linking of the literary legacies of Özdamar and Lasker-Schüler highlights a literary archive of migration beyond national confines while uncovering Turkish German/Jewish German literary intersections.

In "Jewish Tales from a Muslim Turkish Pen: Feridun Zaimoğlu and *Moses in Oberammergau*," Joshua Shelly takes up the complex issue of relations between minority groups and traditions, centered on a reading of a 2013 play by Günter Senkel and Feridun Zaimoğlu, performed at Oberammergau. In the aftermath of the Holocaust, performances of Lessing's *Nathan der Weise* (*Nathan the Wise*) established a standard liberal interfaith ideal. Within contemporary German culture, continued marginalization of Turkish Germans and a growing tendency to frame them in religious terms as part of a "Muslim" minority, as well as a complex dynamic of antisemitism and philosemitism, have altered the landscape. Joshua Shelly shows convincingly how the play's use of Jewish and Muslim religious source material allows Zaimoğlu to make a thoughtful literary intervention, aware of the multidirectional historical and political forces that bear upon a minority perspective on the German stage.

Olivia Landry's "*Schwarz tragen*: Blackness, Performance, and the Utopian in Contemporary German Theater" situates Black German theater vis-à-vis postmigrant theater through an analysis of Elizabeth Blonzen's play *Schwarz tragen* (Carrying/Wearing Black, 2013). Drawing on theories of Blackness and its crossovers with being, identity, and relationality from Frantz Fanon to Fred Moten, Achille Mbembe, and Avery Gordon, this essay reads *Schwarz tragen* as a play that scrambles as well as challenges the rubric of the theatrical event, its province of whiteness in the German space, and its inveterately binary structures of stage and house, performance and spectators, spectacle and gaze.

Turning to comedy, Britta Kallin's chapter, "German Comedians Combating Stereotypes and Discrimination: Oliver Polak, Dave Davis, and Serdar Somuncu," engages with three popular comedians: Oliver Polak, Dave Davis, and Serdar Somuncu, whose work she conceptualizes as comedy of integration. In her analysis of their repertoire, reception, and public statements, she focuses on these comedians' reconceptualization of German comedy through their renegotiations of what constitutes Germanness (by also criticizing their own marginalization through ethnonational prescriptions).

In "Dialogue and Intersection in German Holocaust Memory Culture: Stumbling Blocks and the Memorial to the Murdered Jews of Europe," Nick Block analyzes the discomfort that a range of German Jewish community officials, artists, and intellectuals have expressed regarding two of Germany's most visible public memorials to the Holocaust. Similar to Maya Caspari, Block shows that these issues are not simply binaries (of Germans and Jews; of pasts and presents closed off from each other). Block draws our attention to the claims of Jews in Germany to be seen as living parts of a German and European society (which is itself increasingly informed by cosmopolitan and global cultures of memory). At the same time, Block's reading of a biting 2010 satire by Henryk Broder and Hamed Abdel-Samad reveals how relations between Jews and others in German society are shaped by factors, including: the forms and rituals of Holocaust memory in Germany; the enduring centrality of this trauma for Jews everywhere; the fear of a violent "new" antisemitism from both the far right in Europe and radical jihadist-Islamist calls to destroy Israel and attack Jews generally.

Berna Gueneli's contribution, "Young, Diverse, and Polyglot: Ilker Çatak and Amelia Umuhire Track the New Urban Sound of Europe" centers on a new generation of filmmakers. Gueneli argues that directors such as Çatak and Umuhire revive German participation in international film circuits with their distinctly transnational work. Focusing on the films' "sonic heterogeneity" (which includes multilingualism and musical and other sound elements), and to a lesser extent on their visual representation of People of Color, Gueneli highlights how these films offer visions of Europe that counter ideas of Europe as defined by the borders of the EU or the claims of right-wing populist movements. Through her comparative analysis of Black German and Turkish German filmmakers as antiracist countervoices, she puts these filmmakers into dialogue by foregrounding their sonic and linguistic transformation of Europe through film.

Maya Caspari's chapter, "Subjunctive Remembering; Contingent Resistance: Katja Petrowskaja's *Vielleicht Esther*," focuses on one 2014 novel by a Russian-Jewish-German writer. However, Caspari's nuanced readings have implications for thinking more broadly about literatures of migration and diaspora (not only Jewish), as well as about the complex positionality of migrants (including Jews) in relation to the Holocaust past and within a diverse ethnic and political landscape in contemporary German and European society. Caspari demonstrates how Petrowskaja's literary strategies (which she explores through the concept of *contingency*) complicate the theories of Leslie Adelson, Sara Ahmed, Michael Rothberg, and others. Caspari suggests that *contingency* opens new possibilities for political interventions and translations. Indeed, even hazards: the novel's investigation of a contemporary relation to the Holocaust and its memory exposes the fragility of Jewish positionality, its vulnerability to erasure.

In "Posthumanism and Object-Oriented Ontology in Sharon Dodua Otoo's *Synchronicity* and 'Herr Gröttrup setzt sich hin' [Herr Gröttrup sits down]," Evan Torner considers the unique contributions Black German writing makes to contemporary German fiction in two of Sharon Dodua Otoo's prose works, *Synchronicity* (2014) and the Bachmann Prize–winning short story "Herr Gröttrup setzt sich hin" (2016). Torner argues that while Otoo's fiction certainly unpacks everyday German racism, her texts are also reflections on the posthuman that warrant her work being situated within the realms of speculative realism and object-oriented ontology. While posthumanism has often been criticized for not paying enough attention to issues of race, Torner's essay demonstrates how an author like Otoo is able to combine discourses on race, gender, and human/nonhuman in such a way that allows for a pertinent critique of contemporary German society.

While many of the chapters focus on a single subfield, there are a few that attempt to create a dialogue, perhaps even a trialogue between the different minoritized groups at the focus of this volume. One such chapter is Leslie A. Adelson's "Future Narrative as Contested Ground: Emine Sevgi Özdamar's 'On the Train' and Michael Götting's *Contrapunctus*," which compares futurity in two contemporary works, Turkish German author Emine Özdamar's short story "Bahnfahrt" ("On the Train," 2008) and Black German author Michael Götting's novel *Contrapunctus* (2015). Adelson considers how the radical breaks with time employed by Özdamar and Götting in their narratives offer a unique perspective on future-making in twenty-first-century Europe.[94]

It is our hope that the contributions gathered here will prompt yet further dialogue and reflection about a multifaceted, diverse, and increasingly interrelated cultural production in Germany (and the conceptual tools with which students and scholars of German studies analyze it), a creative wave that sets the tone for future directions.

Ela Gezen is an associate professor of German at the University of Massachusetts Amherst. Her first book, *Brecht, Turkish Theater, and Turkish-German Literature* (Camden House, 2018), studies the significance of Bertolt Brecht for Turkish and Turkish German literature. Her current book project examines cultural practices by Turkish artists in West Berlin. She is the coeditor of two special journal issues exploring new directions in the field of Turkish German studies and the editor of a special issue on Aras Ören. In addition, she has published articles on music, theater, and literature, focusing on the intersection between aesthetics and politics in both Turkish and German contexts.

Priscilla Layne is associate professor of German at the University of North Carolina at Chapel Hill. She is the author of *White Rebels in Black: German Appropriation of African American Culture* (University of Michigan Press, 2018). Her current book project is on Afro-German Afrofuturism. She also holds an adjunct appointment in African, African American, and diaspora studies at the University of North Carolina at Chapel Hill and will serve as president of the American Association of Teachers of German (AATG) from 2022–24.

Jonathan Skolnik is associate professor of German at University of Massachusetts Amherst. He has held fellowships from the United States Holocaust Memorial Museum, the Leo Baeck Institute, and the University of Pennsylvania's Katz Center for Advanced Judaic Studies. He is the author of *Jewish Pasts, German Fictions: History, Memory and Minority Culture in Germany* (Stanford University Press, 2014).

Notes

1. Olga Grjasnowa, *Der Russe ist einer, der Birken liebt* (Munich: Carl Hanser Verlag, 2012). English translation from Grjasnowa, *All Russians Love Birch Trees*, translated from the German by Eva Bacon (New York: Other Press, 2014). The interpretation above was published in Jonathan Skolnik, "Memory without Borders? Migrant Identity and the Legacy of the Holocaust Memory in Olga Grjasnowa's *Der Russe ist einer, der Birken liebt*," in *German-Jewish Literature Since 1990: Beyond the Holocaust?* ed. Katja Garloff and Agnes Mueller (Rochester, NY: Camden House, 2018), 123–45.
2. Grjasnowa, *All Russians*, 251. In the German original: "Aber der Kleine wird keinen Scheiß machen, er wird alles lesen und alles verstehen: alle Klassiker der Post Colonial Studies, der Critical Whitness [sic] Studies, der Rassismustheorien, Fanon, Said, Terkessidis" (Grjasnowa *Russe*, 221).
3. These questions have been taken up in several edited volumes over the last twenty years, such as *Spricht die Subalterne deutsch?* (2003), edited by Hito Steyerl; *Mythen, Masken und Subjekte* (2005), edited by Maureen Maisha Eggers, Grada Kilomba, Peggy Piesche, and Susan Arndt (2005); *Weiß-Weißsein-Whiteness* (2006) edited by Martina Tißberger, Gabriele Dietze, Daniela Hrzán, and Jana Husmann; in addition to Fatima El-Tayeb's monograph *European Others* (2011). This book contributes to this scholarship by posing these questions specifically to the ways that Black German, Turkish German, and German Jewish studies might engage them.
4. Zafer Şenocak, *Gefährliche Verwandtschaft* (Munich: Babel Verlag, 2003); Emine Sevgi Özdamar, *Seltsame Sterne starren zur Erde: Wedding-Pankow; 1976–77* (Cologne: Kiepenheuer & Witsch, 2003); Feridun Zaimoğlu, *Kanak Sprak Kanak Sprak: 24 Mißtöne vom Rande der Gesellschaft* (Hamburg: Rotbuch, 1997); and Feridun Zaimoğlu and Günter Senkel, *Moses* (Kiel: Solivagus-Verlag, 2013).
5. In *My Grandfather Would Have Shot Me*, Black German Jennifer Teege describes what it was like when, in her twenties, her mother confessed that her grandfather was the late concentration camp commandant Amon Göth. In *Milli's Awakening*, Diane, a Black German photographer, describes her life growing up in East Germany with a Jewish mother. Jennifer Teege, *My Grandfather Would Have Shot Me: A Black Woman Discovers Her Family's Nazi Past* (New York: The Experiment, 2016).
6. Maxim Biller, "Harlem Holocaust," in *Wenn ich einmal reich und tot bin* (Cologne: Kiepenheuer & Witsch, 1990), 76–122.
7. An enumeration like this will never be "complete." We do not claim to account for all minoritized communities and already made clear above why we focus on these groups/subfields.
8. "das wieder vereinigte deutschland / feiert sich wieder 1990 / ohne immigrantInnen flüchtlinge jüdische / und schwarze menschen." May Ayim, "blues in schwarz weiss," *blues in schwarz weiss* (Berlin: Orlanda Frauenverlag, 1995), 82.
9. Rita Chin, Heide Fehrenbach, Geoff Eley, Atina Grossmann, eds., *After the Nazi Racial State: Difference and Democracy in Germany and Europe* (Ann Arbor: University of Michigan Press, 2009). See also the discussion by Daniel Levy, Review of Rita Chin, Heide Fehrenbach, Geoff Eley, and Atina Grossmann, *After the Nazi Racial State: Difference and Democracy in Germany and Europe*, H-German, H-Net Reviews, July 2011.
10. Fatima El-Tayeb, *Undeutsch: Die Konstruktion des Anderen in der postmigrantischen Gesellschaft* (Bielefeld: transcript, 2016), 9, 36, 164, 146.

11. "Weigerung der Mehrheitsgesellschaft, sich von dem weiß/christlichen Deutschlandbild zu trennen; eine ... Geschichtsauffassung ... in dem ein essenzialistisch definiertes, weißes, christliches Europa immer und zwangsläufig die Norm bleibt." El-Tayeb, *Undeutsch*, 9, 19.
12. Gizem Arslan et al., "Forum: Migration Studies," *The German Quarterly* 90, no. 2 (Spring 2017): 212–34; Chunjie Zhang, ed., "Forum: What Is Asian German Studies?" *The German Quarterly* 93, no. 1 (Winter 2020): 106–41.
13. Bala Venkat Mani, "Migrants, Refugees, Exiles: *Cosmopolitical Claims* beyond *Willkommenskultur*," in "Forum: Migration Studies," *The German Quarterly* 90, no. 2 (Spring 2017): 219–22.
14. David Gramling and Deniz Göktürk, "*Germany in Transit*, Ten Years On," in "Forum: Migration Studies," *The German Quarterly* 90, no. 2 (Spring 2017): 217–19.
15. Bettina Brandt, "Asisa, Fantasia, Germasia," in "Forum: What Is Asian German Studies?" *The German Quarterly* 93, no. 1 (Winter 2020): 120–23.
16. Johanna Schuster-Craig, "Asian German Studies, Muslim German Studies, and Critical Whiteness Studies," in "Forum: What Is Asian German Studies?" *The German Quarterly* 93, no. 1 (Winter 2020): 123–27; Veronika Füchtner, "From Asian German Studies to Global German Studies?" in "Forum: What Is Asian German Studies?" *The German Quarterly* 93, no. 1 (Winter 2020): 131–35.
17. Natasha A. Kelly, *Rassismus: Strukturelle Probleme brauchen struktuelle Lösungen* (Zurich: Atrium Verlag, 2021), 24.
18. Kelly, *Rassismus: Strukturelle Probleme*, 24
19. ISD-admin, "Stellung zu den faschistischen Attacken in Chemnitz," 31 August 2018, retrieved 12 March 2020 from http://isdonline.de/stellungnahme-zu-den-faschistischen-attacken-in-chemnitz/.
20. "Wie viele rassistische Straftaten gibt es?" Mediendienst Integration, retrieved 14 March 2020 from https://mediendienst-integration.de/desintegration/rassismus.html.
21. It is beyond the scope of this introduction to address all aspects of the NSU Complex in detail. For further information, see Stefan Aust and Dirk Laabs, *Heimatschutz: Der Staat und die Mordserie des NSU* (Munich: Pantheon, 2014); Kemal Bozay, Bahar Aslan, Orhan Mangitay, and Funda Özfirat, eds., *Die haben gedacht wir waren das: MigrantInnen über rechten Terror und Rassismus* (Cologne: Papy Roassa, 2016); and Andreas Förster, ed., *Geheimsache NSU: Zehn Morde, von Aufklärung keine Spur* (Tübingen: Klöfer und Meyer, 2014).
22. On the "Klagelieder," see Ela Gezen, "Poetic Empathy, Political Criticism, and Public Mourning: Esther Dischereit's *Klagelieder*," *Gegenwartsliteratur: A German Studies Yearbook* 17 (2018): 313–30
23. Tribunal NSU Komplex auflösen, *Wir klagen an! Anklage des Tribunals* "NSU-Komplex auflösen (2017), 9.
24. On transnational activism in the 1960s, see Quinn Slobodian, *Foreign Front: Third World Politics in Sixties West Germany* (Durham, NC: Duke University Press, 2012), and Quinn Slobodian, ed., *Comrades of Color: East Germany in the Cold War* (New York: Berghahn Books, 2015).
25. Natasha A. Kelly details several incidents of Black people who died in police custody in Germany in *Rassismus: Strukturelle Probleme*.
26. We decided not to spell out M-word throughout in order not to reproduce the racism inherent in this term. For an explanation of the history behind this term, see Susan

Arndt and Antje Hornscheid, eds., *Afrika und die deutsche Sprache: Ein kritisches Nachschlagwerk* (Münster: Unrast, 2004), 168–171.
27. Ika Hügel-Marshall, Chris Lange, May Ayim, Ilona Bubeck, Gülşen Aktaş, and Dagmar Schultz, "An unsere LeserInnen," in *Entfernte Verbindungen: Rassismus, Antisemitismus, Klassenunterdrückung*, ed. Ika Hügel-Marshall et al. (Berlin: Orlanda Verlag, 1993), 11.
28. Hügel-Marshall et al., "An unsere LeserInnen," 12.
29. Hügel-Marshall et al., "An unsere LeserInnen," 12.
30. "Kulturelle Produktionen von Migrantinnen, Schwarzen und jüdischen Frauen ... in den bislang über sie geführten politischen und kulturellen Diskurs einen, neuen, selbstbestimmten Platz einnehmen," 7.
31. "sich nicht den Zwängen der vorgeschriebenen Rollenmodelle zu beugen." Olumide Popoola and Beldan Sezen, "Zu diesem Buch," in *Talking Home: Heimat aus unserer eigenen Feder, Frauen of Color in Deutschland* (Amsterdam: Blue Moon Press, 1999), 1.
32. "intellektuell verkümmern," Thilo Sarrazin, *Deutschland schafft sich ab: Wie wir unser Land aufs Spiel setzen* (Munich: Deutsche Verlags-Anstalt, 2010), 393.
33. "Demografisch stellt die enorme Fruchtbarkeit der muslimischen Migranten auf lange Sicht eine Bedrohung für der kulturelle und zivilisatorische Gleichgewicht im alternden Europa dar." Sarrazin, *Deutschland schafft sich ab*, 267.
34. Max Czollek, "Gegenwartsbewältigung," in *Eure Heimat ist unser Albtraum*, ed. Fatma Aydemir and Hengameh Yaghoobifarah (Berlin: Ullstein Taschenbuch Verlag, 2020).
35. El-Tayeb, *Undeutsch*, 9–10.
36. "wo Juden_Jüdinnen leben, kann schließlich kein Nationalsozialismus sein." Czollek, "Gegenwartsbewältigung," 168.
37. "Die überwiegend Mehrheit der jüdischen Bevölkerung ist also migrantisch. Gleichzeitig tauchen Juden_Jüdinnen im Kontext der derzeit bestimmenden Binarität von Integrierten vs. Parallelgesellschaft nicht auf." Czollek, "Gegenwartsbewältigung," 171.
38. Ullstein Buchverlage, retrieved 14 March 2020 from https://www.ullstein-buchverlage.de/nc/buch/details/eure-heimat-ist-unser-albtraum-9783548062402.html. "Ein Manifest gegen Heimat – einem völkisch verklärten Konzept gegen dessen Normalisierung sich 14 deutschsprachige Autor_innen wehren."
39. Gorki Studio R., "PostHeimat," retrieved 14 March 2020 from https://www.gorki.de/en/studio-ya.
40. Gorki Studio R., "PostHeimat."
41. Ballhaus Naunynstraße, "10 Jahre Postmigrantisches Theater," retrieved 1 May 2021 from http://www.ballhausnaunynstrasse.de/veranstaltung/10_jahre_postmigrantisches_theater_14.11.2016.
42. Katharina Donath, "Die Herkunft spielt keine Rolle – 'Postmigrantisches' Theater im Ballhaus Naunynstraße. Interview mit Shermin Langhoff," *Bundeszentrale für politische Bildung*, retrieved 14 March 2020 from http://www.bpb.de/gesellschaft/kultur/kulturelle-bildung/60135/interview-mit-shermin-langhoff?p=all.
43. Donath, "Die Herkunft spielt keine Rolle."
44. Leslie Adelson, *The Turkish Turn in Contemporary German Literature: Toward a New Critical Grammar* (New York: Palgrave Macmillan, 2005), 7, 12.
45. This overview of Turkish German sudies is based on an earlier version that has appeared in Gezen, *Brecht, Turkish Theater*.
46. See for example, Adelson, *Turkish Turn*; Ayşe Çağlar, "Mediascapes, Advertisement Industries and Cosmopolitan Transformations: German Turks in Germany," *New*

German Critique 92 (2004): 39–61; Tom Cheesman, *Novels of Turkish German Settlement: Cosmopolite Fictions* (Rochester, NY: Camden House, 2007); Rita Chin, *The Guest Worker Question in Postwar Germany* (Cambridge: Cambridge University Press, 2007); Deniz Göktürk, "Turkish Delight—German Fright: Unsettling Oppositions in Transnational Cinema," EIPCP: European Institute for Progressive Cultural Policies, 2000; Ruth Mandel, *Cosmopolitan Anxieties: Turkish Challenges to Citizenship and Belonging in Germany* (Durham, NC: Duke University Press, 2008); B. Venkat Mani, *Cosmopolitical Claims: Turkish-German Literatures from Nadolny to Pamuk* (Iowa City: University of Iowa Press, 2007); Jennifer Miller, *Turkish Guest Workers in Germany: Hidden Lives and Contested Borders, 1960s to 1980s* (Toronto: University of Toronto Press, 2018); Esra Özyürek, *Being German, Becoming Muslim: Race, Religion, and Conversion in the new Europe* (Princeton, NJ: Princeton University Press, 2014); Azade Seyhan, *Writing Outside the Nation* (Princeton, NJ: Princeton University Press, 2001); Levent Soysal, "Labor to Culture: Writing Turkish Migration to Europe," *South Atlantic Quarterly* 102, nos. 2/3 (2003): 491–508; Beverly Weber, *Violence and Gender in the "New" Europe: Islam in German Culture* (New York: Palgrave Macmillan, 2013); Yasemin Yildiz, *Beyond the Mother Tongue: The Postmonolingual Condition* (New York: Fordham University Press, 2012); Gökce Yurdakul, *From Guestworkers into Muslims: The Transformation of Turkish Immigrant Associations in Germany* (Newcastle upon Tyne: Cambridge Scholars Publishing, 2009).
47. Adelson, *Turkish Turn*, 245.
48. David Gramling, "What Is Turkish-German Studies Up Against? Occidentalism and Thigmotactics," *Colloquia Germanica* 44, no. 4 (2011, published 2014): 387.
49. Revised and extended seminar contributions were published in a special issue, "Turkish-German Studies: Past, Present, and Future," with/of the *Jahrbuch Türkisch-deutsche Studien* in 2015, coedited by Ela Gezen and Berna Gueneli.
50. Mert Bahadir Reisoğlu, "Interlacing Archives: History and Memory in Emine Sevgi Özdamar's *Die Brücke vom Goldenen Horn*," *Colloquia Germanica* 44, no. 4 (2011, published 2014): 422–37; Ela Gezen, *Brecht, Turkish Theater, and Turkish-German Literature: Reception, Adaptation, and Innovation after 1960* (Rochester, NY: Camden House, 2018); Karin Yeşilada, *Poesie der Dritten Sprache* (Tübingen: Stauffenburg Verlag, 2012); Randall Halle, "The Europeanization of Turkish/German Cinema: Complex Connectivity and Imaginative Communities," *Jahrbuch Türkisch-deutsche Studien* (2015): 15–38; Kader Konuk, *East West Mimesis: Auerbach in Turkey* (Stanford, CA: Stanford University Press, 2010); Yildiz, *Beyond the Mother Tongue*; Kristin Dickinson, *DisOrientations: Turkish-German Cultural Contact in Translation (1811–1946)* (University Park: Pennsylvania State University Press, 2021); Deniz Göktürk, "Interrupting Unity: The Berlin Wall's Second Life on Screen—A Transnational Perspective," in *Debating German Cultural Identity Since 1989*, ed. Anne Fuchs et al. (Rochester, NY: Camden House, 2011), 82–99. Berna Gueneli, *Fatih Akin's Cinema and the New Sound of Europe* (Bloomington: Indiana University Press, 2019).
51. Yasemin Yildiz and Michael Rothberg. "Memory Citizenship: Migrant Archives of Holocaust Remembrance in Contemporary Germany," *Parallax* 17, no. 4 (2011): 32–48; Esra Özyürek, "Muslim Minorities as Germany's Past Future: Islam Critics, Holocaust Memory, and Immigrant Integration," *Memory Studies* (June 2019); Adelson, *Turkish Turn*; Yurdakul, *From Guestworkers into Muslims*; Konuk, *East West Mimesis*; Marc D. Baer, *The Dönme: Jewish Converts, Muslim Revolutionaries, and Secular Turks* (Stanford, CA: Stanford University Press, 2010); Karolina Hicke's dissertation in progress,

"Intersections of Migration, Memory, and Gender in Contemporary Jewish Writing in Germany" (University of Massachusetts Amherst), brings German Jewish and literatures of migration in dialogue.

52. Robbie Aitken and Eve Rosenhaft, *Black Germany: The Making and Unmaking of a Diaspora Community* (Cambridge: Cambridge University Press, 2013).
53. Tiffany Florvil, "Writing across Differences: Afro-Germans, Gender, and Diaspora, 1970s–1990s" (PhD diss., University of South Carolina, Columbia, 2013), 54.
54. Iris Wigger, "'Black Shame'— The Campaign against 'Racial Degeneration' and Female Degradation in Interwar Europe," *Institute of Race Relations* 51, no. 3 (2010): 35.
55. Richard J. Evans, *The Third Reich in Power, 1933–1939* (New York: Penguin, 2005), 527.
56. Peter Martin, *Schwarze Teufel, edle M***en: Afrikaner in Geschichte und Bewusstein der Deutschen* (Hamburg: Hamburger Edition, 2001); Mischa Honeck, Martin Klimke, and Anne Kuhlmann-Smirnov, eds., *Germany and the Black Diaspora: Points of Contact, 1250–1914* (New York: Berghahn Books, 2016); Felika Brahm and Eve Rosenhaft, eds., *Slavery Hinterland: Transatlantic Slavery and Continental Europe, 1680–1850* (Woodbridge: Boydell Press, 2016); Eve Rosenhaft and Robbie Aitken, *Black Germany: The Making and Unmaking of a Diasporic Community, 1884–1960* (Cambridge: Cambridge University Press, 2015).
57. Felicitas Jaima, "Adopting Diaspora: African American Military Women in Cold War West Germany" (PhD diss., New York University, 2016).
58. Rosemarie Peña, "The Rekinning: Portrayals of Postwar Black German Transnational Adoption" (PhD diss., Rutgers University, New Brunswick, NJ, 2020).
59. Jamele Watkins, "The Drama of Race: Contemporary Afro-German Theater" (PhD diss., University of Massachusetts at Amherst, 2016), 42.
60. Kevina King's presentation during the conference investigated the pervasiveness of racial profiling and police brutality as linked to the normalization of whiteness. Kevina King, "Tools and Tolls of Germanness: Institutional Racism and Racial Profiling," conference paper presented at the conference "Minorities and Minority Discourses in Germany since 1990: Intersections, Interventions, Interpolations" (University of Massachusetts at Amherst, 3 March 2017). An extended and revised version of this paper, "Black, People of Color and Migrant Lives Should Matter: Racial Profiling, Police Brutality and Whiteness in Germany," appeared in *Rethinking Black German Studies: Approaches, Interventions, Histories*, ed. Tiffany Florvil and Vanessa Plumly (Oxford: Peter Lang, 2018), 169–96.
61. Philipp Khabo Koepsell, "Literature and Activism," in *Arriving in the Future*, edited by Asoka Esuruoso and Philipp Khabo Koepsell (Berlin: epubli, 2014), 36–47.
62. Koepsell, "Literature and Activism," 36–47.
63. Noah Sow, "Diaspora Dynamics: Shaping the Future of Literature," *Journal of the African Literature Association* 11, no. 1 (2017): 28–33.
64. Peggy Piesche and Sara Lennox, "Epilogue: Of Epistemologies and Positionalities. A Conversation, Berlin, October 21, 2014," in *Remapping Black Germany: New Perspectives on Afro-German History, Politics, and Culture*, ed. Sara Lennox (Amherst: University of Massachusetts Press, 2016), 274–82.
65. See Kelly, *Rassismus: Strukturelle Probleme*.
66. See Kelly, *Rassismus: Strukturelle Probleme*; Emily Ngubia Kuria, *eingeschrieben: Zeichen setzen gegen Rassismus an deutschen Hochschulen* (Berlin: w_orten & meer, 2015); and Priscilla Layne, "On Racism without Race: The Need to Diversify *Germanistik* and

the German Academy," in *Who Can Speak and Who Is Heard/Hurt? Facing Problems of Race, Racism and Ethnic Diversity in the Humanities in Germany*, ed. Mahmoud Arghavan, Nicole Hirschfelder, Luvena Kopp, and Katharina Motyl (Bielefeld: transcript, 2019), 217–38.
67. See the discussion by Michael Meyer, "Jewish Self-Understanding," in *German-Jewish History in Modern Times*, vol. 2: *Emancipation and Acculturation*, ed. Michael A. Meyer (New York: Columbia University Press, 1997), as well as David Sorkin, "Emancipation and Assimilation: Two Concepts and Their Application to German-Jewish History," *Year Book of the Leo Baeck Institute* 35 (1990): 17–33; Till van Rahden, "Jews and the Ambivalences of Civil Society in Germany, 1800–1933: Assessment and Reassessment," *Journal of Modern History* 77, no. 4 (2005): 1024–47; and Scott Spector, "Forget Assimilation: Introducing Subjectivity to German-Jewish History," *Jewish History* 20, nos. 3–4 (2006): 349–61.
68. An exception is, for example, Ari Joskowicz, *The Modernity of Others: Jewish Anti-Catholicism in Germany and France* (Stanford, CA: Stanford University Press, 2013).
69. Jonathan M. Hess, "Johann David Michaelis and the Colonial Imaginary: Orientalism and the Emergence of Racial Antisemitism in Eighteenth-Century Germany," *Jewish Social Studies* 6, no. 2 (2000): 56–102; Susannah Heschel "Revolt of the Colonized: Abraham Geiger's Wissenschaft des Judentums as a Challenge to Christian Hegemony in the Academy," *New German Critique*, no. 77 (1999): 61–85; Oliver Lubrich, "Are Russian Jews Post-colonial? Wladimir Kaminer and Identity Politics," *East European Jewish Affairs* 33 (2003): 35–52.
70. Simone Lässig, *Jüdische Wege ins Bürgertum* (Göttingen: Vandenhoeck & Ruprecht, 2004).
71. Hans Mayer, *Außenseiter* (Frankfurt am Main: Suhrkamp, 1975).
72. See, paradigmatically, the influential Sander L. Gilman, *Difference and Pathology: Stereotypes of Sexuality, Race, and Madness* (Ithaca, NY: Cornell University Press, 1985).
73. See Michael Brenner, *A History of Jews in Germany Since 1945* (Bloomington: Indiana University Press, 2018).
74. Jakob Hessing, "Aufbrüche: Zur deutsch-jüdischen Literatur seit 1990," in *Handbuch der deutsch-jüdischen Literatur*, ed. Hans Otto Horch (Berlin: De Gruyter, 2016), 244–45.
75. Y. Michal Bodemann, "A Reemerging of German Jewry?" in *Reemerging Jewish Culture in Germany: Life and Literature Since 1989*, ed. Sander L. Gilman and Karen Remmler (New York: New York University Press, 1994), cited in Hessing, "Aufbrüche," 245.
76. On Jews from the former Soviet Union in Germany, see Larissa Remennick, *Russian Jews on Three Continents: Identity, Integration, and Conflict* (New Brunswick, NJ: Transaction, 2012); Masha Belenky and Jonathan Skolnik, "Russian Jews in Today's Germany: End of the Journey?" *European Judaism* 31, no. 2 (Autumn 1998): 30–44. On post-Soviet Jewish writing and Holocaust memory, it would be desirable to have a study of German-speaking writers that explored the arguments of Karolina Krasuska, "Post Soviet Migrant Memory of the Holocaust," in *The Palgrave Handbook of Holocaust Literature and Culture*, ed. Victoria Aarons and Phyllis Lassner (London: Palgrave Macmillan, 2020), 251–66.
77. In addition to Gilman and Remmler, *Reemerging Jewish Cultural Life in Germany*, see also Thomas Nolden, *Junge jüdische Literatur: Konzentriertes Schreiben in der Gegenwart* (Würzburg: Königshausen & Neumann, 1995), and Hillary Hope Herzog, Todd Herzog, and Ben Lapp, eds., *Rebirth of a Culture: Jewish Identity and Jewish Writing in German and Austria Today* (New York: Berghahn Books, 2008).

78. Katja Garloff and Agnes Mueller, eds., *German Jewish Literature after 1990* (Rochester, NY: Camden House, 2018).
79. Stuart Taberner, "The Possibilities and Pitfalls of a Jewish Cosmopolitanism: Reading Natan Sznaider through Russian-Jewish Writer Olga Grjasnowa's German-Language Novel *Der Russe ist einer, der Birken liebt*." *European Review of History / Revue européenne d'histoire* 23, nos. 5–6 (2016): 912–30.
80. See, for example Sebastian Wogenstein, "Negative Symbiosis? Israel, Germany and Austria in Contemporary Germanophone Literature," *Prooftexts* 33, no. 1 (Winter 2013): 105–32; Ashley Passmore, "Transit and Transfer: Between Germany and Israel in the Granddaughters' Generation," in Aarons and Lassner, *Palgrave Handbook of Holocaust Literature*, 217–32.
81. Christian Heilbronn, Doron Rabinovici, and Natan Sznaider, eds., *Neuer Antisemitismus? Fortsetzung einer globalen Debatte* (Frankfurt am Main: Suhrkamp, 2019).
82. Bruno Schrep, "Anschlag auf Synagoge in Wuppertal: Sechs Brandsätze in der Nacht," *Der Spiegel*, 18 January 2016, retrieved 2 January 2021 from https://www.spiegel.de/panorama/justiz/brandanschlag-auf-synagoge-in-wuppertal-taeter-erneut-vor-gericht-a-1072396.html.
83. "Wir tragen Kippa , weil … : So erleben Juden in Deutschland den Alltag," *Bild-Zeitung*, 27 May 2019, retrieved 2 January 2021 from https://www.bild.de/news/inland/politik-inland/von-bild-gabs-die-kippa-zum-selbstbasteln-wir-tragen-kippa-weil-62228990.bild.html#fromWall.
84. There are politicized debates, linked to anti-immigration discourse, over which presents the "greater" or "real" existential threat to Jews in Germany: Is it antisemitism from the homegrown German neo-Nazi milieu? Or is it a so-called "imported" antisemitism (i.e., by migrants from majority Muslim countries, where antisemitism and Holocaust denial are often inflected with the Arab-Israeli conflict—but also from the former Soviet Union and Southern Europe, where anti-Jewish prejudice is more widespread than in Western Europe)? To move beyond these simplistic and politicized either/or formulations, it is instructive to consult deeply researched studies based on large data sets, which demonstrate convincingly that the discourse of antisemitism cuts across the political and social spectrum in German society. See Jehuda Renharz and Monika Schwarz-Friesel, *Inside the Antisemitic Mind: The Language of Jew-Hatred in Contemporary Germany* (Waltham, MA: Brandeis University Press, 2017).
85. On critical whiteness studies in relation to Jewish Studies in the US context, see, for example, David Shraub, "White Jews: An Intersectional Approach," *AJS Review* 43, no. 2 (November 2019): 379–407. For an important, historically rooted perspective on German Jews, antisemitism, race, refugees, and histories of genocide in a global context, see Marion A. Kaplan, *Dominican Haven: The Jewish Refugee Settlement of Sosua, 1940–1945* (New York: Museum of Jewish Heritage, 2008).
86. Gökçe Yurdakul, "Jews, Muslims and the Ritual Male Circumcision Debate: Religious Diversity and Social Inclusion in Germany," *Social Inclusion* 4, no. 2 (2016): 77–86.
87. For an introduction to the Mbembe affair in English, see Sabine Peschel, "Why Was Achille Mbembe Accused of Antisemitism?" *Deutsche Welle*, 30 April 2020, retrieved 2 January 2021 from https://p.dw.com/p/3bc9N. Mbembe's presentation of his own position is found in Achille Mbembe, "Die Welt reparieren," *Die Zeit* Nr. 18/2020, 22 April 2020, retrieved 2 January 2021 from https://www.zeit.de/2020/18/anti semitismus-achille-mbembe-vorwuerfe-holocaust-rechtsextremisus-rassismus?fbclid =IwAR0MpC_SlrUtHb5ioXJTOKTaf20rU6vTmPoDPyBk_TtUWg1hOrG0wt

QkXJg. One critic of Mbembe who situates the antisemitism issue within a broader critique of postcolonial thought is Ingo Elbe, "Die postkoloniale Schablone," *taz*, 14 May 2020, retrieved 2 January 2021 from https://taz.de/Debatte-um-Historiker-Achille-Mbembe/!5685526/, and Ingo Elbe, "Wenn Linke einen Schlussstrich unter Auschwitz fordern," *Die Welt*, 8 June 2020, retrieved 2 January 2021 from https://www.welt.de/debatte/kommentare/plus209117081/Mbembe-Debatte-Wenn-Linke-einen-Schlussstrich-unter-Auschwitz-fordern.html.

88. Engagement with issues of postcolonial thought in relation to antisemitism and German memory culture was well underway before the Mbembe affair. See Steffen Klävers, *Decolonizing Auschwitz? Komparativ-postkoloniale Ansätze in der Holocaustforschung* (Oldenbourg: De Gruyter, 2019).

89. One group, defining themselves as "Jewish scholars and artists from Israel and elsewhere," issued an open letter calling for the removal of Germany's Federal Commissioner for Jewish Life in Germany and the Fight against Antisemitism, Felix Klein, who had opined on the Mbembe affair. Another group, "Scholars for Peace in the Middle East," declared their support for Klein. It is notable that both groups, the former consisting of about fifty individuals, the latter claiming a membership of fifty thousand, are largely composed of academics working in Israel and North America. The Central Council of Jews in Germany, which is the main community organization representing more than one hundred thousand Jews in Germany, is supportive of Klein. References and links to the statements are found here: https://www.kathradafoundation.org/2020/06/08/letter-call-to-replace-felix-klein-as-the-federal-government-commissioner-for-the-fight-against-antisemitism/ and https://www.jpost.com/bds-threat/50000-scholar-ngo-slams-antisemitic-bds-prof-supports-german-rep-627079.

90. Some of their important related work on the subject is found in Christine Achinger and Robert Fine, eds., *Antisemitism, Racism and Islamophobia: Distorted Faces of Modernity* (New York: Routledge, 2015); Farid Hafez, "Comparing Anti-Semitism and Islamophobia: The State of the Field," *Islamophobia Studies Journal* 3, no. 2 (Spring 2016): 16–34; Susannah Heschel, "Orientalist Triangulations: Jewish Scholarship on Islam as a Response to Christian Europe," in *The Muslim Reception of European Orientalism: Reversing the Gaze*, ed. Susannah Heschel and Umar Ryad (London: Routledge, 2019), 147–67. Achinger and Fine note that "Islamophobia" is a now-common shorthand for a range of phenomena that are largely more accurately described as "anti-Muslim racism."

91. Damani J. Partridge, "Monumental Memory, Moral Superiority, and Contemporary Disconnects: Racisms and Noncitizens in Europe, Then and Now," in *Spaces of Danger: Culture and Power in the Everyday*, ed. Heather Merrill and Lisa M. Hoffman (Athens: University of Georgia Press, 2015), 101–32; Rothberg and Yildiz, "Memory Citizenship," 32–48.

92. The German original version, "Geflüchtet_Zugereist_Eingewandert," is included in the essay collection *Mama darf ich das Deutschlandlied singen: Politische Texte*, edited by Mandelbaum Verlag (Mandelbaum Verlag, 2020), retrieved 14 March 2020 from https://www.mandelbaum.at/buch.php?id=973&menu=buecher.

93. "Einmischungen in die politischen und moralischen Angelegenheiten der Gesellschaft und stellen sich der Frage, wie demokratische und solidarische Prozesse vorankommen können." Dischereit, *Mama darf ich das Deutschlandlied singen*.

94. This chapter was originally printed in *Gegenwartsliteratur: A German Studies Yearbook*, vol. 17, in 2018.

Bibliography

Achinger, Christine, and Robert Fine, eds. *Antisemitism, Racism, and Islamophobia: Distorted Faces of Modernity*. New York: Routledge, 2015.
Adelson, Leslie. *The Turkish Turn in Contemporary German Literature: Toward a New Critical Grammar*. New York: Palgrave Macmillan, 2005.
Aitken, Robbie, and Eve Rosenhaft. *Black Germany: The Making and Unmaking of a Diaspora Community, 1884–1960*. New York: Cambridge University Press, 2013.
Arndt, Susan, and Antje Hornscheid, eds. *Afrika und die deutsche Sprache: Ein kritisches Nachschlagwerk*. Münster: Unrast, 2004.
Arslan, Gizem, et al. "Forum: Migration Studies." *The German Quarterly* 90, no. 2 (Spring 2017): 212–34.
Aust, Stefan, and Dirk Laabs. *Heimatschutz: Der Staat und die Mordserie des NSU*. Munich: Pantheon, 2014.
Aydemir, Fatma, und Hengameh Yaghoobifarah, eds. *Eure Heimat ist unser Albtraum*. Berlin: Ullstein Verlag, 2019.
Ayim, May. *blues in schwarz weiss*. Berlin: Orlanda Frauenverlag, 1995.
Baer, Marc David. *The Dönme: Jewish Converts, Muslim Revolutionaries, and Secular Turks*. Stanford: Stanford University Press, 2010.
Ballhaus Naunynstraße. "10 Jahre Postmigrantisches Theater." Retrieved 1 May 2021 from http://www.ballhausnaunynstrasse.de/veranstaltung/10_jahre_postmigrantisches_theater_14.11.2016.
Belenky, Masha, and Jonathan Skolnik. "Russian Jews in Today's Germany: End of the Journey?" *European Judaism* 31, no. 2 (Autumn 1998): 30–44.
Bild.de. "Wir tragen Kippa, weil . . ." 27 May 2019. Retrieved 2 January 2021 from https://www.bild.de/news/inland/politik-inland/von-bild-gabs-die-kippa-zum-selbstbasteln-wir-tragen-kippa-weil-62228990.bild.html#fromWall.
Biller, Maxim. *Wenn ich einmal reich und tot bin*. Cologne: Kiepenheuer & Witsch, 1990.
Bodemann, Y. Michal. "A Reemerging of German Jewry?" In *Reemerging Jewish Culture in Germany: Life and Literature Since 1989*, edited by Sander L. Gilman and Karen Remmler, 46–61. New York: New York University Press, 1994.
Bozay, Kemal, Bahar Aslan, Orhan Mangitay, and Funda Özfirat, eds. *Die haben gedacht wir waren das: MigrantInnen über rechten Terror und Rassismus*. Cologne: Papy Roassa, 2016.
Brahm, Felika, and Eve Rosenhaft, eds. *Slavery Hinterland: Transatlantic Slavery and Continental Europe, 1680–1850*. Woodbridge: Boydell Press, 2016.
Brandt, Bettina. "Asia, Fantasia, Germasia." In "Forum: What Is Asian German Studies?" *The German Quarterly* 93, no. 1 (Winter 2020): 120–23.
Brenner, Michael. *A History of Jews in Germany Since 1945*. Bloomington: Indiana University Press, 2018.
Çağlar, Ayşe. "Mediascapes, Advertisement Industries and Cosmopolitan Transformations: German Turks in Germany." *New German Critique* 92 (2004): 39–61.
Campt, Tina. *Other Germans: Black Germans and the Politics of Race, Gender, and Memory in the Third Reich*. Ann Arbor: University of Michigan Press, 2004.
Cheesman, Tom. *Novels of Turkish German Settlement: Cosmopolite Fictions*. Rochester, NY: Camden House, 2007.
Chin, Rita. *The Guest Worker Question in Postwar Germany*. Cambridge: Cambridge University Press, 2007.

Chin, Rita, Heide Fehrenbach, Geoff Eley, and Atina Grossmann. *After the Nazi Racial State: Difference and Democracy in Germany and Europe*. Ann Arbor: University of Michigan Press, 2009.

de Faria, Yara-Col Lemke Muniz. *Zwischen Fürsorge und Ausgrenzung: Afrodeutsche "Besatzungskinder" im Nachkriegsdeutschland*. Berlin: Metropol, 2002.

Dickinson, Kristin. *DisOrientations: Turkish-German Cultural Contact in Translation (1811–1946)*. University Park: Pennsylvania State University Press, 2021.

Dischereit, Esther. *Mama darf ich das Deutschlandlied singen; Politische Texte*. Edited by Mandelbaum Verlag. Vienna: Mandelbaum Verlag, 2020. Retrieved 14 March 2020 from https://www.mandelbaum.at/buch.php?id=973&menu=buecher.

Donath, Katharina. "Die Herkunft spielt keine Rolle—'Postmigrantisches' Theater im Ballhaus Naunynstraße: Interview mit Shermin Langhoff." *Bundeszentrale für politische Bildung*, Retrieved 14 March 2020 from http://www.bpb.de/gesellschaft/kultur/kulturelle-bildung/60135/interview-mit-shermin-langhoff?p=all.

Düzyol, Tamer, and Taudy Pathmanathan. *Haymatlos: Gedichte*. Münster: edition assemblage, 2020.

Eggers, Maureen Maisha, Grada Kilomba, Peggy Piesche and Susan Arndt, eds. *Mythen, Masken und Subjekte: Kritische Weissseinforschung in Deutschland*. Münster: Unrast, 2005.

El-Tayeb, Fatima. *Undeutsch: Die Konstruktion des Anderen in der postmigrantsichen Gesellschaft*. Bielefeld: transcript, 2016.

———. *Schwarze Deutsche: Der Diskurs um "Rasse" und nationale Identität, 1890–1933*. Frankfurt am Main: Campus, 2001.

Evans, Richard J. *The Third Reich in Power, 1933–1939*. New York: Penguin, 2005.

Fehrenbach, Heide. *Race after Hitler: Black Occupation Children in Postwar Germany and America*. Princeton, NJ: Princeton University Press, 2005.

Florvil, Tiffany. "Writing across Differences: Afro-Germans, Gender, and Diaspora, 1970s–1990s." PhD diss., University of South Carolina, Columbia, 2013.

———. *Mobilizing Black Germany: Afro-German Women and the Making of a Transnational Movement*. Champaign: University of Illinois Press, 2020.

Förster, Andreas, ed. *Geheimsache NSU: Zehn Morde, von Aufklärung keine Spur*. Tübingen: Klöfer und Meyer, 2014.

Füchtner, Veronika. "From Asian German Studies to Global German Studies?" "Forum: What Is Asian German Studies?" *The German Quarterly* 93, no. 1 (Winter 2020): 131–35.

Garloff, Katja, and Agnes Mueller, eds. *German Jewish Literature after 1990*. Rochester, NY: Camden House, 2018.

Gelbin, Cathy S., Kader Konuk, and Peggy Piesche, eds. *AufBrüche—Kulturelle Produktionen von Migrantinnen, Schwarzen und jüdischen Frauen in Deutschland*. Königstein/Taunus: Ulrike Helmer Verlag 1999.

Gezen, Ela. *Brecht, Turkish Theater, and Turkish-German Literature: Reception, Adaptation, and Innovation after 1960*. Rochester, NY: Camden House, 2018.

———. "Poetic Empathy, Political Criticism, and Public Mourning: Esther Dischereit's *Klagelieder*." *Gegenwartsliteratur: A German Studies Yearbook* 17 (2018): 313–30.

Gezen, Ela, and Berna Güneli, eds. "Turkish-German Studies: Past, Present, and Future." Special issue, *Jahrbuch Türkisch-deutsche Studien* (2015).

———. "Transnational Hi/Stories: Turkish-German Texts and Contexts." Special issue, *Colloquia Germanica* 44, no. 4 (2011, published December 2014).

Gilman, Sander L. *Difference and Pathology: Stereotypes of Sexuality, Race, and Madness.* Ithaca, NY: Cornell University Press, 1985.

Gilman, Sander L., and Karen Remmler, eds. *Reemerging Jewish Culture in Germany: Life and Literature Since 1989.* New York: New York University Press, 1994.

Gorki Studio R. "PostHeimat." Retrieved 14 March 2020 from https://www.gorki.de/en/studio-ya.

Gramling, David. "What Is Turkish-German Studies Up Against? Occidentalism and Thigmotactics." *Colloquia Germanica* 44, no. 4 (2011, published 2014): 382–95.

Gramling, David, and Deniz Göktürk. "Germany in Transit, Ten Years On." In "Forum: Migration Studies," *The German Quarterly* 90, no. 2 (Spring 2017): 217–19.

Göktürk, Deniz. "Turkish Delight—German Fright: Unsettling Oppositions in Transnational Cinema." EIPCP: European Institute for Progressive Cultural Policies, 2000.

———. "Interrupting Unity: The Berlin Wall's Second Life on Screen—A Transnational Perspective." In *Debating German Cultural Identity Since 1989*, edited by Anne Fuchs et al., 82–99. Rochester, NY: Camden House, 2011.

Grjasnowa, Olga. *Der Russe ist einer, der Birken liebt.* Munich: Carl Hanser Verlag, 2012.

———. *All Russians Love Birch Trees.* Translated from the German by Eva Bacon. New York: Other Press, 2014.

Güneli, Berna. *Fatih Akin's Cinema and the New Sound of Europe.* Bloomington: Indiana University Press, 2019.

Hafez, Farid. "Comparing Anti-Semitism and Islamophobia: The State of the Field." *Islamophobia Studies Journal* 3, no. 2 (Spring 2016): 16–34.

Halle, Randall. "The Europeanization of Turkish/German Cinema: Complex Connectivity and Imaginative Communities." *Jahrbuch Türkisch-deutsche Studien* (2015): 15–38.

Heilbronn, Christian, Doron Rabinovici, and Natan Sznaider, eds. *Neuer Antisemitismus? Fortsetzung einer globalen Debatte.* Frankfurt am Main: Suhrkamp, 2019.

Herzog, Hillary Hope, Todd Herzog, and Ben Lapp, eds. *Rebirth of a Culture: Jewish Identity and Jewish Writing in German and Austria Today.* New York: Berghahn Books, 2008.

Heschel, Susannah. "Revolt of the Colonized: Abraham Geiger's Wissenschaft des Judentums as a Challenge to Christian Hegemony in the Academy." *New German Critique* 77 (1999): 61–85.

———. "Orientalist Triangulations: Jewish Scholarship on Islam as a Response to Christian Europe." In *The Muslim Reception of European Orientalism: Reversing the Gaze*, edited by Susannah Heschel and Umar Ryad, 147–67. London: Routledge, 2019.

Hess, Jonathan M. "Johann David Michaelis and the Colonial Imaginary: Orientalism and the Emergence of Racial Antisemitism in Eighteenth-Century Germany." *Jewish Social Studies* 6, no. 2 (2000): 56–102.

Hessing, Jakob. "Aufbrüche: Zur deutsch-jüdischen Literatur seit 1990." In *Handbuch der deutsch-jüdischen Literatur*, edited by Hans Otto Horch, 244–45. Berlin: De Gruyter, 2016.

Hicke, Karolina. "Intersections of Migration, Memory, and Gender in Contemporary Jewish Writing in Germany." PhD diss., University of Massachusetts Amherst, forthcoming.

Honeck, Mischa, Martin Klimke, and Anne Kuhlmann-Smirnov, eds. *Germany and the Black Diaspora: Points of Contact, 1250–1914.* New York: Berghahn Books, 2016.

Hügel-Marshall, Ika, et al., eds. *Entfernte Verbindungen: Rassismus, Antisemitismus, Klassenunterdrückung.* Berlin: Orlanda Verlag, 1993.

Hügel-Marshall, Ika, Chris Lange, May Ayim, Ilona Bubeck, Gülşen Aktaş, and Dagmar Schultz. "An unsere LeserInnen." In *Entfernte Verbindungen: Rassismus, Antisemitismus, Klassenunterdrückung*, edited by Ika Hügel-Marshall et al., 11–14. Berlin: Orlanda Verlag, 1993.
ISD-admin. "Stellungnahme zu den faschistischen Attacken in Chemnitz," 31 August 2018. Retrieved 12 March 2020 from http://isdonline.de/stellungnahme-zu-den-faschistischen-attacken-in-chemnitz/.
Jaima, Felicitas. "Adopting Diaspora: African American Military Women in Cold War West Germany." PhD diss., New York University, 2016.
Joskowicz, Ari. *The Modernity of Others: Jewish Anti-Catholicism in Germany and France.* Stanford, CA: Stanford University Press, 2013.
Kaplan, Marion A. *Dominican Haven: The Jewish Refugee Settlement of Sosua, 1940–1945.* New York: Museum of Jewish Heritage, 2008.
Kelly, Natasha A. *Rassismus: Strukturelle Probleme brauchen struktuelle Lösungen.* Zurich: Atrium Verlag, 2021.
King, Kevina. "Tools and Tolls of Germanness: Institutional Racism and Racial Profiling." Paper presented at the conference "Minorities and Minority Discourses in Germany since 1990: Intersections, Interventions, Interpolations" (University of Massachusetts Amherst, 3 March 2017.
———. "Black, People of Color and Migrant Lives Should Matter: Racial Profiling, Police Brutality and Whiteness in Germany." In *Rethinking Black German Studies: Approaches, Interventions, Histories*, edited by Tiffany Florvil and Vanessa Plumly, 169–96. Oxford: Peter Lang, 2018.
Klävers, Steffen. *Decolonizing Auschwitz? Komparativ-postkoloniale Ansätze in der Holocaustforschung.* Oldenbourg: De Gruyter, 2019.
Koepsell, Philipp Khabo. "Literature and Activism." In *Arriving in the Future*, edited by Asoka Esuruoso and Philipp Khabo Koepsell, 36–47. Berlin: epubli, 2014.
Konuk, Kader. *East West Mimesis: Auerbach in Turkey.* Stanford, CA: Stanford University Press, 2010.
Krasuska, Karolina. "Post-Soviet Migrant Memory of the Holocaust." In *The Palgrave Handbook of Holocaust Literature and Culture*, edited by Victoria Aarons and Phyllis Lassner, 251–66. New York: Palgrave Macmillan, 2020.
Kuria, Emily. *eingeschrieben: Zeichen setzen gegen Rassismus an deutschen Hochschulen.* Berlin: w_orten & meer, 2015.
Lässig, Simone. *Jüdische Wege ins Bürgertum.* Göttingen: Vandenhoeck & Ruprecht, 2004.
Layne, Priscilla. "On Racism without Race: The Need to Diversify *Germanistik* and the German Academy." In *Who Can Speak and Who Is Heard/Hurt? Facing Problems of Race, Racism and Ethnic Diversity in the Humanities in Germany*, edited by Mahmoud Arghavan, Nicole Hirschfelder, Luvena Kopp, and Katharina Motyl, 217–38. Bielefeld: transcript, 2019.
Levy, Daniel. Review of Rita Chin, Heide Fehrenbach, Geoff Eley, and Atina Grossmann, *After the Nazi Racial State: Difference and Democracy in Germany and Europe.* H-German, H-Net Reviews, July 2011.
Lubrich, Oliver. "Are Russian Jews Post-colonial? Wladimir Kaminer and Identity Politics." *East European Jewish Affairs* 33 (2003): 35–52.
Lusane, Clarence. *Hitler's Black Victims: The Historical Experiences of Afro-Germans, European Blacks, Africans, and African Americans in the Nazi Era.* New York: Routledge, 2002.

Mandel, Ruth. *Cosmopolitan Anxieties: Turkish Challenges to Citizenship and Belonging in Germany.* Durham, NC: Duke University Press, 2008.
Mani, Bala Venkat. *Cosmopolitical Claims: Turkish-German Literatures from Nadolny to Pamuk.* Iowa City: University of Iowa Press, 2007.
———. "Migrants, Refugees, Exiles: *Cosmopolitical Claims* beyond *Willkommenskultur*." In "Forum: Migration Studies," *The German Quarterly* 90, no. 2 (Spring 2017): 219–22.
Martin, Peter. *Schwarze Teufel, edle M***en: Afrikaner in Geschichte und Bewußtein der Deutschen.* Hamburg: Hamburger Edition, 2001.
Mayer, Hans. *Außenseiter.* Frankfurt am Main: Suhrkamp, 1975.
Mediendienst Integration. "Wie viele rassistische Straftaten gibt es?" Retrieved 14 March 2020 from https://mediendienst-integration.de/desintegration/rassismus.html.
Meyer, Michael. "Jewish Self-Understanding." In *German-Jewish History in Modern Times.* Vol. 2: *Emancipation and Acculturation*, edited by Michael A. Meyer. New York: Columbia University Press, 1997.
Miller, Jennifer. *Turkish Guest Workers in Germany: Hidden Lives and Contested Borders, 1960s to 1980s.* Toronto: University of Toronto Press, 2018.
Nolden, Thomas. *Junge jüdische Literatur: Konzentriertes Schreiben in der Gegenwart.* Würzburg: Königshausen & Neumann, 1995.
Oguntoye, Katharina. *Eine afrodeutsche Geschichte zur Lebenssituation von Afrikanern und Afro-Deutschen in Deutschland von 1884 bis 1950.* Berlin: Hoho Verlag Christine Hoffmann, 1997.
Özdamar, Emine Sevgi. *Seltsame Sterne staren zur Erde: Wedding-Pankow; 1976–77.* Cologne: Kiepenheuer & Witsch, 2003.
Özyürek, Esra. *Being German, Becoming Muslim: Race, Religion, and Conversion in the New Europe.* Princeton, NJ: Princeton University Press, 2014.
———. "Muslim Minorities as Germany's Past Future: Islam Critics, Holocaust Memory, and Immigrant Integration." *Memory Studies* (June 2019).
Partridge, Damani J. "Monumental Memory, Moral Superiority, and Contemporary Disconnects: Racisms and Noncitizens in Europe, Then and Now." In *Spaces of Danger: Culture and Power in the Everyday*, edited by Heather Merrill and Lisa M. Hoffman, 101–32. Athens: University of Georgia Press, 2015.
Passmore, Ashley. "Transit and Transfer: Between Germany and Israel in the Granddaughters' Generation." In *The Palgrave Handbook of Holocaust Literature and Culture*, edited by Victoria Arons and Phillis Lassner, 217–32. London: Palgrave Macmillan, 2020.
Peña, Rosemarie. "The Rekinning: Portrayals of Postwar Black German Transnational Adoption." PhD diss., Rutgers University, New Brunswick, NJ, 2020.
Piesche, Peggy, and Sara Lennox. "Epilogue: Of Epistemologies and Positionalities. A Conversation, Berlin, October 21, 2014." In *Remapping Black Germany: New Perspectives on Afro-German History, Politics, and Culture*, edited by Sara Lennox, 274–82. Amherst: University of Massachusetts Press, 2016.
Popoola, Olumide, and Belda Sezen, eds. *Talking Home: Heimat aus unserer eigenen Feder, Frauen of Color in Deutschland.* Amsterdam: Blue Moon Press, 1999.
van Rahden, Till. "Jews and the Ambivalences of Civil Society in Germany, 1800–1933: Assessment and Reassessment." *Journal of Modern History* 77, no. 4 (2005): 1024–47.
Reich, Annika, and Lina Muzur, eds. *Das Herz verlässt keinen Ort, an dem es hängt: Weiter Schreiben—Literarische Begegnungen mit Autorinnen und Autoren aus Krisengebieten.* Berlin: Ullstein, 2018.

Reisoğlu, Mert Bahadır "Interlacing Archives: History and Memory in Emine Sevgi Özdamar's *Die Brücke vom Goldenen Horn*." *Colloquia Germanica* 44, no. 4 (2011, published 2014): 422–37.

Remennick, Larissa. *Russian Jews on Three Continents: Identity, Integration, and Conflict.* New Brunswick, NJ: Transaction, 2012.

Renharz, Jehuda, and Monika Schwarz-Friesel. *Inside the Antisemitic Mind: The Language of Jew-Hatred in Contemporary Germany.* Waltham, MA: Brandeis University Press, 2017.

Sarrazin, Thilo. *Deutschland schafft sich ab: Wie wir unser Land aufs Spiel setzen.* Munich: Deutsche Verlags-Anstalt, 2010.

Schuster-Craig, Johanna. "Asian German Studies, Muslim German Studies, and Critical Whiteness Studies." "Forum: What Is Asian German Studies?" *The German Quarterly* 93, no. 1 (Winter 2020): 123–27.

Şenocak, Zafer. *Gefährliche Verwandtschaft.* Munich: Babel Verlag, 2003.

Seyhan, Azade. *Writing Outside the Nation.* Princeton, NJ: Princeton University Press, 2001.

Shraub, David. "White Jews: An Intersectional Approach." *AJS Review* 43, no. 2 (November 2019): 379–407.

Skolnik, Jonathan. "Memory without Borders? Migrant Identity and the Legacy of the Holocaust Memory in Olga Grjasnowa's *Der Russe ist einer, der Birken liebt*." In *German-Jewish Literature Since 1990: Beyond the Holocaust?* edited by Katja Garloff and Agnes Mueller, 123–45. Rochester, NY: Camden House, 2018.

Slobodian, Quinn. *Foreign Front: Third World Politics in Sixties West Germany.* Durham, NC: Duke University Press, 2012.

Slobodian, Quinn, ed. *Comrades of Color: East Germany in the Cold War.* New York: Berghahn Books, 2015.

Sorkin, David. "Emancipation and Assimilation: Two Concepts and their Application to German-Jewish History." *Year Book of the Leo Baeck Institute* 35 (1990): 17–33.

Sow, Noah. "Diaspora Dynamics: Shaping the Future of Literature." *Journal of the African Literature Association* 11, no. 1 (2017): 28–33.

Soysal, Levent. "Labor to Culture: Writing Turkish Migration to Europe." *South Atlantic Quarterly* 102, nos. 2/3 (2003): 491–508.

Spector, Scott. "Forget Assimilation: Introducing Subjectivity to German-Jewish History." *Jewish History* 20, nos. 3–4 (2006): 349–61.

Steyerl, Hito, ed. *Spricht die Subalterne deutsch? Migration und postkoloniale Politik.* Münster: Unrast, 2003.

Still, Eric. *Prophetic Remembrance: Black Subjectivity in African American and South African Trauma Narratives.* Charlottesville: University of Virginia Press, 2014.

Taberner, Stuart. "The Possibilities and Pitfalls of a Jewish Cosmopolitanism: Reading Natan Sznaider through Russian-Jewish Writer Olga Grjasnowa's German-Language Novel *Der Russe ist einer, der Birken liebt*." *European Review of History / Revue européenne d'histoire* 23, nos. 5–6 (2016): 912–30.

Teege, Jennifer, Nikola Sellmair, and Carolin Sommer. *My Grandfather Would Have Shot Me: A Black Woman Discovers Her Family's Nazi Past.* New York: The Experiment, 2016.

Thurman, Kira. *Singing like Germans: Black Musicians in the Land of Bach, Beethoven, and Brahms.* Ithaca, NY: Cornell University Press, 2021.

Tißberger, Martina, Gabriele Dietze, Daniela Hrzán, and Jana Husmann, eds. *Weiß-Weißsein-Whiteness: Kritische Studien zu Gender und Rassismus*. Frankfurt am Main: Peter Lang, 2006.

Tribunal NSU Komplex auflösen. *Wir klagen an! Anklage des Tribunals "NSU-Komplex auflösen* (2017).

Ullstein Buchverlage. "Aydemir, Fatma und Hengameh Yaghoobifarah (Hrsg.). *Eure Heimat ist unser Albtraum.*" Retrieved 14 March 2020 from https://www.ullstein-buchverlage.de/nc/buch/details/eure-heimat-ist-unser-albtraum-9783548062402.html.

Watkins, Jamele. "The Drama of Race: Contemporary Afro-German Theater." PhD diss., University of Massachusetts at Amherst, 2017.

Weber, Beverly. *Violence and Gender in the "New" Europe: Islam in German Culture*. New York: Palgrave Macmillan, 2013.

Weg sein—hier sein: Texte aus Deutschland. Zurich: Secession Verlag, 2016.

Wigger, Iris. "'Black Shame'—The Campaign against 'Racial Degeneration' and Female Degradation in Interwar Europe." *Institute of Race Relations* 51, no. 3 (2010): 33–46.

Wogenstein, Sebastian. "Negative Symbiosis? Israel, Germany and Austria in Contemporary Germanophone Literature." *Prooftexts* 33, no. 1 (Winter 2013): 105–32.

Yeşilada, Karin. *Poesie der Dritten Sprache*. Tübingen: Stauffenburg Verlag, 2012.

Yildiz, Yasemin. *Beyond the Mother Tongue: The Postmonolingual Condition*. New York: Fordham University Press, 2012.

Yurdakul, Gökçe. *From Guestworkers into Muslims: The Transformation of Turkish Immigrant Associations in Germany*. Newcastle upon Tyne: Cambridge Scholars Publishing, 2009.

———. "Jews, Muslims and the Ritual Male Circumcision Debate: Religious Diversity and Social Inclusion in Germany." *Social Inclusion* 4, no. 2 (2016): 77–86.

Zaimoğlu, Feridun. *Kanak Sprak Kanak Sprak: 24 Mißtöne vom Rande der Gesellschaft*. Hamburg: Rotbuch, 1997

Zaimoğlu, Feridun, and Günter Senkel. *Moses*. Kiel: Solivagus-Verlag, 2013.

Zhang, Chunjie, ed. "Forum: What Is Asian German Studies?" *The German Quarterly* 93, no. 1 (Winter 2020): 106–41.

CHAPTER 1

Refugee—Migrant—Immigrant

ESTHER DISCHEREIT

Rahel lives around the corner on the other side of the street. There is a downstairs apartment she owns right under her own that she allowed a mother and two children to use for a long time. At first the children were alone with Rahel. The mother and father had separated, and the children had been sent on ahead until the mother, who came from Sudan, could follow. The three of them have now moved out and settled in Kreuzberg, and the youngest child is going to a preschool that was founded by ADEFRA—an initiative for Black women and "Women of Color" it says on the homepage.

Rahel . . . really she could . . . She takes a young man in. He is only a little older than her son, who could do with another "brother" around anyhow. Especially since his own brother has left home. Maher arrives, hardly speaks, seems reluctant to do so, and is completely unpolitical. She lives with him now, and the three of them do not fit together. They sit squashed in her tiny kitchen. The authorities cover Maher's rent up to three hundred euros. Rahel has been worried for years that she will not be able to keep working if she doesn't get a qualification. She is caught in the nonqualification trap, and the paperwork is piled up on her desk. Maher's room is cheaper than a bed in refugee housing. Rahel has cared for refugees professionally, something she started during the Balkan Wars. She's always done it. She says that being Jewish has something to do with it. She also says that she has only known sort of "run-of-the-mill" refugees up until now. Now it is different. Now it is people with university degrees. She offers Maher free tickets to the theater. Maher says no thanks.

I receive an email from Gh. Two friends from Syria have been living in a small Bavarian village for months. They are now able to take a German course, or rather, they would be able to take a German course if they could find a teacher nearby. There are no teachers in the village. The nearest city is a long way off. They don't have a car because social services do not support that. No train ticket either. They walk up and down the main street, lie on their beds, listen to music on their cellphones, or try to get news from home over the internet. They have full status as asylum seekers, which allows them to stay and to travel, and they are dependent on social services. My neighbor's flat on the floor above has just been rented out. Shame. She rented it to some Israelis. There are lots of them. Lots of young people. Gh. writes that they have to get away or they will go crazy. I call a woman I know who has a flat in Kreuzberg. She lives in Italy, works there, wanted to live in Berlin, really, but has changed her mind—she has a doctor's practice. I say to her, would you like to rent your flat to some asylum seekers? She writes back, saying, unfortunately, she has to get as much money as she can for her flat so that she can cover her costs . . . Alessandra is a survivor; a child survivor of the Holocaust.

Gh. speaks to Rahel. Actually, now Rahel only has one room free. After Gh.'s visit, her friends will come, both of them. My daughter says that she has to leave early today and transport some people's luggage. She is always transporting somebody's luggage. I ask her to stay. She says that the two of them have arrived, that she saw them . . . Oh okay, I say. She needs thermoses. She is organizing a tea stand for the people waiting outside the reception facility. There are long queues. I have hardly used my designer thermos. Actually, I have never used it. Should I give it to her? I give her three thermoses. Normal thermoses. I'm not some sort of field kitchen. Why on earth did she have to take the night shift starting at eleven o'clock?

The two of them move in with Rahel. Rahel says that they are good people and that at last something is happening in her house. They move around the heavy pieces of furniture that have been left behind and carry things in and out. At last something is happening. The whole tea stand business has come to an end. There were only about thirty refugees at the reception facility today. Some of them are sleeping here. In tents. In the middle of Berlin. Thousands of them have registered but have not been able to apply for asylum. Where are they supposed to find a bed or get social assistance? They start queueing up very early in the morning. At first it was almost all men. Now there are women and children. In January alone new arrivals were said to have been around 55 percent women and children. That was 34 percent more than in 2015. Europol—the European police authority—estimates that, of the eighty-five thousand unaccompanied juveniles who arrived in the previous year, around ten thousand of them are regarded as missing in the EU. "We don't know where they are," says the head of Europol, Rob Wainwright.

I know where one of them is. A few days ago, a seventeen-year-old boy from Egypt jumped out of a moving train near Munich. The authorities had already sent him back to Austria once. When they tried to take him with them again, he opened the window. His mother will open a letter. She will not know exactly what stretch of track it was on which her son died or whether the train was stopped or whether somebody held him in their arms.

Whereas last autumn 10,000 refugees crossed the border in a single day, it went down to a few thousand, and now it is only 150. That could change again when the weather improves and the Mediterranean is less stormy. Italy is predicting 50,000. On top of that there are those who are returning—people who have been refused asylum in Austria and want to try Italy. Almost all of those who arrive here set off from Libya. Their route: Lampedusa to Sicily.

Gh. came for an interview for a shared flat, and she brought a tray of cakes with her. The white members of the shared flat had decided to take someone from "somewhere else." They didn't want any more "potato heads." She came to Germany after her boyfriend was killed by a car bomb. They welcomed the Arab Spring, demonstrated, talked, sang. Her father was a lowly official in the civil service until someone denounced him as an Assad opponent. He himself had never said a word, just carried on with his work and was not involved in anything. Now Gh.'s mother and father live on what the children occasionally send them. The two sisters and a brother are already living in Germany. One is a journalist, and Gh. says that she does not want to apply for asylum. She wants to go home one day and help with reconstruction. She has permission to stay as a student but nothing more. A German friend of her sister's had provided a guarantee that she would not become a burden to the state. I know her. She doesn't have a fixed job and lives from hand to mouth. The word "affidavit" had a sort of magical sound to it in the stories that my mother—who survived the Nazis—told me later. After 1945. The word came too late for my mother. She had no affidavit and was not able to escape Nazi Germany. Later Gh. asked me if I could provide an affidavit for her best friend. I said yes. It was a hesitant yes. She doesn't need it now anyway. She made it to France.

At first Gh. had two or three jobs paying significantly less than the minimum wage, until she got a stipend from a foundation. Gh. studies all day. She wants to become a biochemist, and she wants to pass her exams. She earns a little on top of her stipend by giving Arabic lessons. She is also a member of a group that wants to try to make it easier for refugees to go to German universities. She calls me "mother," and she calls my daughter "sister." She is twenty years old. She telephones home once a week. She cannot visit her parents because that would put them in danger, and her parents cannot leave. There wouldn't be enough money for that. If ISIS were to reach them: Gh. draws her finger across her throat. "We are Druze."

I am invited to a birthday party in the evening. Many people have come to the hall where it is being held, which was in the old French zone when the Allies still occupied the city. Elke's cellphone rings. She stands, says that she is going to have to go soon. She is on a list of people who have signed up to take in others who arrive at night in the buses. All of the authorities' offices are closed, there is no information, no help. She would have liked to have stayed, says: "But I don't take in any men. I only take women or families. Nobody can expect me to take in strange men." Young men make up the majority of the refugees. Or they did back then. Later I put myself on the list. In the many months since then the phone has only rung once: "In one hour please come to camp such and such." Central Processing, Berlin. I have room for two people in my study. "People who know each other," I wrote. They will have to sleep in one bed. I check the box for men. And children. I don't have the car today. My daughter took it with her. How am I supposed to get there in the middle of the night and bring people back the next morning? The cellphone tells me: "Stand down." "Only three buses today." I delete the texts.

At the print shop, I discuss the details about the newspaper we're publishing. "The View of the Other," a festival in Vienna. Six unaccompanied young refugees, men, are standing on the stage. The director says that they have no way of getting to the rehearsals. They have been put somewhere outside of town. Most of them have. They get nothing. Somebody will have to organize a ride. At the rehearsal the director says that the actors have to hold hands. It's part of the role. She thinks that the young boys from Afghanistan are shocked about that. Because of the girls. She believes that they are all going to be expelled but that nobody has told them. Nobody here is older than seventeen. At the age of eight my daughter didn't want to have anything more to do with boys ... They have never been to the theater, the director says. I think of the parallel German society. There are some Germans, too, who have never been to the theater ... The number of asylum seekers who are getting official recognition is around 50 or 60 percent. "It has never been higher," says my friend who is working for Aydan Özoğuz, the official in charge of migration, refugees, and integration. She is the first non-German German to occupy this role. The percentage is higher than it was during the Balkan Wars. It is a legal provision that people have to be taken in if they are fleeing war or persecution. The Geneva Refugee Convention and the right of asylum. It is not about assessment or interpretation. It is about the law.

Every other week, the typographer goes to a café that an artist is renting. She offers coffee, tea, and an opportunity to get to know others. She is Ukrainian. The typographer is very taken with a thirteen-year-old boy. Everyone is talking, and somehow it's quite comical, this strangeness, and then everyone breaks out in peals of laughter. So, she goes off once every two weeks to talk and laugh with strangers. I once went to laughter yoga. This café business can't be any funnier than that.

Rahel says that she can't come today. A friend of hers who makes documentaries and Martin W. are probably coming over. W. is an actor. W. is famous. The documentary maker probably wants to make a film with the new residents. And maybe W. can do something for them as well. I am jealous because both of them—Gh.'s friends—will meet Martin W. I always wanted to meet him.

I can't talk to Nehmat either. She is sixty-seven years old and was a very important journalist in Syria, with a sharp tongue, who wrote under a pen-name until the Muhabarat discovered her identity and she had to flee. First to Turkey, then in a rubber dinghy, Mediterranean. Nehmat can't swim. I'm not able to speak to her today. Somebody is making a film about her. I know she lived in Damascus, in Yarmuk, the Palestinian quarter. Nehmat believes that the authorities give intellectuals a particularly hard time. My Palestinian friend, who must have been in Germany for over thirty years now, does not agree. Neither do I. The authorities probably give everyone a hard time.

It was the business with Nehmat that made me realize how crazy it is that she is here in Germany, in Berlin, here, where thousands of young Israelis are also living. People who also want to be far from the place they come from. The writer Lizzi Doron also prefers to be here since she wrote about the expulsion of Palestinians from East Jerusalem. If Nehmat were able to return to the land of her parents, she would not have had to have undertaken this dangerous journey. There are about 350,000 settlers living on her land. They live there illegally. Everyone knows that; the UN, everyone in the world. They're living there illegally and have built up a functioning infrastructure. Palestinian returnees could easily manage there, and the Israelis could save face. They wouldn't have to grant the Right of Return, just take in the people of Yarmouk. And what about the illegal settlers? They would have to go back to the United States, where they came from. That would mean that the United States would have to come to terms with its own fundamentalists, and maybe the young Israelis would regain some sort of hope. My friend M. asks if it isn't the responsibility of the Americans anyway, after waging so many wars, to deal with the consequences? Frank-Walter Steinmeier, the German foreign minister, said recently that this view of things could not simply be dismissed. I can remember the Soviet invasion of Afghanistan. I thought it was a disgrace. And then the Taliban came along . . . but you all know that. If the settlements in Israel were to go, then not only would the routes the refugees have to take be shorter but I would also be able to speak kindly of Israel. That would be good too.

There is a widespread view in Germany that you Americans, that your nation is responsible for most of the terrible things in the world today. That's what my physiotherapist Herr Erdmann says: that internet servers in the United Kingdom and the United States have been sending millions of "welcome" messages out into the world. "So you can see what's what and who wants to finish off whom" Herr Erdmann says. It's also a relic of the defeated and humiliated generation. Or—and this is how it seemed to me recently—it is a demonization of US potency as a sort of Golem figure. Personally, I'm made very uneasy by Mr. Putin's presence in Syria. A few Pussy Riots in Los Angeles don't really help. Not everything people say can be true. The VW scandal helped in this regard. We learned that the emissions guidelines are stricter in the United States than they are in Germany. We wouldn't have believed that either. But I'm getting off the point.

Io. is visiting her sisters. The older one is teaching hip-hop to the girls who fled unaccompanied, and the young one takes them shopping. At the checkout, Io. pretends she doesn't know that the girls are buying fashionable shoes instead of warm coats. She pays, but it's not her private money, it's social support. She talks about her coworker, that they . . . , not, that they . . . Well, they have gotten quite close . . . Very close in fact, but it's all true, all of it, only . . . apart from one thing, apart from one thing . . . The youngest sister was born in Frankfurt am Main. Sixteen relatives, living in two rooms, fled the Balkan Wars. The mother had never been given a work permit to practice medicine in Germany. When she was small, the older sister told them about "Granata" and the big dinosaur bite out of their grandparents' house. She likes her coworker, really likes him, not that anything happened . . . but . . . it's just that he's a Muslim, she says.

The harmlessness test for Berlin-Wilmersdorf has to be done. "Wilmersdorf Helps" is a gigantic business, founded and run by people who have ended up spending their lives involved in it. Volunteers, young people, an efficient business unmatched by any other. They have extraordinary logistics; they know exactly when they need beds, how many, and whether they are going get extra ones—and tomorrow we will need diapers. They distribute things, they post things, they get things done. J. has arrived from the United States with a PhD, but she has no time now, has to get to the health ministry so that it can appear innocuous when she distributes food. Hundreds of meals a day. J. has passed her harmlessness test. J. also teaches a course in advanced German. It had been her intention that everyone would speak freely, not relying on a textbook. She won't try that again, she says. She couldn't bear the stories that her adult students—remarkably they are mostly doctors here—she couldn't stand the stories that they told her. Watching the death of one's own child . . . Other things . . . J. belongs to the third Shoah generation. She went back to the textbook.

Cologne. Because of Cologne some of my friends have turned away from the refugees. One of them writes that he has a daughter who is at an age where she could be raped. And so, they. . . these people . . . they have to understand the rules here. The refugees go around their small communities with their heads hanging and are ashamed. As if we haven't always been afraid for our daughters . . . always that fear when we watched them going out, when we were reluctant to go and pick them up. I read my poem:

> don't touch me
> you make me sick
> I can't
> do not come in the dark
> to my bed
> I shout

show me your face
never ever
without asking me
and if I say
that it's not okay
then that's that
do you get me?

This was published in 2001 in *Hoarfrosted Mouth and Other News*. My friend from Ramallah emails that for decades she has always kept her head down and hurried through the streets when she goes out because, in her society, it is normal for women to be molested. She is outraged about the racialized apportioning of blame to Arabs and Muslims. I sign a petition against racism and sexism.

The Swiss have prevented anyone with two passports from being deported if they get caught riding the tram without a ticket or other such minor offenses. What if somebody were to get involved in a schoolyard fight? We have emphasized democracy, law, the rule of law over the rule of blood and soil. We are relieved. Others are not. In Zirndorf a Black pastor leaves his parish because he can no longer stand the constant death threats. The parish is supporting him, but many others are not, and things are getting more militant. It is as if Germany is even catching up with the Ku Klux Klan, something that we have been aware of since at least the case of the NSU (National Socialist Underground) murders in Baden-Württemberg. The man has done nothing wrong. He is Black, nothing more.

There is an average of 3.3 attacks on asylum seekers' accommodation every day. "Generation Terror," which has been able to constitute itself almost free of any legal constraint since the attacks on asylum seekers' homes in the 1990s, is now acting quite brazenly. They have grown up in a "culture of impunity" (as the journalist Heike Kleffner has called it). There has been an enormous increase in attacks compared to last year and the year before that. I see Jus.'s mother at a reading. The young author escaped a fundamentalist Jewish sect in Williamsburg, New York. She describes a world of Hasidic patriarchal darkness. In Berlin she is asked whether she still considers herself, after everything that has happened, to be a Jew. While the young author and mother explained patiently that she goes with her son to the synagogue, that she loves the city, and that she is sometimes too lazy to go to the synagogue . . . Jus.'s mother whispers in my ear: did I know that there are six hundred crimes a year motivated by antisemitism? I say nothing.

Before the group with the tea canisters arrives, they hand out the medications that they've collected. The two representatives of the local Protestant deaconry, which has replaced the hundreds of volunteers, decline the offer. Some of the medicine is beyond its use-by date, and the law prevents people from handing out medicine without a prescription. I take the medicines to Vienna, to one of the emergency reception facilities. They take them gladly and sort them according to their type. A doctor comes to the center a few times a week as well as other volunteer service providers. There are eight hundred people accommodated there in a former Ministry building. The building does not have adequate bathroom facilities. People who work at the tax office don't often take a shower during the day. The refugees are given tokens, then a bus arrives and takes them to the swimming pool.

Here, too, volunteers are in the majority. Team Austria. You can just drop in. A lot of the helpers are multilingual and have refugee and migrant backgrounds themselves. A student with a Turkish background is very tired in class. He spent the night working in a house for refugees. We organize German-language classes at the university. As much German as they need for now anyway ... In UNIKO, the association of Austrian Universities, member institutions have set themselves the joint task of getting proper recognition and access to university for all those who have fled their countries. I get an Excel table every semester. I can enter the classes that I will be offering in the coming semester and for how many students. Right-wingers have brought a case against this procedure on the grounds that it discriminates in favor of the refugees. Insufficient knowledge of German is still a very high barrier. Notice has been given on the showerless building. Now we are afraid that the refugees will be moved somewhere outside the city, to some sort of camp from which it will be impossible to get away because they have no money and no tickets for the bus or train and are in the middle of nowhere. They are making things as difficult as possible. Yesterday there was a man here from Iraq, and, using the translation app on his cellphone, he managed, eventually, to tell one of the helpers that he wanted to go home. A group of us from the course went once to offer our help. They were all asking about somewhere to live, a room, how do they get away from here? I am looking for a retired rector or someone who would be enthused by an idea that has already been put into practice in the United States: Black Mountain College. It is a place where the refugees who have an educational background in science or art can work together with locals—an experimental laboratory, if you will, and at the same time a sort of first destination for assistance. It offered refugees from Nazi Germany and the rest of Europe a temporary place to stay and work. With the cooperation of American artists, there was a notable synthesis between art and science that lasted well into the 1950s. Merce Cunningham, Albert Einstein. The list of eminent instructors is long. We need the same sort of "Black Mountain" college in Europe. The mountains are already here. And I am trying to scrape together the money for a college like that. Students from Lüneburg managed to make a start with the "No Border Academy" initiative, which is addressing the needs of refugees everywhere. Professors give all classes in English. It is volunteer work. At our little department we have established remedial language classes too. Anyone can come. They don't need to be registered at the university. We have reached the stage where all Austrian universities have joined the Initiative MORE, which organizes German courses for refugees and gives people opportunities to participate in university classes.

The accordion player from Sound Forum Vienna has to get to Germany. There is an announcement every fifteen minutes at the central station. All train service from Salzburg to Germany has been canceled. He takes the train via Passau. Stop. Forty-five minutes. Wait. The border police patrol every train car and remove any refugee they find. He took this route once before, and two young men had laid themselves on the floor, covered themselves, and kept as still as pieces of furniture. The border police pretended not to notice them. The accordion player bought them both bread rolls and coffee. They wanted to get to Munich.

It's no longer possible to do this. Identity checks before entering the country or moving on anywhere else are carried out rigorously. For a little while the Austrians sent buses full of people off in the direction of Germany, at night, in the cold, and dumped their human cargo out into the fields flanking the Danube. People jumped into the water, regardless of the snow and ice.

A few months later. At the Vienna airport one of the Austrian Airline staff croaks into a microphone: due to the recent suspension of the Schengen agreements in Europe all passengers are requested to have their valid travel documents with them. The microphone is turned off. When the passengers present their documents, the stewardess turns away. There is no time for that before departure. The economy is afraid of costs, delays, economic damages. People who work on the other side of the border now need twice as long to get to work. It says in the newspapers that they are hoping to reintroduce the Schengen agreement by the end of the year. The fear of economic damages presents a stroke of good fortune.

Even though Sweden erected the first barriers and the so-called "people smuggler" trials are underway in Austria—trials in which refugees who had long been occupying the Votive Church were dragged before the judge and accused of being smugglers themselves—Germany was only really able to rely on Austria and Sweden within the EU. The smuggler, well, the smuggler smuggles people from point A to point B even if there is a legal barrier between those two points. The writer Abasse Ndione wrote about people smuggling in his book *The Piragua,* in which he says: "There is a member of just about every family in Senegal who has got in a boat and tried to make their way to Europe to seek their fortune." If they could, people would almost certainly drag Europe's fortune back to Senegal. Of course they would. I don't have to tell you that these processes not only have to do with dictatorships and corruption but are also about the distribution of wealth in the world. If you have to go, you have to go, and nothing will stop you. Raoul Schrott, my Austrian fellow writer, has reported how he found a young man from Eritrea in the deserts of Egypt who had died of thirst and who had a slip of paper in his trouser pocket with the address of his aunt in Mannheim on it. And he is full of sadness about this courageous young man who set off on his own and didn't make it.

Do we have to arrest someone who lets a refugee get into his taxi so that that refugee can register at the next police station? Was the taxi driver paid, and if so is he a smuggler, and what if he picked others up on the way, and should he not charge for the ride in order to avoid doing anything illegal? My friends are occupied with such questions as well. They organized a private convoy from Austria to Hungary because Orbán's government torpedoed the refugees' chances of further travel by stopping the buses and other forms of transport. But the convoy was successful, and the people were brought out in private cars. Later they received the Lisa Fittko Prize—*Escape through the Pyrenees*—and were celebrated in the Munich Theatre. Lisa Fittko helped refugees. She was an Austrian resistance fighter against the Nazi dictatorship. Now NATO ships are deployed in the Mediterranean to take action against people smugglers. When you take action against the smugglers, then you are also taking action against the refugees—those who are stranded in Turkey, some of them for a long time. Why have no official visa offices been opened in these countries: threefold occupation? Why has Nehmat not been able to use the legal opportunities open to her? If she had been able to get a visa, then she would have been legally guaranteed. She would have boarded a plane and not a rubber dinghy.

A small group of Jews living in Germany meets. It is a sort of salon, nothing official. The theme is refugees. I attend, want to think about how Jewish people ... One of them says, "When we arrived nobody bothered about us." The woman has a Russian accent, and she came to Germany in the early 1990s as a permitted refugee. There followed a detailed account of why it was impossible to stay in Tajikistan, the rundown, broken system, and whether we could even imagine, and extremists of all kinds ... The woman now has an important position in the education system of the Jewish Community. This forms the basis of some serious doubts that Germany should take in people from Syria. Can we know who they are? Later we discovered that donations have been collected in school and that her own son hardly comes home at night any more. Without telling his mother, he has joined "Wilmersdorf Helps" and is active day and night. A woman rabbi reports how she took Muslims in to her congregation at Hanukkah. She has to be careful. She doesn't want to overstep the mark and lose her job. Some have already lost their jobs in the Jewish Community, particularly in Berlin. A former editor explains that one has to take the people's concerns seriously. Oh yes, you have to do that. This kind of language and the codes that it contains point to Pegida, the populist right-wing movement that has been on the streets recently and that is against the state, against democracy, against the police, and against Islam in Germany. Islam doesn't belong in

Germany ... And here is an interesting linguistic confusion: a Pegida participant says into the reporter's microphone that six million Muslims are too many. That is a number that is far bigger than the actual number of Muslims living in Germany. What am I supposed to think? Is there a link between the Muslims living in Germany and the six million dead Jews? They had to be made into "aliens" first and blamed for making Germany not Germany anymore. And at the end of the slogans there came mass murder.

A Jewish Russian German writer reports that it is all made up anyway. Her Syrian husband simply went to the embassy and got a proper visa for Germany. That is the way to leave the country. A communist woman is very disappointed in the people who have been accommodated in the bunk beds and gym halls. "They just lie around playing incessantly with their cellphones and don't even raise their heads." I leave the group. There is nothing to be done here. They will never manage to produce a statement that perhaps the Central Council of Jews in Germany might consider playing a part in the refugee support organizations that are springing up everywhere and in which both of the Christian churches, Catholic and Protestant, and their various support organizations are participating. "But they are enemies of the Jews ... It's a threat to us."

I hear similar things at a meeting in Hamburg. A woman of indistinguishable age begins to tell the story of how she and her family have suffered and how she was still as traumatized as her parents. Auschwitz—how present it is in the family still. They came from the former Czechoslovakia. For that reason she is afraid of the refugees, afraid of the Muslims, the terrorists, and she tells us that antisemitic attacks on Jewish establishments have increased. As a Jew, she rejects Angela Merkel's policies. Supportive murmur in the room. The discussant on the podium with me, third generation, is an eloquent speaker. He is not going to talk about that subject. I only managed meager words. I am still struck by the language I recently heard from the Catholic bishop. He spoke of mercy and of the lowly among us, and I feel drawn to them as well, and he spoke of compassion. He spoke in the name of Jesus. I studied Emmanuel Levinas. Am I free to say *yes* or *no* to taking in the refugees? Levinas speaks of the Face of the Other that is offered to me, naked and vulnerable—an invitation to an act of violence. But it is that very face that also prevents violence. The face speaks, and we encounter each other face-to-face. By looking at him, by looking at her, I am the one who bears responsibility. I cannot hand it on or refuse it. It is our form of sociality.

I don't know if my crazy Jewish friend Wendy has read Levinas. Probably not. She, a Jewish woman from New York, in other words, she is exactly how we in Germany expect Jewish women from the United States to be. She goes around with such shameless Jewish self-confidence of a sort that we don't have. She took her holiday at the end of the year together with a small group of therapists, reflexologists, and yoga teachers. They flew to Vienna, stayed with various people, got up in the mornings and went to the refugee reception facilities. It was Christmas, and so the voluntary workforce was depleted even more than usual. This Christian Christmas is an extraordinarily family-oriented business. My friend, who as an Arab Spring activist only just managed to escape the ruling clique in Bahrain with his life says that he has to leave Germany at Christmas. He can't stand it. It is as if the whole country has imploded and turned into one big family home surrounded by fir trees.

Back to Vienna: Wendy and Birgit and a few other women went around to the centers, usually without any warning. That sort of thing tends to lead to announcements like the one made in Traiskirchen that they were not able to cope with their visit. Not now. They went to lots of other places and showed people how to do acupressure or come to terms with their trauma, drew and sang songs with the children, and there was sometimes a little yoga thrown in. A crash course for those who just wanted to live. In the end it was not only the refugees who profited from their visit but also the voluntary helpers. They joined in. They are still talking about that wonderful Christmas when those women suddenly arrived at the West station in Vienna.

I don't talk to my neighbor much anymore. We used to sit sometimes and drink tea together. What does he want, I thought, when he rang the doorbell? I thought he was going to bring me back a pound of buckwheat flour from France. His wife has her holiday soon. She is a teacher, and the two of them always go to France. They've built a house there. My neighbor is always building something. As long as I've known him, he's been building something. Ten years now. There is a pile of saplings stacked outside his door. He's going to take them with him. They are cheaper in Germany. His mother-in-law and his wife are from Hungary and fled from communism. His house belongs to him. It's not rented. In Germany it is usual to rent rather than to buy. So he is a man of property. His wife earns the money, he gets a small pension for himself, the mother-in-law gets a larger one, and he also gets some money because he is her caregiver. One grown-up son. He didn't bring me any buckwheat flour. He is red in the face when he talks about "that Merkel" and about how she is destroying everything, destroying Germany, destroying Europe, and he says, "I'm going to kill her." Then he says that he hopes someone kills her. And the French are right not to take anyone in. And it will be the ruin of Germany, and this is not a country based on immigration. I question what he's saying. We argue. And then finally he says: "I have had enough of do-gooders. They are going to ruin the country." When he has gone, I wonder whether I should keep the conversation to myself. On the other hand I should probably report him to the police for hate speech and for threatening to kill someone. I mean, aren't you supposed to report such statements? My friend who works for the Minister of Integration and Migration says that the authorities now send all threatening emails on to the police.

Blatant threats and hate speech. They don't even try to hide their names. One teacher asks why asylum seekers are allowed to steal up to ten euros and so on and so on. We parted in bad temper. I didn't report him to the police, but—for the first time in my life—I thought about whether I should report a private conversation and not one held in public.

Some companies have agreed to offer and to finance German courses: a crash course in technical studies for young asylum seekers. The economy has neglected training and education for a long time . . . This could work out well. And they haven't done anything about the education of second- and third-generation Turkish and Arabic immigrants living in Germany. There is probably no other country in the world that has such remarkable discrimination in its education system. Firms are offering one-year apprenticeships followed by one-year crash courses in German. The process is much more time-consuming than they had imagined, and all of them, the refugees and the firms, say that they need some legal certainty. If the procedures are going to take this long and there is still no legal certainty at the end that the people will be able to complete their education, then there is no point to it. The man who fixes my car occasionally nods his head knowingly. At the beginning of the 1990s he trained two young people from Bosnia. When they went back, they were trained mechanics. Somebody proposes that points should be added to some sort of work time account if people do volunteer work. There have never been so many volunteer workers ever. At least a third of my students are volunteer workers, for example. Many of them are very young. They also seem not to have any particular political or religious view of the world. They just do what needs to be done. That is new. For weeks the media ran reports about people who live in Germany and have their own experiences as refugees or expellees. How many left the GDR with nothing but the clothes on their backs? And still there are some who say that there is no comparison. "We're Germans, aren't we?" No Mediterranean to cross, that's true. Just barbed wire and walls.

I have to look after Gh. She is ill with a fever, the flu.

I really wanted to talk some more about jeans and jackets and food that one isn't allowed to serve anymore because it doesn't conform to European food regulations. We don't know what to say to each other now. We wait. The borders have to be opened again. People in need of protection can't simply be rejected without any sort of investigation, can't be deported. We shouldn't be trying to undermine the UN's Universal Declaration on Human Rights. Then I think about the refugee summit in 1938 in Evian to discuss the fate of the Jews from Germany and Austria . . . The Roosevelt initiative was a failure. This time we cannot fail.

My mother and her first husband, the father of my older sister Hannelore, were able to survive Hitler's Germany with the support of thirty-eight different people. That's what's in the files. Strangers took her in and hid her when she was five years old. By doing so they put themselves in danger. I wrote a poem. Deutschlandradio Kultur broadcast it on 13 July 2015.

Escaping Is Forbidden Too

National Trust Oh I do like to be beside the seaside
The Home Secretary writes back to the seaside
Wherever they or you came from
The prison's on land
Transport by air
If somebody opened the hatch
the people would fall into the sea
where they came from
that's forbidden
Escaping is forbidden too
Staying is
Not escaping
Not staying
Disperse
Lock up or disperse
When they were born
their mothers didn't ask permission
it's regrettable their mothers didn't
ask permission
Let them be going
Thousands are going
Going as such
How does the Home Secretary want to lock up going
Will he lift up roads
Bring air down to earth
Make waters run dry
Prisons for all who still keep going
There'll be many to be locked up
Whole countries will have to be locked up
I don't believe these countries
will fit in our prisons
times were when we rejoiced with them
with the people standing on Tahrir Square
on Tiananmen Square
in the souk in Damascus pile up
weapons instead of fruit
He's from the Congo
and he's from Iraq
if their bones no longer find a place
in the earth of their countries
will you be the one who scatters their ash in the wind

Go rather and buy one of them trousers, a new pair
that fits well or an
ironed shirt. That'll do.[1]

People bought these trousers, and the shirts were pressed. I am sitting in the American Memorial Library in Berlin, a gift from the United States in 1954 and a symbol for education and freedom of opinion. And it is a symbol for the young generation of those times. There are some older schoolchildren from Kreuzberg here doing their homework. "A lot of our refugees," says Rahel, "go there too." "Our refugees"? Somebody asks for a Russian translation. Others are sitting here silently in front of German textbooks. It is the friendliest library in Berlin. It is bursting at the seams and needs to be expanded. In some ways I like to see the whole country as being like this library. It needs support. It would help a lot if the United States were to take in more refugees. Maybe that would ease things up for Europe. And maybe you would like to help found a "Black Mountain College" in Europe, to expand the library, if you understand what I mean.

Translation by Peter Thompson

Esther Dischereit is a writer and activist based in Berlin. Dischereit received the prestigious Erich Fried Prize in 2009. She has taught at the University of the Applied Arts (Vienna), served as the DAAD Chair in Contemporary Poetics at New York University, and has been appointed Max Kade Professor several times, most recently at Indiana University, Bloomington in 2021. Dischereit's collection of essays *Mama, darf ich das Deutschlandlied singen. Politische Texte* [Mama, am I allowed to sing the German national anthem? Political texts] appeared in 2020, as well as her poetry book *Sometimes a Single Leaf,* in German and English, translated by Iain Galbraith, followed by the book Dischereit has edited *Hab keine Angst, erzähl alles! Über das Attentat von Halle und die Stimmen der Überlebenden* [Don't be afraid, tell everything! On the Halle Attack and the voices of the survivors] in 2021.

Notes

Thanks to Kizer S. Walker.
1. Translation by Tom Cheesman, 8 December 2015.

CHAPTER 2

"Strange Stars" in Constellation
Özdamar, Lasker-Schüler, and the Archive

KRISTIN DICKINSON

Emine Sevgi Özdamar's *Strange Stars Stare to Earth: Wedding—Pankow 1976/77* (2003) narrates the decision of its protagonist, Emine, to seek out new acting opportunities with the Volksbühne in East Berlin following the 1971 Turkish military coup. Yet Emine's first experiences with this theater do not involve acting. She takes instead to its archives in order to read the rehearsal notes from Benno Besson's production of Bertolt Brecht's *The Good Person of Szechwan* (1943). Traveling daily from West to East Berlin, Emine proceeds to translate these notes into Turkish and then mail them to imprisoned friends in Istanbul. Emine's point of entry into an acting career with the Volksbühne thus occurs through an engagement with its archive that also subjects it to processes of transformation and dislocation.

Starting with this act of dissemination, I read *Strange Stars* as a complex theorization of the archive. Composed of documentary photographs, sketches, diary entries, facsimiles, and other texts, *Strange Stars* defies genre boundaries. By incorporating diverse material from Özdamar's own literary *Vorlaß*[1] into its process of narration, the novel also actively reflects on the boundaries of the archive as both a repository of documents and a mode of cultural production. As such, it also speaks to Özdamar's centrality to the body of Turkish German literature, which has been described in discursive terms as a cultural archive of postwar migration. Özdamar's diverse oeuvre is, however, in no way limited to the descriptor *Turkish German*; as with all of her work, *Strange Stars* is punctuated by a series of intertexts, including newspaper headlines, theatrical texts, song lyrics, and lines of poetry. As the titular reference to "strange stars" indicates, the legacy of Else Lasker-Schüler (1869–1945) constitutes a central intertextual reference within the novel. Through an engagement with key images from Lasker-Schüler's poetry—including the star, the moon, and the planet—Özdamar creates a constellation of textual imaginaries across East and West Berlin, Jerusalem, and Istanbul that span the twentieth century. In my examination of these diverse cosmic bodies, I show how *Strange Stars* engages in a planetary aesthetic, or "a multi-centric and pluralizing worldly structure of relatedness,"[2] that interrogates the diverse East/West divides in the novel and the archival frameworks that condition them. By employing techniques of simultaneity and the collapsing of distances, I argue that *Strange Stars* does not seek to recuperate the past but rather asks us to read the past in the present. As such, Özdamar does not simply align herself with Lasker-Schüler or a German-Jewish legacy in a teleological manner but explores new modes of being-in-relation for Turkish German and Jewish German studies.

Strange Stars and the Archival Turn

An "archival turn" in contemporary scholarship can be traced at least to the publication of Jacques Derrida's *Archive Fever* (1995), which gave theoretical impulse to a movement that was already underway.[3] In the words of Ann Stoler, this turn has entailed a shift in emphasis from the "archive-as-source" to the "archive-as-subject."[4] Drawing our attention to the power dynamics at work in selection and categorization processes, theorists of the archive ask why specific histories have been documented over others, noting that the archive has both the power to validate and to render invisible.[5] In particular, postcolonial studies has called attention to the role state archives have played in sustaining political domination and has taken to the archives to uncover alternative histories that incorporate the voices of subjugated and minority communities.

In the realm of literary and cultural studies, scholars have further challenged our traditional understanding of the archive as a repository of documents and called attention to its metaphoric dimensions as a site where the interrelationship of narrative, memory, and the past come into play. In her examination of the archival turn in feminism, Kate Eichhorn further describes the archive not as "a destination or an impenetrable barrier to be breached, but rather a site and practice integral to knowledge making [and] cultural production" in the present.[6] In her focus on women as agents of the archive, Eichhorn thus turns our attention from "women being archived" to "women archiving."[7]

Through Emine's engagement with preexisting archival materials at the Volksbühne, and the later incorporation of her own notes and sketches into this same archive, *Strange Stars* also raises pertinent questions about the agency of women in the archive. Following her initial engagement with Besson's notes, Emine eventually receives a position as intern at the Volksbühne, during which she documents rehearsals for Manfred Karge and Matthias Langhoff's production of Johann Wolfgang von Goethe's *The Citizen General* (1778). As intern, she observes and documents rehearsals, taking detailed notes and sketches that are then incorporated into the narrative flow of the novel. These sketches are later put on display for the premiere of *The Citizen General* and ultimately purchased for the archives of the Volksbühne. To whom do Emine's materials—which are a reproduction of notes taken by Özdamar during her time with the Volksbühne in 1976—ultimately belong? Notably, the majority of these materials make their way into the second half of the novel, which is composed in diary format. Yet this shift in narrative style does not entail a corresponding shift in tone; short, matter-of-fact sentences thwart any expectations for an increased level of introspection. On the contrary, the diary entries fulfill a more formal purpose, insofar as they call attention to the dual status of archival documents as institutional property and personal history.

Emine's diary entry from 27 September 1976 is significant in this manner. Set in italics, it consists solely of Emine's rehearsal notes:

> *Citizen General Rehearsal. Schnaps. We tried out the moments of fear, curiosity, desire, excitement, like in a movie, everything quick and near. Schnaps heads to the cabinet where the jug full of milk is sitting. But the speeches about freedom and revolution that he makes in front of the cabinet are essentially those of a village barber. Today his topic is revolution. The barber shops in Istanbul are also places where people can unload their ideas about politics, morality, and the economy in front of the mirror while getting a shave. Goethe in Istanbul.*[8]

Whereas Goethe's burlesque play satirizes the direct importation of French revolutionary ideas to Germany, the descriptors *angst, curiosity, desire,* and *excitement* create an association with the aftermath of the Turkish military coup in Emine's description.[9] By reminding us that Schnaps's call for freedom and revolution is actually the amusing chatter of a village barber, Emine then creates a completely different association with the barbershops of Istanbul, a locale where one can freely discuss politics, morality, and the economy. The fragment with which the paragraph ends—"Goethe in Istanbul"—plays on this unlikely association of *The Citizen General* with the barbershop. At the same time its reference to mirrors—and more specifically the viewing of one's own self and opinions as if in a mirror—bear striking resemblance to Goethe's own scattered reflections on *Weltliteratur*. In his conversations with Eckermann, Goethe described the international circulation of his own work in translation as a process of mirroring (*Spiegelung*). Arguing that any national literature would exhaust itself without the refreshing counterperspective of a foreign literature, Goethe described translation not as an exact reproduction of the image at hand but rather a form of revitalization capable of revealing aspects of an "original" image that would otherwise remain obscured.

Placed at the end of the 27 September diary entry, Emine's tongue-in-cheek fragment "Goethe in Istanbul" thus signals myriad potential geographic, cultural, and historical associations across the narrator's present position as an observer of GDR theater in the making. These include the time period in which the *The Citizen General* is set (1798), the aftermath of the 1971 Turkish military coup, and the formulation of *Weltliteratur* as a concept in the 1820s. Indeed, this brief diary entry is but one example of how Emine both records and stages history in *Strange Stars*. As such, B. Venkat Mani has aptly described her as a "participant observer" of both the Volksbühne productions and of East and West Berlin.[10]

Through Emine's rehearsal notes, multidirectional[11] connections reaching beyond any single national, monolinguistic, or historical framework also become part of the Volksbühne's institutional history. While the inscription of these notes into the institutional archive of the Volksbühne is location specific, they also circulate within the intertexts of *Strange Stars*, and into the hands of readers via the publication of the novel and its translation into multiple languages. Just as the main character Emine translates archival documents and mails them to Turkey, Özdamar also engages in a critical act of archival dissemination. Shedding traditional conceptions of the archive as a site of preservation and protection, *Strange Stars* emerges as a narrativized archive that generates and promotes the circulation of ideas and new modes of cultural intervention in the present.[12] Accordingly, Emine also renders *herself* present in the production notes. During an excursion to Weimar, for example, Emine makes a sketch of the actors relaxing outside, into which she inserts an image of her own shoe.[13] Through this seemingly minor detail, Özdamar offers both an extremely accurate depiction of a production in progress and a personal testament to Emine's (and her own) presence in the theater.

Toward an Archive of Migration

At once observant and factual, hilarious and imaginative, Emine's rehearsal notes also forge a unique "archive of migration" through their incorporation of personal memories and associations with Turkish history. In his brief but poignant essay of the same name, Deniz Utlu envisages an archive of migration without a name or fixed location, one that is yet to be fully compiled and that remains scattered throughout Germany in private residences.[14] Potential contents of this archive include cultural objects, such as the prose and poetry of early guest workers; personal ephemera, including love letters, photographs, and old suitcases; and documentary materials, such as visa applications and expired passports. If actualized, an archive of migration would have the potential to tell an alternative history of the Federal Republic of Germany in which postwar migration plays an integral role. Noting that the first guest workers arrived only six years after the establishment of the republic, Utlu imagines an archive of migration that does not merely form a "footnote" to the larger national history but also demands a coming-to-terms (*Auseinandersetzung*) with the cultural, historical, economic, and social dimensions of postwar German society.[15] The Documentation Center and Museum of Migration (DOMiD) in Cologne is notably the first institution to actively collect and exhibit the kinds of materials Utlu envisions. With its emphasis on migration as a transnational phenomenon that also encompasses countries of origin, DOMiD's planned museum (Haus der Einwanderungsgesellschaft) also speaks to Utlu's assertion that an archive of migration cannot be restricted by nationality or language. *Strange Stars* embraces this idea in literary form: through its multidirectional methods of narration, the novel constructs a nonteleological, narrativized archive that brings disparate events and memories into the same textual space.

Unlike *Life Is a Caravanserai, Has Two Doors, I Came in One, I Went out the Other* (1992) and *The Bridge of the Golden Horn* (1998)—which take place in Anatolia and between Berlin and Istanbul, respectively—*Strange Stars* is unique in Özdamar's *Sun Halfway* trilogy of novels in that it takes place almost exclusively in Berlin. Yet *Strange Stars* is in no way conditioned by an overdetermined moment of arrival. On the contrary, the narrator's "arrival" in Germany sets in motion a period of incessant crossings between East and West Berlin. Temporally, the novel also links and collapses time frames, which include the period of the 1971 Turkish military coup, the German Autumn (1977), and the Holocaust. On 14 May 1976, for example, Emine attends a performance of *The Battle* by Heiner Müller; the final scene, "The Sheet or the Immaculate Conception," takes place in an air-raid shelter shortly before the Red Army's capture of Berlin. From this World War II reference, the novel moves to Emine's memories of her grandmother in a dilapidated wooden house in Istanbul. That night Emine dreams that the Turkish military has arrested her grandmother along with several other women. Within this association of diverse forms of state violence, Emine does not simply project her experience in the theater onto her memories of home or equate the actions of the Nazis with those of the Turkish military. Rather, a nonimmediate and nonteleological association is established across different time frames.

The next diary entry occurs four days later, on 18 May 1976, when Emine recounts her experience walking deep in a forest outside of Weimar:

> A flat landscape, the deer run deep into the depths of the forest. "Now you are in another forest," I thought, "you'll never go back to the old one now." So many deer here. When you scream, they stand still for a moment, then they run off into the heart of the forest. Toward morning I left the house. The others were still sleeping. I wore the blanket around my shoulders, ran into the still woods, far away from the house, and cried. The cranes flew up suddenly into the sky, deer, horses, all were awake. Did my crying wake them? Klaus had told me yesterday evening that the death march of Jews from the Sachsenhausen concentration camp had gone past here. Many died on the way. Klaus said, "Sachsenhausen was

the concentration camp where the entire Holocaust was planned." Now I look at the landscape. Now the deer, the cranes, and the crows are here. Back then it must have looked like being on another planet. People like skeletons under the moonlight. Eyes big. Clothes, torn clothes, that fly across the landscape with the wind.[16]

Though isolated within the narrative, this diary entry recalls an earlier scene in the novel in which Emine's house in an idyllic forest setting outside of Istanbul is recounted.[17] Within this serene landscape, Emine is overcome by grief for victims of the recent military coup and Turkish leftists who are subsequently being tortured in jail. For every action from which she derives even minimal pleasure, Emine feels as if she has betrayed those arrested and confined by the Turkish state.[18] Separated by nearly one hundred pages, Emine's experiences in the German and Turkish forests create a disjointed association between state violence in Turkey and the Holocaust. Rather than conflate two histories or imply a causal relationship between Germany's history of Jewish persecution and Emine's own experience as a Turkish exile living in the divided capital, the novel performs a kind of memory work that places the history of the Holocaust alongside other histories and positions both Emine and Özdamar (as a Turkish German author) in relation to the remembrance of the Nazi past.[19]

How exactly is Özdamar's decision to cite the work of Else Lasker-Schüler in *Strange Stars*, including the titular reference to the poem "Stars of Fate," tied to an engagement with the German past? Through the poem's association with exile, the star of David, and a Community of Fate (*Schicksalsgemeinschaft*), Kader Konuk views Lasker-Schüler as Emine's alter ego. By appropriating Lasker-Schüler and her legacy, she argues, Emine negotiates the role of minorities in postwar Germany and challenges an ethnically defined memory culture.[20] I suggest that Özdamar evokes Lasker-Schüler and her German Jewish legacy in order to reflect on literary lineages in particular, but also to challenge precisely the construction of linear and teleological trajectories between the two authors' works.

My reading builds further on the work of both Gizem Arslan and Ela Gezen. In her focus on moments of transformation, transposition, and performance, Arslan examines diverse translation practices in *Strange Stars* that do not strive for equivalence and are thus marked by creativity and newness rather than pathos or loss.[21] Rather than the recuperation of lost histories, Arslan thus stresses the productive dimension of Özdamar's narrative practice. Gezen in turn focuses not on the physical act of migration but on the role of the theater and theatricality in the construction of the novel's narrative. Through the practice of montage, she argues, Özdamar engages in a "narrative staging of the past"[22] that brings disparate elements into direct contact and creates a sense of simultaneity in the present. Emphasizing analeptic references to the past, Gezen shows how *Strange Stars* superimposes snapshots and soundscapes from

Istanbul onto the narrator's experiences in Berlin; sutured together in the text, the narrator thus experiences her Turkish past simultaneously with her present in both East and West Berlin.[23]

In the following, I highlight precisely such productive simultaneities through attention to the cosmic imagery in *Strange Stars*, which not only links Turkey to Germany but also introduces the third geographic location of Jerusalem. More precisely, by linking the literary legacies of Özdamar and Lasker-Schüler across times and locations, I show how the images of the star and the moon call attention to a planetary aesthetic on which, I argue, the novel relies. With its focus on the problem of relationality, the discourse of planetarity interrogates in turn the very tendency to draw causal links between each author's work, encouraging instead a dynamic and constellative reading practice.

Toward a Planetary Aesthetic

The astrological definition of a constellation, or *Sternbild*, denotes a fixed group of stars in a recognizable pattern:[24]

> Constellations [*Sternbilder*] ... are a composition of phenomena that are not caused by these phenomena in and of themselves—in the sense of a genetic, historical or structural relationship—but rather merely from the contingent position of the observer. The stars of a constellation are among themselves discontinuous but can be perceived as a constellation and noticed in relation to their position.[25]

By placing her own novel in *dynamic* constellation with the poetry and larger legacy of Lasker-Schüler, Özdamar stresses precisely the constructedness of the *Sternbild*. Just as a fixed constellation of stars only becomes visible in the eye of the reader/observer, Özdamar underscores that a progressive or causal movement from Lasker-Schüler's work to her own is constructed precisely in the practice of reading each author as an ethnoreligious Other in the landscape of "German" literature. Özdamar initiates a reversal of this dynamic through the titular reference to "Stars of Fate": the novel opens with Emine in bed with a book of Lasker-Schüler's poetry. Over the sound of a dog barking, Emine first speaks, and then yells the following lines: "Strange stars stare to the earth / Iron-colored, with trails of desire, / With burning arms, they are looking for love ..."[26] By including this Lasker-Schüler poem in the opening lines of her novel, Özdamar both replays and thwarts the reader's desire for an authentic, female, native informant author.[27] Here it is the *stars* that have the power to desire as they cast their gaze back upon the earth. Via the anthropomorphized image of a star with "burning arms" and "trails of desire," Özdamar references a form of agency in motion that counters the spatially static quality of the astrological constellation. Emine's decision to read these lines aloud further brings the poetry of Lasker-Schüler into the present of the novel, thus setting the stage for a dynamic interplay of Lasker-Schüler's poetry and Özdamar's narrative.

Central to this constellative interplay are the images of the star, the moon, and the planet. Via reference to these diverse cosmic bodies, Özdamar highlights both the discontinuities and simultaneities across the multiple geographic and temporal positions from which she and Lasker-Schüler write. As such, multiple and shifting constellations emerge within *Strange Stars*, including: (1) the figures and literary legacies of Lasker-Schüler and Özdamar, (2) the cosmic imagery each author employs, (3) the sites of Berlin (prewar, divided, and postwar), Istanbul, and Palestine, and (4) the time frames of Lasker-Schüler's early career (1900–1920), the Holocaust, and the present time of *Strange Stars* (1976). These diverse configurations of discontinuous elements correspond loosely to Walter Benjamin's understanding of the constellation. As a tool for understanding history, Benjamin's concept of the constellation does not presuppose a causal relationship between events but allows us to read the past via its simultaneity with the present. According to Benjamin, new ideas arise precisely out of the discontinuous nature of the elements in configuration; the critical power of the constellation thus stems from the ability of the observer to recognize this discontinuity.[28] Similarly, the contemporary field of *Konstellationsforschung* highlights the tensions of reading texts with and against one another.[29] Through an emphasis on movement, decentralization, and polyphony, the field defines itself via processes of collective intellectual creativity, intermediality, and intertextuality.[30]

The concept of a constellation also pertains to the archive and archival praxes. Scholars Azade Seyhan and Leslie Adelson have both described the body of postwar Turkish German literature as a cultural archive where national, ethnic, and linguistic memories are contained and contested,[31] and where "changing perceptions and phantasms of sociality are both tracked and imagined."[32] With both national and transnational dimensions, this archive highlights issues of exile and migration, countermemory, and disorientation.[33] If literature thus forms a cultural archive via the histories and intertexts it chooses to cite, the references to Lasker-Schüler in *Strange Stars* confront the porous borders of this archive through recourse to a planetary aesthetic. In her experience in the woods outside of Weimar, Emine's depiction of the past as another *planet* is striking. It is coupled with a strange sense of simultaneity in which the imagined torn clothes of Holocaust victims seem to fly into the wind over the forested landscape, just like the cranes at the sound of Emine's voice.

What is the relationship between this reference to the past as another planet and the recurring image of the star from which the novel takes its name? Notably, the star often emerges as a symbol of transcendence in Lasker-Schüler's poetry. In Özdamar's novel the image of the star also signals Emine's unique, elevated perspective on a divided Berlin: as a foreigner she enjoys an almost incredible freedom of movement, crossing the border daily throughout large sections of the novel. Similarly, in the space of *Strange Stars*, the image of the star is by no means static. It functions instead in constellation with the moon and the planet as a dialectical image that both links and collapses the multiple geographic and temporal positions from which Özdamar and Lasker-Schüler write.

Benjamin describes this interruptive quality of the dialectical image in "Konvolut N" of *The Arcades Project*: "It is not that which is past that casts its light on what is present, or what is present that casts its light on what is past; rather, image is that wherein what has been comes together in a flash with the now to form a constellation. In other words, image is dialectics at a standstill ... the relation of what-has-been to the now is dialectical: is not progression but image, suddenly emergent."[34] Set against the idea of progression and historical continuity, the image flashes up to reveal a dialectical relationship between past and present moments. Yet in contrast to a process of dialectics that ends in synthesis, Benjamin instead describes a form of radical temporal rupture that hinges on synchronicity.[35]

The contemporary field of planetarity arguably builds on this sense of historical rupture through its emphasis on co-presence and contemporaneity, understood as a "multiplicity of ways of being in time" across the present and past, as well as in future times.[36] Such contemporaneity does not emphasize sameness but rather a sense of coeval connectivity across worlds and places that also accounts for difference.[37] Gayatri Chakravorty Spivak first called attention to the planet in contrast to the globe in her incendiary work *Death of Discipline* (2003): "The globe," she argues, "is on our computers. No one lives there. It allows us to think that we can aim to control it. The planet is in the species of alterity, belonging to another system; and yet we inhabit it, on loan."[38] In contrast to the totalizing view of the globe and the homogenizing forces of globalization, the discourse of planetarity requires an ethical shift in perspective to nontotalist and pluralist structures of relatedness.[39] If the globe implies a closed system of even exchange, the planet is thus characterized by epistemological openness and multiplicity.[40] Similarly, I argue that *Strange Stars* does not seek to recuperate the past, but rather establishes a co-presence between Lasker-Schüler and Özdamar as authors through the images of the star and the moon.

From Mouthwhores to the Harem

The second reference to Lasker-Schüler's poetry in *Strange Stars* also enters directly into the action of the narrative. Vexed by the incessant barking of a dog on Christmas Eve, Emine flips open her book and cries out a verse from the poem "Black Stars": "Why do you look for me in our nights, / In clouds of hate upon wicked stars! / Leave me alone with the ghosts that I fight."[41] In this comic scene, Lasker-Schüler's poem is not simply brought to bear on Emine's situation; Emine literally speaks—or rather shouts—with Lasker-Schüler's words. More than adopting Lasker-Schüler as an alter ego, Özdamar collapses the times and spaces that stand between Lasker-Schüler's work and her own, allowing different constellations of texts and places to come together in the space of the novel. In doing so, Özdamar emphasizes her own position as both a contributor to and agent within the archive of migration.

In a third citation from Lasker-Schüler's poetry, Emine's boyfriend Peter reads aloud the love poem "Senna Hoy." Peter frames this reading with his own limited knowledge of Lasker-Schüler's multifaceted life and legacy: "She lived in Berlin, expressionism. She died in 1945 in Jerusalem. She had to flee the Nazis."[42] As if to emphasize the extremely reductive nature of his portrayal, the text of "Senna Hoy" sets off a series of transpositions and associative connections within the novel. By reading the poem aloud, Peter highlights the poem's emphasis on voice: "All the birds practice / On your lips. / Always-blue, your voice scatters / Across the way."[43] As Peter gives voice to the poem in the present time of the novel, Emine transforms into the lover of the poem's lyric I. This reconfiguration of lover/beloved recalls Lasker-Schüler's later renaming of "Stars of Fate" as "Stars of Love" (*Liebessterne*), and Emine's decision to read it aloud in the opening pages of the novel.

As Emine listens to the text of "Senna Hoy," she also draws an unlikely connection to voices coming from the brothel below her apartment. This leads Emine to recall her mother's statement that prostitutes protect women from hungry men,[44] which also appears in the novel *Caravanserai*. Indeed, prostitutes are a recurrent trope in the work of Özdamar, and this connective line leads me to consider Özdamar's depiction of her protagonist in *Caravanserai* as a "mouthwhore" (*Mundhure*), or someone who whores with her tongue (*sie hurt mit der Zunge*).[45] At a second point in this novel, the protagonist's grandmother is also referred to as a "tonguewhore" (*Zungenhure*) for relating a folk tale as if she had actually experienced it. In response, the grandmother retorts, "Stars can speak with stars, people cannot speak with people."[46] This line is then reformulated in *Strange Stars* in reference to postcoup Turkey, where the political situation has placed extreme restrictions on freedom of expression.[47]

Through the complex association of the voice in Lasker-Schüler's poem with prostitutes in *Strange Stars* and *Caravanserai*, "Senna Hoy" becomes a strange site of relationality between Özdamar and Lasker-Schüler. It creates a loose association with both Lasker-Schüler's unorthodox Bohemian lifestyle and the left-wing politics and sexual practices of the West Berlin *Wohngemeinschaft* where Emine lives in *Strange Stars*. Commonly portrayed on the fringes of society, the figure of the prostitute places superficial emphasis on the marginalized positions of Özdamar and Lasker-Schüler as both women and ethnoreligious Others in the German cultural realm. Yet significantly, Özdamar only ever portrays prostitutes in a positive light. Throughout her novels, plays, and short stories, Özdamar furthermore presents the qualities of infidelity and promiscuity as crucial to the realm of imaginative expression. The terms "mouthwhore" and "tonguewhore"—which refer in *Caravanserai* to a woman whose words and imagination are not limited to the reality of her situation—could thus equally be used to describe both Özdamar's and Lasker-Schüler's unorthodox use of German. Each author employs translation, nonidiomatic phrases, and inverted syntax to enunciate a site of cultural difference that challenges the desire for a homogenous German-language community.

A self-orientalizing, poetic use of German also pervades Lasker-Schüler's collections *The Nights of Tino of Baghdad* (1907) and *The Prince of Thebes* (1914). Composed of images, poems, and short prose sections, these collections bear striking resemblance to the genre-blurring quality of *Strange Stars*. Told from multiple perspectives including first and third person, in both male and female voices, *Tino* and *Prinz* are also permeated by intertextual references and allusions, including to Lasker-Schüler's own life.[48] Rather than form a master and/or linear narrative, each collection constitutes an amalgamated and often contradictory whole that evinces the constellative aesthetic outlined above.

While both collections include references to Constantinople, *Prince* in particular offers a striking intertext to *Strange Stars* that maps its references to prostitutes onto a new East/West divide: "In the harbor of Constantinople lie boats—stars,"[49] writes Aunt Schalome in a letter recounting her experience in the harem of the Ottoman Sultan. Longing for her home city of Baghdad, Schalome gazes out the window and reflects on her experience as a foreigner:

> We aunts from Baghdad smell of old ruins, we princesses from the Tigris dance with mute limbs. And I don't understand the language of the women of the harem. Don't know what provokes them to be happy or to have a falling out with one another. They don't speak their Sultan's language: "We speak Parisian," explains the youngest to me.[50]

Whereas the harem has come to signify a quintessentially Eastern space in the Western imagination, Schalome is estranged by its Europeanness. The women of the harem speak "Parisian," suggesting that their use of French as a language of communication is but one aspect of their immersion in a Western habitus. And yet these women are also "Western" in the sense that they play out the desires of an orientalist imagination. It is precisely on these grounds that Schalome finds her own cultural background to be incongruous with the milieu of the Sultan's harem. Both out of sync with and bored by her surroundings, Schalome is too ashamed to bathe in front of the eunuch, whose piercing gaze she contrasts with the harmlessness of the eunuch in Baghdad. Historically employed in the Ottoman imperial court to guard the women of the harem, eunuchs were castrated before puberty. Due to hormonal deprivation, they generally did not grow facial hair and had unnaturally high voices.[51] If Lasker-Schüler's reference to the harem in Baghdad corresponds to the more typical portrayal of the eunuch as an emasculated figure, the contradictory image of the lustful eunuch in Constantinople also recalls the historical conflation of harem women with prostitutes: stereotypical European portrayals of the harem often reduced it to a house for sexually available women, thus aligning it with the brothel.[52] One of the most prevalent symbols in Western myths depicting Muslim sensuality, the harem of the Ottoman Sultan in particular represents the harem par excellence in the Western imagination.[53]

Lasker-Schüler clearly plays on the imagined, lascivious character of the harem woman. Yet the women in Lasker-Schüler's text do not simply pander to the orientalist imagination but rather act out the libertine fantasies of the Marquis de Sade. Gathering around the eunuch as he opens "a large book with dreadful pictures,"[54] the women of the harem proceed to bare themselves to his whips adorned with lead tips. As the aunt screams murderously while coquettishly showing her teeth, Schalome's cousins bare their breasts in jealousy. Bordering on the burlesque, this scene performs the Western desire for an overly sensualized Orient. Lasker-Schüler's use of metaphoric neologisms only heighten this aspect of the performance: the eunuch brings his whip down on the "Full moon of my feverish aunt,"[55] and the cousins "bloom in sprinkled goldcarnations."[56] At the same time, its reference to the torturous elements of Sadean eroticism also point to the breaking open of ossified social conventions his work sought to enact.[57]

Quietly withdrawing from this gruesome scene, the figure of Schalome is set in contrast to the eroticism of the harem, and thus also to the Western myth of the femme fatale constructed around her own name. Lasker-Schüler's decision to write Schalome with an "sch" alludes to the Hebrew spelling of Salome, daughter of Herodias who requested the head of John the Baptist from Herod after dancing for him. In line with Lasker-Schüler's tendency to orientalize her writing, this spelling suggests an attempt to inscribe the character of Schalome with difference. More importantly, via the figure of *Sch*alome from Baghdad, Lasker-Schüler offers a complex "Eastern" perspective on the Ottoman harem: Schalome reveals the harem as a site of lasciviousness to be a construct of the European imagination even as she is estranged from and horrified by precisely its Europeanness.

At the close of this prose piece, Schalome creeps into the adjoining room and longingly looks out at the Bosporus, stating: "I want to climb into one of the little Starboats (*Sternboote*) on the Bosporus—the sky is one great star."[58] With this, the text circles back to the beginning, but it also transforms the opening reference to "boats—stars" (*Boote—Sterne*) into the neologism "Starboats" (*Sternboote*). Through this chiastic turn of phrase, Lasker-Schüler also highlights the phonetic similarity of the German words for boat (*Boote*) and messenger (*Bote*), suggesting that the star presents a metaphoric means for bridging the distance between Constantinople and Baghdad via a specific method of reading. Through the image of the sky (*Himmel*) as one great star, Lasker-Schüler points to the astrological tradition of reading stars like a sign system in order to ascertain one's horoscope.[59] In contrast to the astronomical constellation, which is static and recurs night after night, the horoscope represents one frozen image of the sky, a snapshot that records the configuration of the heavens at any given moment in time. As with Benjamin's understanding of the dialectical image, this snapshot is dynamic, in that it implies a spontaneous interruption of the fixed-star constellation and is open to interpretation.[60]

By bringing Constantinople into dynamic constellation with Baghdad via the image of the star, Lasker-Schüler challenges its fixity as an assumedly Eastern site. A similarly destabilizing constellation emerges within *Strange Stars* across East/West Berlin, Istanbul, and Jerusalem via the image of the moon: "I cannot find the lips I seek ... / Where are you, distant city, / So rich in fragrant blessings?"[61] Read aloud to Emine again by her boyfriend Peter, this reference to Jerusalem in Lasker-Schüler's poem "Full Moon" (1905) reconfigures Emine as a "distant city," at once orientalizing her as Other and turning her into a recurring trope of Lasker-Schüler's poetry. While Özdamar does not explicitly cite the first stanza of the poem, its neologisms "Wandelhin—Taumelher" (Shifting-here—staggering-there) reference a real and imaginative back-and-forth movement central to the novel, in which Emine is constantly traveling between the two Berlins.[62] Notably, this poem is also prefigured in the novel by clear historical and architectural markers to West and East Berlin: ascending the stairs to her rooftop terrace in West Berlin, Emine recalls the clandestine meetings of Ulrike Meinhof and Horst Mahler in this very spot, all while observing the Berlin Television Tower—a symbol of communism and the GDR—in the distance. As such, the novel imaginatively transposes the geographic tension between Jerusalem and Germany in Lasker-Schüler's poem onto the East/West divide of 1970s Berlin.

Özdamar later employs the image of the full moon to link Istanbul and Berlin in *Strange Stars*. Staring at the full moon from the window of her East Berlin bedroom, Emine explains to colleagues Hermann Beyer and Heide Kipp that the full moon shone so brightly at her forest home in Istanbul, it was as if it were hanging right above her garden.[63] Evoking the tropes of distance and nearness so central to Lasker Schüler's poem, Özdamar also brings Istanbul into a new geographic constellation with Jerusalem and Berlin. As such, the image of the moon in the poem brings different locations and the textual traditions of Lasker-Schüler and Özdamar into a constellation that is not conditioned by a simplistic East/West divide but is marked rather by the techniques of juxtaposition and simultaneity.

In the context of Lasker-Schüler's life, the poem "Full Moon" also evokes the image of the star. Lasker-Schüler traveled to Palestine three times from Zürich, where she emigrated in 1933 following Hitler's rise to power. Despite the fact that Palestine was a central object of her literary and artistic imagination, Lasker-Schüler refused to accept it as a lived reality—even after she was forced to emigrate to Jerusalem for good in 1937. After returning to Switzerland from her first trip to Palestine, Lasker-Schüler referred to herself as having been on another star and continued to describe Palestine as "the farthest country in the world."[64] In her subsequent writing, Palestine remained a metaphorical *Urheimat*, whereas her actual experience there was one of extreme disillusionment. Estranged by the petty bourgeois nature of her surroundings, she was overcome by the fear of writer's block and stifled creativity.[65]

Lasker-Schüler's fears find a counterpoint in *Strange Stars*. Early in the novel, Emine reflects on the state of language in Turkey following the military coup. In one key scene, she describes how the expressive capacity of Turkish has been restricted by the current political situation. As the military subjects leftist dissidents to torture, Emine and her friends find themselves repeating the same sentences over and over: "They will be hung. Where were the heads? No one knows where their graves are. The police did not release the bodies!"[66] In an alternative formulation, Emine states that her Turkish words have become "sick":

> The words are sick. My words need a sanatorium, just like sick mussels. There is a place in the Aegean Sea, where three currents come together. People bring sacks of mussels from Istanbul, Izmir, and Italy that have become sick in dirty waters. The clean water from the three currents heals the sick mussels in a couple of months. The fishermen call this part of the sea the mussel sanatorium. How long does a word need, to become healthy again? We say you lose your mother tongue in foreign countries. Can you also lose your mother tongue in your own country?[67]

This formulation recalls Özdamar's tongue stories (1990), in which the narrator attempts to rediscover the moment she "lost" her mother tongue following her migration to Germany. Rather than ever identifying such a moment, the stories ultimately reveal a sense of traumatic loss that is central to the mother tongue itself.[68] Questions of language and loss are also central to *Bridge*, which closes in Turkey with Mustafa Bülent Ecevit's election to power in 1972 and a general amnesty for those arrested in the aftermath of the 1971 military coup. At this point the protagonist's boyfriend urges her to give up the "slogan language" of the leftist student protest movement they have both participated in and join him in starting a more bourgeois lifestyle. While the protagonist clearly rejects this proposal, she also does not cling to the political ideologies she sought to support in the past. Rather, her mouth contracts an "allergy," such that it peels like an orange: "I couldn't speak anymore. Every word pained my mouth."[69] This image of the protagonist's mouth peeling layer by layer reflects her quest for a form of language that escapes the limitations of pre-given categories, such as those set out by the left-wing political movements of 1970s Turkey.[70] The novel ends with the dismantling of the Bridge of the Golden Horn, from which it takes its name. This negative bridge is arguably also a reflection of language in process. Just as the protagonist must learn to speak anew, the performative language of *Bridge* also resists its own methods of representation.

Emine's predicament in *Strange Stars* ties into both of these previous works. Whereas the tongue stories express the ideological violence of linguistic engineering and the modern Turkish state's desire to forge a linguistically homogeneous populace, *Strange Stars* describes how physical violence exercised against political dissidents in the late 1960s and early 1970s manifests itself in the very forms of expression that are available to speakers of modern Turkish. In this way, *Strange Stars* narrates the flipside of the protagonist's predicament in the closing pages of *Bridge*. Together the novels attest to the restrictions placed on a female narrator's speech from both a subcultural leftist movement and from the state.

If the protagonist of *Strange Stars* is in search of a form of linguistic healing, however, the novel does not provide one. Among the many intertexts Özdamar chooses to cite, the poetry of Lasker-Schüler is central to this idea. Awarded with the prestigious Kleist Prize in 1932, only to be banned under National Socialism shortly thereafter, the work of Lasker-Schüler bears a complex and contested legacy. A central Jewish German woman author of the expressionist movement, Lasker-Schüler sought to imbue her German with a sense of alterity by inflecting it with elements of Hebrew and Yiddish; as these were both languages she did not know, however, her work has often been criticized as self-orientalizing.[71] It was notably also the fantastic and neologistic language of *Caravanserai* that won Özdamar the Ingeborg Bachmann Prize in 1991. Yet it was precisely this language that garnered an undue amount of orientalizing reviews.[72]

By placing her own work into dynamic constellation with that of Lasker-Schüler in *Strange Stars*, Özdamar challenges the manner in which she has been categorized as Other due to precisely her use of linguistic invention. As such, the novel also reflects on the role language plays in the construction of literary lineages and cultural archives. While *Strange Stars* clearly engages in complex transcultural memory work, in placing herself into constellation with another woman minority author of the twentieth century, Özdamar arguably upholds the status of both authors as *German* against reductive and orientalizing portrayals of their work. Before flipping through the book of Lasker-Schüler's poetry in *Strange Stars*, for example, Emine reads the blurb on the inside of its dust jacket aloud: "This was the greatest lyric poet Germany ever had. Her topics were frequently Jewish, her fantasy oriental, but her language was German, an opulent, magnificent, tender German."[73] This blurb—which is still often reprinted today—is taken from a speech held by Gottfried Benn in February of 1953, seven years after Lasker-Schüler's death in exile. Though Benn sought to emphasize the value of Lasker-Schüler's legacy for the postwar German literary landscape following the banishment of her works under National Socialism, his use of the word "but" is crucial in that it upholds an understanding of "Jewish[ness]" and "[oriental] fantasy" as otherwise excluded from the German language.[74]

In many ways Lasker-Schüler's life and work can be read as a performative resistance of this "but."[75] She turned her body into a text by performing her "oriental" male characters Prinz Yussuf and the Prinz of Thebes in her everyday life; she defied genres by building poetry and sketches into her prose work and by writing prose that bordered on poetry; she imbued her Jewish characters with Arab and ancient Egyptian names and traits; she infused her German with neologisms and inverted syntax to the point that she at times claimed her texts were actually written in Hebrew (a language she did not know); and she created a fictional *Ursprache*, in which she was known to give entire sermons. In short, Lasker-Schüler tirelessly resisted any strict categorization of her work as "German," "Jewish," "oriental," or otherwise.

The small yet pernicious "but" in the dust jacket description of Lasker-Schüler's poetry finds a counterpoint in the early reception of Özdamar's work, which revealed a strong desire to essentialize Özdamar as an "authentic" voice writing from a position that was distinctly separate from the German cultural sphere. With this history in mind, I argue it is no coincidence that Özdamar chooses to cite Lasker-Schüler precisely in *Strange Stars*—the one literary work of Özdamar's that is *not* characterized by an unorthodox use of German.[76] Özdamar's standard use of German in this novel permeates down to the level of her production notes for the Volksbühne. By correcting many of the grammar mistakes in her original notes,[77] Özdamar brings the reproduced versions in line with the narrative style of *Strange Stars*, which numerous scholars have described as documentary. Noting its relative lack of performative imagination[78] or linguistic invention,[79] others have argued further that the estranging and innovative quality of Özdamar's language decreases across the trilogy *Sun Halfway*, coinciding with the main character's integration into Germany and its literary communities.[80]

In conclusion, I argue that while the trilogy progresses forward in time, it moves backward linguistically, taking us to a point in Özdamar's career when she had only just begun to experiment with German. The fantastic and neologistic elements of a novel like *Caravanserai* are enabled precisely by Özdamar's virtuosic command of German, and the naïve, but playfully performative language of the protagonist in *Bridge* is mediated by Özdamar's insertion of her older self into the narrative, which allows the protagonist at times to view her actions from outside herself. On the contrary, the straightforward style of *Strange Stars* performs the language of a protagonist who is just beginning to learn German.

Just as this double movement challenges a simplistic narrative of progress, the references to Lasker-Schüler in *Strange Stars* consistently collapse times and places. And just as Emine's Turkish-language rehearsal notes unsuspectingly make their way into the institutional archive of the Volksbühne, the diverse poems and references to Lasker-Schüler also circulate with and within *Strange Stars* and the various archival documents it incorporates. As such, Özdamar both puts these poems into dynamic constellation with her own physical archive and suggests that within the discursive archive of postwar migration there is no logical relationship between herself and Lasker-Schüler. The links between these two women's work are rather nonteleological, and, even more importantly, imaginative.

Kristin Dickinson is assistant professor of German studies at the University of Michigan. Her book, *DisOrientations: German-Turkish Cultural Contact in Translation (1811–1946)*, was published by Penn State University Press in 2021. Her translations of authors including Feridun Zaimoğlu, Selim Özdogan, Sabahattin Ali, and Bejan Matur have appeared in *Words without Borders*, *TRANSIT*, *German-Turkish Studies Yearbook*, and the *PEN Poetry Slam*.

Notes

This chapter was completed during a research fellowship at the International Research Center for Cultural Studies (IFK), University of Art and Design Linz.
1. Özdamar donated her own archival materials to Berlin's Akademie der Künste in December 2017. Özdamar's personal estate includes manuscripts, notes, and sketches from her time at the Volksbühne and other Berlin theaters, correspondence, notes from reading tours, as well as secondary literature on her work.
2. Amy J. Elias and Christian Moraru, ed., *The Planetary Turn: Relationality and Geoaesthetics in the Twenty-First Century* (Evanston, IL: Northwestern University Press, 2015), xxiii.
3. An archival turn was further inspired by translations of Walter Benjamin's work into English in the 1970s and by the broader scope of Michel Foucault's theoretical work, which prompted a rethinking of the terms of knowledge production in relation to the archive. Ann Stoler, *Along the Archival Grain* (Princeton, NJ: Princeton University Press, 2010), 44–46.
4. Stoler, *Along*, 43.
5. Harriet Bradley, "The Seductions of the Archive: Voices Lost and Found," *History of the Human Sciences* 12, no. 2 (1999): 108–9.
6. Kate Eichhorn, *The Archival Turn in Feminism: Outrage in Order* (Philadelphia: Temple University Press, 2013), 2.
7. Eichhorn, *Archival Turn*, 2.

8. Unless otherwise noted, all translations in this chapter are my own. "Probe Bürgergeneral. Schnaps. Wir probierten die Momente der Angst, Neugier, Lust, Aufregung, wie in einem Film, alles kurz und nah. Schnaps geht auf den Schrank los, in dem der volle Milchkrug steht. Aber die Reden, die er über Freiheit und Revolution vor dem Schrank führt, sind im Grunde die Reden eines schwatzlustigen Dorfbarbiers. Heute ist sein Thema die Revolution. Auch die Barbiersalons in Istanbul sind die Orte, wo die Leute ihre Ideen über Politik, Moral und Ökonomie vor dem Spiegel einfach loswerden können, während sie rasiert werden. Goethe in Istanbul"; Emine Sevgi Özdamar, *Seltsame Sterne starren zur Erde: Wedding—Pankow 1976/77* (Cologne: Kiepenheuer & Witsch, 2003): 171.
9. B. Venkat Mani, *Cosmopolitical Claims: Turkish-German Literatures from Nadolny to Pamuk* (Iowa City: University of Iowa Press, 2007), 115.
10. Mani, *Cosmopolitical Claims*, 106, 112, 186.
11. My use of this term is inspired by Michael Rothberg's concept of "multidirectional memory." In his examination of Holocaust remembrance in the wake of decolonization, Rothberg challenges the idea that memories can be owned by a given group; his focus lies rather on the productive negotiation of memory through processes of cross-referencing and borrowing across different histories and time frames. Michael Rothberg, *Multidirectional Memory: Remembering the Holocaust in the Age of Decolonization* (Stanford, CA: Stanford University Press, 2009).
12. I borrow this dynamic depiction of the archive from the work of Kate Eichhorn. See Eichhorn, *Archival Turn*, 2.
13. Özdamar, *Seltsame Sterne*, 143.
14. Deniz Utlu, "Das Archiv der Migration," in *Der Freitag: Das Meinungsmedium*, 31 October 2011, retrieved 15 May 2018 from https://www.freitag.de/autoren/der-freitag/das-archiv-der-migration.
15. Utlu, "Archiv."
16. "Eine flache Landschaft, die Rehe rennen in die Tiefe des Waldes. 'Du bist jetzt in einem anderen Wald' dachte ich, 'du wirst jetzt nie zu dem alten zurückkehren.' So viele Rehe hier. Wenn man schreit, bleiben sie stehen, dann rennen sie wieder los in das Herz der Wälder. Gegen Morgen bin ich aus dem Haus gegangen. Die anderen schliefen noch. Ich trug die Bettdecke um meine Schultern, lief in den stillen Wald, weit weg von dem Haus, und weinte. Die Kraniche flogen plötzlich zum Himmel, Rehe, Pferde, alle waren wach. Hat mein Weinen sie geweckt? Klaus hatte mir gestern Abend erzählt, daß hier der Todesmarsch der Juden aus dem KZ Sachsenhausen entlanggegangen war. Viele starben auf dem Weg. Klaus sagte: 'Sachsenhausen war das KZ, in dem der ganze Holocaust geplant worden ist.' Jetzt schaue ich auf diese Landschaft. Jetzt sind die Rehe, die Kraniche und die Krähen hier. Damals muß es hier wie auf einem anderen Planeten ausgesehen haben, Menschen wie Skelette unterm Mondschein. Die Augen groß. Kleider, zerrissene Kleider, die mit dem Wind über die Landschaft fliegen." Özdamar, *Seltsame Sterne*, 114.
17. Kader Konuk first pointed out this connection between the two forests. Kader Konuk, "Taking on German and Turkish History: Emine Sevgi Özdamar's *Seltsame Sterne*," *Gegenwartsliteratur: Ein germanistisches Jahrbuch* (2006/7): 243.
18. Özdamar, *Seltsame Sterne*, 25.
19. In addition to the Holocaust, John Pizer has also analyzed the depiction of East Germany in *Strange Stars* through the lens of countermemory, or the articulation of memories and histories otherwise in the process of being forgotten. Without whitewashing

the history of the GDR or engaging in *Ostalgie*, he argues, Özdamar successfully highlights East Berlin as a site of tolerance, openness, and artistic energy. The novel thus recuperates a different image of the city, in the face of otherwise negative portrayals in the postunification era.

20. In her examination of Emine's reenactment of Jews as victims of the Holocaust, Konuk sees Özdamar as collapsing the distance between Self and Other, past and present. She thus in no way portrays the narrative of *Strange Stars* as sequential but rather as a form of palimpsestic layering that creates narrative depth. At the same time, she argues that Emine's symbolic entrance into the German national community "is linked to appropriating the memory of the exiled and murdered Jew" and that "the implied analogies between the tortured Turk, the persecuted Jew, and the Turkish immigrant [in *Strange Stars*] are what make this act of 'borrowed memory' especially problematic." Konuk, "Taking on German," 245.
21. Gizem Arslan, "Animated Exchange: Translational Strategies in Emine Sevgi Özdamar's *Strange Stars Stare to Earth*," *The Global South* 7, no. 2 (2014).
22. Ela E. Gezen, *Brecht, Turkish Theater, and Turkish-German Literature: Reception, Adaptation, and Innovation after 1960* (Rochester, NY: Camden House, 2018), 86.
23. Ibid., 96.
24. Consider, for example, the following historical definition of *Konstellation* from *Meyers Konversationslexikon* (1885): "die Stellung von Sternen gegeneinander, von der Erde aus betrachtet."
25. "Sternbilder sind nicht nur Erscheinungen, deren Sichtbarkeit an den Einbruch der Dunkelheit gebunden ist. Sie sind vor allem eine Anordnung von Phänomenen, die nicht von diesen Phänomenen selbst—im Sinne einer genetischen, historischen oder strukturellen Verwandtschaft—gestiftet wird, sondern lediglich von dem kontingenten Standort ihres Beobachters." Nicolas Pethes, "Konstellationen: Erinnerung als Kontinuitätsunterbrechung in Walter Benjamins Theorie von Gedächtnis, Kultur und Geschichte," Manuscript, 5. Retrieved 3 December 2021 from http://idsl1.philfak.unikoeln.de/leadmin/IDSLI/dozentenseiten/Pethes/Pethes_Benjamin_Konstellationen.pdf.
26. "Seltsame Sterne starren zur Erde / Eisenfarbene mit Sehnsuchtsschweifen, / Mit brennenden Armen die Liebe suchen." Özdamar, *Seltsame Sterne*, 9.
27. Venkat Mani also addresses the novel's rejection of the German desire for a native informant female author. Mani, *Cosmopolitical Claims*, 97–98.
28. Walter Benjamin, *Das Passagen-Werk*, in *Gesammelte Schriften 5, Band 1*, ed. Rolf Tiedemann (Frankfurt am Main: Suhrkamp, 1982), 576.
29. Helmut Lethen, Annegret Pelz, and Michael Rohrwasser, eds., *Konstellationen—Versuchsanordnungen eines Schreibens* (Vienna: Vienna University Press, 2013), 8.
30. Marcelo Stamm, "Konstellationsforschung—Ein Methodenprofil: Motive und Perspektiven," in *Konstellationsforschung*, ed. Martin Mulsow and Marcelo R. Stamm (Frankfurt am Main: Suhrkamp, 2005), 32.
31. Azade Seyhan, *Writing Outside the Nation* (Princeton, NJ: Princeton University Press, 2001), 12, 18.
32. Leslie Adelson, *The Turkish Turn in Contemporary German Literature: Toward a New Critical Grammar of Migration* (New York: Palgrave Macmillan, 2005), 15.
33. Seyhan understands the cultural archive of Turkish German literature as a place where countermemories of the home country can be preserved. Adelson in turn seeks to counter the perception of guest workers in Germany as helpless and disoriented by showing how Turkish German literature of the 1990s attests instead to an epochal sense of disorientation in German society at large.

34. Walter Benjamin, *The Arcades Project*, trans. Howard Eiland and Kevin McLaughlin, (Cambridge, MA: Harvard University Press, 1999), 462. "Nicht so ist es, daß das Vergangene sein Licht auf das Gegenwärtige oder das Gegenwärtige sein Licht auf das Vergangene wirft, sondern Bild ist dasjenige, worin das Gewesene mit dem Jetzt blitzhaft zu einer Konstellation zusammentritt." Benjamin, *Das Passagen-Werk*, 576.
35. Terry Smith, "Defining Contemporaneity: Imagining Planetarity," *Nordic Journal of Aesthetics* 24, no. 49 (2015): 156.
36. Smith, "Defining Contemporaneity," 155.
37. Smith, "Defining Contemporaneity," 167.
38. Gayatri Chakravorty Spivak, *Death of a Discipline* (New York: Columbia University Press, 2005), 72.
39. Elias and Moraru, *Planetary Turn*, xxiii.
40. Christian Moraru, "'World,' 'Globe,' 'Planet': Comparative Literature, Planetary Studies, and Cultural Debt after the Global Turn," *State of the Discipline Report*, 3 December 2014, retrieved 3 December 2021 from https://stateofthediscipline.acla.org/entry.
41. "Warum suchst die mich in unseren Nächten, / In Wolken des Hasses auf bösen Sternen! / Laß mich allein mit den Geistern fechten." Özdamar, *Seltsame Sterne*, 15.
42. "Sie hat in Berlin gelebt, Expressionismus. 1945 ist sie in Jerusalem gestorben. Sie mußte vor den Nazis fliehen." Özdamar, *Seltsame Sterne*, 58.
43. "Alle Vögel üben sich / Auf deinen Lippen. / Immerblau streut deine Stimme / Über den Weg." Özdamar, *Seltsame Sterne*, 58.
44. "Sie schützen uns vor den hungrigen Männern, sie sind unsere Heiligen." Özdamar, *Seltsame Sterne*, 59.
45. Emine Sevgi Özdamar, *Das Leben ist eine Karawanserei hat zwei Türen, aus einer kam ich rein, aus der anderen ging ich raus* (Cologne: Kiepenheuer & Witsch Verlag, 1992), 117.
46. "Die Sterne können mit den Sternen sprechen, die Menschen können mit den Menschen nicht sprechen." Özdamar, *Karawanserei*, 257.
47. "Wo der Morgen kein Morgen zu sein scheint, wo nur die Sterne mit Sternen sprechen können, aber nicht Menschen mit Menschen." Özdamar, *Seltsame Sterne*, 25.

    Prostitutes also appear in different guises in *The Bridge of the Golden Horn*. At one point, for example, the narrator is assigned to play a madam in a political *Hurenstück*. In preparation for her role, the narrator visits local brothels, the prostitutes of which then attend her premiere. Later in the novel, the narrator dons her prostitute costume at the height of a military coup in order to legitimate her presence on the street. To this end, Karin Lornsen argues that Özdamar leverages "gender clichés, which [otherwise] limit female participation and reinforce gender stereotypes, [to] strategically ... expand a woman's space of action. The whore costume ultimately blurs the line between authenticity and performance since it was inspired by real-life prostitutes, was then acted out on stage, and finally, was utilized in daily life to keep up appearances. Consequently, the image of the whore is stripped of its pejorative stigma by being declared as a set of stereotypes that can be acted out in the arena of everyday life." Karin Lornsen, "The City as Stage of Transgression: Performance, Picaresque Reminiscences, and Linguistic Incongruity in Emine S. Özdamar's *The Bridge of the Golden Horn*," in *Gender and Laughter: Comic Affirmation and Subversion in Traditional and Modern Media*, ed. Gaby Pailer, Andreas Böhn, Stefan Horlacher, and Ulrich Scheck (New York: Rodopi, 2009), 214.
48. Alternately, Lasker-Schüler's life could be understood as a reference to her texts; she notably adopted the titular characters of these stories as alter egos, by dressing up, acting as, and referring to herself in correspondence accordingly.

49. "Im Hafen von Konstantinople liegen Boote—Sterne." Else Lasker-Schüler, *Gesammelte Werke in Drei Bänden: Prosa und Schauspiele 2* (Frankfurt am Main: Suhrkamp, 1998), 107.
50. "Wir Basen aus Bagdad duften nach altem Gemäuer, wir Prinzessinnen vom Tigris tanzen mit stummen Gliedern. Und ich verstehe die Sprache der Frauen des Harems nicht. Weiß nicht um was sie veranlaßt, sich zu freuen oder sich gegenseitig zu überwerfen. Sie sprechen nicht ihre Sultansprache: 'Wir sprechen parisisch,' erklärt mir die Kleinste . . ."; Lasker-Schüler, *Gesammelte Werke*, 107.
51. Jane Hathaway, "Out of Africa, into the Palace: The Ottoman Chief Harem Eunuch," in *Living in the Ottoman Realm: Empire and Identity, 13th–20th Centuries*, ed. Christine Isom-Verhaaren and Kent F. Schull (Bloomington: Indiana University Press, 2016), 225. Barring the sultan, no other uncastrated men were allowed in the harem.
52. Joan Del Plato, *Multiple Wives, Multiple Pleasures: Representing the Harem, 1800–1875* (Vancouver: Fairleigh Dickinson University Press, 2002), 182.
53. Leslie Pierce, *The Imperial Harem: Women and Sovereignty in the Ottoman Empire* (New York: Oxford University Press, 1993), 1.
54. "Ein großes Buch mit grausamen Bildern." Lasker-Schüler, *Gesammelte Werke*, 108.
55. "Vollmond meiner fiebernden Tante." Lasker-Schüler, *Gesammelte Werke*, 108.
56. "Blühen in gesprenkelten Goldnelken." Lasker-Schüler, *Gesammelte Werke*, 109.
57. James M. Glass, "The Modernity of the Marquis de Sade: A Question of Action and Lifestyle," *Political Studies* 19, no. 3 (September 1971): 308.
58. "Ich möchte in eins der kleinen Sternboote steigen, auf dem Bosporus—der Himmel ist ein einziger großer Stern." Lasker-Schüler, *Gesammelte Werke*, 109.
59. Sylke Kirschnick, *Tausend und ein Zeichen: Else Lasker-Schülers Orient und die Berliner Alltags- und Populärkultur um 1900* (Würzburg: Königshausen und Neumann, 2007), 120.
60. Anthony Auerbach, "Imagine No Metaphors: The Dialectical Image of Walter Benjamin," *Image and Narrative: Image [&] Narrative* [e-journal] 18 (2007), retrieved 15 May 2018 from http://www.imageandnarrative.be/inarchive/thinking_pictures/auerbach.htm.
61. "Ich kann deine Lippen nicht finden . . . / Wo bist du, ferne Stadt / Mit den segnenden Düften?" Özdamar, *Seltsame Sterne*, 71.
62. The stanza reads: "Leise schwimmt der Mond durch mein Blut . . . / Schlummernde Töne sind die Augen des Tages / Wandelhin—taumelher" (The moon swims softly through my blood . . . / The eyes of day are slumbering tones / Shifting-here—staggering-there). Else Lasker-Schüler, *Sämtliche Gedichte* (Frankfurt am Main: Suhrkamp, 2016), 78.
63. Özdamar, *Seltsame Sterne*, 142.
64. "Das fernste Land der Welt." Lasker Schüler, *Gesammelte Werke*, 787.
65. Edda Ziegler, *Verboten—verfremt—vertrieben: Schriftstellerinnen im Widerstand gegen den Nationalsozialismus* (Munich: dtv Verlagsgesellschaft, 2010), 147.
66. "Sie werden sie aufhängen. Wo waren die Köpfe? Man weiß nicht, wo ihr Grab ist. Die Polizei hat die Leiche nicht freigegeben!" Özdamar, *Seltsame Sterne*, 23.
67. "Die Wörter sind krank. Meine Wörter brauchen ein Sanatorium, wie kranke Muscheln. Es gibt eine Stelle am Ägäischen Meer, wo drei Ströme zusammenkommen. Man bringt Säcke mit Muscheln aus Istanbul, Izmir, Italien dorthin, die im schmutzigen Wasser krank geworden sind. Das saubere Wasser aus den drei Strömen heilt in ein paar Monaten die erkrankten Muscheln. Dieses Stück Meer nennen die Fischer Muschelsanatorium. Wie lange braucht ein Wort, um wieder gesund zu werden? Man

sagt, in fremden Ländern verliert man die Muttersprache. Kann man nicht auch in seinem eigenen Land die Muttersprache verlieren?" Özdamar, Seltsame Sterne, 23.
68. Yasemin Yildiz, Beyond the Mother Tongue: The Postmonolingual Condition (New York: Fordham University Press, 2012), 143–68.
69. "Ich konnte nicht mehr reden. Jedes Wort tat meinem Mund weh." Özdamar, Die Brücke vom goldenen Horn (Cologne: Kiepenheuer & Witsch, 1998), 254.
70. Read within these terms, the protagonist's decision to return to the Volksbühne expresses commitment to a form of art that is political precisely in its refusal to express explicit political ideology.
71. Such criticism is also based on the fact that Lasker-Schüler produced an ahistorical and syncretic depiction of the Orient in her prose.
72. For a concise reception history, see Karen Jankowsky, "'German' Literature Contested: The 1991 Ingeborg-Bachmann-Prize Debate, 'Cultural Diversity,' and Emine Sevgi Özdamar," The German Quarterly 70, no. 3 (Summer 1997): 261–76.
73. "Dies war die größte Lyrikerin, die Deutschland je hatte. Ihre Themen waren vielfach jüdisch, ihre Phantasie orientalisch, aber ihre Sprache war deutsch, ein üppiges, prunkvolles, zartes, Deutsch." Özdamar, Strange Stars, 15.
74. Uljana Wolf, "Nachwort," in Else Lasker-Schüler: Sämtliche Gedichte (Frankfurt am Main: Fischer Klassik, 2016), 395.
75. Wolf, "Nachwort," 394.
76. Mother Tongue (1990) is marked throughout by the critical and creative incorporation of grammatical mistakes and literal translations from Turkish; similarly, Caravanserai (1992) is replete with neologisms and direct translations from Turkish, incorporates elements of traditional Turkish story telling, and at times borders on magic realism. While Bridge (1998) is more rooted in the everyday experiences of its protagonist as a guest worker in West Berlin, it is also marked by a playful and performative linguistic register.
77. For specific examples, see Moray McGowan, "'Sie Kucken beide an Milch Topf': Goethe's Bürgergeneral in Double Refraction," in Language, Text, Bildung: Essays in Honour of Beate Dreike, ed. Beate Monika Dreike, Andreas Stuhlmann, Patrick Studer, and Gert Hofmann (New York: Peter Lang, 2005), 79–88.
78. Despite what he views as a shared artistic and political telos with Caravanserai and Bridge, Pizer describes the style of Strange Stars as factual, arguing that it does not come across as a work of fiction. John Pizer, "The Continuation of Countermemory: Emine Sevgi Özdamar's Seltsame Sterne starren zur Erde," in German Literature in a New Century: Trends, Traditions, Transitions, Transformations, ed. Katharina Gerstenberger and Patricia Herminghouse (New York: Berghahn Books, 2008), 135.
79. Mani, Cosmopolitical Claims, 103.
80. Leopold Federmair, "Der neue Diamant: Verfremdungseffekte bei E. S. Özdamar," Arcadia: International Journal of Literary Culture 47, no 1 (June 2012): 153.

Bibliography

Adelson, Leslie A. The Turkish Turn in Contemporary German Literature: Towards a New Critical Grammar of Migration. New York: Palgrave Macmillan, 2005.
Arslan, Gizem. "Animated Exchange: Translational Strategies in Emine Sevgi Özdamar's Strange Stars Stare to Earth." The Global South 7, no. 2 (2014): 191–209.

Auerbach, Anthony. "Imagine No Metaphors: The Dialectical Image of Walter Benjamin." *Image and Narrative: Image [&] Narrative* [e-journal] 18 (2007). Retrieved 15 May 2018 from http://www.imageandnarrative.be/inarchive/thinking_pictures/auerbach.htm.

Benjamin, Walter. *Das Passagen-Werk*. In *Gesammelte Schriften 5, Part 1*, edited by Rolf Tiedemann. Frankfurt am Main: Suhrkamp, 1982.

———. *The Arcades Project*. Translated by Howard Eiland and Kevin McLaughlin. Cambridge, MA: Harvard University Press, 1999.

Bradley, Harriet. "The Seductions of the Archive: Voices Lost and Found." *History of the Human Sciences* 12, no. 2 (1999): 107–22.

Del Plato, Joan. *Multiple Wives, Multiple Pleasures: Representing the Harem, 1800–1875*. Vancouver: Fairleigh Dickinson University Press, 2002.

Eichhorn, Kate. *The Archival Turn in Feminism: Outrage in Order*. Philadelphia: Temple University Press, 2013.

Elias, Amy J., and Christian Moraru, eds. *The Planetary Turn: Relationality and Geoaesthetics in the Twenty-First Century*. Evanston, IL: Northwestern University Press, 2015.

Federmair, Leopold. Der neue Diamant: Verfremdungseffekte bei E. S. Özdamar. *Arcadia: International Journal of Literary Culture* 47, no. 1 (June 2012): 153–72.

Gezen, Ela E. *Brecht, Turkish Theater, and Turkish-German Literature: Reception, Adaptation, and Innovation after 1960*. Rochester, NY: Camden House, 2018.

Glass, James M. "The Modernity of the Marquis de Sade: A Question of Action and Lifestyle." *Political Studies* 19, no. 3 (September 1971): 303–15.

Hathaway, Jane. "Out of Africa, into the Palace: The Ottoman Chief Harem Eunuch." In *Living in the Ottoman Realm: Empire and Identity, 13th–20th Centuries*, edited by Christine Isom-Verhaaren and Kent F. Schull, 225–38. Bloomington: Indiana University Press, 2016.

Jankowsky, Karen. "'German' Literature Contested: The 1991 Ingeborg-Bachmann-Prize Debate,'Cultural Diversity,' and Emine Sevgi Özdamar." *The German Quarterly* 70, no. 3 (Summer, 1997): 261–76.

Kirschnick, Sylke. *Tausend und ein Zeichen: Else Lasker-Schülers Orient und die Berliner Alltags- und Populärkultur um 1900*. Würzburg: Königshausen und Neumann, 2007.

Konuk, Kader. "Taking on German and Turkish History: Emine Sevgi Özdamar's *Seltsame Sterne*." *Gegenwartsliteratur: Ein germanistisches Jahrbuch* (2006/7): 232–55.

Lasker-Schüler, Else. *Sämtliche Gedichte*. Frankfurt am Main: Fischer Klassik, 2016.

———. *Gesammelte Werke in Drei Bänden: Prosa und Schauspiele 2*. Frankfurt am Main: Suhrkamp Verlag, 1998.

Lethen, Helmut, Annegret Pelz, and Michael Rohrwasser, eds. *Konstellationen—Versuchsanordnungen eines Schreibens*. Vienna: Vienna University Press, 2013.

Lornsen, Karin. "The City as Stage of Transgression: Performance, Picaresque Reminiscences, and Linguistic Incongruity in Emine S. Özdamar's *The Bridge of the Golden Horn*." In *Gender and Laughter: Comic Affirmation and Subversion in Traditional and Modern Media*, edited by Gaby Pailer, Andreas Böhn, Stefan Horlacher, and Ulrich Scheck, 201–19. New York: Rodopi, 2009.

Mani, Venkat B. *Cosmopolitical Claims: Turkish-German Literatures from Nadolny to Pamuk*. Iowa City: University of Iowa Press, 2007.

McGowan, Moray. "'Sie Kucken beide an Milch Topf': Goethe's *Bürgergeneral* in Double Refraction." In *Language, Text, Bildung: Essays in Honour of Beate Dreike*, edited by

Beate Monika Dreike, Andreas Stuhlmann, Patrick Studer, and Gert Hofmann, 79–88. New York: Peter Lang, 2005.

Moraru, Christian. "'World,' 'Globe,' 'Planet': Comparative Literature, Planetary Studies, and Cultural Debt after the Global Turn." State of the Discipline of Comparative Literature, 2014. Retrieved 3 December 2021 from https://stateofthediscipline.acla.org.

Özdamar, Emine Sevgi. *Seltsame Sterne starren zur Erde: Wedding—Pankow 1976–77*. Cologne: Kiepenheuer & Witsch, 2003.

———. *Die Brücke vom Goldenen Horn*. Cologne: Kiepenheuer & Witsch, 1998.

———. *Das Leben ist eine Karawanserei hat zwei Türen, aus einer kam ich rein, aus der anderen ging ich raus*. Cologne: Kiepenheuer & Witsch, 1992.

———. *Mutterzunge*. Berlin: Rotbuch Verlag, 1990.

Pethes, Nicolas. "Konstellationen: Erinnerung als Kontinuitätsunterbrechung in Walter Benjamins Theorie von Gedächtnis, Kultur und Geschichte." Manuscript, 1–21. Retrieved 3 December 2021 from http://idsl1.philfak.unikoeln.de/fileadmin/IDSLI/dozentenseiten/Pethes/Pethes_Benjamin_Konstellationen.pdf.

Pierce, Leslie. *The Imperial Harem: Women and Sovereignty in the Ottoman Empire*. New York: Oxford University Press, 1993.

Pizer, John. "The Continuation of Countermemory: Emine Sevgi Özdamar's *Seltsame Sterne starren zur Erde*." In *German Literature in a New Century: Trends, Traditions, Transitions, Transformations*, edited by Katharina Gerstenberger and Patricia Herminghouse, 135–52. New York: Berghahn Books, 2008.

Rothberg, Michael. *Multidirectional Memory: Remembering the Holocaust in the Age of Decolonization*. Stanford, CA: Stanford University Press, 2009.

Seyhan, Azade. *Writing Outside the Nation*. Princeton, NJ: Princeton University Press, 2001.

Smith, Terry. "Defining Contemporaneity: Imagining Planetarity." *Nordic Journal of Aesthetics* 24, no. 49 (2015): 155–74.

Spivak, Gayatri Chakravorty. *Death of a Discipline*. New York: Columbia University Press, 2005.

Stamm, Marcelo R. "Konstellationsforschung—Ein Methodenprofil: Motive und Perspektiven." In *Konstellationsforschung*, edited by Martin Mulsow and Marcelo R. Stamm, 31–73. Frankfurt am Main: Suhrkamp, 2005.

Stoler, Ann Laura. *Along the Archival Grain*. Princeton, NJ: Princeton University Press, 2010.

Utlu, Deniz. "Das Archiv der Migration." In *Der Freitag: Das Meinungsmedium*, 31 October 2011. Retrieved 15 May 2018 from https://www.freitag.de/autoren/der-freitag/das-archiv-der-migration.

Wolf, Uljana. "Nachwort." In *Else Lasker-Schüler: Sämtliche Gedichte*, 387–401. Frankfurt am Main: Fischer Klassik, 2016.

Yildiz, Yasemin. *Beyond the Mother Tongue: The Postmonolingual Condition*. New York: Fordham University Press, 2012.

Ziegler, Edda. *Verboten—verfremt—vertrieben: Schriftstellerinnen im Widerstand gegen den Nationalsozialismus*. Munich: dtv Verlagsgesellschaft, 2010.

CHAPTER 3

Jewish Tales from a Muslim Turkish Pen
Feridun Zaimoğlu and Moses in Oberammergau

JOSHUA SHELLY

In 2013 German newspapers eagerly reported a premiere taking place on the stage of the Passionstheater in Oberammergau in Bavaria, the famed location of once-a-decade passion plays, a tradition first begun in 1634. This performance, however, was no passion play.[1] Instead, Oberammergau's director Christian Stückl had commissioned coauthors Günter Senkel and Feridun Zaimoğlu to write a new script for the stage to tell the story of the legendary biblical figure Moses.[2]

The play *Moses*, divided into two acts, was unique not only because of the writers' heterogenous religious backgrounds—Muslim and Catholic—but also because of the sources from which they drew when composing their adaptation.[3] As a basis, the authors used the biblical narrative shared by Christians and Jews, beginning with a retelling of Moses's murder of an Egyptian overseer (found in Exodus 2) and ending with a confrontation between Balaam, a false prophet, and the Israelites (found in Numbers 22–24). Zaimoğlu and Senkel built on this foundation by incorporating sections of postbiblical, Rabbinic Jewish traditions about Moses into their play, drawing them from three major early twentieth century collections of *Aggadot* (Jewish legends), which bring together sources dating back to the first millennium CE. A cross-religious endeavor undertaken by a major German author and staged in world-renowned Oberammergau, *Moses* received positive press coverage that celebrated the seeming ecumenical harmony underlying the collaboration. But what does it mean for this multireligious, non-Jewish team to speak through Jewish sources as they retell a well-known story for a largely Christianized, German audience in the twenty-first century? What are the implications of a playwright of Muslim background who puts "Jewish" words into the mouths of his characters?

And what can it tell us about interfaith dialogue in the contemporary German context?

In what follows, I provide a close reading of Moses, interpreting it as an homage to the power of words to produce action. Through an examination of several passages, I argue that Moses's words only gain efficacy because he carries God's message and not his own; moreover, Moses is only able to conquer the contrary speech acts of his opponent—Pharaoh, who wields political power—because he serves as a conduit for God's words. In the second part of my argument, I pivot to the articles about and interviews conducted with Zaimoğlu in anticipation of the play's premiere. I argue that newspaper accounts present the relationship of the playwright to his specifically Jewish source material as a mirror of Moses's own relationship to the words of God. Moses, the quintessential outsider and stutterer, has impeded and ineffective speech until the power of God's message gives his words power and legitimacy; likewise, Zaimoğlu, the Turkish Muslim migrant to Germany whose German-language ability is constantly questioned and tagged as insufficient, gains literary legitimacy through participation in a liberal interfaith conversation by appealing to Jewish legendary source texts. In the final section of the chapter, I highlight Zaimoğlu's ambivalence toward his Jewish sources, even as he uses them to establish a form of social legitimacy. I then end by examining the strong similarities between Muslim and Jewish traditions about Moses and discuss how these affinities evade our gaze when reading Moses and looking at the presentation of Zaimoğlu's authorship. I conclude by suggesting how an appreciation for the shared Jewish-Muslim biblical imagination allows us as German studies scholars to reconsider the way we discuss dialogue across difference in Germany in the twenty-first century.

Moses as Play: A Battle of Words

Moses opens with a conversation between two Egyptian overseers about the events leading to Israelite[4] enslavement. The first overseer recalls, "with gentle words, clever Pharaoh brought the Hebrews into servitude."[5] The overseer explains how one day the Egyptian ruler proposed that both Egyptians and Israelites, subject and king alike, should work together to mix the mud of the Nile with water to produce bricks. They proceeded to do so, and after the day's work, the Pharaoh withdrew, set taskmasters above the Hebrews, and left them enslaved and bound to a brick quota determined by the first day's production. In response to this story, the second overseer responds: "A clever deception [kluge List]" (9).

This opening exchange serves two main purposes. First, it exposes the audience to the first of many Jewish legends. In the biblical text, one only reads that

Pharaoh enslaves the Hebrews, but not how. In his script, however, Zaimoğlu relies on the legends to fill in the backstory of the Hebrews' enslavement.[6] Second, these lines foreground the importance of (gentle) words as the motor behind the *Moses* plot. The Pharaoh entraps the Israelites through deception and cleverness rather than brute force and overt physical violence; only afterward does he "place overseers" above them (9). Throughout the script, the narration repeatedly relies on words to produce action and conflict in the place of direct deeds.

In the next scenes, Moses appears and avenges an enslaved Israelite by murdering an Egyptian; he thus awakens Pharaoh's wrath and flees into the desert. His brute action is impotent in the face of Pharaoh's words. The audience then learns that Moses, born an Israelite and raised in the Egyptian palace as the child of Pharaoh's daughter, exists in the interstitial space between Egyptian and Israelite, enslaved and free. In a conversation between Pharaoh and the priest Balaam, the audience discovers Moses's own relationship to words: he is a stutterer.[7] As a child, the young Moses had often sat in Pharaoh's lap and grasped for his crown. In response, Balaam prophesied that Moses would usurp Pharaoh's throne. The court magicians then proposed to test the child's understanding to see whether Moses was indeed capable of future treachery. They placed a basin of scorching coals before him, among which lay a piece of gold. If Moses grasped for the gold, he would be deemed "savvy" (*verstandesbegabt*; literally: gifted with understanding) and would later usurp the Pharaoh; if not, he would be considered a simpleton and safe. The child Moses chose a scorching coal, thus saving his life. He then placed the coal in his mouth, injuring his tongue, and became a lifelong stutterer (15–16).[8]

This incident, contrasted with the Pharaoh's deception discussed above, sets up a clear diptych between two models of word usage in the scenes that follow. Pharaoh, with his "gentle words," wields language as a weapon, issuing commands and exhibiting confidence in his ability to orchestrate action in his world through speech. Moses, however, fights his reputation as a stutterer throughout the play but nonetheless proves effective at wielding words because of the higher source behind his message: God.[9]

In the final lines of act 1, scene 4, the audience discovers just how important words are to the functioning of Pharaoh's realm. Having heard Moses's initial demand to free the Israelites and witnessing the loss of his magicians to Moses in a supernatural duel, Pharaoh sends Moses and Aaron off to await his judgment (*Richtspruch*). He then turns to his vizier, exclaiming:

> PHARAOH: I *command*: No more straw for bricks for the Hebrews. Drive them into the desert, so that they may gather dry undergrowth and twigs. Each vassal [will] work as appointed. Flay the negligent with the whip.
>
> HISKIL: May this, Your *word*, be sealed.

PHARAOH: Vizier, I *command*: I *declare* the Sabbath, on which they unroll *their texts*, abolished. They will stir mud and cut bricks. Lazy vassals are good *prophesiers* [*Kündiger*; literally: those who declare]. Break their bones in response to any protest [*Widerwort*; literally: contrary word]. If they *snap* at you, knock out their *teeth*. (25, emphasis added)

Pharaoh responds to Moses's challenge to his authority by doubling down on the use of words to continue and intensify the Israelites' enslavement. Without descending from his throne, he commands swift retribution. His vizier, Hiskil, responds with an affirmation of his word and depicts the image of words set down on paper, given authority by the seal marking them. Meanwhile, the Pharaoh robs the Israelites of their Sabbath, the day on which they study the words from God written on their scrolls. Furthermore, he silences potential protestations by threatening to negate their spoken words and protests by violently removing their teeth. In a few short lines, the Pharaoh clearly shows how power functions in his kingdom: by the effective use and control of language.

If Pharaoh relies on words built on the threat of violence, Moses also battles with words. Moses's words, unlike Pharaoh's, however, are not supported by political power but by a different source: God. The audience first learns of Moses's relationship to the words of God when he stands before the burning bush in the third scene. Moses begins, "I hear You Lord, You who speak," and later he tells Aaron, his brother, "He [God] speaks through me" (17, 19).

The contrast between these two approaches becomes evident in the scene preceding Pharaoh's above commands, when Moses approaches Pharaoh directly to demand that he free the Israelites. Moses presents himself as the "Messenger [*Gesandte*] of the One God," and Pharaoh responds,

PHARAOH: He sends you to me without gifts?

MOSES: [It is] me He has gifted you.

PHARAOH: With what?

MOSES: With *His word* . . .

. . . the God of Israel, *He says*, "Let my people go!"

PHARAOH (*enraged*): You tread in competition with Your King [God]. *I speak*: It is resolved, it is sealed, the seal will not be broken . . . (21, emphasis added)

Moses's few words introduce his consistent claim throughout the play to speak on behalf of the God of Israel, using "His Word." Meanwhile, Pharaoh directly represents himself with his own words, emphasizing, "I speak." In this competition, words are the medium of action, and their efficacy determines who gains power.

As an example of the important role of words in this play, we need only consider the presentation of the plagues later on in act 1, scene 5 (28–29). Rather than relying on a major buildup on stage with multiple scenes where the actual plagues are depicted individually, Moses simply declares, "It will occur," and proceeds to list the plagues in a single monologue. The script relies on these utterances to present the ten plagues as a speech act whose power emanates from Moses's simple words. Two scenes later, in response to the leveling of his kingdom, Pharaoh refers to Moses with the epithet "Stutterer" and demands his head. Pharaoh's decision to attack Moses for his inability to wield language effectively, even as he is conquered by the plagues sent by God and mediated through Moses's words, reveals, once again, the nature of the conflict at hand.

Finally, in the last scene of the first act, Moses learns from Bithiah, his adoptive mother and the daughter of Pharaoh, that the Egyptians will no longer "concern themselves with *your* [Moses's] words" (39, emphasis added). The consequences of this decision to no longer attend to his words are made clear shortly thereafter with the closing of the first act, as the Israelites cross the Red Sea on dry land, and the Egyptians, who follow in pursuit, are washed away by the waters that close in upon them. The final act of spite contained in Bithiah's statement is especially revealing: rather than acknowledging the source of Moses's message as God, she chooses instead to diminish it as simply "*your* [Moses's] words" and not the words of God.

Just as multiple characters frequently discredit Moses's words by calling him a stutterer, the *source* of Moses's message is also frequently called into question by his opponents. The audience encounters this again in the second act, whose focus is the theophany on Mount Sinai and Moses's presentation of God's law to the people. Unlike the first act, where Pharaoh acts as the main antagonist, the second act focuses on the opposition to Moses's leadership from within the Israelite community. Like Bithiah, Moses's main internal opponent, Korah, attacks the laws as coming directly from Moses after he descends Mount Sinai. Surrounded by a crowd, Korah cries out:

KORAH: ... Moses, ... I ask you: Is *your leadership* wise?

MOSES: *The Lord* directs me.

WIDOW: Does He cheat orphans out of their bread? ...

KORAH (*to the Israelites*): Her husband died and left her two daughters and a small field. She stood at the plow—then *Moses* came and *said?*

WIDOW: "You shall not simultaneously till your field with an ox and an ass." I obeyed.

KORAH: She began to sow. Then *Moses* came and *said?*

WIDOW: "You shall not sow your field with two types of crop." I obeyed.

KORAH: The field bore fruit. *Moses said?*

WIDOW: "You shall not harvest the corners of your field. Leave unripe fruit as the poor's portion."

KORAH: She obeyed. (63, emphasis added)

In a dialogue that builds up over the course of several more lines, Korah attacks Moses's words as unreasonable, accusing him of representing his own interests rather than the actual words of God. Quickly, the tension peaks, and Moses's partisans draw swords to defend him. In a final, powerful gesture toward the tent of revelation where God reveals himself, Moses declares, "God [written as the Tetragrammaton] lives there. Before him have you slandered me and the high priest [Aaron]. May your race be snuffed out" (65). The script then directs that the ground "tear open" and consume Korah and his wife.

Like Pharaoh before him, Korah proves powerless before Moses's words. Moses accuses Korah of slander—an untruthful, accusatory speech act—and on those grounds he performs his own speech act that results in an opening of the earth and the extinguishing of a whole family line. What, however, is the source of the slander? It is not that Moses did not declare the things; they are, indeed, commands found in the biblical text. Instead, like Bithiah before him, Korah's slander is his accusation that Moses's commands are his own and have no external source. Korah supposes Moses's words are simply his own and thus impotent, only to be swallowed up by the ground beneath his feet.

Thus, whether examining Korah, Pharaoh, or the other opponents of Moses who appear throughout Zaimoğlu's adaptation, the play continually returns to the way in which Moses engages in a battle of words and is effective in wielding words precisely because they stem from a more powerful source, the Hebrew God. More than a message internal to the *Moses* script, however, I propose that the presentation of this *Moses* adaptation in the press in 2013 was also connected to a rhetoric about who has the power to wield language and the source of that authority.

Zaimoğlu as Author: Performance of Revelation

When *Moses* premiered in Oberammergau in mid-2013, articles and news reports highlighted the unique collaboration, giving special attention to the multireligious team tasked with bringing it to the stage. The cultural programming on Südwestrundfunk captured the general celebration, heralding the team behind *Moses* with the headline, "Catholic-Muslim-Jewish-Heathen Passion Theater."[10] The Catholic theater director, Christian Stückl, sounded a similar note when the newspaper *Die Welt* published an article quoting him as saying, "We are using Jewish material with a Muslim playwright and Catholic director." He concluded: "You don't get more Lessing than that."[11]

Stückl's invocation of Lessing's ring parable from the famed play of religious tolerance, *Nathan the Wise* (1779), underscored his hope for *Moses* to provide a space for "abrahamic trialogue."[12] Yet amid the celebratory cries of ecumenicism, the focus on Zaimoğlu, the writer of this ring parable in a Passionstheater, revealed much about the nature of language and the limits different minority voices confront in modern-day Germany.

Feridun Zaimoğlu first appeared on the German literary scene in 1995 with his "mock ethnography" *Kanak Sprak: 24 Mißtöne vom Rande der Gesellschaft* (Kanak Sprak: 24 notes of discord from the margins of society), where he both "satirized and appropriated ... 'authentic migrant voices.'"[13] Celebrated and maligned as the publication that recorded and semi-legitimized the "incorrect" German of migrants in Germany, *Kanak Sprak* cemented Zaimoğlu's status as a key figure and *enfant terrible* of (Turkish) German literature. *Kanak Sprak*, the title, simultaneously became the name for the German spoken by migrants by combining the once-derogatory and now-reclaimed term for German guest workers, *Kanake*, and a variation of the German term for language (*Sprak*).

Nearly twenty years after its publication, reporters interviewing Zaimoğlu about *Moses* still referred back to his first publication. The *Süddeutsche Zeitung* review commented, perhaps in relief, "No 'Kanak Sprak' here," and *Der Tagesspiegel* quizzically queried about the role of this "man who once stood out with 'Kanak Sprak'" in the staging of a *Moses* adaptation.[14] The latter article assured its readers that Zaimoğlu is an inventor of words, exclaiming that these invented words were "indeed [*zwar*] in German."[15] This assurance, strengthened by the "indeed," made clear that the audience might still question this author who was born in Turkey, only later arrived in Germany as an infant, and came to fame by "bastardizing" the German language in *Kanak Sprak*.[16] In sum, like Moses of both the play and biblical text, these articles attach their own asterisk to Zaimoğlu's earlier language, something they label as problematic, a kind of stammering so to speak; they conclude by assuring readers that the stammering has subsided, making *Moses* safe to consume.

These interviews and play reviews brought up Zaimoğlu's perceived deficient relationship to the German language and thus drew a parallel between Moses and the playwright. Likewise, Zaimoğlu embraced this association in interviews on different grounds, asserting that he, like Moses, belongs among the prophets. In a July 2013 interview conducted with *Der Tagesspiegel*, he portrays a duality between priests and prophets for the interviewer, defining Moses, as a prophet "to whom God speaks," using the epithet given to him in Muslim tradition. He contrasts this with priests, whom he disparagingly describes as agents of belief (*Glaubensmaklern*), cynically acting as intermediaries between the sacred and profane, implying perhaps that they abuse their positions. In so doing, readers might wonder about the priests to whom Zaimoğlu refers: are these the Egyptian priests in *Moses* or Catholic priests, perhaps even those in twenty-first-century Oberammergau? He then proclaims, "I am of the prophets, not of the priests," showing how his identity as a playwright is interwoven with the identity of the prophets, specifically Moses.[17] In so doing, he positions himself as the directly inspired mouthpiece of God and not some meddling intermediary who impedes access to the divine.

It is unclear whether Zaimoğlu adopts this prophetic pose out of religious conviction or simply as performance of authorship. In either case, the question is: in what manner does Zaimoğlu perform his role as a prophet? Put another way: how does God, or an external authority, speak through him, and through what medium? Moreover, to return to his reputation gained through *Kanak Sprak*, how does Zaimoğlu overcome audience skepticism about his ability to speak proper German? As an answer to these questions, and in accordance with the role of the prophet who conveys the message of another, higher force, Zaimoğlu appeals to the authority of the Jewish legends in a rhetorical move that grants him legitimacy. Like Moses, who continually claims to speak the words of God, Zaimoğlu uses biblical and, more importantly, specifically Jewish source texts to grant his project legitimacy. The legends influence his very *words*, giving them the aura that they come from a more legitimate source of knowledge. Zaimoğlu does this by appealing to two texts with cultural currency in twenty-first-century Germany: first, Luther's biblical text, a major creator of, and influence on, modern standardized German, and second, Jewish source texts, especially revered in the philosemitic atmosphere of post-Shoah Germany.

This appeal to outside sources is no simple happenstance. It is done with a clear triangulation between three different nodes. Zaimoğlu identifies the first node, the biblical text in Luther's translation, as Christian German. Incredibly, he credits the Bible as the site of his own language learning and his almost religious childhood encounter with the German language. In the introduction to his interview on *Deutschland Radio* from 2013, the interviewer makes clear that Zaimoğlu has continuously returned to "the Old and New Testaments, above all for the language [*wohl wegen der Sprache*]."[18] Zaimoğlu clearly labels the text as part of the Christian tradition with his appeal to Luther's Bible translation(s); this identification is buttressed by the interviewer's appeal to *both* the Old *and* New Testaments. In doing this, one sees how the mostly Christianized German public attending a performance in a Christian space views this story as largely belonging to the Christian tradition. Moreover, Zaimoğlu's own pronouncement that his personal experience of the German language can be traced back to an encounter with the biblical text in Luther's translation allows his own life history to become a proxy for the larger history of the German language, whose consolidation and the sense that it constitutes a unified whole can be traced to Luther's work from five hundred years ago.[19]

Zaimoğlu identifies the second node as the Rabbinic Jewish traditions of Moses, included in several collections of Jewish legends. Here, he credits a series of three early twentieth-century collections that bring together Jewish traditions of Moses primarily originating from and recorded in the first ten centuries of the common era. Explaining his process, Zaimoğlu credits his "discovery" of Moses to these legends, recalling:

> I plowed through the Jewish collections of legends together with my co-author, Günter Senkel ... and read through several hundred legends. ... Günter translated the traditions, and there, suddenly, I saw him [Moses]. ... And then ... [after] two, three months of hard research and reading [*Lektüre*] ... I sat down, the sequence of scenes was also hammered out [*abgeklopft*], and in a delirium [*Fieberwahn*], wrote everything down.[20]

Zaimoğlu's mythology of his literary process credits his inspiration to the translated legends; this partially obfuscates his own role as a conscious agent and instead makes him a conduit for a series of scenes that he witnesses as if in a religious trance and then transcribes for the sake of others. That said, Zaimoğlu's depiction also functions as an allusion to the third node of the Abrahamic trialogue: it recalls the prophet Muhammad, who received revelations from an angel and transcribed them into what became the different surahs (chapters) of the Koran. The emphasis on Zaimoğlu's role in this ecumenical triplet as a conduit for the voices of the two other religious traditions, with perhaps minimal contribution of unique content, becomes even clearer in other interviews.

In the aforementioned *Tagesspiegel* interview, one discovers the radical manner in which Zaimoğlu's religious tradition and authorial agency are negated. He states, "Nothing should appear in the play which is not verifiable [*belegbar*]. Thus, no bible thumper [*Bibelfester*] can say: Zaimoğlu, this Moslem [*Muselman*, archaic] is attributing something [from our tradition] to us!"[21] In this clear explication and defense of his artistic process, Zaimoğlu, the well-known author who wields language to incredible effect, effaces his own creative role in the *Moses* project, depicting himself as bound to events as recorded elsewhere.[22] This defensive posture evinces a sense of the unequal footing Zaimoğlu knows himself to be on as a self-declared "heathen-Muslim." Put more bluntly, an observer can clearly understand how true equity does not exist in this Abrahamic trialogue. Indeed, the Muslim participant feels defensive, contributing by channeling other religious traditions.

Zaimoğlu's demonstration of this radical effacement is also on display in the printed script of *Moses*, where he and Senkel go to incredible lengths to prove fidelity to these Jewish legends. In the back of the thin volume, the two meticulously document the location of every Jewish legend used in constructing each aspect of the script. In thirty-three pages, or roughly 50 percent of the length of the script, Zaimoğlu and Senkel produce a citation apparatus with statements such as, "Ginzberg"—one of the anthologies of postbiblical Jewish sources used—"confirms [*bestätigt*] the encounter with the giants" (103). Interestingly enough, the biblical text remains mostly ignored, taken as a shared foundation that warrants no mention.

What at one level appears counterintuitive—citing legendary sources as "proof"—functions as a strategy of legitimation, confirming the Jewish origin of each deviation from the biblical text. One might read this as a mocking of German academic "objectivity," with the use of words such as "verifiable" (*belegbar*) and "confirms" (*bestätigt*) echoing a scientific, systematic investigation of *real events*. This is unclear. What is clear is that the privileging of certain textual witnesses (Christian and Jewish) over others (Muslim) indicates what Zaimoğlu perceives the audience to consider as reliable sources.

While documenting and discussing these Jewish sources proves so important to the presentation of the *Moses* adaptation taking place on the stage at Oberammergau, a closer examination of Zaimoğlu's authorship and of the background of the anthologies and the Jewishness of these stories provides us with a slightly different picture. By muddying the waters of this neat picture of Jewish sources, a clearer understanding of the imbricated nature of religious traditions emerges. In turn, it informs how we think about Jews and Muslims in Germany specifically, as well as more universally.

Back to the Sources: Muslim-Jewish Legendary Resonances

Feridun Zaimoğlu eagerly engages the press and provides extensive commentary on his creative process when promoting his many literary works, producing an output of its own that merits the analysis given above. His strong pronouncements in some interviews can sometimes elide, however, or at the very least obscure, certain aspects and ambivalences underlying his process. While his performance above suggests the use of ancient, purely Jewish tales, as well as a negation of his authorial voice, a closer examination of one of Zaimoğlu's own articles and the anthologies he employed when writing *Moses* renders a more complicated picture. This other article reveals a skepticism toward his sources; an examination of his Jewish sources, in turn, helps us to discover a more complicated legendary history. This complicated history reveals how Jewish legends often have their own Muslim counterparts: counterparts unacknowledged by both Zaimoğlu and newspaper reports. This unacknowledged kinship between Muslim and Jewish traditions is, I would argue, an elision that, if not intentional, is nonetheless emblematic of the manner in which we think about different minority communities in Germany today.

In the citation apparatus provided in the back of the published edition of the *Moses* script, Zaimoğlu and Senkel provide readers with access to a detailed accounting of the English-language sources used when constructing the play. These sources, in turn, have their own complicated back stories. The first and most well-known is by Louis Ginzberg, a German-trained academic who immigrated to the United States around the turn of the century to teach at Hebrew

Union College and, later, Jewish Theological Seminary. Ginzberg's celebrated multivolume *Legends of the Jews*, first authored as a German manuscript, was translated for the Jewish Publication Society and released in five separate volumes from 1909 to 1938.[23] The second source, Hayim Bialik and Yehoshua Ravnitzky's *Book of Legends*, collected and published first in Hebrew, is cited in its popular English translation. Listed finally is Angelo S. Rappoport's collection *Myths and Legends of Ancient Israel*, the only one of the three that first took form in the English language.

As discussed above, Zaimoğlu accords these works the place of documentary-like evidence in his presentation of these sources to the press and in the published script. This is exemplified, for instance, in his use of the terms "confirmed" and "verified" in the citation apparatus. Dovetailing with this approach, these sources act as a check on him as a Muslim, as shown in the earlier discussion about his comment to one interviewer that each source must be explicitly documented so that no person might complain about this "Moslem" attributing things to the Jews.[24] This deliberate use of the archaic, derogatory term for Muslims demonstrates Zaimoğlu's awareness of his precarious placement in a tableau together with Christians and Jews. It demonstrates, I argue, his sense of the lingering suspicion toward him that he senses as the Muslim contributor to an interfaith project.

But these comments together with the print script's citation apparatus, taken alone, obscure a more skeptical posture that Zaimoğlu evinces elsewhere toward these sources. In an article for *Cicero* written about his adaptation of the Moses story and another adaptation he undertook around the same time of the story of the Apostle Paul, Zaimoğlu writes:

> In the anthologies of Jewish legends, I searched in vain for reports of Moses as a young courtier. The five books of Moses give an outline of the deeds and miracles of the prophet. They were written down hundreds of years after his death by priests. The stories of [God's] messenger were cemented together into holy writ. Only biblical literalists consider this to be a faithful rendering; but I wanted to use the existing stories [*vorgefundener Stoff*] as a point of departure . . .

Determined to use these sources, Zaimoğlu later concludes: "According to scripture and the legends, these are true stories. I understood: the old times have not passed away." As a response, he chooses to write his script with "powerful words, without hesitation or doubt [*Glaubenschwäche*]." Zaimoğlu shows himself as determined to read Moses—and Paul—as figures of salvation (*Heilsgestalten*) who "were and are machines of progress [*Fortschrittsmaschinen*]." It is these iconoclasts, prophetic figures in their full audacity, not their pale imitations left in holy writ, that Zaimoğlu views himself as reclaiming. The sources are authoritative, but they are also problematic, written by priests many years after they occurred. Tellingly, it is within this context, again, that he proclaims himself on the side of the prophets, not the priests.

Cast in this light, Zaimoğlu's work takes on a new tone with a particularly Muslim religious resonance. His statements reflect a fidelity to sources paired with a skepticism, common among Muslims, about the reliability of Jewish and Christian scriptural traditions recorded by priests; moreover, it sets Zaimoğlu up as the one who can read between the lines and see the truth behind the legendary sources, and how the "old times have not passed away." He therewith envisions himself as the agent who reanimates these tales while also being the prophetic descendent in the line of Moses. In sum, in this article written in his own voice and not mediated by an interviewer, one discovers that Zaimoğlu indeed envisions for himself a somewhat more robust role than that discussed above.

We gain further appreciation for this role and its Muslim specificity by examining just one exemplary legendary tradition Zaimoğlu uses in his *Moses* adaptation. The sources cited in *Moses* prove complicated and mediated many times over, refracted through multiple sources over multiple traditions. This is obscured by the scant attention given in news articles and interviews to the role of Moses in Islam. For while Zaimoğlu makes much of his consultation of Jewish sources in press accounts, he never mentions Islamic sources and only once thematizes Muslim understandings of Moses. This reticence passes over the fact that Moses is a frequently mentioned character in the Koran, more in fact, than any other prophet, including Muhammad.[25] Moses is indeed honored as second only to Muhammad as a preeminent prophet and called *Kalīm Allāh*, the one "given the privilege of hearing God speak," a role quite consonant with the nature of Zaimoğlu's Moses in the Oberammergau script.[26] Indeed, in the only location in the press accounts where he mentions Islam, Zaimoğlu does mention the phrase "*Kalīm Allāh*," defining it as "he to whom God speaks" and mentioning that next to Muhammad and Jesus, Moses is the most important figure in the Koran.[27] This clarification, appropriately enough, comes right before Zaimoğlu compares himself to Moses as a prophet, supporting the reading given above that argues that Zaimoğlu considers himself a latter-day Moses to whom God speaks.

But despite this small allowance for the importance of Moses in Islamic tradition, there is silence on a more important point: the mutual influences and interrelationship of Jewish and Muslim traditions of Moses. Indeed, though he proclaims the many deviations and extrapolations of his script from the biblical text to be Jewish, many of these same traditions can also be found in Islam as well. Known as *Isra'iliyyat*, these traditions first entered into Islam by way of Jewish converts to Islam and other forms of early Muslim-Jewish contact.[28] Not just simple borrowing, Brannon Wheeler argues in *Moses in the Quran and Islamic Exegesis*: from early on, "Muslims and Jews drew upon a shared set of cultural symbols to imagine themselves and the other ... [and] to establish distinct but overlapping identities."[29]

A closer examination of just one of the tales Zaimoğlu draws on in his script provides an example of this shared Jewish-Muslim imagination. As recounted above, in *Moses*, Balaam recalls how the child Moses would grab Pharaoh's crown, which led to the trial of the scorching coals and gold. Moses reaches for a coal rather than the piece of gold, thus saving his life but causing his stutter forever after. Here, a return to Zaimoğlu's sources is instructive. In Louis Ginzberg's retelling, cited in the script, this legend is followed by a footnote, which mentions: "On the Arabic [i.e., Muslim] version of this legend see Grünbaum."[30] Rappoport also cites Max Grünbaum, though without mentioning what version Grünbaum provides.[31] Turning to Grünbaum, one discovers that al-Tabari (839–923 CE), a well-known Muslim writer and chronicler, records a similar story, complete with a basin of coals and a pearl instead of gold. In this story, however, the provocation is that Moses tugs at Pharaoh's beard instead of grabbing at his crown.[32]

I do not propose to undertake a thorough comparison of all the Jewish legends found in *Moses* and find the corollaries in the Islamic tradition, but I provide an example of this story as simply one of many ways in which the Islamic religious imagination about Moses is similar to the Jewish one, often in ways that remain invisible to a Christianized audience unfamiliar with Islamic Moses traditions. Indeed, in light of these resonances, one might even go so far as to argue that Zaimoğlu's *Jewish* Moses actually takes on a partially Muslim aspect as well. Put another way, one might argue that the distance between "Jewish" Moses and "Muslim" Moses is not quite as great as one might initially think—they may be much closer to each other than either is to a Christian reception of Moses. However, in returning to the German press accounts and Zaimoğlu's several interviews discussed earlier on, one senses an erasure of this shared ground between Islam and Judaism. It is this erasure, or at least effacement, that I would like to dwell on in my conclusion.

Conclusion: Reconceptualizing Conversations among Minorities in Germany

The close readings in the first part of this chapter demonstrated the key dynamic underlying the theme at heart of *Moses* as a text: the question of whose speech acts and rhetorical gestures could be backed up by a higher authority. Moses, both when he confronts Pharaoh in act 1 and in his encounters with an opponent from within the Israelite community, Korah, in act 2, is able to speak authoritatively because of the source from which he draws his message: God.

By themselves, Moses's words are of questionable value when they encounter Pharaoh's political power or the figure of Korah, who leads a rebellion that effectively channels widespread Israelite discontent. But when understood as divine decree, one can see how Moses's words become irresistible and overwhelming for both foes.

Placed next to *Moses* as text, Zaimoğlu's performance of authorship and (possibly divine) inspiration evinces a similar dynamic. Though many Germans might, and indeed do, question Zaimoğlu's relationship to the German language as shown in a variety of responses to *Moses*, the Jewish source texts he uses and documents in his script, together with his appeal to the German Christian Luther Bible, legitimate Zaimoğlu's "questionable" Turkish Muslim voice. The rhetorical appeal to these sources allows Zaimoğlu to draw upon Luther's standing, as well as the standing of Jewish religious tradition, which Turkish Germans and the Muslim religious tradition do not enjoy in German public life. The public standing of Judaism and Jewish citizens within German life is considerable, as evidenced by the many public commemorations of the Shoah, the emergence of multiple societies for Christian-Jewish understanding throughout the country, and the frequent pronouncements by the German presidents and chancellors speaking out against any form of antisemitism. This stands in stark contrast to the standing of Islam in Germany, which is often associated with fundamentalist sects and terrorism and is mapped on to political actors such as Recep Tayyip Erdoğan in Turkey and their repressive governments. While Jewish life in contemporary Germany continues to face challenges, German public figures display significant sensitivities toward any hint of antisemitism; by contrast, no such taboo exists against political statements attacking Muslim women wearing head coverings and religious fundamentalists or newspaper accounts of violent refugees who are inevitably coded as Muslim. In this atmosphere, Zaimoğlu cannot draw on any sort of religious, Muslim background to provide himself legitimacy. Instead, within the public sphere and the presentation of literary works, it is something to be compensated for, if not completely avoided. A careful examination of press accounts about *Moses* shows how Zaimoğlu's appeals to Jewish sources, as well as to Luther, function to grant interfaith legitimacy to his status as Muslim writer and, at least in the minds of outsiders, to distance himself from his earlier, more "questionable" literary output. This legitimacy is manifold. The appeal to the Luther Bible translation provides a culturally acceptable story for how Zaimoğlu's German has moved beyond *Kanak Sprak*. The citation of these Jewish source texts, in turn, protects him from those "Bible thumpers" (*Bibelfester*) who might otherwise attack him for a lack of fidelity to the text, while it also demonstrates a willingness to participate in a liberal, interfaith dialogue. This second point also counteracts claims that Muslim actors are inevitably the main source of antisemitic actions in modern-day Germany.

Zaimoğlu's appeal to this source of legitimacy does not lessen the manner in which he creates room for his own, Muslim voice in this interfaith dialogue. His play depicts a protagonist and hero, Moses, the consummate insider-outsider who belongs fully neither to Egyptians nor to Israelites but can nonetheless authoritatively communicate a message with powerful words that overwhelm his audience. In so doing, he provides an image that evokes his own role as a Turkish German author in contemporary Germany. Moreover, in weaving Jewish *Aggadot* into a story otherwise familiar to a German audience, Zaimoğlu implicitly questions the Christian appropriation of the Hebrew Bible and provides a space for alternative traditions about biblical figures and in so doing participates in a culturally acceptable form of liberal interfaith dialogue. Yes, the traditions found in *Moses* are Jewish, but as a closer examination of their history demonstrates, these traditions resonate with Muslim traditions in a way that can easily elude the Christian gaze.

This lack of any journalistic or authorial comment about the similarities between the Jewish legends Zaimoğlu draws upon and Muslim traditions presents an important lesson for contemporary scholars looking at the interactions between different minority groups in Germany today. Whether looking at contemporary discourses of "imported antisemitism" or the framing of interreligious dialogues just as press accounts framed the *Moses* project, there is often a sense that Germany provides a unique opportunity for groups such as Jews and Muslims to reconcile in a way unparalleled in human history. Underlying this assumption is the belief that there exists between Jews and Muslims an adversarial dialogue and a wide gap, which only the Enlightened world, often coded as Christian, can bridge. Indeed, the Oberammergau production aspires to this by providing the literal physical, Christian location as this seemingly "objective" neutral space where Judaism and Islam can finally meet and, perhaps, reconcile. This, of course, can elide the problems Oberammergau itself has had with antisemitism over the years.

What this deeper exploration of the Moses script and its press reception provides us, however, is a demythologization of the neutral Christian (German) space. It allows us to see that, behind the scenes, both Jews and Muslims share a history of dialogue that the Christians participating in liberal interfaith dialogues can often overlook. This dialogue reaches back beyond the founding of any German-speaking state or even Lessing's famed ring parable to the beginning of Islam in the Arabian peninsula, where Jews and Muslims—and Christians too—were already in a conversation that included a shared set of symbols and a not-too-dissimilar set of stories. While previous German studies scholarship has done an excellent job of looking at the shared commonalities between Jews and Muslims in the German context, this scholarship often considers these concerns from the perspective of German Jews, not German Muslims, and remains overwhelmingly concentrated on events from before

1945.³³ Zaimoğlu's *Moses* provides us with a reminder of the bidirectionality and contemporaneity of this relationship. Moreover, it reminds us scholars looking at minority groups in Germany and multireligious encounters that we need to be sensitive to how interreligious and intergroup dialogues exist beyond the borders of Germany and extend to, and inform, the dialogues going on in neighborhoods in Berlin, markets in Frankfurt, and, indeed, on a stage in Oberammergau. With this knowledge we can begin to comprehend how a Jewish Moses might not be as far away from a German Turk as one might initially expect.

Joshua Shelly is a graduate student in the Carolina-Duke Graduate Program in German Studies. He is currently completing a dissertation on the role of German-language Jewish literature, especially utopian works, in early Zionism.

Notes

1. Oberammergau's 2020 play was eventually delayed because of the COVID-19 pandemic and rescheduled for 2022. See https://www.passionsspiele-oberammergau.de.
2. Moses adaptations and interpretations for a contemporary audience have a storied history in German literature and arts; these are most frequently authored by German and Austrian Jews. Bluma Goldstein explores some of these important adaptations written by four different German and Austrian Jews from the nineteenth and early twentieth centuries. She reads these works as attempts to wrestle with dynamics of Jewish assimilation and emancipation in the German-speaking world. These works come from a quite different sociohistorical milieu from Zaimoğlu's own adaptation. That said, as my argument demonstrates, Zaimoğlu considers himself to share a kinship with Moses, just as these earlier adaptors understood Moses as sharing similarities with them; Goldstein demonstrates how they wrote their works accordingly. See Bluma Goldstein, *Reinscribing Moses: Heine, Kafka, Freud and Schoenberg in a European Wilderness* (Cambridge, MA: Harvard University Press, 1992), 8ff.
3. According to Zaimoğlu, Günter Senkel researched various Jewish legends in English-language sources and then translated the relevant ones into German for him to read. Based on this division of duties and the presentation in press accounts of Zaimoğlu as the chief author, I analyze the implications of Zaimoğlu's rather than Senkel's authorship in the following pages. This is not the first time Zaimoğlu and Senkel have worked together. They first worked as a team on an *Othello* adaptation performed at the Munich Kammerspiele in 2003. For a rather idiosyncratic report of working together with Zaimoğlu, see Günter Senkel, "Recherchen mit / Researching with Feridun Zaimoğlu," in *Feridun Zaimoğlu*, edited by Tom Cheesman and Karin E. Yeşilada (Oxford: Peter Lang, 2012), 259–65.
4. Throughout both the biblical text and Zaimoğlu's play, the terms *Israelites* and *Hebrews* are used interchangeably; I do so as well throughout my analysis.
5. Feridun Zaimoğlu and Günter Senkel, *Moses* (Kiel: Solivagus-Verlag, 2013), 9. The following citations will be given parenthetically throughout the text. Unless otherwise indicated, translations are my own.

6. According to the Exodus narrative, Pharaoh only says, "Behold, the people of Israel are too many and too mighty for us. Come, let us deal shrewdly with them, lest they multiply, and, if war breaks out, they join our enemies and fight against us and escape from the land." The text then describes how "they set taskmasters over them to afflict them with heavy burdens," Exodus 1:8–11 (ESV). What this "shrewd dealing" might be remains uncommented upon in the biblical text.
7. Once again, Zaimoğlu relies on Jewish sources, rabbinic legends, to explain Moses's stammer. The biblical text only states that Moses is "פה־כבד" and "כבד לשון," cf. Exodus 4:10. Most translations render this as "slow of speech, and slow of tongue" (KJV, NIV, NJPS). Robert Alter translates it as "heavy-mouthed and heavy-tongued," thus capturing the main meaning of כבד, "heavy." See Robert Alter, *The Five Books of Moses: A Translation with Commentary* (New York: W. W. Norton & Co., 2004).
8. Though the dialogue does not explain why the child Moses chooses a coal, the textual apparatus in the published script adds that Balaam's remark—"In his hand flowed the evil magic of the enemy"—"refers to the archangel Gabriel who, according to legend, guided the hand of the boy, so that he would not grasp for the gold." Zaimoğlu and Senkel, *Moses*, 84.
9. In this adaptation, Moses's lame tongue continually provides fodder for his opponents, Egyptian and Israelite alike. Pharaoh (ibid., 38), Balaam (ibid., 41 and 73), Israelites (ibid., 45), foreign kings marching against Israel in the desert (ibid., 53), and the enemy king Balak (ibid., 71), all refer to Moses as a stammerer.
10. Katharina Eickhoff, "Katholisch-muslimisch-jüdisch-heidnisches Passionstheater, Interview mit Feridun Zaimoğlu," *Kulturgespräch, Südwestrundfunk* 2, 5 July 2013. Of course, Zaimoğlu's *Moses* is not a passion play, it was only staged in Oberammergau, which is famous for its once-a-decade passion plays.
11. Deutsche Presse Agentur, "Zaimoglu schreibt Moses-Stück für Oberammergau," *Die Welt*, 30 November 2012.
12. Sven Ricklefs, "Moses schwieriger Auszug aus Ägypten: Christian Stückl inszeniert 'Moses' in Oberammergau," *Deutschlandfunk*, 6 July 2013. Although I have chosen not to address Oberammergau as such here, the town has a long, contentious relationship with the Jewish community. Accusations of antisemitic portrayals in its passion plays, as well as personal antisemitism, especially during National Socialism, have occasioned multiple threats of large-scale boycotts from the Jewish community, most often led by representative organizations in the United States. Christian Stückl specifically has been at the forefront of attempts to reconcile the Jewish community and Oberammergau, which makes his participation in this project all the more interesting. For contextualization, see James Shapiro, *Oberammergau: The Troubling Story of the World's Most Famous Passion Play* (New York: Pantheon Books, 2000).
13. From more information, see the short introduction and partial translation of Zaimoğlu's own introduction to the work in *Germany in Transit: Nation and Migration, 1955–2005*, edited by Deniz Göktürk, David Gramling, and Anton Kaes (Berkeley, CA: University of California Press, 2007), 386 and 405–8.
14. Tholl Egbert, "Der erste Gotteskrieger; Heiligengeschichte von unten: Christian Stücke inszeniert Feridun Zaimoğlus und Günter Senkel's 'Moses' im Oberammergauer Passionsspielhaus; Das dürre Alte Testament wird ergänzt durch das erzählerische Fleisch der Legenden," *Süddeutsche Zeitung*, 8 July 2013. Interestingly, the use of *Gotteskrieger* (religious warrior) in the first headline cited here evokes negative images

of jihad that seem to undermine the celebratory tone and hope for religious reconciliation that this collaboration might seem to portend.
15. Kerstin Decker, "Zaimoğlu in Oberammergau: Im Niemandsland der Religionen," *Der Tagesspiegel*, 7 July 2013.
16. Decker, "Zaimoğlu in Oberammergau."
17. Decker, "Zaimoğlu in Oberammergau"; Zaimoğlu repeats his assertion that he is "of the prophets" in an article in the magazine *Cicero*. See Feridun Zaimoğlu, "Paulus und Moses: Im Glauben gibt es kein Expertentum," *Cicero: Magazin für Politische Kultur*, 1 September 2018.
18. Britta Bürger, "Ein erschreckendes Bühnenspektakel, Der Schriftsteller Feridun Zaimoglu über sein Stück 'Moses,'" *Deutschlandradio Kultur*, 5 July 2013; see also, Ricklefs, "Moses schwieriger Auszug aus Ägypten," and Eickhoff, "Katholisch-muslimisch-jüdisch-heidnisches Passionstheater."
19. In a 2013 article in *Die Welt*, "Jesus kam nur bis Unterammergau," the journalist even makes a connection between the Jewish legends and the biblical story, claiming it as German when he writes, "The tone of the stories, like those we Germans are familiar with from Luther's Bible translation, has been preserved." The mention of Zaimoğlu's "tone" refers to the archaic *Lutherdeutsch* in which Zaimoğlu writes his Moses script. His interest in Luther and his German is even more evident in his 2017 novel *Evangelio: Ein Luther-Roman*, which he authored in an artistically rendered, deliberately archaic German to evoke the language of Luther's Bible translation(s). See Eckhart Fuhr, "Jesus kam nur bis Unterammergau," *Die Welt*, 26 July 2013, and Feridun Zaimoğlu, *Evangelio: Ein Luther-Roman* (Cologne: Kiepenheuer & Witsch, 2017).
20. "Ein erschreckendes Bühnenspektakel." The delirium in which Zaimoğlu authors *Moses* also recalls his portrayal of Luther's translation work in *Evangelio*.
21. "Zaimoğlu in Oberammergau." Although I foreground the anxiety this statement communicates for Zaimoğlu speaking as a German of Turkish and Muslim background in modern-day Germany, it also reveals a second anxiety: the (perceived) absence of Jews in modern-day Germany who can speak for themselves. The absence of Jews in this production is notable, and the choice to represent Jewish perspectives through texts rather than individuals cannot but bring up the specter of the Shoah. The *Jüdische Allgemeine Zeitung* pointed out this absence, commenting, "A third, Jewish author would have been perfect. One was not to be found, perhaps not sought out." It continues, rather skeptically, in reference to the antisemitic history of Oberammergau, suggesting that the town is not actually "koshered." See Michael Wuliger, "Oberammergauer Multikulti-Moses; Inszenierung; Das bayerische Passionstheater bringt das Buch Exodus auf die Bühne, dramatisiert von Feridun Zaimoglu," *Jüdische Allgemeine Zeitung*, 27 June 2013.
22. This is not the first time Zaimoğlu has framed his literary output as simply recording others' words. In the forward to *Kanak Sprak*, Zaimoğlu presents the book as the product of interviews that he then transcribed in poetic language after the fact (*Nachdichtung*). See Feridun Zaimoğlu, *Kanak Sprak: 24 Mißtöne vom Rande der Gesellschaft* (Berlin: Rotbuch Verlag, 2013), 12–19. He has also made similar claims when discussing his earlier collaboration with Günther Senkel, *Schwarze Jungfrauen*. See here, "Schwarze Jungfrauen," Gorki, retrieved 4 September 2018 from https://gorki.de/de/schwarze-jungfrauen.
23. For a historical overview of the project, see Rebecca Schorsch, "The Past in the Service of the Present: Rabbinicizing Folklore or Folklorizing the Rabbis?" In *Louis Ginzberg's*

Legends of the Jews: Ancient Jewish Folk Literature Reconsidered, edited by Galit Hasan-Rokem and Ithamar Gruenwald (Detroit: Wayne State University Press, 2014), 1–16.
24. See note 21.
25. Annabel Keeler, "Moses from a Muslim Perspective," In *Abraham's Children: Jews, Christians, and Muslims in Conversation*, edited by Norman Solomon, Richard Harries, and Tim Winter (New York: T&T Clark, 2005), 56.
26. Keeler, "Moses," 66. Interestingly enough, while Jesus is honored in Islam, one wonders whether Zaimoğlu includes Jesus in this list for his Christian audience and not because of his unique place among the prophets of Islam.
27. "Zaimoğlu in Oberammergau."
28. Keeler, "Moses," 63.
29. Brannon Wheeler, *Moses in the Quran and Islamic Exegesis* (London: RoutledgeCurzon, 2002), 6.
30. Louis Ginzberg, *Legends of the Jews*, trans. Henrietta Szold and Paul Radin (Philadelphia: Jewish Publication Society, 2003), 1:484n65.
31. Angelo S. Rappoport, *Myth and Legend of Ancient Israel* (London: Gresham Publishing Company, Ltd., 1928), 2:223n1.
32. Max Grünbaum, *Neue Beiträge zur Semitischen Sagenkunde* (Leiden: E. J. Brill, 1893), 156.
33. Just a brief, representative sample of these works includes: Donna K. Heizer, *Jewish-German Identity in the Orientalist Literature of Else Lasker-Schüler, Friedrich Wolf, and Franz Werfel* (Columbia, SC: Camden House, 1996); Susannah Heschel, *Abraham Geiger and the Jewish Jesus* (Chicago: University of Chicago Press, 1998); Susannah Heschel, *Jüdischer Islam: Jüdisch-deutsche Selbstbestimmung*, trans. Dirk Hartwig, Mortiz Buchner, and Georges Khalil (Berlin: Matthes & Seitz Berlin, 2018); Ivan Davidson Kalmar and Derek J. Penslar, eds., *Orientalism and the Jews* (Waltham, MA: Brandeis University Press, 2005); Ulrike Brunotte, Anna-Dorothea Ludewig, and Axel Stähler, eds., *Orientalism, Gender, and the Jews: Literary and Artistic Transformations of European National Discourses* (Berlin: De Gruyter, 2015). Other than a few chapters in the volume edited by Brunotte et al., these excellent works focus almost exclusively on Jewish approaches to, and appropriations of, Islam. A volume that makes steps toward rectifying this imbalance is Susannah Heschel and Umar Ryad, eds., *The Muslim Reception of European Orientalism: Reversing the Gaze* (New York: Routledge, 2019).

Bibliography

Alter, Robert. *The Five Books of Moses: A Translation with Commentary*. New York: W. W. Norton & Co., 2004.

Bialik, Hayim N., and Yehoshua H. Ravnitzky. *The Book of Legends, Sefer Ha-Aggadah: Legends from the Talmud and Midrash*. Translated by William G. Braude. New York: Schocken Books, 1992.

Brunotte, Ulrike, Anna-Dorothea Ludewig, and Axel Stähler, eds. *Orientalism, Gender, and the Jews: Literary and Artistic Transformations of European National Discourses*. Berlin: De Gruyter, 2015.

Bürger, Britta. "Ein erschreckendes Bühnenspektakel, Der Schriftsteller Feridun Zaimoglu über sein Stück 'Moses.'" *Deutschlandradio Kultur*, 5 July 2013.

Decker, Kerstin. "Zaimoğlu in Oberammergau: Im Niemandsland der Religionen." *Der Tagesspiegel*, 7 July 2013.
Deutsche Presse Agentur. "Zaimoglu schreibt Moses-Stück für Oberammergau." *Die Welt*, 30 November 2012.
Egbert, Tholl. "Der erste Gotteskrieger; Heiligengeschichte von unten: Christian Stückl inszeniert Feridun Zaimoglus und Günter Senkels 'Moses' im Oberammergauer Passionsspielhaus; Das dürre Alte Testament wird ergänzt durch das erzählerische Fleisch der Legenden." *Süddeutsche Zeitung*, 8 July 2013.
Eickhoff, Katharina. "Katholisch-muslimisch-jüdisch-heidnisches Passionstheater, Interview mit Feridun Zaimoğlu." *Kulturgespräch, Südwestrundfunk 2*, 5 July 2013.
Fuhr, Eckhart. "Jesus kam nur bis Unterammergau." *Die Welt*, 26 July 2013.
Ginzberg, Louis. *Legends of the Jews*. Translated by Henrietta Szold and Paul Radin. 2 vols. Philadelphia: Jewish Publication Society, 2003.
Göktürk, Deniz, David Gramling, and Anton Kaes, eds. *Germany in Transit: Nation and Migration, 1955–2005*. Berkeley: University of California Press, 2007.
Goldstein, Bluma. *Reinscribing Moses: Heine, Kafka, Freud, and Schoenberg in a European Wilderness*. Cambridge, MA: Harvard University Press, 1992.
Gorki. "Schwarze Jungfrauen: Von Feridun Zaimoğlu und Günter Senkel." Retrieved 4 September 2018 from https://gorki.de/de/schwarze-jungfrauen.
Grünbaum, Max. *Neue Beiträge zur Semitischen Sagenkunde*. Leiden: E. J. Brill, 1893.
Heizer, Donna K. *Jewish-German Identity in the Orientalist Literature of Else Lasker-Schüler, Friedrich Wolf, and Franz Werfel*. Columbia, SC: Camden House, 1996.
Heschel, Susannah. *Abraham Geiger and the Jewish Jesus*. Chicago: University of Chicago Press, 1998.
———. *Jüdischer Islam: Jüdisch-deutsche Selbstbestimmung*. Translated by Dirk Hartwig, Mortiz Buchner, and Georges Khalil. Berlin: Matthes & Seitz Berlin, 2018.
Heschel, Susannah, and Umar Ryad, eds. *The Muslim Reception of European Orientalism: Reversing the Gaze*. London: Routledge, 2019.
Kalmar, Ivan Davidson, and Derek J. Penslar, eds. *Orientalism and the Jews*. Waltham, MA: Brandeis University Press, 2005.
Keeler, Annabel. "Moses from a Muslim Perspective." In *Abraham's Children: Jews, Christians, and Muslims in Conversation*, edited by Norman Solomon, Richard Harries, and Tim Winter, 55–66. New York: T&T Clark, 2005.
Rappoport, Angelo S. *Myth and Legend of Ancient Israel*. Vol. 2. London: Gresham Publishing Company, Ltd., 1928.
Ricklefs, Sven. "Moses schwieriger Auszug aus Ägypten: Christian Stückl inszeniert 'Moses' in Oberammergau." *Deutschlandfunk*, 6 July 2013.
Schorsch, Rebecca. "Introduction: The Past in the Service of the Present; Rabbinicizing Folklore or Folklorizing the Rabbis?" In *Louis Ginzberg's Legends of the Jews: Ancient Jewish Folk Literature Reconsidered*, edited by Galit Hasan-Rokem and Ithamar Gruenwald, 1–16. Detroit: Wayne State University Press, 2014.
Senkel, Günter. "Recherchen mit / Researching with Feridun Zaimoğlu." In *Feridun Zaimoğlu*, edited by Tom Cheesman and Karin E. Yeşilada, 259–65. Oxford: Peter Lang, 2012.
Shapiro, James. *Oberammergau: The Troubling Story of the World's Most Famous Passion Play*. New York: Pantheon Books, 2000.
Wheeler, Brannon M. *Moses in the Quran and Islamic Exegesis*. London: RoutledgeCurzon, 2002.

Wuliger, Michael. "Oberammergauer Multikulti-Moses; Inszenierung Das bayerische Passionstheater bringt das Buch Exodus auf die Bühne, dramatisiert von Feridun Zaimoglu." *Jüdische Allgemeine Zeitung*, 27 June 2013.
Zaimoğlu, Feridun. *Evangelio: ein Luther-Roman*. Cologne: Kiepenheuer & Witsch, 2017.
———. *Kanak Sprak: 24 Mißtöne vom Rande der Gesellschaft*. Berlin: Rotbuch Verlag, 2013.
———. "Paulus und Moses: Im Glauben gibt es kein Expertentum." *Cicero: Magazin für Politische Kultur*, 1 September 2018.
Zaimoğlu, Feridun, and Günter Senkel. *Moses*. Kiel: Solivagus-Verlag, 2013.

CHAPTER 4

Schwarz tragen
Blackness, Performance, and the Utopian in Contemporary German Theater

OLIVIA LANDRY

> Those clothed in the name "Black"
> are well aware of its external provenance.
> —Achille Mbembe, *Critique of Black Reason*

At the start of the new theater season in the late summer of 2013, Berlin-Kreuzberg's independent theater, the Ballhaus Naunynstraße, opened its doors anew. The departure of the theater's former artistic director and visionary, Shermin Langhoff, who had recently taken up a new position as the *Intendantin* of the Maxim Gorki Theater in central Berlin, left the future of the Ballhaus somewhat in question. This was compounded by the fact that the postmigrant theater work that had become synonymous with the Ballhaus since its reopening in 2008 had also been transplanted to the larger and more centrally-located, state-funded Maxim Gorki Theater with Langhoff and her team of playwrights, directors, and actors. Seeking a newfound sense of relevance, the then co-*Intendanten* of the Ballhaus Naunynstraße, Wagner Carvalho and Tunçay Kulaoğlu, embraced a slightly different transnational tradition and future. With its erstwhile emphasis on Turkish German performances and representations, which corresponded directly to the theater's historical and geographical positioning in Berlin-Kreuzberg, the Ballhaus has come to take up a more explicit interest in broader narratives of People of Color, especially Black, Afro-German, and those of African diasporic communities. To inaugurate this new turn, the Ballhaus started its 2013 season with the decisively representational festival Black Lux—Home Festival from Black Perspectives. The festival, which ran from 28 August to 30 September, was a collection of theater plays, dramatic readings, dance presentations, exhibitions, performances, video exhibits, and installation art pieces and included important framing through academic talks and panel discussions. It brought together artists and scholars from Germany and abroad to reflect on Black identity in Germany and Europe. Among other things, the festival sought to further scrutinize contemporary debates about race and anti-Black racism in Germany, specifically in the theater. It directly raised issue with the significant underrepresentation of People of Color in German theater ensembles compared to the United States, France, and the United Kingdom. Finally, it addressed the exceedingly racist and recurring use of blackface in German theater.[1]

This chapter explores the play *Schwarz tragen* (Carrying/wearing Black), which was an in-house production commissioned by Carvalho as part of the Black Lux Festival, written by Elizabeth Blonzen and directed by Branwen Okpako. *Schwarz tragen* is a chamber play in three acts about the life of four roommates in a shared Berlin *Wohngemeinschaft* (hereafter abbreviated WG). But this is not exactly a typical Berlin WG; it is an all-Black WG. In this setting, whiteness becomes that absent Other (on stage). The play begins with the tragic and unexpected death of one of the roommates and the attendant concern of trying to find an appropriate person to replace him, which subsequently raises a spate of issues about identity, society, and racism in Germany. I consider *Schwarz tragen* as representative of a new movement within contemporary German theater that expands the possibilities and the temporal parameters of postmigrant theater, which at the time was rooted in the Ballhaus Naunynstraße and (traditionally) in Turkish German performance communities. As I analyze it here, this new movement, Black German theater, turns more explicitly to the utopian as both a future hope for change and a lateral relish of what the present can offer. Indeed, in much postmigrant, pre-Gorki theater there has been a tendency to thematize the past and to reconstruct historical narratives of migration in order to make visible histories long rendered invisible.[2]

Simultaneously, this chapter calls attention to the potential of the theater, with its formidable orchestration of stage, bodies, gesture, and audience, as an important site for performing and scrutinizing the complexity of Blackness and the relationality at its crux. *Schwarz tragen* tracks and plays with the category of Blackness and its German equivalent, *Schwarzsein*. Already the play's title brings into relief the urgency of troubling the ontology of Blackness, one that invokes myriad definitions. Embracing an ambiguity that jolts the audience into thought, *Schwarz tragen* asks what it means "to carry" or "to wear" black/Black. How do these imperatives displace or reinforce the "*being* (of) Black" inherent in the category of Blackness (*Schwarz-sein*)? Engaging these questions, the play ultimately disturbs the (white) gaze and turns it back on itself by bringing forth the important bilateral nature of the performer-spectator relationship and its capacity for fluidity and transgression.

A Utopian Postmigrant Theater?

Schwarz tragen fluctuates between a utopia of a better future—if simply a more livable one, as most notably articulated in recent years by José Esteban Muñoz (2009)—and a utopia that manifests itself as an alternative to the mainstream present, a utopia of the margins, conceptualized by Avery Gordon as "being-in-difference" (2018). As a matter of course, the most utopian figure of *Schwarz tragen*, the carefree student, is named Joy (Thelma Buabeng). Frivolous and ebullient, Joy is not only always "positive," as she herself declares, she is also obsessed with becoming pregnant because, in her words, "The only possibility to change the world is to have as many Black babies as possible."[3] While her utopian mission is a source of comedy in the play, as it seems she is regularly convinced that she is pregnant even when she is not, it is also an explicit example of the practice and performance of futurity. Introduced slightly later in act 1, Joy, who has forgotten her key, arrives late and enters the stage, immediately climbing atop the centrally positioned kitchen table, reclining in a pose of self-spectacle while facing the audience, and announcing with great animation: "I'm pregnant."[4] Promptly, the female Black body is presented as an agent of resistance and hope for change.[5] Although Joy is apparently not pregnant in this first scene, as she eventually concedes that it might not be true, she does become pregnant by the close of the play. The child is of course one of the oldest utopian tropes, one that curiously recurs as a failed enterprise in a later play by Sasha Marianna Salzmann, *Meteoriten* (*Meteorites*, 2016), which also stars Thelma Buabeng. The utopian charge of the child here is not comparable to the culture of the child, polemicized by Lee Edelman in his 2006 book *No Future*. Instead, it is, paraphrasing the final lines of Hortense Spiller's pathbreaking essay "Mama's Baby, Papa's Maybe" (1987), the empowering act of claiming a status and a legitimacy historically denied Black women—the status of motherhood. As such, Joy's performance may be read as the assertion of self through self-propagation in a society that otherwise adjures one's existence. This carries resonance both in (German) society and in the theater.

Emerging scholarship on the concurrently incipient phenomenon of Black German theater does not completely demarcate it from postmigrant theater, but it does seek new rubrics of analysis. Through an examination of the plays *real life: Germany* (2008), *Heimat, bittersüße Heimat* (Home, bittersweet home, 2010), *Also By Mail* (2013), and *Mais in Deutschland und anderen Galaxien* (Corn in Germany and other galaxies, 2015), Jamele Watkins establishes the roots of Black German theater (or, as she terms it, "Afro-German theater") in Afro-German literature.[6] Priscilla Layne examines Black German theater through its aesthetic and narrative manifestations of Afrofuturism as a critical intersection of technoculture and racial justice, with a look to plays such as Olivia Wenzel's *Mais in Deutschland und anderen Galaxien* (directed by Atif

Hussein), which premiered at the Ballhaus Naunynstraße as part of the 2015 performance festival We Are Tomorrow. For Layne, an Afrofuturist pursuit is particularly apt in this context, for it spurs Black German theater beyond the limited scope of national borders. Her approach similarly attends to hope for the future, in which science fiction becomes a kind of utopian horizon.[7] I am beholden to these studies and the compelling dialogue they provide.

When the Black Lux festival declared itself an occupation of postmigrant theater, it indicated both a continuity and a break.[8] The adoption of a space and a tradition speaks to lines of continuity. Black German theater resonates with early postmigrant theater's radical modality of struggle, which sought to provide other forms of making and experiencing theater in the culturally exclusionary zone of German (national) theater. Postmigrant theater did not make claims for a theater that had moved past the realities of migration as a phenomenon now over and done with; rather, it insisted on the recognition of and radical engagement with the ways migration continues to condition the present. The objectives of Black German theater are consonant with those of postmigrant theater insofar as these objectives are a struggle and demand for recognition within an institution that has been hitherto predominantly white and ethnically German. But Black German theater also seeks its own narratives, genres, and designs. Its intervention has been an assertion of this individuality, self-determination, and self-positioning.

What perhaps most distinguishes *Schwarz tragen* as an example of the possibilities of Black German theater from much postmigrant theater is its greater purport of utopian temporalities. This is in part a utopia not yet realized, that is, a utopia enfolded in a futurity full of anticipation and heady promise, similar to what Muñoz imagines as the not-yet-there of queer possibility. If postmigrant theater adheres to a certain temporality, I argue, it is by contrast often from past to present in the effort to form a common history around which identity might be both established and legitimated.[9] Attunement to the future is often marginal. This is not to propose that postmigrant theater is not forward-looking or stuck in the past but that its inceptive projects often aspired to new dramatic historiographies.

Diversely, futurity is frequently presented as the hope of Black German theater, in which the collective possibilities of a Black WG will be not only thinkable but also a reality both in theater and society. Yet *Schwarz tragen* itself is not exclusively about future projection. That is, the here and now is not altogether the "prison house" that Muñoz imagined it to be.[10] If utopia is spatiotemporal, then the setting of the play in an all-Black WG in Berlin, a "safe space" in a less-than-welcoming world, proffers a livable (utopian) alternative on a smaller scale. This is in many ways an example of what Davina Cooper calls "everyday utopias"—"networks and spaces that perform regular daily life, in the global North, in a radically different fashion."[11] When an argument erupts about whether the roommates should welcome a white person into the fold of their "safe space" to take the spot of Frank, whose sudden death shakes the opening of the play, Cyrus (Thomas B. Hoffmann), the oldest and wisest of the group, lucidly explains his misgivings about this: "We need a place, where we can be who we are without having to constantly place ourselves in relationship to the 'Others.' We have that all the time outside of these walls."[12] At the same time, this utopian place where race does not seem to exist, or at least must not constantly be accounted for, this Black WG, "needs," in Blonzen's own words, "at least one more generation."[13]

The play thus performs what it simultaneously seeks. In Blonzen's first version of the play, there were white characters, and Carvalho asked her to change it.[14] Both setting and stage should be a safe space in an otherwise white society and (theater) institution. Ultimately, Avery Gordon's conceptualization of utopia as one manifested within zones of exclusion, which is invested in both the present and the future, is informative to *Schwarz tragen*. Gordon writes: "In the zone of exclusion, the utopian is a standpoint for the here and now—not only the future—which registers and incites the works, the thoughts, and the better worlds inhabited by those who always, as Raymond Williams put it, 'meanwhile carry on.'"[15] Building especially (but not exclusively) on Herbert Marcuse's notion of "The Great Refusal" and its embrace of a resistance untethered to historical materialism and a dialectical "waiting out" or "biding time" for change, Gordon calls her version of utopia "being-in-difference."[16] It is about the practices of people living in the present and making this living livable, even meaningful. It is about creating a better world in the space of the one that is there. Such a description adroitly encapsulates the utopian quality of *Schwarz tragen*, which is both about hope for a better future and about carrying on in the present in a way that finds (even) pleasure in the lateral. Working against the grain of much contemporary scholarship on utopia, and its exclusive focus on futurity against a lateral present, *Schwarz tragen* is both a practice and performance of intervention and interjection in the theater (not dissimilar to the project of postmigrant theater, termed a *Kampfbegriff*, a "fighting concept" in its early days) and an enduring spectacle of that better world that comes after this successful intervention. Put another way, *Schwarz tragen* is the utopian "post" of postmigrant theater. It is that futurity, that promise of something good to come, as well as the performance of a meaningful and exciting existence in the margins of the present.

Performing Blackness / *Schwarzsein/tragen*

Suffice to say, utopian discourse and Blackness have had a troubled relationship. While Gordon's pursuit of the utopian intersects with the abolitionist imaginary and radical acts of fugitivity, which are generally conceived within the discourse of Black optimism (such as in the works of Daphne Brooks, E. Patrick Johnson, and Fred Moten), Blackness does not readily lend itself to utopian thought. *Schwarz tragen*'s titular concern with Blackness as a burdened and unwieldy category is not subsumed by the utopian ethos of the play. Rather, it opens up this trouble, even confounds it. Here the polyvalence of Blackness is stripped of its more unequivocal ontological imperative in the German vernacular *Schwarzsein* and is, I argue, more aptly figured into the unstable meaning of the German *Schwarz tragen*. This is especially evident in its indirect transivity, for one cannot technically carry or wear black, unless it is a "black *bag*" or a "black *sweater*," because the verb demands a direct object. Even as a noun, "black" is a descriptor of something else and not an object. Carrying and wearing "black" thus adopt metonymical qualities that may only be read symbolically by means of the frame of relationality within which they appear. Similarly, as I will show, *tragen* invites the ambiguity inherent in the category of Blackness as at once pathological and performative.

In its definition "to carry Black," *Schwarz tragen* promptly implies a burden not easily shed, by way of which "Black" must symbolize either a psychopathological or phenomenological weightiness. You carry it. Carrying is always a task, desirable or not. It is often a task thrust upon a person by another. In the case of Blackness, this can be the burden of hypervisibility. In May Ayim's words, "Earlier, I believed that I didn't fit in anywhere because I would always totally attract attention. I thought I can't just be me, I always walk around with this skin color."[17] Hypervisibility is the result of exposure to the oppressive gaze of the Other. As Achille Mbembe argues by way of Frantz Fanon, "the Black Man was a figure, an 'object,' invented by Whites and as such 'fixed' by their gaze, gestures, and attitudes."[18] Such is the burden of relationality of Blackness, of the inescapable Hegelian moment of "being for others," that, according to Fanon, for the Black Man never settles in ontology.[19] When the roommate Vicki (Sheri Hagen) unavailingly attempts to convince her other roommates that not wanting to live with a white person is also a form of racism—it is, what she calls, "Ghetto"—her rhetorical question deftly brings forth the relationality of Blackness: "You need white people in order to realize that you are not white, or what."[20] This questioning indictment calls to mind the double-consciousness of Blackness notably described by W. E. B. Du Bois as "the sense of always looking at one's self through the eyes of others, of measuring one's soul by the tape of a world that looks on in amused contempt and pity."[21] These words are echoed in somewhat humorous manner by Joy when she expresses her skepticism about inviting a white person to come and live in the WG. "When I imagine that in the morning I come to breakfast and then there's a white person sitting there ... who lives here ... then even before my first coffee I am reminded that I am not white. You know?"²² This pronouncement elicited some subdued chuckles from the audience and mixed miens from the other roommates. Ultimately, it distills the humor of the play as always enfolded in racial consciousness, a negating relationality.

Under the white gaze, Fanon asserts, "the image of one's body is solely negating. It's an image of a third person."²³ The burden of "carrying black/Black," then, can entail both the negating consciousness of one's body and the racist episteme that is already part of visibility itself—that is, that the gaze is always white. The interpellated identity linked to "Blackness" is, as Fanon expresses, dispensed as being outside oneself—part of but also apart from oneself, what Mbembe refers to as a "body of extraction."²⁴ It is not something that simply *is* but something that is apart, alien even, something that must be carried (like a burden). But the double meaning of "tragen" in standard German vernacular, as also "to wear," adds an asterisk of uncertainty to this negating definition. The instability of Blackness as a signifier is underscored.

Certainly, a number of Black studies scholars have sought paths beyond what Fred Moten critically calls "Fanon's pathontological refusal of blackness."²⁵ In its other definition of "*wearing* black/Black," the play's title proposes an alternative that does not completely dismantle the negating tenor of "*carrying* black/Black" but does proffer a more avowing approach. "Wearing black/Black" may in fact infer a willful act and an assertion of the agency that appears altogether lost in the case of "carrying." Wearing might be read as performance. While Judith Butler reminds us that performance can certainly also be the result of oppressive expectations and ascriptions, "wearing black/Black" seems to imply a performance of identity and an action that in contrast to "carrying black/Black" may be read as subjective and affirmative.²⁶ To wear black can metonymically indicate an act of pride and solidarity that assumes alternate modes of knowledge and volitional forms of subjectivization. E. Patrick Johnson cautiously but affirmatively observes that performing Blackness is not exclusively an act of disavowal; it can also be avowing and expansive.²⁷ In this context, two respective statements given by Blonzen and the play's director, Okpako, require close scrutiny. In an interview with the daily newspaper *Der Tagesspiegel*, Blonzen asserts, "I had to learn to be Black."²⁸ In a separate interview with the English-language magazine, *ExBerliner*, Okpako remarks of the title of the play that "it's also wearing blackness, as in wearing identities: you can try them on and you can take them off. The mere fact that it's addressed as something you're just wearing immediately shows you that it's not who you are."²⁹ Both assertions appear to treat Blackness not only as a fluid category but also as performance, insofar as performance is, in Tavia Nyong'o's illuminating turns of phrase, "the dramaturgy of newness" or "the ambivalent actualization of a troubling potential."³⁰ Such conditions of transformation are present in the play, in which wearing Black slides into a performance of Blackness in all of its vicissitudes and possibilities. For Blonzen, "learning to be Black" means learning about Black culture and social life in an otherwise colorblind society (Germany) where they had long been absent.

But wearing Black bears additional significance in the context of the play. It is also a performance of mourning. At the beginning of the second act, all of the performers are dressed in black to mourn the death of their roommate, Frank. The sartorial display of death and mourning visibly contrasts with the first act, in which all of the performers conspicuously don white clothing. Whereas the first act presents a typical morning in the WG kitchen with coffee, breakfast, teasing, and amusing banter, the second act is tinged with tragedy. There is no funeral scene as such in *Schwarz tragen*; instead, the work of mourning takes the form of a dramaturgy of trauma and bitter disclosure. In particular, Vicki reveals a harrowing story of racialized sexual violence in the law firm where she works as a legal intern. A character of strength but also of intransigence, Vicki attempts to distance herself from the trauma and the shame of victimhood and narrates the event in the third person as a terrible violation that has befallen one of her colleagues. However, it is her own wrist that has been hurt and bandaged, and she is the one who is visibly shaken by the event. Finally, when verbal narration turns to physical performance and Vicki embodies the role of her attacker, forcing herself in a hurtle onto a bewildered and flailing Joy, Vicki's fictional third-person account shatters. Performing her racist boss, who enjoys calling her "my non-Aryan" ("meine Nicht-Arierin"), Vicki reenacts the assault scene in excruciating detail, gesturing his thrusting, and repeating his words: "Women like you like that ... You slut. You pig. Slut. You pig."[31] The scene is ominous in its violence and in the tremendous scope of its displayed violation. The two other roommates, Cyrus and Eric (Ernest Allan Hausmann), are perplexed and can only look on in horror at this shocking performance within a performance, unsure of what to do. To speak of performance within performance is not to speak of a meta-performance, or simply what James Naremore refers to as professional acting versus a Goffmanian presentation of self in society.[32] Instead, a performance within a performance can also designate a performance scenario with an embedded and dynamic audience, a kind of theatrical mise en abyme. Thus, the violence entangled in wearing Black becomes a theatrical modality of mimesis and reflection. These performers as spectators try to convince Vicki in vain to go to the police. Her defeated response is simply: "We know how that goes."[33] The theatrical layers of this entire scene, its emphatic mimetic principle, galvanizes a reflection on Blackness and theater that implicitly addresses the spectators' participation and, as a matter of course, challenges them to recognize their own culpability as bystanders to this re-performance of injustice.

Schwarz tragen and Blackface

The play's text opens with an instruction and a caveat: "The figures are all Black. Blackface is not permitted in the performance of this play."³⁴ Olumide Popoola's slightly earlier dramatic text, *Also by Mail* (2013), similarly calls for such heedfulness in the performance of its text at its close. This is an expressed response to the preposterous (continued) use of blackface in German theater. Further, it reflects the assertion of sovereignty and responsibility of the playwright over her material and the way in which it is performed. In the case of *Schwarz tragen*, it is an unambiguous imperative: this play must be performed by Black actors or not at all. As such, it not only condemns the practice of blackface but also performatively affirms the sufficient presence of Black actors and actors of color in Germany to perform the roles in *Schwarz tragen*.

This brings us to yet another possible reading of the play's title: the recurring use of blackface on German stages. What happens when white actors "wear black," that is, play Black roles? More specifically, what happens when white actors paint their faces black? While performance does open up the possibility to question one's own a priori assumptions, it is always a delicate matter. *Schwarz tragen* obliquely alludes to the 2011–12 (and ongoing) firestorm of controversy surrounding the practice of blackface in Germany and in German theaters, in particular. In late September 2011, Michael Thalheimer's production of Dea Loher's play *Unschuld* (Innocence) premiered at the Deutsches Theater, in which two white actors played the roles of Black undocumented migrants in highly theatricalized blackface. A half a year later in March 2012, a German production of Herb Gardner's *I Am Not Rappaport* (1985) (*Ich bin nicht Rappaport*) directed by Dieter Hallervorden premiered at the Schlosspark Theater in Berlin, in which a white actor in blackface played the role of the African American character, Midge Carter. As the English Theatre of Berlin detailed on its website at the time, detractors rightly declared the production (of *Ich bin nicht Rappaport*) racist and drew "parallels between the use of blackface in this play with the minstrelsy and the decidedly racist tradition of blackface within 19th century minstrel shows in the United States, where white performers applied black make-up to themselves to present a deeply stereotyped caricature of a black person."³⁵ The most notorious example of American minstrelsy, "Jim Crow," created and performed by Thomas Dartmouth Rice, eventually came to personify the officially sanctioned racial segregation and oppression in the southern United States in the postbellum period. Without the comparable historical resonance, blackface in Germany is often reduced to a performance of Blackness that is simply a dehistoricized and apolitical spectacle of otherness. Many Germans have even defended the use of blackface in theater and elsewhere as a blameless act of artistic expression.³⁶

Without endorsing the practice of blackface by any means, Katrin Sieg pursues a more nuanced approach to the debate, as it has unfolded in Germany beginning with the case of Thalheimer's production of *Unschuld* glossed above. Building on Jonathan Wipplinger's argument that blackface has yet to be fully analyzed and conceptualized in the German context (2011), Sieg expounds that the use of blackface had existed in Germany heretofore as a culturally and historically overlooked phenomenon. It seems that only with the emergence of recent massive protest against this practice did it simultaneously co-opt not only its loaded name in the German vernacular "blackfacing," clearly borrowed from the English word, but also a history of slavery, segregation, and racism that is uniquely American.[37] Sieg is certainly right to point out the potential risks of misreading and projection when national histories are homogenized. In the case of Black and Afro-German discourses more broadly, the influence of African American culture and identity formations have for better or for worse been significant in shaping and even defining Black German discourses. According to Sander Gilman, (white) Germans have at least since the postwar era relied on the "American image of the Black" as a way "to deal with the idea of Blackness."[38] El-Tayeb too has cautioned against the uncritical co-option of African American history by Black German communities. She notes that "too easily are differences erased again as Afro-Germans are integrated into dominant narratives of diaspora in which they appear as merely imitative of the paradigmatic U.S. experience."[39] However, attunement to the universalist approach of Black history, as encouraged by Fanon's approach to postcolonial theory, does not necessarily obscure the importance of the particular and the local.[40] If anything, for Fanon, these two—the national and the international—are inextricably linked, because colonialism's condemnation was not only national but also international (certainly, continental) in scale.[41] I propose that, in the case of blackface, taking a universalist approach can offer a heuristic starting place and a basic language and discourse from within which this practice may be addressed in the German (national) context. The racist mechanics of blackface in the German tradition cannot be denied. The fact that blackface as a practice has existed unremarked for so long appears inherent of what El-Tayeb refers to as the dogma of European "colorblindness." In a colorblind society, "difference is marked along lines of nationality and ethnicized Others are routinely ascribed a position outside the nation, allowing the permanent externalization and thus the silencing of a debate on the legacy of racism and colonialism."[42] Although indirect, colorblindness is still an active form of racism that perpetuates both an internalist view of race and a deeply problematic mechanism of denial of both colonial history and the persisting existence of racism in European society. This denial is routinely reflected in culture and cultural production. As Julia Lemmle explains, "The use of blackface in the almost exclusively white environment of German theater speaks always about the continuity of the colonial imaginary in Germany, where colonial history has not been worked off at all."[43]

Practically speaking, the use of blackface in theater as a substitute for hiring Black actors and actors of color, of which there are significant number in Germany despite the argument to the contrary made by many theaters in defense of the use of blackface, is not only insulting and hurtful but also frustrating. That Black actors and actors of color already encounter immense challenges finding work to play roles traditionally cast as white, the practice of blackface is a double affront. Lara-Sophie Milagro, an actor and the founder of Label Noir, a network and collective to support Black actors and actors of color, observes that whereas in the United Kingdom and the United States theater ensembles are frequently racially and culturally diverse, including the somewhat more traditional Royal Shakespeare Company and the National Theatre in London, this is still simply not the case in Germany. A perusal through the ensembles of the nation's copious list of theaters doubtless supports such a claim. While white actors can be cast for any role, Black actors and actors of color are routinely passed over even for traditionally Black roles. The heinous practice of blackface aside, this is, as Milagro manifestly asserts, a transparent circumstance of racism in German theater.[44]

While written, produced, and performed in the swell of the blackface controversy in Germany, *Schwarz tragen* is not simply a play about and against blackface. It practices resistance but it also expansively asserts itself as part of a theater intent on self-expression, experimentation, and reflexivity. As a significant example of an emergent theatrical mode, *Schwarz tragen* attunes itself to the generative powers of solidarity in precarity and of possibilities to be found in the vagaries of performance.

Finding Their Self-Expressive Mode

In the wake of the blackface debate in 2012, Blonzen gave an interview with Bühnenwatch (Stage Watch), an organization and internet platform of artists, journals, and activists established in 2011 to address racism in theater. When asked what action needs to be taken to improve the situation for Black actors and actors of color in theater, Blonzen offers an affirmative, even hopeful, response:

> Like their white colleagues, Black actors should also ensure that they are well-trained, they present themselves with confidence, not let themselves be told that color is a blemish, sometimes turn a deaf ear, [have] thick skin and always look forward, never give up. And to reassess each stupid comment as motivation for the right cause. And most of all to confront the theater folks. Never bow down, rather challenge, fight, grapple with it. But above all: do not lose one's sense of humor![45]

The purport of Blonzen's proclamation of the significance of self-presentation and self-expression returns in theatrical form in *Schwarz tragen* with its utopian confluence of hope for a better future and a carrying on in the present with a generous dose of humor. At no point is this most evident as in the final act of the play.

In the midst of a group discussion about what Joy should do with her baby, which in reality is suddenly not as desirable to her as it was in fantasy (at the beginning of the play), there is a coup de théâtre. Cyrus directly breaks the fourth wall and alights to the house. Even the small space of the Ballhaus Naunynstraße had been partitioned in preparation for this final act. A pathway cutting right through the audience space had been physically devised. The spatial strategy aimed to draw the spectators into the performance by creating flexibility and flow for spectator-performer interaction. Reminiscent of the design of Richard Schechner's environmental theater and the living space of theater, the pathway allowed the performers to easily move through the house in order to encroach on the space of the audience and directly interact with individual spectators. The physical crossing of boundaries set up the breakdown of "the usual agreements between performer and spectator."[46] The spectators—by choice or not—become implicated in the actions of the play, insofar as the audience's presence is made present. For Schechner, the entire theater space is performance space. Performance is not isolated to the stage; it is everywhere. This is the living space of theater and its entirety.[47] With the area lights suddenly alit, Cyrus walks up and then down the pathway, speaking directly to audience members, making eye contact, shooting smiles, even shaking hands. He introduces himself and briefly narrates his personal story: "Listen up friends I'm Cyrus I hmm I want to apply as your new roommate. I was once the king of marketing but that's a long time ago. Then I founded this safe space with Frank . . ."[48] Addressing the audience as he walks up and down the aisle, his introduction and application as a "roommate" ("Mitbewohner"), which in the German literally means "coinhabitant," seems to speak to a broader context of both the theater and society. Cyrus appeals to German theater and society to accept him as a "co-inhabitant." Likewise, physically and phenomenologically expanding the performance space, the final line of Cyrus's monologue is performatively mirrored in his action: "A safe space is good but one also has to go out in the world."[49] Movement from stage to house and the violation of the fourth wall at once opens up the threshold of the contingent and the crossing over of two worlds.

Reworking the possibilities of performative theater, Cyrus's physical movement from stage to house, his encroachment on the audience, also evokes a history of Black performance of the American postbellum period, in which theater, and especially the galvanic and interactive performance of cabaret, would facilitate the encounter between a Black performer and a predominantly white audience. Daphne Brooks describes this phenomenon as the creation of a "contact zone," in which performance had the capacity to trouble that otherwise unyielding color line and its power dynamic.[50] A possible reminder of that history, this transgressive crossing of spaces, crossing lines, crossing thresholds carries its own weightiness, notwithstanding the ostensible levity of the scene. Ultimately, this dynamism directly confounds the simple separation of spectacle and spectator, even the dialectic of the white spectator and the Black performative experience.[51]

Cyrus's performative monologue is copied sequentially by Vicki, Eric, and then Joy. Interaction with the audience in this contact zone continues with a variation of gestures, from Eric's winking at certain female audience members to Joy's subsequent scowling at the same. The performance of volitional subjectivity quite literally comes to the fore in this scene. Although the performers remain in character, this particular scene feels intimate, improvised, and certainly phenomenologically real. This literal turn to the audience in the play is this explicit turn to performance. The deliberate break in the flow of the narrative and drama of *Schwarz tragen*, not to mention the ideological and physical break with the fourth wall, crosses over into the performative. Bert O. States's concept of the self-expressive mode in theater offers a possible point of reference for reading this final act as a performance of the actor on her or his own behalf.[52] The self-expressive mode keys into the "I" of the performer without completely breaking character. It is about showing the audience what the actor can do through the simultaneous performance of character and self (as actor). While States uses the example of the star performance in which the actor's presence and display of self are routinely components, the same could apply here as the assertion of identity and virtuosity of each performer as a Black actor in a German theater. It is the expressive declaration of a presence often ignored and marginalized: an unflappable "Here I am!" It is the insistence of Blackness in the overwhelmingly white space of theater and, by extension, German society.

The self-expressive mode is also a reflexive mode, insofar as it reckons with the mechanics of the gaze. In a way, all performance is reflexive. But the self-expressive mode is also responsive. An awareness of being observed, even judged, is returned with a self-presentation that may or may not coincide with the spectator's impression. This is a return, or at least a reorientation, of the gaze. In a German theater, in which the audience is predominantly white, even in a smaller, more experimental, some might even say "utopian" theater such as the Ballhaus Naunynstraße, the scopic regime is always racialized. However, perhaps it is also in the theater, in the space of performance, where the (white) gaze and its condemning and obscene relationality can be put under duress. In the final act of *Schwarz tragen*, in which there is an expansion of the performance space and a merging of actor-spectator roles when the performers alight one by one to the house and make direct contact with the spectators, the site of the spectacle is transferred to the audience, and as a matter of course the performers become spectators and seize control of the gaze. One might be inclined to consider this reversal of the gaze as simply theatrical and therefore also artificial; however, its performative charge is significant and residual. The community of shared experience and knowledge shaped by the participation in this performance endures, even if only as ephemera or traces of something. Immediacy, common situatedness, and the constant reorientation of bodies and gazes between performers and spectators: these are the qualities that condition this performance community, one that in its afterlife ultimately spills out beyond the world of the theater.

Concluding with the Utopian

Schwarz tragen concludes with a communal dinner and the return to the (utopian) quotidian collectivity of the characters. Still in the space of the kitchen, the roommates collectively prepare a stew of vegetables and herbs. Smells waft soothingly from stage to house, creating a flow of olfactory experience. While the others are occupied with cooking, Cyrus once more positions himself downstage and faces the audience. Throughout the play, Cyrus communicates with the deceased Frank (played virtually by Tyron Ricketts as a digital ghost projected on a makeshift screen, constructed with long leather tassels, that hangs upstage), who was not only his friend and roommate but also his lover. Throughout the play Cyrus struggles to reveal his true identity to his roommates—to come out to them. In a final monologue, he instead comes out to the audience with the concluding line: "I am gay."[53] That Cyrus comes out to the audience in a monologue instead of coming out directly to his friends is a startling act that emphasizes the authority of the performer-spectator encounter and the function of the theatrical feedback loop initiated moments earlier when the performers physically entered the house. While Joy's Black pregnant body can be read as an agent of utopian resistance, so too can the queer or the sexually nonconforming body. Both are at once what Muñoz calls "the rejection of a here and now and insistence on potentiality or concrete possibility for another world"[54] and the manifestation of Gordon's "being-in-difference." The Black pregnant body and the queer body in this play are ultimately, though in exceedingly different ways, performances of the utopian. An intersection of Blackness and queerness in this final act is salient. Both reject the ascendancy of white heteronormativity and assert a future that is perhaps uncertain but nonetheless full of promise. Yet the play does not conclude with Cyrus's testimonial-style monologue. Instead, he is called back to the kitchen, to the present, to the everyday, by his roommates for the communal meal. Again,

Schwarz tragen underscores a utopian spirit that does not only strive toward a better future but also rests in an optimism of the present. This is not exclusively an optimism for a better future; rather, it is one that unravels in the present, inasmuch as performance, solidarity, and the strength of resistance allow it to. *Schwarz tragen* importantly demonstrates how performance is, in the words of Johnson, useful both "in deconstructing essentialist notions of selfhood" and "provid[ing] a space for meaningful resistance of oppressive systems."[55]

Through a framing with utopian politics, the preceding pages have sought to examine Blonzen's play, and Okpako's sophisticated production thereof, as a complex drama of Blackness and performance. Not the first and certainly not the last example of Black German theater, *Schwarz tragen* is nonetheless exhilaratingly archetypal in its ability to speak to contemporary politics both within and outside of the theater. It expands the possibilities of postmigrant theater but also goes in its own directions. Finally, grappling with the muddy residue of subjugating imperatives of Black consciousness under colonialism, slavery, apartheid, and diasporic identity, not to mention persisting structures of racism, *Schwarz tragen* searches for new conditions of possibility in the utopian present and future.

Olivia Landry is assistant professor of German in the Department for Modern Languages and Literatures at Lehigh University.

Notes

1. For fuller details about the festival, see http://www.ballhausnaunynstrasse.de/veran staltung/black_lux__ein_heimatfest_aus_schwarzen_perspektiven_28.08.2013.
2. Consider for instance (in chronological order) Hakan Savaş Mican's *Die Schwäne vom Schlachthof* (The swans of the slaughterhouse, 2009), Lukas Langhoff's *Die lange Nacht der Generationen* (The long night of generations, 2012), Nurkan Erpulat's *Lö bal Almanya* (2012), Michael Ronen's *Perikızı* (Fairy, 2012, an adaptation of Emine Sevgi Özdamar's *Die Brücke vom Goldenen Horn*), Hakan Savaş Mican's adaptation of Orhan Pamuk's *Schnee* (Snow, 2012), Tuğsal Moğul and Antje Sachwitz's *Das Summen der Montagswürmer* (The buzz of the Monday worms, 2013), Anestis Azas and Prodromos Tsinikoris's *Telemachos—Should I Stay or Should I Go?* (2014), and İdil Üner's *Süpermänner* (Supermen, 2014).
3. "Die einzige Möglichkeit, die Welt zu verändern ist, möglichst viele schwarze Babies zu bekommen" (act 2). All citations from the play are taken from my personal notes from three different performances attended in September 2013 and corroborated by an unpublished, working-draft version of the play, dated 21 September 2013. I am grateful to Priscilla Layne, Philipp Khabo Koepsell, and Elizabeth Blonzen for sharing this material. All translations from the German are my own unless otherwise indicated.
4. "Ich bin schwanger" (act 1).
5. It bears noting that, with regard to US history, this argument becomes more complex, even polemical. Under slavery, it was the Black woman's role to reproduce children for

the enslaver and, as Hortense Spillers writes, "'motherhood' [was] not perceived in the prevailing social climate as a legitimate procedure of cultural inheritance." Hortense J. Spiller, "Mama's Baby, Papa's Maybe: An American Grammar Book." *Diacritics* 17, no. 2 (1987): 80. Further, more recent studies on maternity in the US context reveal the startlingly high maternal mortality rate among African American women compared to white women, which presents a counterargument for the resistant Black pregnant body. See Mary Beth Flanders-Stepans, "Alarming Racial Differences in Maternal Mortality," *Journal of Perinatal Education* 9, no. 2 (2000): 50–51.
6. Jamele Watkins, "The Drama of Race: Contemporary Afro-German Theater" (PhD diss., University of Massachusetts, Amherst, 2017).
7. Priscilla Layne, *White Rebels in Black: German Appropriation of Black Popular Culture* (Ann Arbor: University of Michigan Press, 2018): 177–81.
8. On the Ballhaus Naunynstraße webpage dedicated to the festival, it is stated that "Vier Wochen im Spätsommer *besetzt* das Festival Black Lux—Ein Heimatfest aus Schwarzen Perspektiven das postmigrantische Theater" (my emphasis). (Four weeks in late summer the Festival Black Lux—Home Festival from Black Perspectives will occupy postmigrant theater.) See http://www.ballhausnaunynstrasse.de/veranstaltung/black_lux__ein_heimatfest_aus_schwarzen_perspektiven, retrieved 12 August 2018.
9. This is certainly the case for earlier postmigrant theater examples enumerated in the first section.
10. José Esteban Muñoz, *Cruising Utopia: The Then and There of Queer Futurity* (New York: New York University Press, 2009): 1.
11. Davina Cooper, *Everyday Utopias: The Conceptual Life of Promising Spaces* (Durham, NC: Duke University Press, 2014), 2.
12. "Wir brauchen einen Ort, wo wir so sein können, wie wir sind ohne uns ständig ins Verhältnis setzen müssen zu den 'Anderen.' Das haben wir da draußen den ganzen Tag" (act 2).
13. "... braucht mindestens noch eine Generation." Elizabeth Blonzen, "Ein sicherer Ort: 'Schwarz tragen' am Ballhaus Naunynstraße," interview with Patrick Wildermann, *Tagesspiegel*, 14 September 2013, retrieved 12 November 2021 from http://www.tagesspiegel.de/kultur/elizabeth-blonzen-ein-sicherer-ort-schwarz-tragen-am-ballhaus-naunynstrasse/8834734.html.
14. Blonzen, "Ein sicherer Ort."
15. Avery F. Gordon, *The Hawthorn Archive: Letters from the Utopian Margins* (New York: Fordham University Press, 2018), viii.
16. Gordon, *Hawthorn Archive*, 34. It may be noted that Marcuse charts his notion of "the Great Refusal" (against all prevailing methods of control) particularly in his texts *One-Dimensional Man* (1964) and *An Essay on Liberation* (1969).
17. "Früher glaubte ich, ich passe nirgendwo hin, weil ich überall total auffallen würde. Ich dachte, ich kann nie einfach mal ich sein, ich laufe immer mit dieser Hautfarbe rum." Cited in Katharina, Oguntoye, May Opitz, and Dagmar Schultz, eds., *Farbe bekennen: Afro-deutsche Frauen auf den Spuren ihrer Geschichte* (Frankfurt am Main: Fischer, 1992): 135.
18. Achille Mbembe, *Critique of Black Reason* (Durham, NC: Duke University Press, 2014): 43.
19. Frantz Fanon, *Black Skin, White Masks*, trans. Richard Philcox (New York: Grove Press, [1952] 2008): 77–78.

20. "Du brauchst Weiße, um zu merken, dass du es nicht bist, oder wie" (act 2).
21. W. E. B. Du Bois, *The Souls of Blackfolk: Essays and Sketches* (Chicago: A. C. McClurg & Co., 1904): 8.
22. "Wenn ich mir vorstelle, dass ich morgens zum Frühstückstisch komme und dann sitzt da ein Weißer . . . der hier . . . wohnt dann ist mir noch vor dem ersten Kaffee klar, dass ich nicht weiß bin. Weißt du?" (act 2).
23. Fanon, *Black Skin*, 90–92.
24. Mbembe, *Critique of Black Reason*, 40.
25. Fred Moten, "The Case of Blackness," *Criticism* 50, no. 2 (2008): 187.
26. This is of course one of the main arguments of Butler's pathbreaking text, *Gender Trouble*. See Judith Butler, *Gender Trouble: Feminism and the Subversion of Identity* (London: Routledge, 1990).
27. Patrick E. Johnson, *Appropriating Blackness: Performance and the Politics of Authenticity* (Durham, NC: Duke University Press, 2003): 2.
28. "Ich musste ja auch lernen, schwarz zu sein." Blonzen, "Ein sicherer Ort."
29. Branwen Okpako, in "This Is Your Country: If You Don't Like It, Make It Better," interview by Summer Banks, *ExBerliner*, 6 November 2014, retrieved 12 November 2021 from http://www.exberliner.com/whats-on/stage/this-is-your-country-if-you-don pe rcentE2 percent80 percent99t-like-it-make-it-better/.
30. Tavia Nyong'o, *The Amalgamation Waltz: Race, Performance, and the Ruses of Memory* (Minneapolis, MN: University of Minnesota Press, 2009): 14–15.
31. "Frauen wie du mögen so was. . . . Du Schlampe. Du Sau. Schlampe. Du Sau" (act 3).
32. James Naremore, *Acting in the Cinema* (Berkeley, CA: University of California Press, 1988): 70.
33. "Wir wissen doch wie das läuft" (act 2).
34. "Die Figuren sind alle Schwarze. Blackfacing ist bei der Aufführung dieses Stückes nicht gestattet."
35. "Colorblind?" English Theatre Berlin, retrieved 22 December 2014 from http://www.etberlin.de/production/colorblind/.
36. Matthias Heine, "Rassismusvorwurf gegen Dieter Hallervorden," *Die Welt*, 10 January 2012, retrieved 12 November 2021 from http://www.welt.de/kultur/article13 807516/Rassismusvorwurf-gegen-Dieter- Hallervorden.html.
37. Katrin Sieg, "Race, Guilt and *Innocence*: Facing Blackfacing Contemporary German Theater." *German Studies Review* 38, no. 1 (2015): 117–18.
38. Sander L. Gilman, *On Blackness without Blacks: Essays on the Image of the Black in Germany* (Boston, MA: Hall and Co., 1982), xii.
39. Fatima El-Tayeb, *European Others: Queering Ethnicity in Postnational Europe* (Minneapolis: University of Minnesota Press, 2011): 64.
40. Frantz Fanon, *The Wretched of the Earth*, trans. Richard Philcox (New York: Grove Press, [1963] 2004): 149–50.
41. Fanon, *Wretched of the Earth*, 150.
42. El-Tayeb, *European Others*, xix; 13–14.
43. Julia Lemmle, "'Ich bin kein Nazi!'—The Blackface Debate in the German Mainstream Media," *Textures*, 20 May 2014, retrieved 12 November 2021 from http://www.tex tures-platform.com/?p=3142.
44. Lara-Sophie Milagro, "Die Bequemlichkeit der Definitionshoheit," *Nachtkritik*, 28 March 2012, retrieved 12 November 2021 from https://www.nachtkritik.de/in

dex.php?option=com_content&view=article&id=6740:die-blackfacing-debatte-iii-man-muss-kein-neonazi-sein-um-rassistisch-zu-handeln&catid=101:debatte&Itemid=84.
45. "Schwarze Schauspieler-Innen sollten, wie ihre weißen Kollegen auch, darauf achten, gut ausgebildet zu sein. Selbstbewusst auftreten, sich nicht aufschwatzen lassen, dass die Farbe ein Makel ist, manchmal weghören, dicke Haut und immer weitermachen. Nie aufgeben. Und jeden blöden Kommentar als Zuspruch umwerten für die richtige Sache. Und vor allem Theaterleute konfrontieren. Nie den Kopf einziehen, sondern fordern, kämpfen, auseinandersetzen. Aber bei allem: den Humor nicht verlieren!" Elizabeth Blonzen, "Interview with Elizabeth Blonzen," Bühnenwatch, 16 February 2012, retrieved 12 November 2021 from https://web.archive.org/web/20131214054603/http://buehnenwatch.com/interview-mit-elizabeth-blonzen/.
46. Richard Schechner, *Environmental Theater* (New York: Applause, [1973] 1994): 40.
47. Schechner, *Environmental Theater*, 1–2.
48. "Hört zu Freunde ich bin Cyrus ich hmm ich will mir hier bei euch bewerben als neuer Mitbewohner. Ich war mal der König der Werbebranche aber das ist lange her. Dann hab ich mit Frank diesen Schutzraum gegründet . . ." (act 3).
49. "Ein Schutzraum ist gut aber man muss auch hinausgehen in die Welt" (act 3).
50. Daphne A. Brooks, *Bodies in Dissent: Spectacular Performances of Race and Freedom, 1850–1910* (Durham, NC: Duke University Press, 2007): 301–2.
51. Brooks, *Bodies in Dissent*, 301.
52. Bert O. States, "The Actor's Presence: Three Phenomenal Modes." *Theatre Journal* 35, no. 3 (1983): 361.
53. "Ich bin schwul" (act 3).
54. Muñoz, *Cruising Utopia*, 1.
55. Johnson, *Appropriating Blackness*, 9.

Bibliography

Banks, Summer. "This Is Your Country: If You Don't Like It, Make It Better." *ExBerliner*, 6 November 2014. Retrieved 12 November 2021 from http://www.exberliner.com/whats-on/stage/this-is-your-country-if-you-don percentE2 percent80 percent 99t-like-it-make-it-better/.

Blonzen, Elizabeth. "Ein sicherer Ort: 'Schwarz tragen' am Ballhaus Naunynstraße." Interview with Patrick Wildemann. *Tagesspiegel*, 14 September 2013. Retrieved 12 November 2021 from http://www.tagesspiegel.de/kultur/elizabeth-blonzen-ein-sicherer-ort-schwarz-tragen-am-ballhaus-naunynstrasse/8834734.html.

———. "Interview with Elizabeth Blonzen." Bühnenwatch, 16 February 2012. Retrieved 12 November 2021 from https://web.archive.org/web/20131214054603/http://buehnenwatch.com/interview-mit-elizabeth-blonzen/.

———. "Schwarz tragen." Working draft from Branwen Okpako, Ballhaus Naunynstraße, 2013.

Brooks, Daphne A. *Bodies in Dissent: Spectacular Performances of Race and Freedom, 1850–1910*. Durham, NC: Duke University Press, 2007.

Butler, Judith. *Gender Trouble: Feminism and the Subversion of Identity*. London: Routledge, 1990.

Cooper, Davina. *Everyday Utopias: The Conceptual Life of Promising Spaces.* Durham, NC: Duke University Press, 2014.
Du Bois, W. E. B. *The Souls of Blackfolk: Essays and Sketches.* Chicago: A. C. McClurg & Co., 1904.
Edelmann, Lee. *No Future: Queer Theory and the Death Drive.* Durham, NC: Duke University Press, 2004.
El-Tayeb, Fatima. *European Others: Queering Ethnicity in Postnational Europe.* Minneapolis: University of Minnesota Press, 2011.
Fanon, Frantz. *Black Skin, White Masks.* Translated by Richard Philcox. New York: Grove Press, [1952] 2008.
———. *The Wretched of the Earth.* Translated by Richard Philcox. New York: Grove Press, [1963] 2004.
Flanders-Stepans, Mary Beth. "Alarming Racial Differences in Maternal Mortality." *Journal of Perinatal Education* 9, no. 2 (2000): 50–51.
Gilman, Sander L. *On Blackness without Blacks: Essays on the Image of the Black in Germany.* Boston: Hall and Co., 1982.
Goffman, Erving. *The Presentation of Self in Everyday Life.* New York: Anchor Books, 1959.
Gordon, Avery F. *The Hawthorn Archive: Letters from the Utopian Margins.* New York: Fordham University Press, 2018.
Heine, Matthias. 2012. "Rassismusvorwurf gegen Dieter Hallervorden." *Die Welt,* 10 January 2017. Retrieved 12 November 2021 from http://www.welt.de/kultur/article13807516/Rassismusvorwurf-gegen-Dieter- Hallervorden.html.
Johnson, E. Patrick. *Appropriating Blackness: Performance and the Politics of Authenticity.* Durham, NC: Duke University Press, 2003.
Layne, Priscilla. *White Rebels in Black: German Appropriation of Black Popular Culture.* Ann Arbor: University of Michigan Press, 2018.
Lemmle, Julia. "'Ich bin kein Nazi!'—The Blackface Debate in the German Mainstream Media." *Textures,* 20 May 2014. Retrieved 12 November 2021 from http://www.textures-platform.com/?p=3142.
Marcuse, Herbert. 1969. *An Essay on Liberation.* Boston: Beacon Press, 1969.
———. *One-Dimensional Man: Studies in the Ideology of Advanced Industrial Society.* Boston: Beacon, 1964.
Mbembe, Achille. *Critique of Black Reason.* Durham, NC: Duke University Press, 2014.
Milagro, Lara-Sophie. "Die Bequemlichkeit der Definitionshoheit." *Nachtkritik,* 28 March 2012. Retrieved 12 November 2021 from https://www.nachtkritik.de/index.php?option=com_content&view=article&id=6740:die-blackfacing-debatte-iii-man-muss-kein-neonazi-sein-um-rassistisch-zu-handeln&catid=101:debatte&Itemid=84.
Moten, Fred. "The Case of Blackness." *Criticism* 50, no. 2 (2008): 177–218.
Muñoz, José Esteban. *Cruising Utopia: The Then and There of Queer Futurity.* New York: New York University, 2009.
Naremore, James. *Acting in the Cinema.* Berkeley, CA: University of California Press, 1988.
Nyong'o, Tavia. *The Amalgamation Waltz: Race, Performance, and the Ruses of Memory.* Minneapolis: University of Minnesota Press, 2009.
Oguntoye, Katharina, May Opitz, and Dagmar Schultz, eds. *Farbe bekennen: Afro-deutsche Frauen auf den Spuren ihrer Geschichte.* Frankfurt am Main: Fischer, 1992.
Popoola, Olumide. *Also By Mail.* Berlin: Assemblage, 2012.
Schechner, Richard. *Environmental Theater.* New York: Applause, [1973] 1994.

Sieg, Katrin. "Race, Guilt and *Innocence*: Facing Blackfacing Contemporary German Theater." *German Studies Review* 38, no. 1 (2015): 117–34.

Spiller, Hortense J. "Mama's Baby, Papa's Maybe: An American Grammar Book." *Diacritics* 17, no. 2 (1987): 64–81.

States, Bert O. "The Actor's Presence: Three Phenomenal Modes." *Theatre Journal* 35, no. 3 (1983): 359–375.

Watkins, Jamele. "The Drama of Race: Contemporary Afro-German Theater." PhD diss., University of Massachusetts, Amherst, 2017.

Wipplinger, Jonathan. "The Racial Ruse: On Blackness and Blackface Comedy in 'fin-de-siècle' Germany." *The German Quarterly* 84, no. 4 (2011): 457–76.

CHAPTER 5

German Comedians Combating Racist Stereotypes and Discrimination
Oliver Polak, Dave Davis, and Serdar Somuncu

BRITTA KALLIN

The Black German comedian Dave Davis comes on stage as the fictitious African character Motombo Umbokko and says to his audience during a comedy show: "I was told that Bavaria is a state where blacks are in charge, and I arrive and see that they are all white."[1] The character Umbokko confronts his mostly white viewers with wordplay focusing on the official color of the CDU/CSU governing party in Bavaria, which happens to be black. Davis pretends—as Umbokko—to be unaware that it is not the individuals in the Bavarian government who are Black but that black is the party color of conservative Bavarians. Davis's use of humor here utilizes satire to draw for his German audience the disconnected and cognitive gap between *Schwarze* as a designation for Black people and *Schwarze* as a shorthand description for a conservative political party with a well-known anti-immigrant and anti-Black bias. He does something that is typical of a new wave of nonwhite, non-Christian German comedians who confront existing taboos about religions, ethnicity, national belonging, gender, and other identity markers. Here, the two different meanings of black (as party color) and Black (as racial identity) overlap, and the semantic overlap and possible misinterpretation causes the punchline to reach his audience.

This chapter examines how the German comedians Oliver Polak, Dave Davis, and Serdar Somuncu deploy humor to renegotiate norms around religious, national, ethnic, and cultural belonging in Germany. All three comedians theorize national, religious, and ethnic identity formation by making jokes about "Germans" and what it means to be "German," which can include Black

German, Jewish German, Turkish German, or other racialized identities. The comedy they deliver has potential for positive cultural impact and change by questioning established norms of the German national narrative and by showing bold comedy that problematizes the idea of a homogenous German identity. They problematize the different statuses of migrant workers who arrived in the past centuries and those who have come to Germany for generations through transnational labor migration. Some of these migrants, mostly white Christians from European countries, have been integrated without any issues. Other migrants, who are marginalized based on race, ethnicity, or religion, have faced a long history of discrimination and more hurdles to achieve the same status. First-, second-, and third-generation immigrants as well as newly arrived refugees have started a transcultural dialog that is changing the German national narrative, and they have created a multiethnic society in contemporary Germany, which includes cultural, linguistic, ethnic, and religious diversity.

All three comedians try to provide opportunities for this transcultural dialog in their shows and their writings when they, for example, use satire to critique ethnonational typecasting. Given the twenty-first-century resurgence of populism and neofascism in Central Europe, these prominent comedians are providing a counternarrative that pokes fun at a traditional image of Germany and Germans as white, sausage-eating, polka-dancing Christians. They question the notion of a German blood lineage (*jus sanguinis*) and forms of *völkisch* belonging as well as religious, ethnic, and cultural associations of Germany during the twentieth century. More importantly, they also demand that we engage with a German national and religious discourse that is not based on the Shoah but on what is happening in twenty-first-century Germany (cf. Nick Block's chapter in this volume), namely "radical diversity,"[2] as Max Czollek calls it, and the normalization of a multiethnic Germany. They also wish for the audience to laugh along with comedians who are making fun of different groups of Germans and German stereotypes.

Each of these comedians uses unique strategies to highlight marginalized groups and the groups' contributions to and active participation in German society. While none of the three are without fault in reinforcing various stereotypes in their comedy, they all challenge received patterns of German comedy as well as social and institutional racism. Their acts, as well as their public statements, hold out the promise of social transformation and a future that is more tolerant toward People of Color in German media and the German national narrative. Through transgressive humor, these comedians break taboos and shine a light on the narratives of racial and religious exclusion within Germany.

While Polak, Davis, and Somuncu do not perform together or see themselves as a cohort, looking at them side by side allows us to compare and contrast their successful approaches to comedy in Germany. All of them offer the perspective of a Person of Color in their shows and writings. Just as there is not just one white German ethnonational narrative and not one alternative PoC German narrative, examining these three comedians allows us to engage with comedy as an arena where Germany emerges as a modern, multiethnic, and multireligious nation in the center of Europe. The rationale for bringing the three comedians together is not that they have all been assigned the status and category of "ethno-comedians" in the German media but that they are all People of Color and speak from different perspectives of oppression and discrimination.³ Calling all three men People of Color acknowledges that in the early twenty-first century the discourse of race and belonging is not confined to a few countries like Great Britain or the United states but rather to all former colonizers, including Germany, as a transnational phenomenon. All three may be aware of the PoC rhetoric, and they might recognize that the term also applies to them:

> The term people of colour was coined in the United States during the emergence of the Black Power movement in the late sixties. As an anti-racist self-definition, it became a political term which was intended to mobilise and connect racially marginalised groups and their members beyond the boundaries of their "own" ethnic, national, cultural and religious group membership. It does not describe persons based on an ethnic classification but according to racism as it is experienced in its everyday and institutional forms.... The term people of colour refers to all racialised persons who, to varying degrees, are of African, Asian, Latin American, Pacific, Arab, Jewish or indigenous origin or background. It connects those who are marginalised by the culture of white dominance and collectively degraded by the force of colonial traditions and presence.⁴

People of Color face different forms of "racism as it is experienced in its everyday and institutional forms," as Sharifi frames it. These patterns of discrimination and racism go back to colonial times. The domination over the centuries of German comedy by white, Christian men parallels the unquestioned dominant social and political hierarchy in Germany during that time. Migrant groups and comedians of Color occupy a valuable position as part of the mainstream culture, and they deploy comedy as a critical tool to renegotiate their status in Germany. As Fatima El-Tayeb argues in her study of marginalization of various nonwhite ethnic groups in Europe, these "minoritized" groups draw attention to the process of marginalization and construction of the "Other." El-Tayeb has shown in *European Others* how European belonging and the imaginary narrative of European whiteness are being renegotiated by People of Color and migrant groups that illustrate and give voice to the growing nonwhite and non-Christian European populations. Her work helps to explain what issues the comedians address in their shows as she has analyzed the marginalization and *Migrantisierung* of various groups of populations in European countries. In

Undeutsch: Die Konstruktion des Anderen in der postmigrantischen Gesellschaft (Ungerman: The construction of Otherness in the postmigrant society), El-Tayeb states that it is important to unearth the silencing and erasure of nonwhite races and religious minority groups because, as she argues "[t]here is a causal connection between the failure of Europe's multicultural presence and the continental racism amnesia."[5] Especially, by *queering* ethnicity—changing European understanding of national belonging—People of Color show resistance to the "hegemonic memory" that exists in mainstream contemporary Europe.[6] So, for example, when Dave Davis performs his sketch about Blacks in Bavaria, we can see him engaging with what El-Tayeb refers to as "continental racism amnesia." His comedy forbids his audience to ignore or refuse to acknowledge racial power differentials.

Research on marginal humor can help explain how artists positioned on the margins of society see the center, including their role as outsiders and insiders, and how they contribute to an ever-changing and evolving German culture. Existing scholarship such as the contributions in the volume *Komik der Integration* (The humor of integration) by Özkan Ezli, Deniz Göktürk, and Uwe Wirth are helpful in the analysis of what the three German comedians try to achieve through satire, parody, polemics, and wit, namely using language and rhetoric in working against stereotypes and discrimination. Humor from People of Color has long been situated at the margins of society, which slowly changes national narratives. The comedians comment on the center by engaging in conversations where they actively participate in the public debate about positioning themselves as PoC and where they take up center stage so they can no longer be ignored as standing on the sidelines. These three comedians are engaged in creating what Wirth, Ezli, and Göktürk call a "transcultural comedy of integration." The editors write in their introduction to *Komik der Integration* that "one can observe the spreading of a special type of transcultural comedy, one that makes those implicitly functioning ways of negotiating belonging and border practices explicit and thus makes the performance aspect of the double dynamic of integration and desintegration visible."[7] Uwe Wirth suggests that integration itself—still the goal of German governments that invited immigrant laborers into the country—is worthy of critique. He describes the situation in which the nonwhite person, whose "skin color does not conform to the standard set around 1900 by racist and colonialist Europe," becomes a potential laughingstock. "Those who stand out and are culturally peculiar [*auffällig*] in this way can become the butt of the joke because they did not make enough of an effort to fit in—or because they have tried very hard but still cannot assimilate in an un-peculiar [*unauffällig*] way."[8] Here, Wirth draws our attention to one part of the distinction between "laughing at" versus "laughing with." The three comedians are forcing the transition from being laughed at to those who make jokes that people laugh with.

Joanne Gilbert examines marginal humor in the United States in *Performing Marginality: Humor, Gender, and Cultural Critique*, and her argument about marginality also applies to the German context:

> The defining characteristics of African American, female, gay/lesbian, and Jewish humor, therefore, are inherently similar. And marginal humor sometimes seems to be a subset of a larger rhetoric—the rhetoric of victimage. Because of the "us against them" nature of marginal humor, marginal comics often construct themselves as victims. In so doing, however, they may subvert their own status by embodying the potential power of powerlessness. Their social critique is potent and, because it is offered in a comedic context, safe from retribution as well.[9]

When a member of a marginalized group, including women and racialized minorities, uses humor to attack a barrier set by society, the comedian is making a social intervention, and if the audience joins the comedian by laughing with him or her, the audience and the comedian can break through this barrier together. Some critics claim that self-deprecatory humor repeats stereotypes. However, as Gilbert argues, "the self-deprecatory humor may be constructed as cultural critique, and ... comics who use self-deprecatory material do not necessarily believe themselves to be the persons they project onstage. ... Humor is a rhetoric unique in its ability to undermine its own power with the 'only joking' disclaimer."[10] Oliver Polak, for example, criticizes those voices that take his jokes too seriously. Marginal humor is not concerned with its popularity but rather its stance on the margins of dominant culture.

Sigmund Freud described Jewish humor as marginal humor and portrayed it as a socially sanctioned means of releasing aggression. This type of humor derived from mocking the ingroup rather than the outgroup. Polak has used this way of releasing aggression in his shows and books. He has used the image of the whining Jew in several of his shows and books, sometimes connecting to US American depictions of Jews in popular culture. Hanni Mittelmann states that "the sitcom-figure Alf became an important identificatory figure for Oliver Polak in his youth." The show *Alf*, which ran from 1986 to 1990, depicted an alien whose spaceship crashed into the garage of a white American, suburban, middle-class family, the Tanners. The Tanners decide to take Alf in, and each episode follows the cultural misunderstandings between the wholesome family and their small, brown, furry alien guest with a large, protruding nose. As Mittelmann continues, "From this 'big-nosed cousin with the body covering sidelocks' ('grossnasiger Vetter mit den Ganzkörper-Gebetslocken'), Polak learned that one can stage the 'alien'—and specifically the Jewish alien, who was and is always eyed by Germans with suspicion—in an engaging way."[11] However, according to Freud, Jewish humor is not simply self-deprecatory but also contains self-praise and self-assertion in a hostile environment in which the Jewish diaspora has lived in Europe and abroad. Comedy from the sidelines of society is described as marginal humor, humor that circulates in marginalized and racialized groups and is often aimed at the mainstream culture. Marginal humor is often critical and geared toward both certain ingroups and some outgroups. For instance, Polak's humor includes aspects of Jewish humor such as his overbearing and overindulgent Jewish mother. He jokes that she always stayed close to him while other mothers left their children unsupervised. Even in his puberty and during his early adult years his mother—as he jokes—denied him time to spend with his girlfriend.[12] As he writes in his show *Krankes Schwein* (Sick pig/Sicko, 2014) Polak has suffered from a breakdown due to depression and mentions his mother's refusal to admit her son's mental health issues.[13]

The US American psychologist Herbert Lefcourt analyzed the pressure of stress and personality characteristics that help humans manage the dangerous effects of stress. He argues in his book *Humor: The Psychology of Living Buoyantly* that "persons who shared the [humorous] event felt much closer to each other after they had laughed together about it."[14] Lefcourt argues that humor enhances social belonging and, therefore, helps minorities assert their status of belonging. In that sense, humor is a coping process that encourages a feeling of community, closeness, and control. The question remains how long the feeling of social belonging remains for viewers of the events, as research has not been able to quantify the duration of these emotional bonds. It is not possible to prove that audiences' opinions change or remain the same after watching comedy shows. Yet, this discourse analysis only aims to examine what the effects are in the moment and in the media reviews in which critics mention a critical yet inclusive message of national and social belonging in the comedy shows.

Davis, Polak, and Somuncu appeal to white Germans, an imaginary group that some have called *Biodeutsche*,[15] as well as to Germans with a *Migrationshintergrund*.[16] The new transcultural comedy situates the comedians within a globalized world and suggests to scholars, and perhaps audiences, that assumptions about the breadth of German humor should be open to renegotiation. The type of marginal humor that all three embrace has been labeled "ethnic comedy" by various media outlets, even though all three are pushing back against this kind of labeling of their art. "Ethnic comedy" in Germany is a complex and controversial term as it automatically and irrevocably racializes the performing comedian. It categorizes groups of artists as "Other" compared to white, Christian German comedians who have been accepted to represent the norm. This, of course, illustrates the problematic "unmarked" nature of whiteness that scholars in critical whiteness studies have pointed out. Cultural movements and critical theories are raising awareness around white privilege and white bias and the role these play in structural racism in Western societies. In her article on the symbolic order of the social construct of whiteness, Susan Arndt argues that the idea of race is a myth that allows whites to legitimize privileges and stay in power positions. "Societal, political, and cultural processes of formation rely on a historical process of racialization which allows whiteness a hegemonial role. These hegemonies and the differences cannot easily be overcome by negating them or ignoring them."[17] Arndt explains that whiteness needs to be addressed and analyzed by those that benefit from the priviliges of whiteness in order to understand the power imbalances in our modern-day societies and to eventually overcome the structural faults of our societies and their systemic racism. In his book *Wie die Deutschen weiß wurden: Kleine (Heimat-)Geschichte des Rassismus* (How Germans became white: Small [homeland] history of racism), Wulf Hund discusses the idea of a connection between Germanness and whiteness that first had to be fabricated:

> Yet, German whiteness was not just ambivalent. It first had to be created in a long-winding and complicated process. In nature, there are no races nor are there any whites. These are ideological mind games of the European expansion that came into being with the help of colonial violence before they were systematized in the eighteenth century by the Enlightenment and turned into scientific categories.[18]

Hund explores how German whiteness was created over the centuries and is now embedded in the German cultural imagination. This in turn has ramifications for contemporary German comedians who use the stage and the word to combat the association of whiteness with German.

The critic Andrej Klahn wrote of German "ethnic comedy" in 2014: "Kaya Yanar and Bülent Ceylan initiated the breathtaking breakthrough of ethnic comedy into mass media after the turn of the century."[19] He continues: "Ethnic comedy is hugely successful. Artists like RebellComedy [Babak Grassim, born in Iran, und Usama Elyas, whose parents are from Saudi Arabia] and Abdelkarim make fun of clichés about their heritage as much as about themselves. The diverse audience likes this."[20] Klahn critically uses the term "ethnic comedy" and calls attention to the pitfalls of the term. "Ethnic comedy" implies that any ethnicity that is not based on racialized whiteness and Christianity is marked as other from the ethnonational discourse around German national belonging. The term assumes outsider status within the broader field of German comedy that over time has aimed to become more inclusive by inviting—and not any longer ignoring—previously neglected groups of comedians onto stages in Germany.

The three comedians, Davis, Polak, and Somuncu, are reshaping German comedy by being successful while expanding the rubric of "German" humor. However, neither of the three comedians actually embraces the term "ethnic comedy" because they resist the "pigeonholing" or "ghettoization" of their art and rightfully and actively claim to be part of and contribute to German comedy, not "ethno-comedy." I use the category of People of Color in comedy because it allows for a degree of strategic essentialism. Strategic essentialism refers to "a political tactic employed by a minority group acting on the basis of a shared identity in the public arena in the interests of unity during a struggle for equal rights. The term was coined by Spivak and has been influential in feminism, queer theory, and postcolonial theory."[21] By grouping Davis, Polak and Somuncu together under the category of People of Color in comedy, critics have been able to highlight their shared intentions of using satire to engage with race, ethnicity, and religious affiliation in a way that has been taboo for white comedians.

One of the most prominent strategies used within comedy by People of Color is the stereotype. According to Homi Bhaba, what makes a stereotype powerful is its "dependence on the concept of 'fixity' in the ideological construction of otherness. Fixity, as the sign of cultural/historical/racial difference in the discourse of colonialism ... connotes rigidity and an unchanging order."[22] Understood as an allegedly fixed sign, the stereotype is "a form of knowledge and identification that vacillates between what is always 'in place,' already known, and something that must be anxiously repeated."[23] As David Huddart states, "Through racist jokes, cinematic images, and other forms of representation, the colonizer circulates stereotypes about the laziness or stupidity of the colonized population."[24] In their comedy, Davis, Polak, and Somuncu demonstrate that these stereotypes may appear stable, but they are actually a "false foundation upon which colonialism bases its power."[25] Utilizing stereotypes, these comedians often use exaggerated fashion, gestures, and speech associated with the marginalized group that is represented in the joke or story they tell. For example, Dave Davis uses stereotypes when he acts as the African migrant Motombo Umbokko, who works as a cleaner in German restrooms and whose German is faulty, but he also uses Bhabha's concept of mimicry (becoming like the dominant culture, but not quite) in the form of another character who exaggerates a Bavarian accent and dresses up in lederhosen and traditional Bavarian attire while singing a song about the dangers of neo-Nazis in Germany. Lars Koch describes ethnic comedy as an unfortunate repetition of stereotypes and clichés of the subaltern character as victim and in an exoticized style with "offensive bodily features."[26] Nevertheless, Koch argues that the transcultural humor that is often used in so-called "ethno-comedy" can lead to discussions about misdirected perceptions or clichés of marginalized groups.

The humor sociologist Antonin Obrdlik suggests in "'Gallows Humor'—A Sociological Phenomenon" that humor can be a sign of "defiance" as well as "an intellectual and emotional escape from the disturbing realities."[27] Obrdlik spent nine months in Nazi-occupied Czechoslovakia during World War II and analyzed how prisoners and soldiers used jokes and humor to combat the difficult and dangerous situation as oppressed, occupied people. He explained that "gallows humor is an index of strength or morale on the part of oppressed peoples" and that it has historically been associated with the persecuted and condemned. Humor, according to him, is "a psychological compensation,"[28] "a powerful weapon," a "shield," and "a reliable index of the morale of the oppressed."[29] He asserts: "The purest type of ironical humor is born out of sad experiences accompanied by grief and sorrow. It is spontaneous and deeply felt—the very necessity of life which it helps to preserve."[30] Oliver Polak, in particular, makes use of gallows humor in his shows, for example, when he jokes about his family's neighbors during the *Reichspogromnacht* or *Kristallnacht* (night of broken glass) on 9 November 1938 who wanted to set fire to his family's house but finally decided not to do so because the neighbor's house might have caught fire as well.[31] In her study on women's use of humor, Gina Barreca notes: "Humor doesn't dismiss a subject but rather often opens that subject up for discussion. Humor breaks taboos by allowing us to talk about those issues closest to us.... Humor is a way to affirm ourselves, to rise to meet the challenge, channel fear into pleasure, translate pain into courage."[32] Davis opens up discussions about Blackness in Germany, Polak asks for discussions about the National Socialist past and "translates" his family's pain into courage to talk about his family's and Germany's past, while Somuncu problematizes positions of German Turks and their roles in German society.

Comedy has the potential to transform social patterns, but it also has always been considered a threat by those in power. Recent political trends, such as the election of right-wing parties, and recent political incidents, such as the printing of ridiculed Muhammad cartoons in Danish and French newspapers followed by the fire-bombing of the offices of *Charlie Hebdo* in 2011 in Paris, France, and the killing of twelve journalists of the satirical magazine in 2015, have shown that comedians, cartoonists, authors, journalists, and actors are not safe from retribution to their spoken, sung, drawn, or otherwise published humor, despite its birth in sadness, grief, and oppression.[33] Indeed, satire is such a potent tool when it comes to criticizing long-standing social and religious beliefs that governments all over the world incarcerate and censor journalists, comedians, cartoonists, and authors.[34] For example, the comedian Jan Böhmermann became embroiled in German-Turkish political tensions after reading his "Schmähgedicht" (taunting poem) about the current Turkish president Recep Tayyip Erdoğan. The ensuing "Böhmermann affair" in 2016 involved the Turkish government requesting criminal prosecution of Böhmermann. According to an outdated German penal code, which has since been eliminated, it was prohibited to mock foreign heads of state.[35]

In an article about satire in Germany titled "Satire in Deutschland—Lachen als Aufklärung" (Satire in Germany—laughter as englightenment), Michael Meyer muses: "In light of the many crises and conflicts in the world and the rise of populists, the viewers escape into satire. No wonder: satire can, may and has to be much more pointed."[36] Meyer refers to the media scholar Benedikt Porzelt, who explains: "Humor is based on disappointing expectations[,] and the breaking of taboos is part of that.... Therefore, one has to experiment with what is allowed."[37] Still, what is allowed or permitted (and by whom) in Germany as a subject of humor is very specific. The approach of the Turkish German author and public intellectual Zafer Şenocak toward cultural and national identity construction is helpful. In *Deutschsein: Eine Aufklärungsschrift* (Germany: An Enlightenment script), he problematizes the ambiguous history of German nation-building, the forming of a German national narrative, and the celebration and/or repression of nationalism and the perennial concept of blood lineage, the concept of the *jus sanguinis* "Volk." According to Senocak, Germany is not yet a nation, a group of people living in a geographic area that, since 1949, is supposed to feel united through the *Verfassungspatriotismus*. Germans, he argues, do not have anything in particular that unites them, *except for what does not belong—the Other*: "The Otherness of Eastern European Jews yesterday and of Muslims from the Middle East today is at the core of the German debate about its identity, which has meanwhile replaced the East German–West German separation debate."[38] While the separation of East and West Germany was still one of the major topics in public debates before the fall of the Berlin Wall, the relationship within Germany between white, Christian Germans and their counterparts that did not fit the internalized description of the imaginary German prevailed after the fall of the Berlin Wall.

Despite the difficulties of being allowed to fit in to the scene in Germany that is dominated by white, non-Jewish comedians, Polak, Davis and Somuncu have won a plethora of media prizes over the past decade, written books, toured their shows, and been invited to some of the most celebrated comedy shows on German television. The shock value that the comedians offer is good for television ratings, and the traditions of satire and comedy that they continue make them a good fit for German TV because they attract publicity despite (or because of) their racialized positions. Among the comedy shows are: *Neues aus der Anstalt* (ARD); *die heute show* (ZDF); *Nightwash* (einsfestival); *Stand-UpMigranten* (SWR, EinsPlus); *Pufpaffs Happy Hour* and *Quatsch Comedy Club* (ProSieben); *Extra3* and *Fat Chicken Club* (Tele 5); *Cindy und die jungen Wilden* (RTL); and *SWR Latenight* and *Spätschicht* (SWR).

The comedians Polak, Davis, and Somuncu exploit a single permissible subject, pushing the limits with their jokes about Jews, Muslims, Black Germans, and other racialized groups. Whereas coming from other Germans such jokes could be deeply offensive and perceived as racist, these three use their position as People of Color—as a German Jew; as a German who was born in Istanbul, Turkey, but migrated to Germany with his parents as a child; and as a Black German born and raised in Cologne by parents from Uganda—to alert their audiences to the deeply ingrained stereotypes regarding racialized groups.

Oliver Polak

Oliver Polak's book *Ich bin Jude, ich darf das* (I am allowed to do that because I am Jewish, 2013) is explicit about exploiting the author's marginality to his comedic advantage. It breaks many taboos, as do his provocative show *Jud süß sauer* (Jew sweet and sour, 2012) in which he pokes fun with and at Jewish humor and contrasts it with an Asian chicken dish. In the other show, *Krankes Schwein*, Polak offers some insights into his personal story with mental illness but also reflects on the difficult state of racialized groups in Germany. He uses the German expression meaning "sick pig" for abhorrent behavior, such as in "sick prick," a pejorative expression, partially and jokingly aimed at himself but also taken from critics' responses to his humor. He sees himself in the tradition of Lenny Bruce or Richard Pryor in the United States ("Psychiatrie-Ansichten"). Lenny Bruce (1926–66, born Leonard Alfred Schneider) integrated politics, religion, sex, and vulgarity into his performance act, which turned the corny humor of the American Borscht Belt, the summer resorts of upstate New York where Jews would vacation between the 1920s to 1960s, on its head. The African American comedian Richard Pryor (1940–2005) was known for uncompromising examinations of racism: he was a social critic who employed vulgarities and profanity, including racial epithets. Polak wants to raise awareness like his idols and provoke his audiences. He claims that comedy in Germany plays it too safe and is thus not as powerful as the comedy of Bruce and Pryor, comedians who saw themselves equally as social critics and as comedians and who faced legal and social trouble for their comedy shows.

Polak, for example, rises to meet the challenge of being considered an outsider as a Jew in contemporary Germany when he channels fear into pleasure and translates his pain into courage in the title of his show and his book *Ich darf das, ich bin Jude*. While non-Jewish Germans do not have the moral right to joke about anything that has to do with the torture, persecution, attempted extinction, and overall horrific treatment of Jews during the Holocaust, Polak claims the right to speak about the crimes that were committed against Jews to remind Germans that Jews are still an integral part of German society and culture and the different perspectives of German Jews need to be heard and acknowledged. In one of his acts, Polak comes on stage and says "I feel so burnt out.... Are Jews allowed to say that on a German comedy show?"[39] Polak sarcastically infers the burning of gassed Jews in concentration camps. When he tells jokes like these, his German audience swallows hard and then laughs. Nick Block has argued that Polak and other German Jewish comedians and authors position themselves in comparison and in relation to Turks in Germany and to Christian, white Germans: "Polak, Salzmann, and Grjasnowa all thematize a friendship between Turks (Achmed, Sedat, and Cem) and Jews (Oli, Aron, and Masha), all of whom position their identities counter to ethnic Germans (the 'white bread' in Salzmann's formulation)."[40] Block analyzes the Jewish-Muslim connections within the German public discourse and accurately states that Polak, for example, relates well with other comedians from religious minority groups because Polak emphasizes different religious affiliations in his jokes and voices. Interestingly, he embodies some of the demographic and cultural changes that have taken place over the past decades toward a more heterogeneous Germany. The number of Jewish people in Germany has risen in past decades due to the fact that Jews of German heritage (*Russlanddeutsche*) from Russia were invited to return and migrate to Germany after the fall of the Berlin Wall. While Polak explains that the openly addressed topic in his comedy of his Jewish family background in Germany was initially an act of freedom, he also condemns his non-Jewish comedian colleagues and representatives of the German media who foreground his Jewishness in introductions and comments and who insist that Polak should mostly focus on the Jewish aspect of his identity in his act. Polak feels that the public discourse in Germany has pigeonholed him as a "Jewish" comedian, an antisemitic act in itself.[41] Polak tried to clarify what he meant in an interview:

> In my show [*Ich bin Jude, ich darf das*], all these stupid questions came up that I had to answer as a Jewish boy. In Germany, people are easily pigeonholed: that is the Black guy, this is the Jewish guy. But I refused this labeling. I was constantly invited to shows like *StandUpMigranten* on the channel EinsPlus. My booker always responded: "Well, Oliver Polak is German, what do you want him to do there?" And I always said: "Why don't you call it by its name: it's a comedy concentration camp." Honestly, why would you want to separate comedians into groups? Either they are funny, or they are not. For me this sounded like a show where you can touch the *Bimbo* [racist term for Black people]. Terrible. I am not up for that.[42]

Polak says he wants to be viewed as a funny or unfunny comedian, not as a Jewish comedian. But at the same time he markets himself as Jewish with a book like *Ich bin Jude, ich darf das*. In highlighting his Jewishness, he opens himself up for being categorized with other racialized comedians whether he wants this or not. Polak is offended to be included in a group of comics "with a migrant background" since that does not describe his identity, as he is German Jewish and not a migrant. By being categorized alongside Davis, Somuncu, and others, he loses part of his status as a white German man and is upset about white Germans' refusal to differentiate between different kinds of racialized Germans.

Oliver Polak compares the *StandUpMigranten* concept to a concentration camp in his polemical statement because the show segregates comedians by ethnicity, race, and religion, just as people were segregated by race, ethnicity, religion, and political party membership from the rest of white, Christian society within concentration camps during the Holocaust. Polak criticizes the approach of the comedy show in a similar manner as does the author Feridun Zaimoğlu, who refers to shows that focus on diversity as "Multikulti Zoos."[43] Referring to the comedy show as a "concentration camp," Polak uses a term for camps that were first introduced by German colonialists in Southwest Africa during the nineteenth century and those that were built and run by the National Socialists during World War II. With this comparison, Polak provokes a morally and ethically objectionable laughter and explicitly "permits" himself to do so because he, unlike his audience, is Jewish. If Polak is labeled a German Jew or a Jew, he possibly cannot speak for all Germans, and his perspective is reduced to that of a religious minority.[44] However, his Jewish perspective makes a difference as a reminder of Germany's past and its German Jewish citizens' efforts to try to overcome discrimination. That perspective allows the audience to see and recognize the few German Jews who survived the Holocaust and stayed in Germany as well as the Jewish migration to Germany and the recreation of Jewish communities in Germany in postwar years. Polak positions himself as a comedian who does not want to be cast within a group of multicultural comedians as he offers a perspective of an insider. In response to being asked whether his comedy can be categorized as "Ethno-Komik" with an immigrant perspective, Polak protests:

> It's all nonsense. Just now we had an inquiry. An organizer had a Turkish and a Black comedian and I was supposed to appear because I would be such a good fit. Obviously, I am not going there. We don't want to go to the comedy concentration camp. I do stand-up comedy. . . . Actually, stand-up comedy comes from people like Bill Murray, Steve Martin, Jim Carrey, or Eddie Murphy. They get up on stage and tell people about uncomfortable things in their lives in an authentic manner.[45]

Polak is upset because the offer to work alongside a Turkish and a Black comedian implies that he is understood as an outsider, which is a form of racialization of Jews as ethnic or religious outsiders to the traditional white Christian ethnonationalist narrative in Germany. Yet German society and media still attempt to overcome this mindset, as can be seen from his experiences. It is not problematic for Polak to refer to the show as a "KZ." Yet, he also wants to provoke his audience by connecting and linking his style of comedy with German Jewish comedy, culture, and history. Polak dismisses this unfortunate, underlying cultural contradiction and relentlessly works to break up the binary opposition between German and Jew. Annika Orich explains this phenomenon by arguing that Polak refuses to be reduced to just a member of one group, namely German Jews: "Even if Polak could claim a family or hereditary relationship to the past, he always tries to shield himself against the categorization through his audience and reductive thinking. 'How do I feel? And I have to admit: Would they offer me the option 'Jew,' 'German,' or 'comedian,' I would probably check off 'comedian.'"⁴⁶ Orich correctly outlines how Polak fights against the pigeonholing and thus the limitation of the media's attention but not necessarily the reach of his satire. After all, comedians from ethnic and religious minority groups make use of marginal humor that targets their racialized status, a kind of humor that is not employed in most shows by nonracialized comedians. Polak thus emphasizes and insists that he is German *and* Jewish and changes his position as a German Jew, and German comedy as such, when he, for instance, insists that he is German and a member of an underrepresented religious (and racialized) minority. Thus, Polak doesn't see himself as a *Jewish* comedian. He is a stand-up comedian who provokes people with uncomfortable topics, and, due to his background, those uncomfortable topics just happen to include Jewishness.

In 2016, Polak was awarded the Deutscher Fernsehpreis in the category of "Best Comedy" for his work in *Das Lachen der Anderen* (The laughing of others), a TV show for the WDR. The title recalls the Academy Award–winning German movie *Das Leben der Anderen* (*The Lives of Others*, 2006, dir. Florian Henckel von Donnersmarck) about the fortunes of the East German Stasi agent Wiesler before and immediately after the fall of the Berlin Wall. On the WDR website of the show *Das Lachen der Anderen*, the TV station explains the goals of the series: "Both men [Polak and Micky Beisenherz] meet special, different, and interesting people, in order to write a stand-up comedy program about these people and for them."⁴⁷ The viewer infers that special people refers to people with disabilities. Despite the jury's debate about the cynicism of the show that became so heated that some members relinquished their duties, Polak was awarded the prestigious Grimme-Preis in 2017 during the controversy. In spite of such accolades, after filming groups of people with multiple sclerosis and seniors in a senior citizen home as part of the project *Das Lachen der Anderen* with his colleague Micky Beisenherz, Polak ran into some controversies, which he defended as follows: "What was new about the show was that we included these groups [i.e., people with disabilities], which was a totally different level. It was not supposed to create a feeling of dread, but rather it is a type of racism if you cannot tell jokes about these people and thus exclude them."⁴⁸ Polak's reference to racism seems ill placed when referring to people with disabilities; what he really is criticizing is ableism and age discrimination. By highlighting society's inability to accept that people with disabilities desire humor too, he points out that all kinds of marginalized groups can be discriminated against. In an intersectional approach, all of these identity markers are intertwined, and add to the marginalization of disabled people and seniors and cannot be viewed separately. Polak considers himself a social critic and refers to Germany as disabled when it comes to accepting humor (*humorbehindert*) from different angles and about various groups. He wants to create a dialog about different forms of privilege, resistance, and oppression.⁴⁹

During the late-night show *Applaus und Raus*, which Polak hosted from October to November 2016 on ProSieben, he also ran into trouble. A segment of the show was titled with the Twitter name #Gastoderspast, which translates to "guest or spastic person." *Spast* is to this day still a derogatory term in German, one that groups with disabilities have not fully reclaimed. Polak's way of using the term was criticized to such an extent that the TV station immediately changed the Twitter handle. Lilian Masuhr, who works for the project Leidmedien [suffering media], helps media outlets with newscasts aim to avoid discriminatory speech. She claims that the term "spastic" in Polak's show should not become acceptable to describe people who are not suffering from a disease of muscle spasms because that is discriminatory and ableist:

> The term "spastic" becomes socially acceptable if the host can label guests who are boring "spastic" and can kick them off the show. No matter how badly the guest has been offended prior to this, to be called "spastic" is the ultimate insult. Not only does the term discriminate against persons with disabilities but it also weakens the current efforts against hate speech in social media.[50]

Here, it becomes obvious again that it matters who speaks, who makes the joke. As a comedian and a member of a minority group, Polak claims the right to make jokes about all minority groups. In the case of Polak's show, it is not a person with a disability who is using the label of *Spast* to describe him- or herself: Polak is referring to unwanted guests on the show as *Spastis*.[51] His use of language has long been criticized as being too offensive and politically incorrect. In his research on disability humor, Tom Coogan argues about ableist jokes:

> Laughter directed at a disabled person on account of her or his disability is not a release from disability, but part of its continuing social construction. This "comic discourse of projected ridicule" portrayed as positively subversive by Stronach and Allan is, Corker argues, actually "pitted against" the liberating transgression offered by "Bakhtin's inside-out carnivalesque subversion."[52]

The joke about people with disabilities in *Das Lachen der Anderen* does not automatically include them in the laughter, nor does it release any close-minded social narrative about disabled people as represented in the media. A common view in the media is that Polak should be more sensitive to the difficulties of other minorities. Coogan argues that the person making the joke has more freedom in provoking his or her audience than the audience members: "While a joker is liberated by the social rules around joking practice (he or she is 'only joking'), the audience is rigidly constrained by them, responsible for any social difficulty (upset or challenge) the joke causes, lest they be accused of lacking a sense of humour."[53] These social constraints can, for instance, be seen in white German audience members who are aware of Germany's racist and colonialist *Völkerschauen* (ethnological exhibitions), in which Africans were displayed in nineteenth-century German zoo enclosures alongside animals, who respond with irritation and disorientation. The next comedian tackles the history of German colonial phantasies and creates comedy around the perception of Blackness in German society.

Dave Davis

The Black German comedian Dave Davis was born in 1973 in Cologne after his parents migrated to Germany from Uganda. After graduating from high school, Davis completed a trainee program as an insurance agent but then wanted a professional change. He started his show portraying the fictitious toilet man "Motombo Umbokko," but he has since morphed into several other personae who offer social commentaries. In a hyperstylized role mimicking the figure of an African migrant that is in itself a parody of an ethnic stereotype, Davis plays with cultural norms and includes typical German humor, German idiomatic expressions, and German social codes that he sometimes inverts to show his audience the implicit racism that he and other Black Germans have to confront on a daily basis.

At the beginning of the show *Verstehen Sie Spaß?* in 2011, Davis greeted his audience with a witty twist of a colonialist stereotype when coming on stage: "Boy oh boy, there are so many albino monkeys here in the audience, this is going to be fun. My name is Motombo Umbokko."[54] Davis plays with the common colonialist image of Africans as monkeys and returns the favor by addressing the audience as white (albino) monkeys. Germans still have to learn about the abuse, assault, and terror of German colonial history, as it has been mostly ignored in German schools. As a result of the Black Lives Matter demonstrations and movement, there are a variety of efforts underway to decolonize school and university curricula. In another reference to slavery, colonial occupation, and racist behavior in twenty-first-century Germany, Davis alludes to racist attacks on Blacks in Germany when using parody and making jokes such as: "I was in Leipzig. Three Blacks were chased by fifty whites.... It was a marathon."[55] He superimposes successful African marathon runners with the victimized Blacks hunted by Germans. In 2019, there was a discussion in the German media about Blacks on foot being attacked by racists and white supremacists in German cities like Chemnitz, for example. Davis reminds his audience repeatedly that a postcolonial or decolonial turn in German society has yet to take place and that Blacks face overt and covert racism in both the former East Germany as well as the Western federal German states where Black Germans are discriminated and treated with less respect than white Germans. On a talk show, Davis explains that he created the character Motombo Umbokko, whose work is to clean public toilets and who speaks incorrect German with an African accent, because he wanted to be politically incorrect and because he believes Germans listen to an underdog more than to an academic who tries to tell them in sophisticated German how racist they are due to their racist history. The history of discrimination of Black Germans may be a factor that constrains his choice of comedic persona and compels him to downplay his education and pretend to speak from a less educated position to engage his audience who also come from different classes and educational backgrounds. Davis knows that the jokes are only received as funny as long as the audience accepts the comedian as a member of their inside or outside group, as the jokes only have an impact in the social context they are told. Davis emphasizes both his family's migration history and his regional upbringing and belonging to Cologne via his humor and his regional dialect. He knows that an implicit rule for comedians is that those who have taken on a regional sense of belonging in Germany and have attained the ability to speak a regional dialect can justly claim the status of belonging to Germany in linguistic and cultural terms.

Davis's shows are called *Spaß um die Ecke* (Fun around the corner, 2009), *Live & in Farbe* (Live and in color, 2010), *Afrodisiaka* (Afrodisiac; a word-play of "Afro" and "aphrodisiac," 2014), *Blacko Mio!* (My Black; with an Italian connotation, 2016), and *Genial Verrückt* (Genial Craziness, 2018). In his acts, he warns his audience of the evils of capitalism, racism, and populism and comments on the dangers of right-wing terrorist groups like the NSU (Nationalsozialistischer Untergrund). He also warns his audience of the instrumentalization of Islam: "But using this to stoke fears against everyone who is associated with Islam. I believe that is very dangerous. We create an image of an enemy."[56] Like his colleagues, Davis loves to play with language and repeatedly uses idiomatic expressions that include color of any kind, in particular *schwarz* (black).[57] Thus, he follows in a tradition of other Black German activists before him, like the poet and sociologist May Ayim, who also used *schwarz, weiß,* and cognates as well as homophones in her poetry to draw attention to racialization in German society. Talking about why he became a comedian, he replies: "I am a typical German and wanted to do something solid. ... I have always been creative. ... I put all my eggs into one basket, and I hit the mark right on [*ins Schwarze getroffen*]."[58] The play on the expression *ins Schwarze treffen* is both self-referential and implies the (financial) success of his choice; by extension, this refers to his identity, thus highlighting positive associations of "blackness" in the German language in addition to negative associations that make up the majority of expressions. Part of his act also sees him purposefully adopting an ignorant view—the white German perspective—of Africans when he jokes about his grandfather and tells his audience what he calls African proverbs. These instead are German aphorisms that he changes into African-sounding proverbs, such as "Too much mush spoils the cook," which is a play on "Too many cooks spoil the mush," or "The fat bird breaks the branch" instead of "The sparrow in your hand is better than the pigeon on the roof."⁵⁹ Davis goes back to the alleged roots of his ethnic heritage as his audience anticipates African stories, but he intentially misquotes African proverbs to show the humor of mixing up German proverbs and undermining Germans' expectations of African Otherness.

Davis's idols are the freedom fighter and politician Nelson Mandela and the comedian, writer, and producer Dave Chappelle, whose comedy plays with complicated race relations in the United States. Similar to other comedians, Davis also draws on a history of Black German literature as well as comedy and humor in contemporary Black German theater. Jamele Watkins has noted in her dissertation *The Drama of Race: Contemporary Afro-German Theater* (2017) that Black German authors such as May Ayim and others have often used humor to approach themes of racism and belonging in Germany, and their writings are "examples of diasporic iconography."⁶⁰ According to Davis, talking about race as a comedian is not as simple in Germany as it is in the United States. He is aware of his German Turkish colleague, who has received threats from German Turks: "Bülent Ceylan, for example, cannot leave the house in Mannheim without bodyguards anymore."⁶¹ Davis makes white Germans consider the ways in which marginalized groups are treated differently: "People come up to me and ask if I speak German. So, the other day I asked the blond salesperson in the bakery if she speaks German. After she confirmed I ordered a croissant."⁶² The humor here is that Davis changes sides and pretends that it could be normal for blond Germans to be asked if they belong to the nation of Germany and if they speak the language, finishing his joke by using a French word rather than a German one. He parodies the dialogue about German-language abilities by adding a French word that has become part of the German vocabulary. Davis points out that the German language is not a pure Germanic language but that it has changed and has been influenced over centuries, having incorporated many expressions from Greek, Romance languages, and other European and non-European languages.

Davis and Polak reshape German comedy by engaging with the difficult task of "staging" and problematizing racialized characters that have been underdogs and have not made it to a stage presence. Davis has been criticized by Oliver Polak, who sees Davis's stage figure of Motombo Umbokko as a tragic character that reproduces stereotypes of uneducated African migrants. Yet, Polak himself has been accused of reproducing negative stereotypes of Jews. Davis's comedy has made it possible to create a character like Motombo Umbokko who reminds Germans of the discrimination of People of Color within contemporary German society and its racist culture. Thematically similar to Polak and Davis and yet different in his approach to comedy, the next comedian has run for public office. He creates comedy around racilized Turks and other

Muslims in Germany who have been set apart from dominant German culture through a narrative of so-called Christian national values.

Serdar Somuncu

The German author, musician, and politician Serdar Somuncu (b. 1968), has made a name for himself as a stellar yet controversial German comedian. After his *Mein Kampf* (1996) tour, during which he read excerpts of Adolf Hitler's book and commented on them, he received death threats from right-wing Germans. He has also been blasted by German Turks for denouncing reactionary Islamic views. Somuncu has been criticized for taking on German history as someone whose ancestors did not live in Germany during the Holocaust, as if he does not fully belong to Germany. Leslie Adelson argues in her book *The Turkish Turn in Contemporary German Literature* that German Turks and Turkish intellectuals have made and are making valuable contributions to German history, literature, and culture and constitute "a threshold that beckons, not a tired bridge 'between two worlds.'"[63] As Maha El Hissy and Erol Boran contend, Somuncu's humor has been influenced by decades of German Turkish 'Kabarett' such as *Knobi Bonbon* (1985–97) and the *Bodenkosmetikerinnen* (1991–99), which also actively addressed the varied experiences of migration through comedy.[64]

After showing solidarity with Jan Böhmermann following the recitation of his poem against Erdoğan, Somuncu likewise received death threats from some members of the Turkish community, who claimed that he is a traitor and does not support his parents' homeland of Turkey. He embarked on several comedy tours, including performances of his show *Der Hassprediger* (2008). Somuncu wittlily draws parallels between German society during the time of National Socialism and its modern form in the twenty-first century. For example, during a performance of *Der Hassprediger* he recalls that he wanted to do something "cool" in high school: "I wanted to be elected to the class council. I arranged the speech in the diction of my greatest idol." And then he mimics Adolf Hitler's diction and starts his speech by copying Hitler's style of speaking and rhetoric: "One day ... ," breaking off the sentence once he hears the laughter of the audience when they recognize that he uses Hitler's particular way of orating. And Somuncu asserts that his German classmates agreed, "This guy knows what he is talking about."[65] His audience immediately breaks into laughter because of the contradiction of a German Turkish high schooler who uses Hitler's rhetorical devices and runs for class council but also because of the ongoing struggle of Germans to overcome Hitler's legacy and the infatuation with populist politics and rhetoric. Somuncu breaks taboos by discussing violent German history and ridiculing Hitler's voice and texts as someone without a German lineage.

However, despite the liberal politics exhibited in his critique of right-wing extremism, some of his jokes also offend a progressive perspective. In some of his shows, Somuncu uses misogynist language when making fun of vegans and bashing middle-aged women who, for example, shop in local, organic food stores as "eco-bitches" and "whores." What stands out in Somuncu's comedy is that he is breaking taboos when it comes to language that is mostly used for bodily functions and that he has brought to the stage, which El Hissy refers to as "the grotesque of the fecal language."[66] Since September 2016, Somuncu has had his own weekly two-hour radio talk show called *Blaue Stunde* (Blue hour) on the Berlin-Brandenburg radio station Radio Eins, now also available as a podcast.

He has also hosted the TV show *So! Muncu!* on n-tv and sees himself as following in the tradition of Christoph Schlingensief rather than Anne Will or Frank Plasberg, because his aim is to deconstruct the traditional talk show genre and the white, liberal, political engagement as embodied by Anne Will and others.[67] The parallels to Schlingensief are obvious because Somuncu sees himself as a performance artist, not simply a stand-up comedian. He approaches his performances with costumes, music, and stage art, and he fully engages with his audience in a similar way as Schlingensief, who was a provocateur with political goals.[68] The idea of spectacle, shock, and radical gestures that can be seen in Somuncu's acts were also part of Schlingensief's aesthetic approach in his stage and film productions. Schlingensief and some of his actors ran through the theater at times and yelled "try to escape" to the audience, while Somuncu insults his audience as part of his *Aggro-Comedy*,[69] escalating his rhetoric to a level of vulgarity and profanity that shocks them. Paul David Young asserts that Schlingensief's "blunt, campy tastelessness that is directed toward social good through provocation" was done with the goal of changing and positively influencing the social fabric and the national narrative in Germany, very similar to Somuncu's goals.[70]

Somuncu has had several run-ins with the media. For years he has claimed that public and private TV stations and other media outlets are censoring his shows. In particular, he accused the WDR of editing out, without permission, controversial parts of his comedy act for a TV broadcast. He then accused a reporter and the WDR: "These assholes assume that they can censor us in the name of those who pay their TV and radio fees. And that was—for me—the breeding ground of fascism."[71] Subsequently, the WDR filed a lawsuit against Somuncu that detailed why they reprimanded the comedian for calling their reporter and TV station "fascist." Even on his Facebook page, Somuncu has tried to combat censorship when he created the expression "WDRdogan" and marked his photo with the stamp "CENSORED." Christian Buß writes of Somuncu that he is not a traditional comedian and that he is difficult to work with because he questions the German media apparatus and its hierarchy as well as its portrayal of racialized members in German society:

The case remains confusing. That has to do with the fact that the borders between performer and private person in the case of Serdar Somuncu are fluid. They book the comedian as—funny!—verbally abusive angry Turk for the shoot and they get—not funny!—a verbally abusive business partner who loses control. In addition, he criticizes the structural problems of public radio and TV and uses derogatory terms like "asshole."[72]

Somuncu obviously wants to question the terminologies that are used to refer to him as a comedian and an artist but also as a German of Turkish heritage. Asked about his categorization as a "German Turkish" comedian, Somuncu responded in an indirect manner by problematizing the meaning of "Turkishness" and "comedian" and the role of the "token Turk."

> For the editorial departments of comedy shows I am not Turkish enough to act as the stereotypical Turk. For the editorial departments of talk shows I have spent too little time as a cabaret performer in order to be a comedian, and too little time as a politician to be a politician. Only after I sat in *Anne Will* and *Maybrit Illner* did they realize that, hey, this guy doesn't have to define himself. He has an opinion, that's enough. At first, I was invited to debates around integration, as a token Turk.[73]

Somuncu uses satire to probe the narrative of not being Turkish enough even though he is asked to act as a model or token Turk. Kathrin Bower has examined Somuncu's "Transnational Politics of Satire" and has concluded that he regularly "questions the fixity of Germanness and Turkishness using his own position—as 'eingedeutschter Kanake'—to complicate both terms[, and yet] ... he has not found an alternative semantics for cultural difference and continues to refer to Germans and Turks."[74] This quest for an alternative semantics for cultural difference and national narratives is a quest that comedians, politicians, and scholars share. Bower has drawn attention to Somuncu's "transnational intervention" in comedy and to "integration as inside joke."[75] She has shown how Somuncu contributes through artistic means to the representation of PoC in Germany and how he contributes his views by participating in Germany's public debates and by intervening into and making steps toward a more inclusive way of discussing national belonging through comedy: "Somuncu may be the most compelling example of the hybrid as the identificatory model for Turkish German performers, not only because of his demonstrated ability to engage with Germany's past as well as contemporary signs of mixed identity."[76] In his jokes, Somuncu tries to provoke and highlight the divide between and within some ethnic minorities in Germany.

Somuncu has indicated that he intentionally wants to irritate and incite anger on all sides because he believes that his audience will engage in discussions when he breaks taboos and talks about difficult subjects that are often untouched. Despite his efforts to raise awareness and support open discussions, he has repeatedly been accused of spreading misogyny and homophobia with his on-stage jokes. Both sexist and homophobic jokes reaffirm stereotypes of a hypermasculinity or toxic masculinity that is allegedly represented by Muslim men. Nevertheless, his colleague Oliver Polak considers Somuncu to be a powerful comedic voice: "I wouldn't want Dieter Nuhr, for example. In contrast to him, Serdar Somuncu is the only one in Germany who makes intelligent, relevant comedy. That's why he is always invited to Anne Will's show."[77] Timo Steppat confirms the discrepancy between Somuncu's vulgarity and his political sincerity in his portrait of the comedian who is hard to categorize and wants to be regarded as a serious performance artist:

> It is difficult to believe, but Serdar Somuncu has turned into a voice that demands to be taken seriously. He sits on the *Anne Will* or *Hart aber fair* shows and talks with Edmund Stoiber or Claudia Roth. He is smart and analytical, a good speaker. On the other hand, he is also—at least in his solo shows—too vulgar to be the model migrant. That is the area of tension that makes him unusual and successful.... It is not comedy or cabaret: what he does is too loud and too vulgar for that. Somuncu sees his performances as short theatrical plays, he claims he is an artist first.[78]

The critic states that Somuncu cannot easily be put into a category as a model migrant because his performance act is too vulgar, but that role is also part of his success story. People realize that they have to take him seriously because he wants to involve his audience and the wider public in sophisticated discussions about developments in German society and the changing German national narrative.

Somuncu's claim that his performances are small plays also displays his affinity with Christoph Schlingensief's approach to performance as a political act. David Hughes has observed that "Schlingensief moved on to theater, as though the very medium of film had consumed itself. Yet, within a few years, he pronounced that 'theater is dead. You can't achieve anything with it. I am founding my own political party, called Chance 2000.'"[79] Just like Schlingensief's political campaign in 1998, Somuncu ran as candidate for the German parliamentary election in September 2017 for Martin Sonneborn's satire party Die Partei (The Party) in the Berlin district of Friedrichshain-Kreuzberg.

Similar to Schlingensief, who appropriated and changed the xenophobic slogans of the Free Party Austria and of the candidate Jörg Haider, Somuncu also earmarks some of Hitler's, the AfD's, and right-wing groups' slogans to confront his audience with the blatant bigotry and hatred that has led one group of people to racialize and persecute another group. Somuncu explained his political and professional ambitions and the intersections of politics and satire: "I am only the designated candidate for chancellor.... If we try to remember how close the reality of Böhmermann and Erdoğan came to politics, it is only appropriate and timely to recognize how Sonneborn views politics. Satire makes good politics, and sometimes politics is satire."[80] Asked about his statement concerning the need for more discussions with neo-Nazis and members of the AfD, Somuncu explained: "I want a debate about content. You cannot avoid the arguments for fear of the populists."[81] Somuncu was not elected as chancellor in Germany in September 2017 but received 7.2 percent of all of the votes for his electoral district, Berlin Friedrichshain-Kreuzberg/Prenzlauer Berg East, and pointedly identified the satirical traits in German politics at the time.

Conclusion

All three comedians—Oliver Polak, Dave Davis, and Serdar Somuncu—use satire and parody to break taboos and combat racist and antisemitic stereotypes and discrimination through outdated concepts of what is considered "German." At times they fall into the trap of reproducing stereotypes, and they can exacerbate and complicate the debates around humor and racialized groups when they use stereotypes and homophobic, ableist, and misogynist jokes. Yet, each of their shows present German audiences with alternative and much more inclusive definitions of "German" as well as "German comedy." Each of them offers a different form and different degrees of subversion in his comedy. Polak confronts his audience head-on about the Holocaust; Davis engages with colonialist clichés; Somuncu problematizes what it means for him to be a German with Turkish heritage and flouts the taboo of Hitler's *Mein Kampf*, a volume that was not readily available for purchase in Germany when he went on tour. All three comedians successfully use parody, wordplay, satire, and subversion as tools of overcoming stereotypes, discrimination, belonging to the German nation, and what it means to be "German." While the stereotypical misogynist, homophobic, and ableist comments are questionable strategies of the comedians who want to reach out to certain groups of people in the audience in order to build alliances, the comedians' strategies and their subversion of stereotypes is successful when it comes to ethnonational discourses that their comedy critiques. In times of populist and growing right-wing movements in Germany, Europe, the United States, and Latin America, Polak, Davis, and Somuncu provide comedy from a position of People of Color—which they contest and at the same time invoke—that continues to spark and fuel public debates about the benefits of democratic systems, free speech, comedy, and art as a political tool, as well as about the dangers of microaggressions, systemic racism, and discrimination of racialized groups.

Britta Kallin is associate professor of German at the Georgia Institute of Technology, Atlanta, Georgia. She has published articles on authors Christa Wolf, Günter Grass, Elfriede Jelinek, Marlene Streeruwitz, and others. Her monograph *The Presentation of Racism in Contemporary German and Austrian Plays* was published in 2007. Her research focuses on gender, race and ethnicity, national identity, religious minorities, and intersectional theory. Currently, she is working on a book manuscript about contemporary feminist adaptations of fairy tales in German-language literature.

Notes

1. "Bayern ist Bundesland, wo regieren die Schwarzen, und ich komme an, sind alle weiß" (Dave Davis intentionally uses incorrect German grammar here).
2. Max Czollek, "Gegenwartsbewältigung," in *Eure Heimat ist unser Alptraum*, ed. Fatma Aydemir and Hengameh Yaghoobifarah (Berlin: Ullstein, 2019), 179.
3. Not all German Jews necessarily consider themselves People of Color as opposed to "racialized Germans."
4. Azadeh Sharifi, "Theatre and Migration Documentation, Influences and Perspectives in European Theatre," in *Independent Theatre in Contemporary Europe Book Subtitle: Structures—Aesthetics—Cultural Policy*, ed. Manfred Brauneck and ITI Germany (Bielefeld: transcript, 2017), 328.
5. Fatima El-Tayeb, *Undeutsch: Die Konstruktion des Anderen in der postmigrantischen Gesellschaft* (Bielefeld: transcript, 2016), 26. "Es besteht ein kausaler Zusammenhang zwischen dem Scheitern von Europas multikultureller Gegenwart und der kontinentalen Rassismusamnesie."
6. Fatima El-Tayeb, *European Others: Queering Ethnicity in Postnational Europe* (Minneapolis: University of Minnesota Press, 2011), 27.
7. Ezli Özkan, Deniz Göktürk, and Uwe Wirth, eds., "Vorwort," *Komik der Integration: Grenzpraktiken und Identifikationen des Sozialen* (Bielefeld: Aisthesis, 2019), 10. "..., dass man in den letzten 20 Jahren die Verbreitung eines besonderen Typus von *transcultural comedy* beobachten kann, die implizit ablaufende Zugehörigkeitsverhandlungen und Grenzpraktiken explizit macht und damit die doppelte Dynamik von Integration und Desintegration performativ zur Schau stellt."
8. Uwe Wirth, "Komik der Integration," *Komik der Integration: Grenzpraktiken und Identifikationen des Sozialen* (Bielefeld: Aisthesis, 2019), 34. "Die nicht dem gesetzten Standard des rassistisch-kolonialistisch geprägten Europas um 1900 entsprechende Hautfarbe wird damit zum Symptom einer kulturellen Unangepasstheit, die der Korrektur bedarf. Und das bedeutet auch: Wer in dieser Weise *kulturell auffällig* wird, der wird potentiell auch zum Lachgegenstand, weil er nicht genügend Aufwand betrieben hat, um sich anzupassen – oder weil er es *trotz* eines immensen Aufwandes, nicht geschafft hat, sich *unauffällig* anzupassen."
9. Joann R. Gilbert, *Performing Marginality: Humor, Gender, and Cultural Critique* (Detroit: Wayne State University Press, 2004), 137.
10. Gilbert, *Performing Marginality*, 140. Humor as a rhetorical tool and its role in social interactions, literary contributions, and cultural performance is difficult to define. As Sean Zwagerman writes in *Wit's End: Women's Humor as Rhetorical and Performative Strategy*, "Humor's use of multiple meanings, of indirection and implication, its play with language and conventions—in a word, its shiftiness—seems to confound every attempt to contain humor within clear categories, definitions, or theories." Sean Zwager-

man, *Wit's End: Women's Humor as Rhetorical and Performative Strategy* (Pittsburgh: University of Pittsburgh Press, 2010), 1.
11. Hanni Mittelmann, "Reconceptualization of Jewish Identity as Reflected in Contemporary German-Jewish Humorist Literature," *Being Jewish in 21st-Century Germany*, ed. Haim Fireberg and Olaf Glöckner (Berlin: De Gruyter, 2015), 137.
12. Compare Gerald Beyrodt, "Jüdische Witze: Genervt von der Übermutter," *Deutschlandfunk Kultur*, 6 May 2016, retrieved 30 November 2021 from https://www.deutsch landfunkkultur.de/juedische-witze-genervt-von-der-uebermutter-100.html.
13. Compare Frederic Schwilden, "Tagebuch eines Onanisten: Oliver Polak ist der Meister der geschmackvollsten geschmacklosen Witze," *Die Zeit*, 24 October 2018, retrieved 30 November 2021 from https://www.zeit.de/kultur/literatur/2014-10/oliver-polak-der-juedische-patient.
14. Herbert Lefcourt, *Humor: The Psychology of Living Buoyantly* (New York: Kluwer Academic, 2001), 133.
15. The term *Biodeutsche* is itself problematic but has been used to describe ethnic Germans who are supposedly a white ethnic group. The term reinscribes the idea that a nation is made up of a biological group that belongs together and thus constitutes a homogenous group.
16. The term *Migrationshintergrund* also has a problematic connotation and separates those who have a different ethnic background and darker skin color or darker hair from those with white *Migrationshintergrund*, who come from other countries but whose integration has not been considered a problem.
17. Susan Arndt, "'Rassen' gibt es nicht, wohl aber die symbolische Ordnung von *Rasse*: Der Racial Turn als Gegennarrativ zur Verleugnung und Hierarchisierung von Rassismus," *Mythen, Masken und Subjekte: Kritische Weißseinsforschung in Deutschland*, ed. Maureen Maisha Eggers, Grada Kilomba, Peggy Piesche, and Susan Arndt (Münster: Unrast, 2017), 348. "Gesellschaftliche, politische und kulturelle Formationsprozesse fußen auf einem historischen Rassialisierungsprozess, bei dem Weißsein eine hegemoniale Rolle zukommt. Diese Hegemonien und Differenzen können nicht einfach nur dadurch überwunden werden, dass sie negiert oder ignoriert werden."
18. Wulf D. Hund, *Wie die Deutschen Weiß Wurden: Kleine (Heimat-)Geschichte des Rassismus* (Metzler, 2017), 6. "Doch deutsches Weißsein war nicht nur ambivalent. Es hatte in einem langwierigen und komplizierten Prozess allererst erzeugt werden müssen. Denn von Natur aus gibt es weder Rassen noch Weiße. Die sind ideologische Kopfgeburten der europäischen Expansion und mit Hilfe kolonialer Gewalt zur Welt gekommen, ehe sie im 18. Jahrhundert von der Aufklärung systematisiert und zu wissenschaftlichen Kategorien gemacht wurden."
19. Andrej Klahn, "Warum wir plötzlich über Ausländer lachen dürfen," *Die Welt*, 29 November 2014, retrieved 30 November 2021 from https://www.welt.de/regionales/nrw/article134786771/Warum-wir-ploetzlich-ueber-Auslaender-lachen-duerfen.html. "Mit Kaya Yanar und Bülent Ceylan gelang der sogenannten Ethno-Comedy nach der Jahrtausendwende der massenmediale Durchbruch."
20. Klahn, "Warum wir plötzlich." "Ethno-Comedy hat großen Erfolg. Künstler wie RebellComedy und Abdelkarim ziehen die Klischees über ihre Herkunft genauso ins Lächerliche wie sich selbst. Dem bunt gemischten Publikum gefällt es."
21. Oxford Reference, "Strategic Essentialism," retrieved 28 November 2020 from https://www.oxfordreference.com/view/10.1093/oi/authority.20110803100536145.

22. Homi Bhabha, "The Other Question: Homi Bhabha Reconsiders the Stereotype and Colonial Discourse," *Screen* 24, no. 6 (1983): 18.
23. Bhabha, "Other Question," 18.
24. David Huddart, *Homi K. Bhabha* (New York: Routledge: 2006), 24.
25. Huddart, *Bhabha*, 24.
26. Lars Koch, "Das Lachen der Subalternen: Die Ethno-Comedy in Deutschland," in *Wie die Welt lacht: Lachkulturen im Vergleich*, ed. Waltraud Wende (Würzburg: Königshausen & Neumann, 2008), 210.
27. Antonin J. Obrdlik, "'Gallows Humor'—A Sociological Phenomenon." *American Journal of Sociology* 47, no. 5 (1942): 710.
28. Obrdlik, "Gallows Humor," 712.
29. Obrdlik, "Gallows Humor," 716.
30. Obrdlik, "Gallows Humor," 715.
31. Manuel, Gogos, "Fallhöhe: Jüdischer Humor in Deutschland," *Deutschlandfunk Kultur*, 1 December 2019, retrieved 30 November 2021 from https://www.hoerspielundfeature.de/juedischer-humor-in-deutschland-fallhoehe-100.html.
32. Gina Barreca, *They Used to Call Me Snow White but I Drifted: Women's Strategic Use of Humor* (New York: Penguin, 1992), 210.
33. In Denmark, journalists of *Jyllands Posten* faced death threats after depicting Islamic religious figures in cartoons in 2005.
34. In authoritarian countries, censorship restricts the freedom of speech and expression through cartoon art or other forms of satire. Satirical portrayals of governments, rulers, and governing heads of state have a long tradition, and cartoonists have for centuries used satire to criticize governments.
35. While Böhmermann is a well-known German comedian who has his own TV show and has also hosted Somuncu and Polak, Oliver Polak has claimed in one of his books that Böhmermann has exhibited antisemitic behavior and made aggressive comments about his Jewishness toward Polak before and after one of Polak's skits. Compare Stefan Niggemeier, "Ein Gag, der keiner war: Oliver Polak wirft in seinem Buch einem Moderator antisemitisches Verhalten vor," *Freitag* 43 (2018), retrieved 30 November 2021 from https://www.freitag.de/autoren/der-freitag/ein-gag-der-keiner-war.
36. Michael Meyer, "Satire in Deutschland: Lachen als Aufklärung." *Deutschlandfunk*, 7 January 2017, retrieved 30 November 2021 from http://www.deutschlandfunk.de/satire-in-deutschland-lachen-als-aufklaerung.761.de.html?dram:article_id=375790. "Angesichts der vielen Krisen und Konflikte in der Welt und dem Vormarsch der Populisten, flüchten sich die Zuschauer in die Satire. Kein Wunder: sie kann, darf und muss natürlich viel stärker zuspitzen."
37. Qtd. in Meyer, "Satire in Deutschland." "Humor basiert immer auf einem Erwartungsbruch, und dazu kann ja auch der Tabubruch gezählt werden. . . . Dementsprechend muss da auch immer ein bisschen mit dem Erlaubten gespielt werden."
38. Zafer Senocak, *Deutschsein: Eine Aufklärungsschrift* (Edition Körber, 2011), 65. "Die Andersartigkeit von osteuropäischen Juden gestern und nahöstlichen Muslimen heute steht im Mittelpunkt einer deutschen Identitätsdebatte, die inzwischen die deutsch-deutsche Teilung als Thema verdrängt hat."
39. "Ich fühl mich so burnt out. . . . Dürfen Juden das eigentlich in einer deutschen Comedy Show sagen?"
40. Nick Block, "A Berlin Republic Convevencia? Ethnic Tensions in the Turkish-German-Jewish Triangle," *German Studies Review* 40, no. 2 (May 2017): 356.

41. Compare Niggemeier, "Ein Gag, der keiner war."
42. Oliver Polak, "Es geht auch um Onanie bei Sartre und Camus," interview with Kathrin Rosendorff, *Die Welt*, 11 March 2014, retrieved 30 November 2021 from https://www.welt.de/kultur/buehne-konzert/article125669873/Es-geht-auch-um-Onanie-bei-Sartre-und-Camus.html. "In meiner Show [*Ich darf das, ich bin Jude*] ging es dann um all die dummen Fragen, die ich mein Leben lang als jüdischer Junge beantworten musste. In Deutschland drückt man ja gerne den Stempel drauf: Das ist der Schwarze, das ist der Jude. Ich habe mich aber sehr dagegen gewehrt. Ständig bekam ich Einladungen zu Shows wie *StandUpMigranten* auf EinsPlus. Mein Booker hat immer geantwortet: 'Äh, Oliver Polak ist Deutscher, was soll er da?' Und ich sage dann immer: 'Dann nennt es doch gleich, was es ist: ein Comedy-KZ.' Jetzt mal ehrlich, warum soll man bitte Comedians in Shows separieren? Entweder ist man lustig oder eben nicht. Für mich klang das wie eine Show, wo es die Bimbos zum Anfassen gibt. Grauenvoll. Hab ich keinen Bock drauf."
43. Feridun Zaimoglu, *Kanak Sprak: 24 Misstöne vom Rande der Gesellschaft* (Rotbuch, 1995), 11.
44. Jewish identity can function in different ways, i.e., not everyone who identifies as Jewish is religious. Max Czollek and Sasha Maria Salzmann critically engage with the question of what it means to be Jewish in Germany in their project of a "Disintegrationskongress," "Gedächtnistheater," and "Integrationsparadigma." Sasha Maria Salzmann, "Sichtbar," in *Eure Heimat ist unser Alptraum*, ed. Fatma Azdemir and Hengameh Yaghoobifarah (Berlin: Ullstein, 2019), 18–26; Czollek, "Gegenwartsbewältigung," 168–81.
45. Thomas Lindemann and Cl. Schumacher, "Wir kriegen auf die Fresse, die anderen die Preise," interview with Oliver Polak, *Die Welt*, 14 April 2010, retrieved 30 November 2021 from https://www.welt.de/welt_print/kultur/article7172678/Wir-kriegen-auf-die-Fresse-die-anderen-die-Preise.html. "Das ist alles Unsinn. Gerade erst kam eine Anfrage: Da hatte ein Veranstalter einen türkischen Komiker und einen schwarzen und ich sollte auch auftreten, weil ich angeblich so gut reinpassen würde. Natürlich gehe ich nicht hin. Wir wollen nicht ins Comedy-KZ. Ich mache Stand-up-Comedy. . . . Eigentlich aber kommt der Stand Up von Leuten wie Bill Murray, Steve Martin, Jim Carrey oder Eddie Murphy. Die gehen auf die Bühne und erzählen authentisch auch Unbequemes aus ihrem Leben."
46. Annika Orich, "'Wir wollen nicht ins Comedy-KZ': Serdar Somuncu, Oliver Polak, Ethno-Komik und deutsche Zugehörigkeits- und Erinnerungskultur," in *Komik der Integration: Grenzpraktiken und Identifikationen des Sozialen*, ed. Özkan Ezli, Deniz Göktürk, and Uwe Wirth (Bielefeld: Aisthesis, 2019), 292. "Auch wenn Polak eine familiäre, hereditäre Beziehung zur Vergangenheit für sich in Anspruch nehmen könnte, versucht er immer wieder sich gegen eine derartige Einordnung durch sein Publikum und reduzierendes Denken zu stellen. 'Als was fühle ich mich? Und da muss ich zugeben: Würde man mir die Option 'Jude,' 'Deutscher' oder 'Komiker' anbieten, ich würde wohl den 'Komiker' ankreuzen."
47. "Beide lernen spezielle, besondere und interessante Menschen kennen, um für und über diese Menschen ein Stand-up-Comedy-Programm zu schreiben."
48. Meyer, "Satire in Deutschland." "Was neu war an der Sendung war, dass man diese Gruppen selber getroffen hat, und da gab es nochmal eine ganz andere Ebene, dass es nicht so ein Betroffenheitsding war, sondern, es ist ja auch eine Form von Rassismus, wenn man keine Witze über diese Menschen machen würde und die ausgrenzen würde."

49. Compare Frank Meyer, "Deutschland ist humorbehindert: Der Stand-up-Comedian Oliver Polak über seine Depressionen und deutsches Kabarett," *Deutschlandfunk Kultur*, 5 November 2014.
50. Daniel Lücking, "*Applaus und raus:* Eine Provokation zu viel," *Der Tagesspiegel*, 26 October 2016, retrieved 30 November 2021 from https://www.tagesspiegel.de/medien/applaus-und-raus-eine-provokation-zu-viel/14742780.html. "'Mit dem Konzept, dass Gäste, die den Moderator langweilen, dann einfach zum Spast erklärt und rausgeschmissen werden, wird der Begriff wieder als Schimpfwort salonfähig. Egal wie der Gast vorher schon beleidigt wurde, ein "Spast" zu sein, wird jedes Mal zur größten Beleidigung.' Damit würden nicht nur Menschen diskriminiert, die eine Spastik haben, sondern auch das aktuell so wichtige Engagement gegen Hate Speech in den Sozialen Medien geschwächt."
51. Compare Andrea Hanna Hünninger, "Herr Polak, wie macht man Gags über Randgruppen?" *Die Welt*, 31 August 2015, retrieved 30 November 2021 from https://www.welt.de/kultur/medien/article145844993/Herr-Polak-wie-macht-man-Gags-ueber-Randgruppen.html.
52. Tom Coogan, "'Usually I Love *The Onion*, but This Time You've Gone Too Far': Disability Humour and Transgression," *Journal of Literary & Cultural Disability Studies* 7, no. 1 (2013): 6.
53. Coogan, "'Usually I Love *The Onion*," 6–7.
54. "Junge, Junge, hier so viele Albino-Äffchen, da hab ich doch Spaß. Mein Name ist Motombo Umbokko."
55. "Ich war in Leipzig. Drei Schwarze wurden von 50 Weißen gejagt . . . war ein Marathon-Lauf."
56. Thomas Kölsch, "Kabarettist Dave Davis im Interview: Stärker polarisieren," interview with Dave Davis, *Rhein Zeitung*, 19 October 2014, retrieved 30 November 2021 from https://www.rhein-zeitung.de/kultur_artikel,-kabarettist-dave-davis-im-interview-staerker-polarisieren-_arid,1221713.html. "Aber damit dann hier in Deutschland Ängste gegen jeden zu schüren, der dem Islam zugehörig ist, halte ich für sehr gefährlich. Da werden Feindbilder kreiert."
57. The terms for Black Germans have evolved over time from the "N" word and "Moor" to "colored" (*Farbiger*) to, finally, "Afro-German" (Afro-Deutscher) and "Black German" (Schwarzer Deutscher).
58. Dave Davis, "Kabarettist Dave Davis: Der Bayer ist Deutschlands Afrikaner," interview with Tobias Röber, *Aachener Zeitung*, 28 August 2014, retrieved 30 November 2021 from http://www.aachener-zeitung.de/lokales/eschweiler/kabarettist-dave-davis-der-bayer-ist-deutschlands-afrikaner-1.903368. "Ich bin da typisch deutsch und wollte erstmal was Solides machen. . . . Ich habe alles auf eine Karte gesetzt und ins Schwarze getroffen."
59. "Zu viel Brei verdirbt den Koch" instead of "zu viele Köche verderben den Brei" and "Der fette Vogel bricht den Ast," a saying that was commonly used as a funny pun in 2010 and that plays with "Lieber ein Spatz in der Hand als die Taube auf dem Dach."
60. Jamele Watkins, "The Drama of Race: Contemporary Afro-German Theater" (PhD diss., University of Massachussetts, Amherst, 2017), 100.
61. Dave Davis, "Kabarettist Dave Davis: Der Bayer ist Deutschlands Afrikaner." "Bülent Ceylan zum Beispiel kann in Mannheim nicht mehr ohne Bodyguard aus dem Haus gehen."

62. "Leute sprechen mich an und fragen, ob ich Deutsch spreche. Dann frage ich die blonde Verkäuferin: 'Sprechen Sie Deutsch?' Dann hab ich gesagt, ein Croissant, bitte."
63. Leslie Adelson, *The Turkish Turn in Contemporary German Literature* (New York: Palgrave Macmillan, 2005), 269.
64. Maha El Hissy, *Getürkte Türken: Karnevaleske Stilmittel im Theater, Kabarett und Film deutsch-türkischer Künstlerinnen und Künstler* (Bielefeld: transcript, 2012) 145–84; Erol Boran, *Eine Geschichte des türkisch-deutschen Theaters und politischen Kabaretts* (PhD diss., Ohio State University, 2004), 201–90.
65. "Ich lass mich zum Klassensprecher wählen. Die Rede habe ich in der Diktion meines größten Vorbilds gehalten. Eines Tages. ... Die sagten, der Typ hat was drauf." *Der Hassprediger*, 13 September 2013.
66. Maha El Hissy, *Getürkte Türken*, 177. "Das Groteske der Fäkalsprache."
67. Christoph Schlingensief was a controversial German performance artist, Anne Will is the host of a German political TV talk show, and Frank Plasberg is the host of the TV show *Hart aber fair*, on which political issues are discussed.
68. Compare David Hughes, "Everything in Excess—Christoph Schlingensief and the Crisis of the German Left," *Germanic Review* 81, no. 4 (2007): 317–39; Paul David Young, "Tasteless, Crude, and Politically Progressive," *PAJ: A Journal of Performance and Art* 36, no. 3 (2014): 73.
69. Kathrin Bower, "Serdar Somuncu: Turkish German Comedy as Transnational Intervention," *Transit* 7, no. 1 (2011), retrieved 30 November 2021 from https://transit.berkeley.edu/2011/bower/.
70. Young, "Tasteless, Crude, and Politically Progressive," 73.
71. "Diese Arschlöcher nehmen sich raus, im Namen der Gebührenzahler, uns zu zensieren. Und das war für mich die Keimzelle des Faschismus." Bernhard Jarosch, "Klage gegen Satiriker: Unerhörter Witz," *Frankfurter Allgemeine Zeitung*, 11 January 2017, retrieved 30 November 2021 from http://www.faz.net/aktuell/feuilleton/medien/klage-gegen-satiriker-unerhoerter-witz-14620636.html.
72. Christian Buß, "Zensurvorwurf von Serdar Somuncu: Wut-Türke gegen WDRdogan," *Der Spiegel*, 12 January 2017, retrieved 30 November 2021 from http://www.spiegel.de/kultur/tv/serdar-somuncu-zensurvorwurf-gegen-den-wdr-wegen-pussy-terror-a-1129627.html. "Der Fall bleibt also unübersichtlich. Und das hat auch mit dem Umstand zu tun, dass bei Serdar Somuncu die Grenzen zwischen Bühnenperson und realer Person fließend sind. Man bucht den Kabarettisten als—lustig!—verbal voll entgleisenden Wut-Türken vor die Kamera und bekommt—unlustig!—den verbal voll entgleisenden Wut-Türken auch als Geschäftspartner. Und oben drauf auch noch als Kritiker struktureller Probleme im öffentlich-rechtlichen Rundfunk, der dabei mit Begriffen wie 'Arschloch' operiert."
73. Serdar Somuncu, "Ich glaube diese ganze Refugee-Welcome-Kacke nicht," interview with Markus Ehrenberg, *Der Tagesspiegel*, 29 January 2016, retrieved 30 November 2021 from https://www.tagesspiegel.de/medien/interview-mit-serdar-somuncu-ich-glaube-diese-ganze-refugees-welcome-kacke-nicht/12893066.html. "Den Comedian-Redaktionen bin ich zu untürkisch, um Klischee-Türke zu sein. Den Talkshow-Redaktionen war ich zu lang zu wenig Kabarettist, um Kabarettist zu sein und zu wenig Politiker, um Politiker zu sein. Erst als ich mal bei *Anne Will* und *Maybrit Illner* saß, hat man gemerkt, he, der Mann muss sich gar nicht definieren. Der hat eine Meinung, das reicht. Am Anfang bin ich immer zu Integrations-Themen eingeladen worden, als der Quoten-Kanake."

74. Kathrin Bower, "Serdar Somuncu: Reframing Integration through a Transnational Politics of Satire," *The German Quarterly* 85, no. 2 (2012): 204.
75. Kathrin Bower, "Made in Germany: Integration as Inside Joke in the Ethno-comedy of Kaya Yanar and Bülent Ceylan," *German Studies Review* 37, no. 2 (2014): 357. Compare also Bower, "Serdar Somuncu: Reframing Integration," 213.
76. Bower, "Serdar Somuncu: Turkish German Comedy."
77. Oliver Polak, "Zu Applaus und raus: Ich bin der perfekte Moderator," interview with Gunda Bartels, 24 October 2016, retrieved 30 November 2021 from https://www.tagesspiegel.de/medien/oliver-polak-zu-applaus-und-raus-ich-bin-der-perfekte-moderator/14722576.html. "Auf Dieter Nuhr beispielsweise hätte ich keinen Fall Bock. Im Gegensatz zu Serdar Somuncu, der derzeit als Einziger in Deutschland schlaue, inhaltlich relevante Comedy macht. Deswegen sitzt er auch ständig bei *Anne Will*."
78. Timo Steppat, "Serdar Somuncu im Porträt: Weil er einfach Bock drauf hat," *Frankfurter Allgemeine Zeitung*, 14 July 2016, retrieved 30 November 2021 from http://www.faz.net/aktuell/gesellschaft/menschen/serdar-somuncu-im-portraet-14333078.html. "Es fällt schwer, es so ganz zu glauben, aber Serdar Somuncu ist in den vergangenen Jahren zu einer ernstzunehmenden Stimme geworden, einerseits. Er sitzt bei 'Anne Will' oder 'Hart aber fair' und diskutiert mit Edmund Stoiber oder Claudia Roth. Er ist klug und analytisch, ein guter Diskutant. Er ist aber andererseits auch— zumindest in seinen Soloshows—zu vulgär, um als Vorzeige-Migrant zu firmieren. Das ist das Spannungsfeld, das Somuncu ungewöhnlich und erfolgreich macht. . . . Es ist nicht Comedy, was Somuncu macht, ebenso wenig wie Kabarett, dafür ist er zu laut und vulgär. Somuncu sieht seine Auftritte als kleine Theaterstücke, er selbst sei in erster Linie ein Künstler."
79. Hughes, "Everything in Excess—Christoph Schlingenseif and the Crisis of the German Left," 324.
80. Serdar Somuncu, "Ist Serdar Somuncu der nächste Sonneborn?" interview with Jan Sternberg, *Märkische Allgemeine*, 29 January 2017, retrieved 30 November 2021 from http://www.maz-online.de/Nachrichten/Kultur/Ist-Serdar-Somuncu-der-naechste-Sonneborn. "Ich bin lediglich designierter Kanzlerkandidat . . . wenn man sich noch mal daran erinnert, wie nahe die Realität in Sachen Böhmermann und Erdoğan an die Politik rangerückt ist, dann finde ich es nur zeitgemäß, wie Sonneborn Politik macht. Satire macht eben auch Politik, und Politik ist manchmal auch Satire."
81. Somuncu, "Ist Serdar Somuncu der nächste Sonneborn?" "Ich will eine inhaltliche Debatte. Man darf aus Angst vor den Populisten nicht die Argumente scheuen."

Bibliography

Adelson, Leslie. *The Turkish Turn in Contemporary German Literature*. New York: Palgrave Macmillan, 2005.

Arndt, Susan. "'Rassen' gibt es nicht, wohl aber die symbolische Ordnung von *Rasse*: Der Racial Turn als Gegennarrativ zur Verleugnung und Hierarchisierung von Rassismus." In *Mythen, Masken und Subjekte: Kritische Weißseinsforschung in Deutschland*, edited by Maureen Maisha Eggers, Grada Kilomba, Peggy Piesche, and Susan Arndt, 340–62. Münster: Unrast, 2017.

Barreca, Gina. *They Used to Call Me Snow White but I Drifted: Women's Strategic Use of Humor*. New York: Penguin, 1992.
Beyrodt, Gerald. "Jüdische Witze: Genervt von der Übermutter." *Deutschlandfunk Kultur*, 6 May 2016. Retrieved 30 November 2021 from https://www.deutschlandfunkkultur.de/juedische-witze-genervt-von-der-uebermutter-100.html.
Bhabha, Homi. "The Other Question: Homi Bhabha Reconsiders the Stereotype and Colonial Discourse." *Screen* 24, no. 6 (1983): 18–36.
Block, Nick. "A Berlin Republic Convevencia? Ethnic Tensions in the Turkish-German-Jewish Triangle." *German Studies Review* 40, no. 2 (May 2017): 353–71.
Böhmermann, Jan. "Neo Magazine Royale." Vimeo, 31 March 2016. Retrieved 30 November 2021 from https://vimeo.com/161209329.
Boran, Erol. *Eine Geschichte des türkisch-deutschen Theaters und politischen Kabaretts*. PhD diss., Ohio State University, 2004.
Bower, Kathrin. "Made in Germany: Integration as Inside Joke in the Ethno-comedy of Kaya Yanar and Bülent Ceylan." *German Studies Review* 37, no. 2 (2014): 357–76.
———. "Serdar Somuncu: Reframing Integration through a Transnational Politics of Satire." *The German Quarterly* 85, no. 2 (2012): 193–213.
———. "Serdar Somuncu: Turkish German Comedy as Transnational Intervention." *Transit* 7, no. 1 (2011). https://transit.berkeley.edu/2011/bower/.
Buß, Christian. "Zensurvorwurf von Serdar Somuncu: Wut-Türke gegen WDRdogan." *Der Spiegel*, 12 January 2017. Retrieved 30 November 2021 from http://www.spiegel.de/kultur/tv/serdar-somuncu-zensurvorwurf-gegen-den-wdr-wegen-pussyterror-a-1129627.html.
Coogan, Tom. "'Usually I Love *The Onion*, but This Time You've Gone Too Far': Disability Humour and Transgression." *Journal of Literary & Cultural Disability Studies* 7, no. 1 (2013): 1–17.
Czollek, Max. "Gegenwartsbewältigung." In *Eure Heimat ist unser Alptraum*, edited by Fatma Aydemir and Hengameh Yaghoobifarah, 167–94. Berlin: Ullstein, 2019.
Davis, Dave. "Kabarettist Dave Davis: Der Bayer ist Deutschlands Afrikaner." Interview with Tobias Röber. *Aachener Zeitung*, 28 August 2014. Retrieved 30 November 2021 from http://www.aachener-zeitung.de/lokales/eschweiler/kabarettist-dave-davis-der-bayer-ist-deutschlands-afrikaner-1.903368.
El Hissy, Maha. *Getürkte Türken: Karnevaleske Stilmittel im Theater, Kabarett und Film deutsch-türkischer Künstlerinnen und Künstler*. Bielefeld: transcript, 2012.
El-Tayeb, Fatima. *European Others: Queering Ethnicity in Postnational Europe*. Minneapolis: University of Minnesota Press, 2011.
———. *Undeutsch: Die Konstruktion des Anderen in der postmigrantischen Gesellschaft*. Bielefeld: transcript, 2016.
Gilbert, Joanne R. *Performing Marginality: Humor, Gender, and Cultural Critique*. Detroit: Wayne State University Press, 2004.
Gogos, Manuel. "Fallhöhe: Jüdischer Humor in Deutschland." *Deutschlandfunk Kultur*, 1 December 2019. Retrieved 30 November 2021 from https://www.hoerspielundfeature.de/juedischer-humor-in-deutschland-fallhoehe-100.html.
"Grimme-Preis für Polak und Böhmermann." *Der Spiegel*, 8 March 2017. http://www.spiegel.de/kultur/tv/grimme-preis-2017-auszeichnungen-fuer-jan-boehmermann-oliver-polak-nsu-film-a-1134911.html
Huddart, David. *Homi K. Bhabha*. New York: Routledge, 2006.

Hughes, David. "Everything in Excess—Christoph Schlingenseif and the Crisis of the German Left." *Germanic Review* 81, no. 4 (2007): 317–39.

Hund, Wulf D. *Wie die Deutschen weiß wurden: Kleine (Heimat-)Geschichte des Rassismus.* Stuttgart: Metzler, 2017.

Hünninger, Andrea Hanna. "Herr Polak, wie macht man Gags über Randgruppen?" *Die Welt*, 31 August 2015. https://www.welt.de/kultur/medien/article145844993/Herr-Polak-wie-macht-man-Gags-ueber-Randgruppen.html.

Jarosch, Bernhard. "Klage gegen Satiriker: Unerhörter Witz." *Frankfurter Allgemeine Zeitung*, 11 January 2017. Retrieved 30 November 2021 from http://www.faz.net/aktuell/feuilleton/medien/klage-gegen-satiriker-unerhoerter-witz-14620636.html.

Klahn, Andrej. "Warum wir plötzlich über Ausländer lachen dürfen." *Die Welt*, 29 November 2014. Retrieved 30 November 2021 from https://www.welt.de/regionales/nrw/article134786771/Warum-wir-ploetzlich-ueber-Auslaender-lachen-duerfen.html.

Koch, Lars. "Das Lachen der Subalternen: Die Ethno-Comedy in Deutschland." In *Wie die Welt lacht: Lachkulturen im Vergleich*, edited by Waltraud Wende, 208–23. Würzburg: Königshausen & Neumann, 2008.

Kölsch, Thomas. "Kabarettist Dave Davis im Interview: Stärker polarisieren." Interview with Dave Davis. *Rhein Zeitung*, 19 October 2014. Retrieved 30 November 2021 from https://www.rhein-zeitung.de/kultur_artikel,-kabarettist-dave-davis-im-interview-staerker-polarisieren-_arid,1221713.html.

Lefcourt, Herbert. *Humor: The Psychology of Living Buoyantly.* New York: Kluwer Academic, 2001.

Lindemann, Thomas, and Cl. Schumacher. "Wir kriegen auf die Fresse, die anderen die Preise." Interview with Oliver Polak. *Die Welt*, 14 April 2010. Retrieved 30 November 2021 from https://www.welt.de/welt_print/kultur/article7172678/Wir-kriegen-auf-die-Fresse-die-anderen-die-Preise.html.

Lücking, Daniel. "*Applaus und raus*: Eine Provokation zu viel." *Der Tagesspiegel*, 26 October 2016. Retrieved 30 November 2021 from https://www.tagesspiegel.de/medien/applaus-und-raus-eine-provokation-zu-viel/14742780.html.

Meyer, Frank. "Deutschland ist humorbehindert: Der Stand-up-Comedian Oliver Polak über seine Depressionen und deutsches Kabarett." *Deutschlandfunk Kultur*, 5 November 2014.

Meyer, Michael. "Satire in Deutschland: Lachen als Aufklärung." *Deutschlandfunk*, 7 January 2017. Retrieved 30 November 2021 from http://www.deutschlandfunk.de/satire-in-deutschland-lachen-als-aufklaerung.761.de.html?dram:article_id=375790.

Mittelmann, Hanni. "Reconceptualization of Jewish Identity as Reflected in Contemporary German-Jewish Humorist Literature." In *Being Jewish in 21st-Century Germany*, edited by Haim Fireberg and Olaf Glöckner, 131–41. Berlin: De Gruyter, 2015.

Niggemeier, Stefan. "Ein Gag, der keiner war: Oliver Polak wirft in seinem Buch einem Moderator antisemitisches Verhalten vor." *Freitag* 43 (2018). Retrieved 30 November 2021 from https://www.freitag.de/autoren/der-freitag/ein-gag-der-keiner-war.

Obrdlik, Antonin J. "'Gallows Humor'—A Sociological Phenomenon." *American Journal of Sociology* 47, no. 5 (1942): 709–16.

Orich, Annika. "'Wir wollen nicht ins Comedy-KZ': Serdar Somuncu, Oliver Polak, Ethno-Komik und deutsche Zugehörigkeits- und Erinnerungskultur." In *Komik der Integration: Grenzpraktiken und Identifikationen des Sozialen*, edited by Özkan Ezli, Deniz Göktürk, and Uwe Wirth, 273–97. Bielefeld: Aisthesis, 2019.

Özkan, Ezli, Deniz Göktürk, and Uwe Wirth, eds. "Vorwort." *Komik der Integration: Grenzpraktiken und Identifikationen des Sozialen*, 7–18. Bielefeld: Aisthesis, 2019.

Polak, Oliver. "Es geht auch um Onanie bei Sartre und Camus." Interview with Kathrin Rosendorff. *Die Welt*, 11 March 2014. Retrieved 30 November 2021 from https://www.welt.de/kultur/buehne-konzert/article125669873/Es-geht-auch-um-Onanie-bei-Sartre-und-Camus.html.

———. "Psychiatrie-Ansichten eines Clowns." Interview with Barbara Mader. *Der Kurier*, 21 October 2014. Retrieved 30 November 2021 from https://kurier.at/kultur/oliver-polak-psychiatrie-ansichten-eines-clowns/92.316.315.

———. "Zu Applaus und raus: Ich bin der perfekte Moderator." Interview with Gunda Bartels. *Der Tagesspiegel*, 24 October 2016. Retrieved 30 November 2021 from https://www.tagesspiegel.de/medien/oliver-polak-zu-applaus-und-raus-ich-bin-der-perfekte-moderator/14722576.html.

Salzmann, Sasha Maria. "Sichtbar." In *Eure Heimat ist unser Alptraum*, edited by Fatma Azdemir and Hengameh Yaghoobifarah, 13–26. Berlin: Ullstein, 2019.

Schwilden, Frederic. "Tagebuch eines Onanisten: Oliver Polak ist der Meister der geschmackvollsten geschmacklosen Witze." *Die Zeit*, 24 October 2018. Retrieved 30 November 2021 from https://www.zeit.de/kultur/literatur/2014-10/oliver-polak-der-juedische-patient.

Senocak, Zafer. *Deutschsein: Eine Aufklärungsschrift*. Edition Körber, 2011.

Sharifi, Azadeh. "Theatre and Migration Documentation, Influences and Perspectives in European Theatre." In *Independent Theatre in Contemporary Europe Book Subtitle: Structures—Aesthetics—Cultural Policy*, edited by Manfred Brauneck and ITI Germany, 321–415. Bielefeld: transcript, 2017.

Somuncu, Serdar. "Ich glaube diese ganze Refugee-Welcome-Kacke nicht." Interview with Markus Ehrenberg. *Der Tagesspiegel*, 29 January 2016. Retrieved 30 November 2021 from https://www.tagesspiegel.de/medien/interview-mit-serdar-somuncu-ich-glaube-diese-ganze-refugees-welcome-kacke-nicht/12893066.html.

———. "Ist Serdar Somuncu der nächste Sonneborn?" Interview with Jan Sternberg. *Märkische Allgemeine*, 29 January 2017. Retrieved 30 November 2021 from http://www.maz-online.de/Nachrichten/Kultur/Ist-Serdar-Somuncu-der-naechste-Sonneborn.

Steppat, Timo. "Serdar Somuncu im Porträt: Weil er einfach Bock drauf hat." *Frankfurter Allgemeine Zeitung*, 14 July 2016. Retrieved 30 November 2021 from http://www.faz.net/aktuell/gesellschaft/menschen/serdar-somuncu-im-portraet-14333078.html.

Watkins, Jamele. "The Drama of Race: Contemporary Afro-German Theater." PhD diss., University of Massachussetts, Amherst, 2017.

Wirth, Uwe. "Komik der Integration." In *Komik der Integration: Grenzpraktiken und Identifikationen des Sozialen*, edited by Özkan, Ezli, Deniz Göktürk, and Uwe Wirth, 19–42. Bielefeld: Aisthesis, 2019.

Young, Paul David. "Tasteless, Crude, and Politically Progressive." *PAJ: A Journal of Performance and Art* 36, no. 3 (2014): 73–79.

Zaimoglu, Feridun. *Kanak Sprak: 24 Misstöne vom Rande der Gesellschaft*. Rotbuch, 1995.

Zwagerman, Sean. *Wit's End: Women's Humor as Rhetorical and Performative Strategy*. Pittsburgh: University of Pittsburgh Press, 2010.

CHAPTER 6

Dialogue and Intersection in German Holocaust Memory Culture
Stumbling Blocks and the Memorial to the Murdered Jews of Europe

NICK BLOCK

Berlin's layered history is acutely evident at the intersection of Brunnenstraße and Bernauer Straße, the northern border of the central Mitte district. The open-air Berlin Wall Memorial (Gedenkstätte Berliner Mauer) is situated just down the block from a synagogue complex with an elementary school and a yeshiva in former East Berlin's newly reconstituted Jewish community. Here passersby read names on plaques embedded in the ground, not the familiar names of Holocaust victims on stumbling blocks (*Stolpersteine*) but those of East Germans who fled to West Berlin over Bernauer Straße.[1] These plaques, installed between 2010 and 2014, only differ from the stumbling blocks in that they are circular rather than square, but they clearly echo the earlier memorialization project and indicate a shift in discourse to include German victimhood alongside Jewish victimhood. The names of Else Luft and Walter Michaelis, who were deported from Brunnenstraße to Theresienstadt and Auschwitz, are just a few feet away from the names of Gabriele M. and Frank K., arrested in the same street in the 1980s for attempting to escape. Figures 6.1 and 6.2 show two plaques that stare at each other from across the street.

In the twenty-seven years since Gunter Demnig began laying the stumbling blocks, his project has spread throughout Germany and Europe with over seventy-five thousand stones. The funding model for the stumbling block proj-

Dialogue and Intersection ~ 153

Figure 6.1. Plaque on ground in front of 141A Brunnenstraße commemorating the arrest of Gabriele M., who attempted to flee East Germany in 1989. © Nick Block.

Figure 6.2. Plaque on ground in front of 50 Brunnenstraße commemorating the arrest, deportation, and murder of Walter Michaelis in 1943. © Nick Block.

ect relies on individual donors to sponsor the setting of a stone, usually on the donor's own street of residence.[2] The project's success can be read from this public financial support, the number of plaques, and its influence on other unrelated memorials in the public sphere, as seen at Brunnenstraße. The echoes of Holocaust memorials that mostly commemorate Jewish victims, like the stumbling blocks, resonate throughout Germany's capital city in other contexts and result in a layering of memorialization. Another echo in addition to the Berlin Wall memorial is the Memorial to Homosexuals Persecuted under Nazism (Denkmal für die im Nationalsozialismus verfolgten Homosexuellen) in the Tiergarten, which sits across the street from the football-field-sized Memorial to the Murdered Jews of Europe (Denkmal für die ermordeten Juden Europas). The memorial to homosexuals, opened in 2008, explicitly mimics one of the 2,711 concrete stelae in the Memorial to the Murdered Jews of Europe, which opened in 2005. The similarities in form create a parallel narrative of victimization as designers seek to replicate successful memorials. These new claims of German victimhood are compelling in the face of past scrutiny of memorials such as those for the postwar German expellees from Eastern Europe.[3] The trend of formal elements in Jewish Holocaust memorials being appropriated for disparate victim groups and historical periods marks a new space alongside the singularity of Jewish victimhood that has dominated postwar discourse. Despite the positive public reception (a city council approves the design for every monument after public input), it is ironic that many German Jewish public figures have gone on record against the stumbling block project and other Jewish Holocaust memorials. This chapter seeks to account for this tension between, on the one hand, a seemingly productive dialogue between memorials and, on the other hand, the critiques some Jews in Germany have levied since 2000. Jewish criticism has not been directed, as one might expect, at the appropriation of Holocaust memorials by later memorials nearby but rather at the form of the original Holocaust memorials for Jewish victims. In the following, criticism by Jewish politicians, artists, and authors levied against Gunter Demnig's stumbling blocks and Peter Eisenman's Memorial to the Murdered Jews of Europe will be analyzed, together with recent scholarship on Holocaust memory. This perspective adds to our understanding of working through the past (*Vergangenheitsbewältigung*), showing how the living voices of contemporary Jews in Germany contour the ways in which ethnic Germans confront the past. What roles do "Jewish voices" play in debates about memorials in Germany, and who claims to speak from this perspective? Ultimately, this chapter analyzes these memorials as dialogic, their meaning impregnated with a complex twenty-first-century discourse between Jews, Muslims, and other historically victimized communities (e.g., GDR refugees and homosexuals).

Gunter Demnig's Stumbling Blocks

Every Holocaust memorial has faced opposition.[4] Even before the stumbling blocks started appearing widely in the early 2000s, there were objections to a seeming ubiquity of Holocaust memorials in Germany. In May 1999 federal legislators proposed a bill to shift the planned budget from the grand Memorial to the Murdered Jews of Europe to already standing Holocaust memorials in Berlin.[5] Protests made by Jewish figures, even if they were made for other reasons, thus boosted an existing opposition. Indeed, criticisms by Jews ended up as one of the opposition's main arguments in their campaign to prohibit stumbling blocks in Munich. In 2004, the Munich city council rejected Demnig's project to memorialize the Holocaust with plaques in the sidewalk, citing opposition from the Jewish federation (Israelitische Kultusgemeinde), of which Charlotte Knobloch was the president, as the "democratically legitimate representative of Jews in Munich."[6] Knobloch has been the most vocal and prominent opponent to the stumbling blocks but not the only Jewish one. Family members of those memorialized have themselves protested, using Knobloch's main argument: "I won't allow my family members to be walked on again."[7] Demnig has balked at the suggestion to instead place the memorial stones in the walls of former residences: "The basic thought behind this project is that it is about 'stumbling blocks,' which passersby perchance stumble upon and then begin to ask questions."[8] The Munich city council has opposed Demnig's installations since 2004, and in 2015 it actively removed illegally installed plaques from public streets. In 2017, the council backed a proposal by Kilian Stauss for an alternative memorial that indeed places the square plaques vertically on walls or on freestanding columns to avoid the trampling of the names. Munich is unique as a major German city for its lone holdout stance. Where Munich has none, the five thousandth stone was laid in Berlin in 2013.[9] Of note is that Munich approved an in-ground Holocaust monument for homosexuals. The artist Ulla von Brandenburg opened her installation, known as the Monument to the Gays and Lesbians Persecuted under the Nazi Regime (Denkmal für die im Nationalsozialismus verfolgten Lesben und Schwulen), on 27 June 2017, with approval from the Munich city council in 2011.[10] The monument consists of an array of rainbow colors that have transformed the sidewalk around the former location of the Schwarzfischer bar, known as a gay hangout in Nazi Germany. Though both this monument and the stumbling block project are embedded in the ground for people to walk over, the Munich memorial to homosexuals lacks names. The postwar German term *Mahnmal* (warning memorial) suggests Holocaust memorializations are a warning for non-Jewish citizens rather than something that addresses the needs of the Jewish community. It could be in response to such a viewpoint that the Munich

Jewish community insisted upon sensitivity to the ways that living Jews also perceive these memorials.

Beyond political figures like Knobloch, Jewish artists have criticized the stumbling blocks along similar lines in a series of cultural products. The Jewish comedian Oliver Polak performed the cabaret show *Jud Süß Sauer Die Show* from 2008 to 2012. Polak included the following skit on the stumbling blocks: "On Tuesday I went jogging, . . . went out the door and I slip in front of the door to my building, fell straight on my face. Some murderers put this metal protrusion in front of the door. I called the city right away. I said, 'Hello, what's wrong with all of you? You want to kill me or something?!'" After Oliver explains to the city employee what he is talking about, the official explains:

> "Those are the stumbling blocks."
> "Exactly, that's my problem."
> "Young man, a little more respect. They are there for the Jews . . . for our former Jewish citizens, who lived in those buildings before their deportation. [*whispering*] And can I tell you something, between you and me? They made them from real leftover Nazi gold, because of their value."
> So I went to Obi [Hardware Store], got myself a crowbar. Next week I'm getting crowns put on. My aunt Rachel always said, "Oliver, the gold has to stay in the family."[11]

Polak's fictitious exchange exaggerates, of course, to absurdity. The stumbling blocks do not actually cause people to trip since they lie flat on the ground, and they are made of brass not gold. He suggests the memorial is made of gold as a commentary on the questionable choice of material. Polak plays with the idea that his character could remove the German-consecrated items for himself, claiming to be the rightful owner as a Jew. He references antisemitic stereotypes of gold-hoarding Jews in order for his largely non-Jewish audience to break the taboo of laughing at antisemitic jokes. Also embedded in the exchange is a question of reception—whether the Holocaust memorial is "for the Jews" or for Germans. Polak's comedy reveals a sore spot in German reconciliation, namely that Holocaust memorials have left out living Jews in Germany as an intended audience.

The facetious idea of using a crowbar on the stumbling blocks is also the comic relief in a cartoon by the Hamburg Jewish artist Daniel Haw. In "Based on Wilhelm Busch," (2008), the Jewish-inflected cartoon character Moishe Hundesohn and his duck, Ruthi, are shown pulling the stumbling blocks out of the ground so that they do indeed trip passersby as they are named (figure 6.3).[12] In the frame that follows, a cartoon Demnig shakes his fist at Moishe and Ruthi in the distance as they leave behind a street full of unearthed stumbling blocks. Wilhelm Busch, of the cartoon's title, is a nineteenth-century cartoonist known for his prankster characters Max and Moritz. Moishe Hundesohn

Figure 6.3. Daniel Haw's Jewish-inflected cartoon characters Moishe Hundesohn and Ruthi pull up one of the stumbling blocks in "Based on Wilhelm Busch" (2008). © Daniel Haw.

and Ruthi had been planning this prank for some time. Two years earlier, in "Moishe Hundesohn and the Stumbling Block" (2006), the dog character first levels the charge of "false advertisement" against the monument without doing anything about it at the time.[13]

The humor of Polak's and Haw's criticism, expressed through the "low" media of stand-up comedy and cartoons, aligns with Knobloch's political protest. Polak's cynical suggestion that the stones were installed outside his home without his knowledge raises the issue of Jewish consent in memorial construction. Similarly, Haw does not feel the memorial of names goes far enough in compelling Germans to work through the past. He imagines a scenario that both undoes Demnig's sanctified work and causes physical harm as a more sufficient way to "remember" the Holocaust.

The author Esther Dischereit has also joined the chorus of German Jewish voices critical of this famous decentralized Holocaust exhibit. Unlike other critics of Holocaust memorials, Dischereit has proactively created a memorial of her own, which she showcased in the book *Vor den Hohen Feiertagen gab es ein Flüstern und Rascheln im Haus* (*Before the High Holy Days the House was Full of Whisperings and Rustlings*, 2009).[14] Dischereit's memorial, opened in 2008, is a sound installation in the town of Dülmen, Germany. Visitors approach motion-activated speakers, which triggers a short audio recording of a vignette about Jewish life: a woman reading a recipe; a memory from a holiday. At one of Dischereit's book readings, comparatist Kader Konuk posed a question to

Dischereit in relation to her Holocaust memorial: "Are the stumbling blocks something you were thinking about as you were creating this sound space?"[15] Dischereit answered by listing five reasons she opposed the stumbling blocks, in order to clarify that she did not consider them as an inspiration for her installation (Dischereit's response reflects her non-native English):

> I personally oppose the stumbling blocks. I don't participate in these actions.... They made it cheap—placed [them] on common ground. And if you live in the near[by vicinity] and you're an inhabitant of one of these houses, and in front of your house there were these things, and you could show something.... There were people living [in there] who at least could afford six hundred euro to pay for one of these stones. So [that's] one thing. Second—I think there are a lot of problems throughout this action—who is chosen to be mentioned or not? It turns out that people really like to adopt the killed Jews. They [the dead Jews] cannot say, "I don't want this. I don't like this." So people would really learn this biography, they would come to like these people. And for me, this is not the point. You don't have to like the killed German Jews or other Jews. This is not the point. It could have been an ugly, nasty, I-don't-know-what [type of] person.... Third, you have in certain areas even something like, "Oh, now we are complete." "You completed it! Brilliant! For every person!" Such a thing. For me, this is very, very strange. Fourth, . . . how does it look like? It looks like golden metal. For me, this reminds me of what else was gold and metal. It's just not possible that they chose this material. There were even school groups, groups of children that came and clean this and make it more shiny. Fifth, . . . even in the word, it is "stolpern über die Steine" [stumble over the stones]. I don't think they can *stolpern über* Auschwitz. This is just not the way it should be. . . . If you really want to help, collect money for a new Torah, a Torah scroll. Why not? In a German discussion, this is totally absurd. There were lots of stolen Torah scrolls, so why couldn't you just collect money . . . ? It doesn't happen. It has to be these stone pieces outside.

Dischereit's five objections to the stumbling block memorial can be summarized as: (1) the display value of the plaque for the sponsors; (2) the selectivity of the victims chosen; (3) the catharsis Germans feel for doing something in response to the Holocaust; (4) the ill-suited choice of gold-colored material, because of the association between Jews and gold in antisemitic narratives and the Nazi plunder of Jewish gold and gold fillings; (5) the name "stumbling blocks," which underplays the enormity of the Holocaust crimes and the work needed in its postgenerational processing. The introduction to the volume on Dischereit's Holocaust monument reframes her critique of the stumbling blocks:

> Dülmen has not erected a monument on the "Eichengrün" plaza. Something else occurs here. Something that sheers off from the rituals of the German Federal Republic's culture of remembrance. Jews lived in Dülmen. As they did in so many German villages and cities. In one of her fifty-five soundmarks Esther Dischereit has given the names of those who in the last century were born, lived, worked

and died here. ... The objects, the stories are not given a coordinating sense. And so they diverge from the rituals of memorialization. Monuments, reflecting walls, "Stolpersteine," stumbling blocks, can comfort and reassure. Something is being done, visibly, not to be ignored. As if there were an appropriate way to counter what happened in Germany and in the countries occupied by Germany. Quietly the installation objects to such an encounter with history. That is its great courage.[16]

The book sets up Dischereit's aural monument as a countermemorial, counter to the physical or visual memory culture set up by non-Jewish Germans. The one monument explicitly named as representative of mainstream German ritualized memorialization is the stumbling blocks. For Dischereit, German society should remember Jewish life as opposed to Jewish death.

Peter Eisenman's Memorial to the Murdered Jews of Europe

Henryk Broder's critique of Eisenman's Berlin Memorial to the Murdered Jews of Europe is similar to Dischereit's discontent with the stumbling blocks, in that it argues that remembering Jewish life should be prioritized over a fetishization of Jewish deaths. Broder presented his view on the TV show *Entweder Broder*, which ran for three seasons from 2010 to 2012. The series starred a duo of journalists, Broder and Hamed Abdel-Samad, one Jewish and the other Egyptian.[17] Broder and Abdel-Samad drive around Germany and Europe discussing their perspectives on minority issues. The show provides an irreverent analysis of minority issues. One scene in the second episode takes place at Eisenman's memorial. This scene demonstrates the limits of discourse between Jews and others in Germany, including between Jews and members of other minorities. The field of gray stelae that constitute the Eisenman memorial, abstract in form, appears in a long shot. One of the stelae in the foreground pivots on its axis to reveal Broder's face peeking through a cutout. Broder is wearing a costume, weighing twenty-five kilograms, that approximates in detail one of the stelae in the monument (see figure 6.4).[18]

Broder walks up to Abdel-Samad, who apparently had not been let in on the joke. Abdel-Samad asks him what he is doing. Broder informs him of a celebration that day on the fifth

Figure 6.4. Henryk Broder attends the fifth anniversary of the Memorial to the Murdered Jews of Europe dressed as one of the concrete stelae. © Zorro Medien.

anniversary of the monument's opening and that he decided to celebrate along with everyone else by going to the ceremony dressed as a "mobile monument." Abdel-Samad inquires further about Broder's intentions before saying that he does not feel comfortable accompanying Broder: "That's my line in the sand. ... No, I can't do this. Really, I can't." While the camera rolls, Broder convinces his partner to walk a little way with him, after which Abdel-Samad goes to sit in the car while Broder continues his shenanigans at the ceremony with its speeches and klezmer band. The episode then cuts to the car where Broder debriefs Abdel-Samad and explains his actions and opposition to the memorial:

> I was always against the [Eisenman] monument. First because it reopens the Nazis' death hierarchy: Jews first! ... Second, because it suggests that without the Jewish genocide the Third Reich would not have been half as bad. And third, because there is not even a hint of a connection made between the last Holocaust and the next one that could play out in the Middle East, if the Europeans continue to treat [Mahmoud] Ahmadinejad as they did Hitler between 1933 and 1939. ... The last Holocaust interests me as much as the exodus from Egypt or the Battle of Verdun or the sinking of the *Titanic*. I am interested in whether the next Holocaust is prevented or if the world peacefully looks on as a regime that has women stoned to death gets itself into the position to produce nuclear weapons.[19]

Broder drives home the point of his costume antics at the anniversary celebration as a protest against ignoring contemporary antisemitism, which is also the main argument in Broder's book *Vergesst Auschwitz!* (Forget Auschwitz!). In the book, Broder draws attention to a court in Cologne that determined imagery used in a protest of Israel was not antisemitic because it was politically contextualized. Broder contrasts this verdict with plans for a Jewish museum to be built in the same city: "The museum will incidentally cost over 50 million euros, of which the city of Cologne will pay 37 million. Cologne might be broke, but the city council will think of something. Because *it* is about dead Jews. And those are the good ones."[20] Broder calls out Cologne's hypocrisy for recognizing past antisemitism but not antisemitism affecting Jews today.

Another Jewish author to fault the Eisenman memorial is Maxim Biller, who writes: "Whenever I stand at the Holocaust Memorial in central Berlin, I think to myself, this is not a memorial at all. This is a triumphal arch. And then there is also this state-ordered antifascism. If you're drumming into people all day long: we were Nazis and you can't be ... now if I were fifteen and not me, I would have the biggest desire to go out and be a Nazi."[21] The juxtaposition of the Eisenman memorial immediately next to the Brandenburg Gate, an actual triumphal arch in eighteenth-century neoclassical style, supports Biller's unlikely assessment. Biller, like Dischereit and Broder, see German Holocaust memorials as top-down. For Biller it is a "state-ordered antifascism," for Dischereit the "Federal Republic's culture of remembrance," and for Broder "mainstream."[22] These arguments run counter to the praise heaped upon the memorials, especially the decentralized stumbling blocks that specifically have been seen as a response to "the top-down and largely non-dialogic character of [earlier] monuments."[23] The critics argue that the stumbling blocks reinscribe the same problematic as Eisenman's memorial.

Taboo arises again and again with these public criticisms of Holocaust monuments. Gunter Demnig's laying of the names of Jewish Holocaust victims with brass stumbling blocks has taken on the air of an ersatz religious ceremony in Germany. Similar to the Jewish ritual of unveiling the headstone a year after burial, this delayed recognition of the deceased is attended by Demnig, neighbors, and sometimes family and press and is accompanied by a speech. Each of the tens of thousands of stones comes with this performative hallowed ritual.[24] Polak's humor in his skit on the stumbling blocks relies on breaking two taboos: laughing at antisemitic stereotypes and questioning the Holocaust memorial. Broder's performance art at the Eisenman memorial is a commentary on the lack of Jewish input into Holocaust memorialization and exposes the limits of discourse between German groups, like that between Muslims and Jews. Abdel-Samad does not feel comfortable engaging in this critique alongside Broder. The reasons for Abdel-Samad's reticence are most likely manifold, but among them is the association between calling a Holocaust memorial into question as a non-Jewish German and certain dubious antisemitic politics, where ethnic Germans might be considered neo-Nazis, and Muslims in Germany as extremists with their "imported anti-Semitism."[25] Criticizing Holocaust memorialization strains this Jewish-Muslim friendship, revealing a taboo for all non-Jewish Germans.[26]

Intersections and Dialogue

The dialogics of the Eisenman monument permeate its immediate vicinity, from the adjacent Brandenburg Gate to the homosexual memorial across the street, making Berlin a minefield of *lieux de memoire*. Irit Dekel sees an intrinsic dialogic nature to monument culture in Berlin: "The [Eisenman] memorial is a 'tourist magnet' and portal to other memorials such as the Memorial to Homosexuals persecuted under the National Socialist regime and the Memorial to Sinti and Roma."[27] Similarly, the stumbling block project is a portal to other monuments. A book titled *Stumbling Stones in Berlin: 12 Neighborhood Walks*, published in cooperation with the project, lists a section of "Museums, Exhibitions and Memorials," including the House of the Wannsee Conference, the Eisenman memorial, and Topography of Terror.[28] The reader is encouraged to attend these other sites in the Berlin memorial landscape in tandem with their coordinated walk. German Holocaust monuments are dialogic, relating both geographically and temporally to other local monuments.

The Memorial to Homosexuals Persecuted under Nazism is located across the street from the Eisenman memorial, in the Tiergarten, a park that is also famous as a cruising spot for gay men. Designed by Michael Elmgreen and Ingar Dragset, the memorial to homosexuals (often called the *Homo-Mahnmal*) is one concrete, gray stele set at a slight angle with a recessed window revealing a video of two men kissing, in its original iteration. The brochure for the *Mahnmal* explicitly addresses the intersection of this monument with the Jewish monument across the street:

> The two artists have closely adapted their aesthetic conceptualisation to the monument's immediate surroundings. For their sculptural rendition of the memorial, they have chosen to adopt the formal language of the Holocaust Memorial directly opposite. In Elmgreen & Dragset's version, however, the cubic sculptural shape of Eisenman's stelae acquires an additional layer. With its clear allusion to the monument on the other side of the street, the memorial seems to be saying, we are the same kind of human beings, yet we are also different from each other. And therein lies the challenge to our tolerance and acceptance.[29]

The brochure thus draws attention to the memorial's proximity to the Eisenman memorial and its formal influence. The contact information even lists the foundation for the Eisenman memorial first, only followed by the foundation for the Lesbian and Gay Union in Germany (LSDV), further suggesting that the symbolism of the monument to persecuted homosexuals should be seen in relation to the central locus in German culture for Jewish persecution. An interpretation one could easily draw from the form and location of Elmgreen and Dragset's monument is the intersectional nature of religion or ethnicity (Jewish) and sexuality (gay)—some of the Jewish victims were also homosexual. Yet this is not the focus of the text. The text presents a vague platitude that the "clear reference" to the Eisenman monument is that "all people are equal," making a liberal appeal for equality of sexual, religious, and ethnic minorities. However, this suggestion creates a problematic equivalency of victimhood that the monument itself does not necessarily evoke. The persecution of the two groups was different in scale and measure, which the monument addresses with a singular stela facing the field of stelae across the street.

The Berlin Wall Memorial, introduced at the beginning of this chapter, features plaques, *Ereignismarken*, embedded in the ground to commemorate East German refugees at the locations along Bernauer Straße where they successfully escaped or attempted escape. The markers evoke Demnig's stumbling blocks in color, function, and size, while they are also proximate to actual stumbling blocks. Curator Gerhard Sälter explains the concept of the 2007 winning design for the memorial complex by ON architektur:

> The multi-pronged interpretative approach features a third element, so-called "event markers." ... Between 1961 and 1989 some five hundred escapes and attempted escapes occurred at the Bernauer Strasse alone. If one were to include all of them in our exhibition, the volume of the material would obstruct the visitors' view of both the historic site and the contextual interrelationships we wish to impart to them. The "event markers" present a decentralized way to tell the stories that happened at Bernauer Strasse in keeping with the volume of material; they also offer us the possibility to describe events in almost complete detail. Essential information about each case will be conveyed as unobtrusively as possible, in cavities recessed in the ground. For more information, interested guests will be invited to consult a "field book" about each event describing the stories and fortunes involved.[30]

Unlike in the abstract of the homosexual victims memorial, there is no explicit comparison drawn here from the Berlin Wall Memorial to a Holocaust memorial. Betraying the silence, however, is the word "decentralized," which associatively draws one's mind to Demnig's project that, before this point in time, had long been described as the world's largest decentralized memorial.[31] Of further comparative interest, Sälter pointed out to me that event marker A 330 is the sole marker in the memorial not pertaining to an event between 1961 and 1989. It marks the grave of two brothers of Jewish heritage who were buried in the Sophienfriedhof Protestant cemetery in 1943 but whose grave markers were later erased as they were in the East-West Berlin border zone. The constellation of plaques therefore internally references the Holocaust as it intersected with GDR history at the same time that the plaques take on the form and function of the decentralized stumbling block project. German victimhood of the East German era is almost woven into Jewish victimhood of an earlier period.

The dialogic echoes of Holocaust memorials for Jewish victims in later German monuments to other events and victim groups are increasingly evident. Memorial space in Berlin has to deal with two big histories: Berlin as Hitler's capital and the divided Berlin of the Cold War. Holocaust memorials are thus in dialogue with the memory of the GDR. Issues of historical relativism exist alongside generational change and a more diverse Germany. To understand these developments and the ways that German Jewish voices inflect the changes, I turn to Daniel Levy, Nathan Sznaider, and Michael Rothberg. Whereas Levy and Sznaider speak of a competitive memory theory and a narrative of memories being replaced, Rothberg offers a theory of memory exchanges. I bring their views to bear on the specific influences on the Berlin memorial landscape. In *The Holocaust and Memory in the Global Age*, Daniel Levy and Nathan Sznaider write that the memory of the Holocaust has come to blur the lines between perpetrator and victim, once two immutable categories in a postwar German context that divided ethnic Germans from Jews. In today's "global age," immigrants to Germany, for example, refuse to accept the mantle of perpetrator, and grandchildren of Nazi perpetrators may not take responsibility for the actions of their forebears.[32] Levy and Sznaider focus on representation in visual media and historiographic debates rather than physical memorials, and they globally claim that "the Holocaust is shaping forms of remembrance for the future." One example they reference outside of Germany is the Palestinian moment of silence on Nakba Day that borrows the use of a moment of silence on Holocaust Memorial Day in Israel.[33] Palestinian nationalism has come to shape one of its memorial acts as an appropriation of and opposition to Zionist memory of the Holocaust. Expanding the purview of their argument to physical memorials in Berlin, this chapter therefore strengthens their assertion that the Holocaust has shaped "forms of remembrance," especially where intersectional identities are partially feeding this trend.

Michael Rothberg distinguishes between "competitive memory" and "multidirectional memory," where the latter cross-references, borrows, and is productive.[34] Though similar to Levy and Sznaider's consideration of "cosmopolitan memory," Rothberg's multidirectional memory emphasizes the positive inflection of borrowing.[35] Under cosmopolitan memory, Levy and Sznaider understand the notions of local and global memories in contact with global memory replacing the local, but Rothberg views these two memories as exchanges, not as competition in a zero-sum game. Multidirectional memory "recognizes the dynamic transfers that take place between diverse places and times during remembrance."[36] Attempts to bring the term *Vergangenheitsbewältigung* (working through the past) outside of a Nazi-specific context into debates around East Germany have been dismissed because of a taboo in comparing the Third Reich and East Germany, and yet the nameplates in the ground at the Berlin Wall show that this taboo might be breaking down as the memory becomes increasingly intersectional, multidirectional, and dialogic.[37]

The Jewish voices criticizing German Holocaust memorialization efforts have been directed at the form of Holocaust memorials meant for Jewish victims. These criticisms have not entered into a debate about competitive memory and the repurposing of Holocaust memorials for other victim groups. I have argued that their complaint namely raises the question: In what ways are the needs of the Jewish community addressed in Holocaust monuments? Pinpointing this concern ultimately contributes to an understanding of the twenty-first-century dialogue between Jews and other victimized German groups. James Young in *The Texture of Memory* lays out the function of Holocaust memorialization in various national contexts. In the United States, Holocaust memorialization serves to further the savior narrative of the American military. In Israel, Holocaust memorials promote the idea of Jews as resistance fighters in the context of the strong New Jew in a Jewish country. In the Soviet bloc, Holocaust memorials subsume Jews under the general category of victims of fascism. In Germany, Holocaust memorials speak to perpetrators and their descendants as a warning for the future, a *Mahnmal*.[38] Young's view implies that the German memorials are only secondarily for the families of victims who no longer live in Germany, since it is not likely that such a family member will stumble across the name of their loved one on the public sidewalk. Criticism comes, in part, as a response to this vision of a non-Jewish audience, where living Jews in Germany are ignored in the construction of German memorials. Jews have in fact designed Holocaust memorials in Germany, but oftentimes they are by foreign Jews without German citizenship, like the American Peter Eisenman's Memorial to the Murdered Jews of Europe or the Polish-born American Daniel Libeskind's Garden of Exile.[39] This foreign (and mainly American) substitution led to early criticisms that the Eisenman "memorial was not a Jewish initiative.... Many—like Ignatz Bubis, the president of the Central Council of Jews in Germany between 1992 and 1999, and the 'Jewish Group' in the 1980s—claimed that it is not 'for them.'"[40] Bubis's statement that a Holocaust memorial was not "for them" further articulates the position that German Jews have felt left out of the creation process and the process of working through the past, and it is to this that Germany's now more robust Jewish community is responding. At the beginning of the twenty-first century, there are estimates of upward of two hundred thousand Jews in Germany.[41] Esther Dischereit's sound installation in 2008 was therefore a new model, designed by a German Jew. Charlotte Knobloch's protest in Munich has potentially led to the most enduring conversation to shape a memorial with local Jewish input, finalizing in the 2017 compromise of vertical name plaques. Memorials such as these, however, designed by Jewish artists or expressly taking into account the Jewish community, are emerging in response to public memory projects since the late 1990s and represent a physical manifestation of the goal to recognize a living Jewish presence in Germany.

The comedian Shahak Shapira represents one counterweight to the many critical Jewish voices of German memory culture. Born in Israel, Shapira has lived in Germany since he was a teenager and became a naturalized German citizen in March 2018.[42] His ironic tweet, cited below, encapsulates his engagement in preserving the "mainstream" German Holocaust memory culture that Broder and others attack.[43] Shapira satirizes the way that (mainly young) Germans routinely disrespect the intended hallowed spaces of Holocaust memorials: "DUDE. I'm just coming from a date at the Holocaust monument (with a happy ending, of course). WHAT'S UP???"[44] A reference to a sexual act performed at the Holocaust monument simultaneously criticizes how Germans interact with the memorial sites as everyday Berlin locales and criticizes the role of social media.[45] Shapira has created a stir with a couple of his projects. In one film-recorded operation, he spray-paints the sidewalk outside of Twitter's headquarters in Hamburg with antisemitic and racist tweets that he had reported but that Twitter had failed to take down.[46] A second campaign was #YOLOCAUST, in which Shapira edited pictures he found online of people acting inappropriately while visiting Holocaust remembrance sites. He termed this shaming #YOLOCAUST, combining the fun-loving hashtag #YOLO (You Only Live Once) and Holocaust. Possibly stemming from the tweet above, this 2018 project focused on those who act improperly, in Shapira's view, at Holocaust sites and are brazen enough to post pictures to social media. In one image, Shapira manipulated a photo of two men jumping over the stelae at the Eisenman structure, which had originally been posted with the caption "Jumping on dead Jews @ Holocaust Memorial." Shapira superimposed the individuals in black and white jumping over a historic photo of piles of dead, emaciated bodies. Shapira did the same to several photographs, editing the present-day tourists into archival photographs, including the famous postliberation picture with Elie Wiesel in the bunks at Buchenwald. #YOLOCAUST became a viral sensation and evoked apologies from *almost all* of the twelve individuals involved.[47] Preserving the taboo, Shapira's crusade contrasts with Henryk Broder's indelicate performance at the same monument. Shapira morally shames Germans into respecting the space, where Broder actively disrespects the space in dressing like a Holocaust mascot. Yet both responses are similar in the underlying assumption that living Jews in Germany act as guardians for Holocaust memorialization and the proper message relayed in the work of memory.

The attempt here to boil down the various criticisms from Jewish Germans into just a few unified messages is noteworthy considering the differences that separate the individuals otherwise. Politically, Henryk Broder and Daniel Haw are controversial figures on the right.[48] Broder objects to the Berlin Holocaust memorial for political gain. He writes that he wants Germans to "forget" about past antisemitism and instead focus on current-day antisemitism. In his view, instead of focusing so much on the Holocaust, one should instead focus on Iran's desire to wipe out Israel. This anti-Iran, pro-Israel stance places him on the right, and his objection to the Eisenman memorial is a pawn in his political argument. In comparison, someone like Dischereit does not have any international political goals that can be gleaned from her objection to the stumbling blocks. Though some of these Jewish voices brought here are descendants of pre-Holocaust German Jews (namely, Esther Dischereit, Oliver Polak, and Charlotte Knobloch), others are naturalized Germans (Shahak Shapira was born in Israel, Henryk Broder in Poland, and Maxim Biller in the Czech Republic). Beyond temporal distance, these guardians of Holocaust memory are becoming further distant from the victims, speaking to the community of memory that the German Jewish community represents in the twenty-first century.

This chapter's findings on intersectionality, multidirectionality, and dialogue among memorials center on Jewish communal engagement with other German minorities, including Muslims and historically victimized groups. Levy and Sznaider consider cosmopolitan memory in the global age as a warning against a narrow focus on national narratives in memorial making (Young) and instead advocate for a look at "how global topoi are inscribed into local and national discourse."[49] The collective critical German Jewish voice could represent a pushback against this very real globalism, where the local voices are not being heard at the expense of international Jewish architects. Many of the examples exhibited in this chapter come in the form of comedy and cartoons, genres generally perceived as "low" media, which perhaps furthers the idea of the transgression at stake in breaking national taboos such as criticizing Holocaust memorials. The Jewish criticism directed at the original monuments themselves expresses frustration at a possible echo chamber where other victim groups (GDR refugees, homosexuals) have successively taken on one formal aspect of a Holocaust memorial without Jewish input from the beginning. Where Germans use a form of mourning Jewish victims to relay meaning to other Germans, a German Jewish discourse is lacking. In a volume on German minority discourse such as this one, the specter of Gershom Scholem looms with his famous essay decrying a lack of a pre-Holocaust German Jewish dialogue. Rejecting the notion that there was an idyllic time between Germans and Jews before the Holocaust, Scholem writes: "Who then were the Jews in that much-cited German Jewish dialogue talking to? They were talking to themselves."[50] So too now that Germany has a resurgent Jewish population, these Jewish voices against Holocaust memorialization efforts largely unify around the idea that a dialogue needs to ensue where Jewish concerns are heard. In the words of Henryk Broder in his book *Vergesst Auschwitz!* "Instead of mourning the dead after the fact, I think it's more important to help the living stay alive."[51] Living Jews are just as important as dead Jews.

Nick Block is assistant professor of the practice, German studies and Jewish studies at Boston College. His current book project is *Schlepping Culture: The Jewish Renaissance between German and Yiddish, 1880–1940*.

Notes

1. *Stolperstein* has been translated as "tripping stone" or "stumbling stone." I have chosen the somewhat more colloquial English expression "stumbling block." All further translations my own unless otherwise stated.
2. Gunter Demnig, "Technik," http://www.stolpersteine.eu/de/technik/.
3. Jeffrey Luppes, "'Den Toten der ostdeutschen Heimat': Local Expellee Monuments and the Construction of Post-war Narratives," in *Narratives of Trauma: Discourses of Ger-*

man Wartime Suffering in National and International Perspective, ed. Helmut Schmitz and Annette Seidel-Arpacı (Amsterdam: Rodopi, 2011), 89–110.
4. For example, Gerd Knischewski and Ulla Spittler, "Remembering in the Berlin Republic: The Debate about the Central Holocaust Memorial in Berlin," *Debatte: Journal of Contemporary Central and Eastern Europe* 13, no. 1 (April 2005): 25–42.
5. Bundestag, Drucksache 14/981, 6 May 1999, http://dipbt.bundestag.de/doc/btd/14/009/1400981.pdf. "Der Bundestag wolle beschließen: Auf die Errichtung eines neuen, weiteren Mahnmals in Berlin wird verzichtet. Die vom Bund vorgesehenen Mittel für das Holocaust-Mahnmal sollten für die bestehenden Gedenkstätten zur Verfügung gestellt werden."
6. Münchner Stadtrat, "Projekt 'Stolpersteine,'" 02-08 / A 01704, 16 June 2004; "Formen des dezentralen und individuellen Gedenkens an die Opfer des NS-Regimes in München," 14-20 / A 01258, 29 July 2015, https://www.ris-muenchen.de.
7. Eldad Beck, "Die Familie von Holocaustopfern protestierte gegen die Verewigung," Hagalil.com, trans. from *Yediot Ahronot*, 8 February 2008.
8. Ibid.
9. Aktives Museum Faschismus und Widerstand in Berlin e.V., Koordinierungsstelle Stolpersteine Berlin, and Kulturprojekte Berlin GmbH, *Stumbling Stones in Berlin: 12 Neighborhood Walks*, 2nd ed., trans. Miriamne Fields (Berlin: Rucksaldruck, 2016), 25–27.
10. Landeshauptstadt München Kulturreferat, "Verfolgung von Lesben und Schwulen im Nationalsozialismus: Ein Kunstdenkmal in München," pamphlet, 2017, 10, https://www.muenchen.de/rathaus/Stadtverwaltung/Direktorium/Koordinierungsstelle-fuer-gleichgeschlechtliche-Lebensweisen/Veranstaltungen/Denkmal.html.
11. Oliver Polak, "Stolpersteine," track 29 on *Jud Süß Sauer-Die Show*, Sony Music Entertainment Germany, 2010, compact disc.
12. Daniel Haw, "Frei nach Wilhelm Busch," 14 February 2008, http://www.israeli-art.com/satire/busch.htm. See Nick Block, "A Berlin Republic *Convivencia*? Ethnic Tensions in the Turkish-German-Jewish Triangle," *German Studies Review* 40, no. 2 (May 2017): 353–71, doi:10.1353/gsr.2017.0050.
13. Daniel Haw, "Moishe Hundesohn und der Stolperstein," 5 May 2006, http://www.israeli-art.com/satire/stolperstein.htm.
14. Esther Dischereit, *Vor den Hohen Feiertagen gab es ein Flüstern und Rascheln im Haus*, trans. Iain Galbraith and Lisa Shoemaker (Berlin: AvivA, 2009).
15. I recorded this exchange at the Mobility and Jewish Studies Conference, University of Michigan, 21 September 2010.
16. Barbara Hahn, "'Aufgehobene' Stories," in Esther Dischereit, *Vor den Hohen Feiertagen*, trans. James McFarland, 1–3.
17. Joachim Schroeder, Claudio Schmid, and Tobias Streck, dirs., *Entweder Broder—Die Deutschland-Safari* (Munich: Zorro Medien, 2011), DVD; Henryk M. Broder and Hamed Abdel-Samad, *Entweder Broder: Die Deutschland-Safari*, 3rd ed. (Munich: Knaus, 2010).
18. Henryk M. Broder, *Vergesst Auschwitz! Der deutsche Erinnerungswahn und die Endlösung der Israel-Frage* (Munich: Pantheon, 2013), 177.
19. Broder and Abdel-Samad, *Entweder Broder*, 35–36.
20. Broder, *Vergesst Auschwitz!* 59.
21. Maxim Biller, "Die Deutschen kriegen es ab," interview by Adam Soboczynski, *Die Zeit*, 20 March 2016.

22. Broder and Abdel-Samad, *Entweder Broder*, 43.
23. Natalia Krzyżanowska, "The Discourse of Counter-monuments: Semiotics of Material Commemoration in Contemporary Urban Spaces," *Social Semiotics* 26, no. 5 (2016): 465–85, doi: 10.1080/10350330.2015.1096132.
24. David Hanauer, "The Discursive Construction of the Stolpersteine Memorial Project: Official, Education and Familial Meanings," in *The Holocaust in the Twenty-First Century: Contesting/Contested Memories*, ed. David M. Seymour and Mercedes Camino (New York: Taylor & Francis, 2017), 263–76.
25. Esra Özyürek, "Export-Import Theory and the Racialization of Anti-Semitism: Turkish- and Arab-Only Prevention Programs in Germany," *Comparative Studies in Society and History* 58, no. 1 (2016): 40–65, doi: 10.1017/S0010417515000560.
26. Block, "Berlin Republic *Convivencia?*"
27. Irit Dekel, *Mediation at the Holocaust Memorial in Berlin* (New York: Palgrave Macmillan, 2013), 5.
28. Aktives Museum Faschismus und Widerstand in Berlin e.V., *Stumbling Stones in Berlin*.
29. Bundesregierung für Kultur und Medien, "Information Memorial to the Homosexuals Persecuted under the National Socialist Regime," pamphlet, 2015.
30. Gerhard Sälter, "The Berlin Wall Explained in Context: Rebuilding the Berlin Wall Memorial," in *C'era una volta il Muro: A vent'anni dalla svolta tedesca*, ed. Emilia Fiandra (Rome: Artemide, 2011), 204.
31. Michael Imort, "Stumbling Blocks: A Decentralized Memorial to Holocaust Victims," in *Memorialization in Germany since 1945*, ed. Bill Niven and Chloe Paver (New York: Palgrave Macmillan, 2007), 233–42.
32. Daniel Levy and Natan Sznaider, *The Holocaust and Memory in a Global Age* (Philadelphia: Temple University Press, 2006), 24.
33. Levy and Sznaider, *Holocaust and Memory*, 199.
34. Michael Rothberg, *Multidirectional Memory: Remembering the Holocaust in the Age of Decolonization* (Stanford, CA: Stanford University Press, 2009).
35. Levy and Sznaider, *Holocaust and Memory*, 20.
36. Rothberg, *Multidirectional Memory*, 11.
37. Levy and Sznaider, *Holocaust and Memory*, 70.
38. James Edward Young, *The Texture of Memory: Holocaust Memorials and Meaning in Europe, Israel, and America* (New Haven, CT: Yale University Press, 1993).
39. Peter Eisenman's Memorial to the Murdered Jews of Europe and Daniel Libeskind's Garden of Exile are themselves dialogic in the formal connections through their use of stelae and slanted ground that induces unsteadiness and disorientation, both in Berlin.
40. Dekel, *Mediation*, 15–16.
41. Arnold Dashefsky, Sergio DellaPergola, and Ira Sheskin Berman, eds., *World Jewish Population 2016*, Jewish Databank, no. 17, 57. Germany's 2016 core Jewish pop.: 117,000; pop. with one Jewish parent: 150,000; enlarged Jewish pop.: 225,000; law of return pop.: 275,000.
42. Shahak Shapira, "DIESER MANN GEHÖRT ZU DEUTSCHLAND #Einigkeit UndRechtUndShahaks," Twitter, 20 March 2018, 9:50 a.m., https://twitter.com/ShahakShapira/status/976093649955106816.
43. Broder and Abdel-Samad, *Entweder Broder*, 43.
44. Shahak Shapira, "ALTER. Ich komme gerade von 'nem Date am Holocaust-Mahnmal (mit Happy End, ja). WAS GEHT???," Twitter, 7 August 2017, 5:55 a.m., https://twitter.com/ShahakShapira/status/781665893008994304.

45. For more on how Germans interact with the space at Eisenman's monument, see Dekel, *Mediation*.
46. Shahak Shapira, "I reported about 300 hate tweets. Twitter didn't delete 'em, so I sprayed them in front of their office #HEYTWITTER," Twitter, 29 September 2016, 9:24 p.m., https://twitter.com/ShahakShapira/status/894497226189402112. The tweet provides a link to his YouTube video: Shahak Shapira, "#HEYTWITTER," YouTube, 7 August 2017, https://www.youtube.com/watch?v=jzMTBINILFU&ab_channel=ShahakShapira.
47. Shahak Shapira, "YOLOCAUST," http://yolocaust.de/.
48. Block, "A Berlin Republic *Convivencia?*"
49. Levy and Sznaider, *Holocaust and Memory*, 9.
50. Gershom Scholem, *Briefe*, vol. 2, ed. Thomas Sparr (Beck: Munich, 1995), 88.
51. Broder, *Vergesst Auschwitz!* 178–79.

Bibliography

Aktives Museum Faschismus und Widerstand in Berlin e.V., Koordinierungsstelle Stolpersteine Berlin, and Kulturprojekte Berlin GmbH. *Stumbling Stones in Berlin: 12 Neighborhood Walks*. Translated by Miriamne Fields. 2nd ed. Berlin: Rucksaldruck, 2016.

Beck, Eldad. "Die Familie von Holocaustopfern protestierte gegen die Verewigung." Hagalil.com. Originally published in Hebrew in *Yediot Ahronot*, 8 February 2008.

Biller, Maxim. "Die Deutschen kriegen es ab." Interview by Adam Soboczynski. *Die Zeit*, 20 March 2016, http://www.zeit.de/2016/11/maxim-biller-literarisches-quartett-biografie-roman/seite-3.

Block, Nick. "A Berlin Republic *Convivencia?* Ethnic Tensions in the Turkish-German-Jewish Triangle." *German Studies Review* 40, no. 2 (May 2017): 353–71. DOI: 10.1353/gsr.2017.0050.

Broder, Henryk M. *Vergesst Auschwitz! Der deutsche Erinnerungswahn und die Endlösung der Israel-Frage*. Munich: Pantheon, 2013.

Broder, Henryk M., and Hamed Abdel-Samad. *Entweder Broder: Die Deutschland-Safari*. 3rd ed. Munich: Knaus, 2010.

Dashefsky, Arnold, Sergio DellaPergola, and Ira Sheskin Berman, eds. *World Jewish Population 2016*. Jewish Databank, no. 17.

Dekel, Irit. *Mediation at the Holocaust Memorial in Berlin*. New York: Palgrave Macmillan, 2013.

Dischereit, Esther. *Vor den Hohen Feiertagen gab es ein Flüstern und Rascheln im Haus*. Translated by Iain Galbraith and Lisa Shoemaker. Berlin: AvivA, 2009.

Hahn, Barbara. "'Aufgehobene' Stories." In Esther Dischereit, *Vor den Hohen Feiertagen*, translated by James McFarland, 1–3. Berlin: AvivA, 2009.

Hanauer, David. "The Discursive Construction of the Stolpersteine Memorial Project: Official, Education and Familial Meanings." In *The Holocaust in the Twenty-First Century: Contesting/Contested Memories*, edited by David M. Seymour and Mercedes Camino, 263–76. New York: Taylor & Francis, 2017.

Imort, Michael. "Stumbling Blocks: A Decentralized Memorial to Holocaust Victims." In *Memorialization in Germany since 1945*, edited by Bill Niven and Chloe Paver, 233–42. New York: Palgrave Macmillan, 2007.

Knischewski, Gerd, and Ulla Spittler. "Remembering in the Berlin Republic: The Debate about the Central Holocaust Memorial in Berlin." *Debatte: Journal of Contemporary Central and Eastern Europe* 13, no. 1 (April 2005): 25–42.
Krzyżanowska, Natalia. "The Discourse of Counter-monuments: Semiotics of Material Commemoration in Contemporary Urban Spaces." *Social Semiotics* 26, no. 5 (2016): 465–85. DOI: 10.1080/10350330.2015.1096132.
Levy, Daniel, and Natan Sznaider. *The Holocaust and Memory in a Global Age*. Philadelphia: Temple University Press, 2006.
Luppes, Jeffrey. "'Den Toten der ostdeutschen Heimat': Local Expellee Monuments and the Construction of Post-war Narratives." In *Narratives of Trauma: Discourses of German Wartime Suffering in National and International Perspective*, edited by Helmut Schmitz and Annette Seidel-Arpacı, 89–110. Amsterdam: Rodopi, 2011.
Özyürek, Esra. "Export-Import Theory and the Racialization of Anti-Semitism: Turkish- and Arab-Only Prevention Programs in Germany." *Comparative Studies in Society and History* 58, no. 1 (2016): 40–65. DOI: 10.1017/S0010417515000560.
Polak, Oliver. "Stolpersteine." Track 29 on *Jud Süß Sauer-Die Show*. Sony Music Entertainment Germany, 2010, compact disc.
Rothberg, Michael. *Multidirectional Memory: Remembering the Holocaust in the Age of Decolonization*. Stanford, CA: Stanford University Press, 2009.
Sälter, Gerhard. "The Berlin Wall Explained in Context: Rebuilding the Berlin Wall Memorial." In *C'era una volta il Muro: A vent'anni dalla svolta tedesca*, edited by Emilia Fiandra, 191–206. Rome: Artemide, 2011.
Scholem, Gershom. *Briefe*. Edited by Thomas Sparr. Vol. 2. Beck: Munich, 1995.
Schroeder, Joachim, Claudio Schmid, Tobias Streck, dirs. *Entweder Broder—Die Deutschland-Safari*. Munich: Zorro Medien, 2011. DVD.
Young, James Edward. *The Texture of Memory: Holocaust Memorials and Meaning in Europe, Israel, and America*. New Haven, CT: Yale University Press, 1993.

CHAPTER 7

Young, Diverse, and Polyglot
Ilker Çatak and Amelia Umuhire Track the New Urban Sound of Europe

BERNA GUENELI

Whether due to the 2015 *Charlie Hebdo* terror attack in Paris, the xenophobic Pegida marches that began in 2014 in Germany for a White Christian Europe, or the Islamist terrorist London bombings of 2005, Europe is constantly evaluating its borders, its identity, and its structures.[1] A particularly xenophobic form of these debates has established itself in ultraconservative and populist parties across Europe, for example, in the AfD (Alternative für Deutschland [Alternative for Germany]) in Germany, in the Front National (National Front until 2018; now National Rally) in France, and in the FPÖ (Freiheitliche Partei Österreichs [The Freedom Party of Austria]) in Austria. These parties have all seen significant growth in recent years, which has led to a substantial rise in conservative power.[2] Such political developments have thus provided a sound political platform for right-wing voices across Europe. Certainly, such xenophobic and right-wing sentiments are equally prevalent in a variety of mainstream media and discourse.[3]

Contemporary Europe is torn between concepts of a cosmopolitan "new Europe," with open borders and free movement for its citizens and goods, and such xenophobic and, ultimately, racist constructs of "Fortress Europe,"[4] featuring enforced borders at the edges of the European Union devoted to keeping non-EU citizens out.[5] At stake are not only political borders but also so-called cultural borders. While participants in right-wing movements time and again seek to preserve a homogenous, monocultural definition of German and European culture, there are significant political and cultural movements fighting against the racist forces described above. I am interested in scrutinizing endeavors from within the film industry.

I argue that antiracist countervoices, subtly expressed, for example, in the work of Fatih Akın, İlker Çatak, and Amelia Umuhire, provide a fundamentally different account of European heterogeneity. In this contribution, I ultimately show that there is a select group of German filmmakers—such as Akın, Çatak, and Umuhire—who highlight new diverse visions and understandings of European cities and their people. As my discussion will demonstrate, these Turkish German and Afro-German visions (e.g., transnational themes and aesthetics) and production details (e.g., transnational casting, setting, soundtrack), in fact, go beyond European political and cultural boundaries—as conceptualized by the European Union—as well as beyond the boundaries defined by conservative, nationalist, and populist movements across Europe. Not insignificantly, these films use filmic sound, among other elements, to achieve these novel presentations of European diversity.

I chose these directors precisely because, despite their quite different work, they achieve a similar outcome: the diversification of German/European film on a variety of platforms. Indeed, these directors create their work under very different circumstances—Akın's *Auf der Anderen Seite* (*The Edge of Heaven*, 2007) is a larger-budget European production by a celebrated director who is in the midst of his career; Çatak's *Sadakat* (*Fidelity*, 2014) is a graduation film made by an up-and-coming director at a prestigious film school with access to its material resources; and Umuhire's *Polyglot* (2015) is an independent, zero-budget web series created by a university student in collaboration with family and friends—and at the same time, they facilitate the reception of a very similar audiovisual European urban space, reaching different audiences across Germany, Europe, and the globe.

In the course of this chapter, I will discuss three main points: I will first deliberate on the pioneer of diversification within Turkish German cinema, Fatih Akın. I will present Akın as an early director, juxtaposed with my more recent examples, who through his artistic oeuvre subtly counteracts on the global screen against racist voices in German media and politics. I will refer to sound studies in this context. Second, after giving more specific insights into Akın's soundtrack and his resulting contribution to the diversification of German cinema, I will highlight how examples from Çatak's short film *Sadakat* (*Fidelity*, 2014) engage with the Turkish soundscape first introduced in that manner by Akın. Both directors offer similar treatments of the sonic landscape of Istanbul. Third, and with special emphasis, I will discuss Umuhire's lesser-studied web series *Polyglot* (2015), which offers insights from the perspective of Afro-European sensibilities and experiences.[6]

The directors and their filmic efforts discussed in this chapter are indeed in good company across Europe. Glancing at a larger segment of cinematic productions, we see that there are, in fact, several European filmmakers who partake in the creation of a particular European cinema that diversifies the cinematic image and sound of the continent.⁷ An early example for post–Cold War Eastern European cinema is Emir Kusturica and his multinational (German, French, Serbian) coproductions. In these, he mixes and uses Romani music, languages, and accents, along with other Eastern European languages, thereby shifting the sound of Europe away from a Central/Northern European focus.⁸ Other examples include international coproductions from France, such as the work of Philippe Lioret, Yamina Benguigui, and Tony Gatlif.⁹ These filmmakers also include variations of North African and Romani voices and musical sounds in their films, as scholars such as Will Higbee have discussed.¹⁰ In England's cinema, most impressively the early Hanif Kureishi/Stephen Frears collaborations such as *My Beautiful Launderette* (1985) and *Sammy and Rosie Get Laid* (1987), as well as Frears's *Dirty Pretty Things* (2002) engage with London's multiethnic characters and their socioeconomic inequalities in one way or another. While the topics vary in these films, Frears makes sure that we hear what a global city like London sounds like, thereby helping to normalize non-English languages and a variety of accents in England.¹¹

One of the earlier cinematic examples of a force against one-dimensional understandings of Germany and Europe can be found among Akın's body of work.¹² In 2007 the European Parliament awarded Turkish German director Akın with the first Lux Cinema Prize for his multilingual film *The Edge of Heaven*. The film portrays the transnational lives and works of three parent-child relationships and their emotional, ideological, and physical journeys across Germany and Turkey. With his impressive filmic depiction of European diversity in music, languages, and fashion and his complex figures, facilitated by his focus on the non-EU country of Turkey, Akın offered a much-needed, initial filmic countervoice to populist xenophobic disseminations (which often include the perception of different languages, religions, skin colors, and so forth as threatening) commonly spread by populist parties, organizations, and their followers. Akın's film about the right-wing NSU (National Socialist Underground) murders, *Aus dem nichts* (*In the Fade*, 2017), brought a fictionalized account of racist events in Germany to a wider international cinema audience.¹³ The film received the 2017 Cannes film festival award for best actress, honoring the white German actress Diane Kruger. Kruger plays the film's protagonist, whose Kurdish German family is the target and victim of a right-wing terrorist attack that claims the lives of her husband and young son. The film also received the 2018 Best Picture—Foreign Language award at the Golden Globes, thereby bringing further global attention to the theme of racism in Germany.

Beyond Akın, emerging filmmakers such as Çatak and Umuhire also offer different perspectives on the theme of European diversity and heterogeneity, having surfaced as recent award-winning German participants in the international film circuits and presenting their sonically diverse films that extend well beyond traditional European borders. The work of these directors demonstrates the vast spectrum of topics and aesthetics—related to European susceptibilities in several ways—to an ever-expanding international audience. They do so, in particular, through the sound of their films.

Film sound scholarship has already devoted significant attention to how the soundtrack of films can be used to effectively present quotidian aspects of urban life across the globe. Selmin Kara, for example, analyzes the filmic sound of James Longley's documentary *Iraq in Fragments* (2006) by examining the urban noise of Baghdad as it relates to Sunnis, Shiites, and the Kurds of Iraq under occupation. She finds that these diverse sounds help to reassemble the city.[14] In a different geographical context, Amanda Holmes and Tania Gentic both discuss Fernando Pérez's 2003 documentary *Suite Habana* and its effective use of soundtrack to recreate the everyday audiovisual dimension of the Cuban city.[15] Holmes states, for example, that "*Suite Habana* does not have a musical composition as an *accompaniment* (with some short exceptions), but rather isolates and captures urban sounds that emanate from the daily activities of the city residents. In this sense, the Cuban film claims an aesthetic voice not only for everyday images of the city but also for everyday urban sounds."[16]

Thus, the sounds of a cinematic city can help to create a sensory experience and understanding of an urban space. Discussing the physical auditory quality of sound, Andrew Czink states that, "unlike the visual domain, auditory experience is fundamentally haptic and brings us into close contact with our environment. We 'feel' our environment and our place in it through hearing." That is, "sound is crucial to fully situating us in our world."[17] In a different context, discussing the film music in contemporary Hollywood cinema as opposed to classic Hollywood films, Anahid Kassabian examines the changes film music has undergone in response to the inclusion of new ethnicities, races, and sexualities in filmic narratives, for example. Kassabian observes that films such as *Malcom X* and *Mi Familia/My Family* allow us to "consider film music's role in the changing pressures of identity formations such as race, ethnicity, sexuality, and gender."[18] Kassabian argues that such films have "not only changed the narrative landscape of mainstream movie making, but they have also significantly broadened its range of musical materials."[19]

The sound of European cities in the works discussed here (*The Edge of Heaven, Fidelity, Polyglot*)—constructed through language use, the film's musical soundtrack, and other particular sounds of the films, all performed and supported by a transnational cast—testifies to a filmic intervention that contributes to normalizing multilingualism, as well as musical and sonic heterogeneity, in this new Europe and its filmic imagining.[20] This new transnational notion of film frequently depicts young, diverse, and polyglot characters as the navigators of a transnational urban European space. By using hip, likeable, and mobile figures (through casting and costume choices) and by creating empathy for the characters (through the plot), the films arguably facilitate a positive identification with the multilingual filmic characters. As such, with their often fashionable, urban, and congenial characters, these films differ from the "accented cinema" that Hamid Naficy defined in 2001.[21]

Faith Akın

A variety of scholars have frequently discussed that Akın's cinema exhibits an array of distinctive musical and other sonic juxtapositions.[22] As I have analyzed elsewhere in more detail, Akın's films sample sounds from a range of European and non-European regions, which offer an experience of a contemporary (filmic) Europe emphasizing multiethnicity and the sensations of multilingualism.[23] More explicitly, through the heterogeneous musical soundtrack and the sound of the diverse voices in his films, Akın enables his audience to become aware of Europe's varied sounds as imagined in his cinema. The soundtrack emphasizes diversity primarily through the dialogue and music. The characters' speech includes, for example, variations of European (Serbo-Croatian, German, English) and non-European (Kurdish, Turkish) languages.[24] The international cast playing a heterogeneous group of characters additionally presents an array of accents. Therefore, the sound and use of languages in general is diversified through the variety of speakers in the films. The same is true for the musical soundtrack: the diegetic music in Akın's films ranges, for example, from Turkish folk to Balkan electronic to German classical music. Providing a glimpse at the broad spectrum of the Turkish musical scene today and its history, Akın's soundtrack includes the music of 1970s Turkish Yeşilçam movie star and singer Neşe Karaböcek, Anatolian rock pioneer Erkin Koray, and pop icon Sezen Aksu, among many others.[25] At the same time, DJ Shantel in *The Edge of Heaven*, for example, creates mixed sounds from the Balkans and dubs Turkish folk musicians such as Kazım Koyuncu.[26]

All of these sounds create an acoustic means of diversifying the aural landscape of European film—which actually presents a highly unique way of normalizing this diversity without exoticizing and othering the sound. In fact, Akın was one of the first to create this type of normalization of diversity in film sound through, for example, his characters' use of any of the abovementioned music and languages and variations thereof in quotidian settings (cooking, eating, commuting, socializing, listening to music) without marking them as dangerous, threatening, or incompatible with the films' European settings. In his films, the sound of difference is thereby naturalized. At this point, this technique is not exclusive to Akın—there are several young and up-and-coming filmmakers who contribute to this type of diversification of European sound in German film. However, this was not always the case.

Throughout German film history—examples include films such as Richard Eichberg's Weimar film *Der Weg zur Schande* (*The Road to Dishonour*, 1930), which featured Chinese-American actress Anna May Wong; Douglas Sirk's Third Reich film *La Habanera* (1937), the musical soundtrack of which featured the Cuban habanera; Robert Stemmle's postwar film *Toxi* (1952), which portrays briefly an African American soldier as the father of Toxi; R. W. Fassbinder's New German Cinema film *Angst Essen Seele auf* (*Ali: Fear Eats the Soul*, 1974), in which the portrayal of Moroccan guest worker figures highlights their perceived otherness; Caroline Link's post-Wall film *Nirgendwo in Afrika* (*Nowhere in Africa*, 2001), which features representations of Kenyan characters[27]—the use of typically non-German music, languages, and/or accents in combination with a nonwhite body and/or exotic costumes often has had a rather exoticizing, and thereby ultimately othering, effect.[28] This is different in Akın's cinematic soundscape and that of the younger generation of filmmakers, who I introduce below, because Akın et al. do not use foreign music and sounds to exoticize their characters.

İlker Çatak

Early in his career, Çatak, the international award-winning graduate of the Hamburg Media School (2014), attracted attention with his short films, particularly with *Fidelity*, his most successful short film to date, for which, among other awards, he received the 2015 Foreign Film Gold Medal from the Student Academy Awards in Los Angeles. *Fidelity* depicts a young Turkish woman who helps an activist hide from the police during antigovernment protests in Istanbul—these scenes recall the actual 2013 Gezi protests and their media depiction in Istanbul, Turkey, where some street scenes for *Fidelity* were filmed. At the intersection of protest movements, divergent ideologies, state power dynamics, and the instinct to protect one's own family, the loyalty of the protagonist Aslı to her husband Gökhan, and ultimately to her entire marriage, is tested.[29]

With *Fidelity*, Çatak manages to put himself in line with filmmakers who expand not only the boundaries of German film but the boundaries of European film in general, as evidenced by the general soundtrack, which includes the sounds of the city of Istanbul, and by the Turkish voices, both presented as nonexoticizing aspects of German and European culture. In this section, I will briefly examine Çatak along with Akın, since both are prominent German directors who use Turkish voices, sounds, and contexts as European soundscapes in their films. By comparing urban sound examples—such as the sounds of Istanbul, presented in Akın's *The Edge of Heaven* (2007) and Çatak's *Fidelity*—I highlight the directors' joint creation of a particular urban sound and image for the city.

In Çatak's and Akın's German-produced films, Istanbul features prominently in sight and sound. Two things are particularly striking: the politicization of the city and the complication and empowerment of the Turkish female characters who are apt and vocal navigators of the city (see figures 7.1 and 7.2). That is, Akın and Çatak prominently portray Turkish-speaking female figures who move with ease through the politicized city of Istanbul. Considering the long-established media and film image of the battered Turkish/Muslim woman,[30] whose Turkish language use is often a sign of linguistic limitation, this image of a mobile, modern, Turkish-speaking female figure is new for Turkish German film. Both films' depictions of the mobility of young Turkish women in the dynamic city of Istanbul normalize their movement in open, urban space and are accompanied by quotidian sounds of the Bosporus—typical Istanbul sounds of seagulls and ferry horns, of urban traffic sounds and the sound of police sirens, etc.

While the sounds of waves, seagulls, and ferry horns create a site-specific, quotidian sonic experience of the city surrounded by the sea, the sound of police sirens and agitated voices is suggestive of past and present political activities in Turkey. These sounds and the setting of protest scenes in and around Taxim Square, for example, automatically invoke government-critical rallies and demonstrations that historically took place at these same sites, recalling events at the time around the military coups of 1960 and 1980, among others, as much as the more recent rallies in contemporary Turkey. Ultimately, through Akın's and Çatak's work, these sounds and historical references become integrated into German film and its discourse.

To summarize, Akın und Çatak create new cinematic images of self-confident, Turkish-speaking urban female figures who are multilingual—*The*

Figure 7.1. Contemplative Aslı (Sanem Öge) is crossing the Bosporus on a ferry in Istanbul in *Fidelity*. Press image, film still, *Fidelity*, Turkey, Germany, 2014. Photo source: Hamburg Media School.

Figure 7.2. Contemplative Ayten (Nurgül Yeşilçay) traverses the Bosporus in *The Edge of Heaven*. Film poster. With kind permission of Pyramide Distribution.

Edge of Heaven features Ayten, who speaks English, and a female translator, who speaks German in addition to Turkish. Ultimately, the plot of both films involves Turkish female figures fighting for things they believe in—such as justice and human rights—in the context of the diverse, vibrant, historicized cityscape of Istanbul. The directors create new quotidian city images of Istanbul—as a space to be navigated by these women—that go beyond tourist or cliché images and depict a heterogeneous, multifaceted city. Both of these depictions are innovative and much-needed interventions in the portrayal of Turkey and Turkish femininity in German film. At the same time, the new urban sound of Istanbul also includes a politicized sound of the city and thereby helps produce a complex character for the Turkish urban space. In both films, this is achieved by the sound of police sirens, shouting by the police, and the sound of footsteps running away from something. Regardless of the stories that are being told in these different films, as German filmmakers, Çatak and Akın project such new images and sounds of Istanbul and new perspectives of female Turkish figures onto global screens in combination with a particular European sound, which includes Turkish language and music.

Regarding the linguistic specificity of the soundtracks, there are further important details about the use of Turkish in the work of these directors. By normalizing the sound of the Turkish language, the language itself becomes normalized in European film. This is accomplished by, for example, creating full, complex characters whose first and preferred language of communication is Turkish, such as Ayten or Yeter in *The Edge of Heaven* and Aslı in *Fidelity*. This is especially relevant because the sound of the language in these films is not associated with stereotypical roles, such as comedic, passive, submissive, pious, victimized, exoticized, or eroticized figures. In this way, films like *The Edge of Heaven* and *Fidelity* change the sound of European film entirely, providing an alternative to the othering effect often invoked by using non-Western European languages and accents such as Turkish. In addition to the history of films exoticizing and/or othering nonwhite characters mentioned above, further examples of such othering effects are frequently found not only in older Turkish German narrative films but also in newer, more mainstream dramas or comedies about immigrants and ethnic minorities. These include the virtually canonized dramas *Yasemin* (1988) and *40 qm Deutschland* (40 Square Meters of Germany, 1986), *Tatort* episodes such as "Voll auf Hass" (Full of hate, 1987), as well as contemporary culture-clash comedies like *300 Worte Deutsch* (300 German words, 2013), or *Einmal Hans mit Scharfer Soße* (Spiced Up Jack, 2013).

In the context of Turkish-language use in European film, we should also consider Turkish French filmmaker Deniz Gamze Ergüven and her first feature film *Mustang* (2015). Ergüven's *Mustang* attracted a 2016 nomination for the Academy Award in the category of Best Foreign Language Film. *Mustang*'s at times exoticizing and orientalist portrayals notwithstanding—especially regarding the dreamy depiction of young Turkish femininities and the othering and vilifying portrayal of Muslim masculinity, respectively—the film nonetheless adds to the diversification of European cinema sound. *Mustang* was primarily made with a Turkish-speaking cast from Turkey and was selected by

France as its nomination for the 2016 Oscars. If we consider this selection against the backdrop of the foreign-language limits France imposes on a different medium—namely radio—which prescribes the amount of non-French languages that can be used on air, the decision to choose *Mustang* to represent France is all the more surprising, given that the soundscape of *Mustang* is entirely Turkish. Certainly, as stated above, we should acknowledge the criticism of the film raised due to its othering elements regarding the depiction of Turkish masculinity as much as the eroticism and exoticism surrounding the five young female protagonists portraying the siblings.[31] However, setting such criticism aside—especially given the fact that other characters in the film do not fit such easy, and problematic, categorizations, such as the character of the urban, secular, female Turkish teacher who lives in Istanbul and is portrayed as a role model for the siblings—*Mustang* is a film that deserves to be included into a discussion of the changed urban sounds of European cinema. Especially in light of Akın and Çatak, who use Turkish language and music among other languages in their soundtrack, without the exoticism associated with some of Ergüven's portrayals, these films all contribute to transforming Turkish into a native part of the French, German, and general European cinematic soundtrack.

Languages and contexts extending far beyond a geographical Europe and its neighboring countries are evoked in the work of filmmaker Amelia Umuhire. Umuhire contributes in similar ways to the changing sounds of German, European, and global film but via a completely different context; thereby, she presents a further, complex example for the construction of the new, diverse, urban sound of Europe.

Amelia Umuhire

Umuhire is a Rwandan-born artist who first moved with her family to the United Kingdom and then, in 1999 when her mother remarried and found employment in Germany, relocated to Neukirchen-Vluyn, a small town near Düsseldorf in Germany. In a personal email message, Umuhire stated that for two semesters she studied theater and film studies in Vienna, switched to international development and then switched again to area studies after moving to the Humboldt University in Berlin, where she currently lives and works. She has no formal training in filmmaking and had not applied to film school when she began working on *Polyglot* (2015). Still a university student, she simply started making the first episode for her web series. Working with no budget at all and relying on the help of family and friends, she directed her award-winning production.[32] While *Polyglot* was traveling the film circuits, Umuhire applied to film school (HFF) in Potsdam, but she was rejected.[33]

Awarded in 2015 at the Geneva International Film Festival, the Webfest Berlin, and the NumbiFest, Atlanta, just to name a few, *Polyglot* is a web series about the experiences of a multilingual Afro-German/Afro-European protagonist and her community of friends living in Berlin and London. While the first two episodes follow protagonist Babiche Papaya (also known as Amanda) in Berlin, the third part, "My Own," depicts Papaya's brother Roger, whom she visits in London. Roger is played by Umuhire's cousin Roger Jean Nsengiyumva, and Papaya is played by Umuhire's sister Amanda Mukasonga.

In general, the web series offers an intimate and emotional portrayal that introduces the particular quotidian experiences of a Rwandan German to a larger audience, including the intersection of multilingual sounds and multiethnic lives, the physical needs, and the inability or difficulty of sharing certain deep emotions and painful experiences such as migration, loss, and possibly the Rwandan genocide. At the same time, the series uses a quasi-realist-documentary style to offer a glimpse into the complex everyday life of a particular, strong, independent, creative, and multilingual Afro-European female figure who lives through different emotions of joy and pain while traversing and experiencing the city of Berlin. Mukasonga, who plays Papaya, states that "if I were in a TV show, normally, as me, a Black woman, I wouldn't get to be this real, as this 3D, as deep as a character."[34]

I focus on the episodes of *Polyglot* that are set in Berlin, Germany, because my main interest is in the audiovisual creation of a particular urban space—in this case, that of Berlin. The content of the first episode, "The Bewerbungsgespräch" (The interview), is centered around Papaya, a young, female person of color, who moved to Berlin and is looking for a room in an apartment. We follow her on her travels to the apartment, riding with her on the subway and walking with her on the streets of Berlin. At the end of the episode, right after she interviews for consideration as a roommate, the group of international and cosmopolitan roommates gather, indicating Papaya's successful interview and imminent move into the new home. The city and its inhabitants are presented in a uniquely intimate but also relaxed and carefree way.

Throughout the series, Berlin and the protagonist are portrayed as intrinsically linked. This episode begins by introducing Papaya speaking English to an acquaintance of hers on her cellphone about her search for an apartment in Berlin (figure 7.3). The establishing shot from a handheld camera is a medium shot of her in an unidentified part of Berlin, but it is clearly identifiable as an urban setting. While we hear her speaking English—the global language of communication and a language of the international city of Berlin—we also hear urban sounds very prominently (e.g., a variety of traffic sounds, including an ambulance and different vehicles of transportation). The unapologetic urbanity of Berlin is also mirrored in Papaya's attire. She is portrayed as a casual, internationally oriented, laid-back, creative person as indicated by her casual

Figure 7.3. Babiche Papaya (Amanda Mukasonga) talks on the phone about her apartment hunt in Berlin. Screen capture, *Polyglot*, "The Bewerbungsgespräch" (2015). With kind permission of Amelia Umuhire.

hipster-chic attire—she wears a dark hoodie beneath a vintage-looking 1980s black/purple track jacket, has fashionably peeling black nail polish, and carries a skateboard and a dark-colored backpack—as much as by her linguistic competencies, which we are exposed to throughout the episodes (in the first episode, she speaks German and English, as do her cosmopolitan future roommates, and shifts to French in the second episode). That is, Papaya's urban look and sound fits well with the urban depiction of Berlin in the film, as more specifically shown in the cross-cuts of the city.

In the subsequent cross-cuts of Berlin, we see sights that are marked by street art on the walls and doors. These are places of transit, such as the light rail Papaya rides on, a variety of specific Berlin streets, and specialty stores such as a former Swiss Lindt store transformed into a clothing boutique, and a Turkish German Döner stand. Papaya is ultimately framed by the graphics and tag-covered walls, trains, and sites of Berlin. In fact, her attire—including particularly her stylish, youthful jacket and nail polish—suggest that she is a vital part of the artistic fabric of Berlin. As an artist, she feels at home in this dynamic city. This is particularly highlighted and culminates when we hear Papaya's powerful performance of her poetry at the end of the episode, aurally marking her as an artist.

As observable by contemporary street art, changing urban design and developments, and continuous gentrification, Berlin is changing constantly and quickly. This is not a new notion of the city but has been a characteristic of Berlin since its early days as a metropolis in the twentieth century. Cultural critic Karl Scheffler wrote in his observations already in 1910 that Berlin is a city that is always in the making—"forever becoming" and never completed ("Berlin [ist] dazu verdammt immerfort zu werden und niemals zu sein").[35] This constant fluctuation is reiterated in the film audiovisually. Among others, Papaya's move into the city, her transportation on the trains, and her cosmopolitan roommates as the new, perhaps transitory, multilingual citizens of Berlin, as much as the ephemeral street art on Berlin's walls and trains, represent these fast-changing developments today. As a city marked by the constantly fluctuating street art, Berlin itself and Papaya the artist share a particular style: they are free-spirited, restless, and intrinsically connected to art. Ultimately, the audiovisual depiction of the urban space and the portrayal of the protagonist seem to overlap as Papaya becomes part of Berlin's vibrant art scene and finds a new home in this city.

The general idea of finding and ultimately creating a home, introduced in the first episode, is more explicitly and emotionally addressed in the second episode of *Polyglot*, "Le Mal du Pays" (Homesickness). Here, the focus and story are slightly different, yet the film is set in the same urban, street-art-filled, mobile, and cosmopolitan Berlin. The film features again a diverse soundtrack. Fitting the cosmopolitanism of Berlin, this time it includes musical sounds by DJ Zhao and musician Cécile Kayirebwa. DJ Zhao's work, for example, is described as bringing together different types of world music.

> DJ Zhao brings contemporary and classic dance music together from all five continents, with focus on Africa. ... [An] ethno-musicologist[,] ... Zhao ... demonstrate[es] ... raw sound experience, the underlying unity of all earth cultures and peoples.[36]

Additionally, Belgian Rwandan musician Cécile Kayirebwa performs the song "Marebe" twice—diegetically and nondiegetically—from the album *Interuro* (2015 [Vol. 1, 1981]), which features traditional Rwandan songs. Kayirebwa, who moved to Belgium in 1973, sings in her music about Rwandan life and themes, wishing to protect Rwandan traditional music. More recently she has stated, "I want to at least work with young Rwandans who are passionate about art, so that I share and pass on the cultural heritage."[37] She has been referred to as "the guardian of traditional Rwandan Music."[38] Thereby, Kayirebwa's song in this episode particularly links the film acoustically to the protagonist and the theme of homesickness; but at the same time, the song also connects to the themes and artistic styles associated with Rwandan musical traditions and integrates them into heterogeneous European cultural experiences as imaged on film.

In "Le Mal du Pays," the complex theme of homesickness is first introduced via text messages. The episode begins with a close-up of a mobile phone message being written (in English). Papaya goes through multiple drafts until the least emotional and most superficial version is finally sent. Beginning with texts such as "I am not well Jerome," "I've been in a weird mood lately," and "You know those days when you can't stop crying?" erasing them one by one, and ultimately sending the message "Hey dude, what's up?" indicates the inability to express (or at least the difficulties associated with expressing) certain feelings and to share them with other people.

The inability to express homesickness via the text messages is juxtaposed with the difficulties of dealing with daily challenges such as hair/body care. After Amanda—a young, fashionable woman—is depicted sitting and smoking at her window while listening to Kayirebwa's song "Marebe," we see her trying to style her hair with the help of a YouTube video. Finally, frustrated, she appears to give up. Later, we follow Amanda through the city of Berlin on a bus trip to a specialty store where she buys hair products (the shop name "Golden Lock" appears on one storefront). The ride through the city and the existence of the store indicate that the city offers alternatives and has a variety of products for its denizens. Yet these exchanges and products, though offering practical help, remain on an impersonal level.

It is only through the actual, physical, intimate presence of another female character who is able to help Amanda style and care for her hair and share her emotional concerns that we see a true expression of her feelings and perhaps begin to understand them. This scene takes place between two Afro-European characters and represents the culmination of an emotional quest through Berlin. The medium and close-up shots of the two women present their close positioning (figure 7.4). The camera frames them both individually and together—Amanda sits on the floor, leaning with her back toward the legs

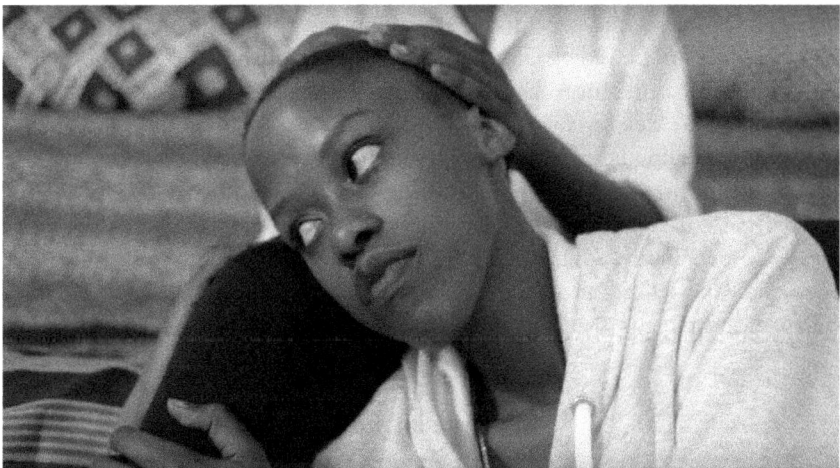

Figure 7.4. Amanda (Amanda Mukasonga) gets her hair done in Berlin. Screen capture, *Polyglot*, "Le Mal du Pays" (2015). With kind permission of Amelia Umuhire.

of the hair stylist, who carefully attends to her hair. These women are physically close to each other due to the act of hair care, but they are also close emotionally as they exchange, albeit minimally, their experiences and feelings about leaving the continent of Africa—expressing loss, sadness, etc. These scenes are very quiet compared to the bustling city of Berlin. The silence allows the protagonist—and the viewer—to dwell in the moment of sorrow. That is, there is a level of understanding between the two women that starts with the hair care and culminates in the quietly shared experience of migration, exile, and loss. The scene ends with the nondiegetic Rwandan song "Marebe" that Amanda also listened to at the beginning of the episode in her apartment.

The camera captures in medium shots the hair care as an act of caressing. The gentle combing and treating of the hair becomes a soothing human touch between the two women, which is highlighted formally through close-ups and extreme close-ups of the faces, the tears, and, ultimately, the sound of the French-speaking voices—a language that is reminiscent of a Belgian colonial past that is linked to Rwandan and German colonial history. This episode highlights that through a specific language—French, spoken in a particular accent—the Rwandan German and Belgian history is evoked, and the aftermath is experienced, in today's Berlin. The Rwandan song by the Belgian Rwandan artist Kayirebwa underlines this connection.

Languages and their sounds are as relevant in this web series as they are in the other films discussed here. The sound of the city (traffic sounds) is augmented with the sound of a variety of languages. In "The Bewerbungsgespräch," English and German are spoken with different accents, indicating once more the cosmopolitan aspects of Berlin's daily life. In the "Le Mal du Pays" episode, we hear German spoken with an accent, for example in the specialty hair product store. At the same time, we hear French as spoken by Amanda and her hairdresser (both played by Umuhire's sisters) or English in the YouTube video. Such linguistic differences, besides evoking different histories or geographies, can be relevant devices for making audible the accented sound of a globalized city. Multilingual filmic characters and their multivalent use of language becomes a normalized way of interacting in globalized urban spaces. While the dramatic narratives of the films unfold, these diversified sounds allow the viewer to experience a multiethnic and multilingual contemporary Europe as lived and experienced on a daily basis in cities such as Berlin, Hamburg, Istanbul, or London.

Conclusion

Ultimately, the films discussed in this chapter resist othering their characters. Rather, the variations of languages become a common factor among the speakers, serving to normalize the existence of accents and thereby expanding the sound of Europe. This sonic diversity is opposed to populist ideas that accents are inherently foreign or unsettling. While the films introduce and calmly lay bare topics such as home, *Heimat*, nostalgia, and the actual lived diversity of Europe in their narratives, the viewers listen to the diverse sounds that express these emotions and ideas in its urban centers. In an NPR Berlin interview, Umuhire states that she noticed that this type of sonic and visual diversity in German media was missing.[39] She adds: "There is this one image of Germany, like you have White people speaking German, if you look at the TV landscape for example. Black people only appear as nurses, or cooks. You don't get to know people, this big part of Germany and Berlin, because they are kind of marginalized in media."[40]

I would like to conclude by referring to this quote in particular. As I have shown in the three different productions above, with their multiethnic casts, urban settings, linguistic diversity, and dubbed and mixed music from various European and non-European regions (such as Rwanda and Turkey), among other sounds, "this part of Germany" does not need to be "marginalized in media" at all. In fact, it can be, and has to be, a regular part of it. These films invite the audience to aurally experience an interrelational Europe. Increasingly, artists such as Akın, Çatak, and Umuhire present a multiethnic and multilingual perspective of "German" film, thereby constructing a heterogeneous transnational concept of European film and media while also creating a countervoice to the existing racist tones across European politics and media.

Some production details that I have focused on in my study—such as setting, casting, and sound—might evoke the transnational nature of the contemporary (European) film industry and its production methods in general.[41] However, in addition to the production details, the directors and their films discussed in this contribution also exemplify the transnational alignment of Germany's and Europe's historical past and present. As I have shown, on the one hand, the production details of these films already extend beyond the conventional borders of Europe. On the other hand, these directors and their work also challenge, and are perhaps capable of ultimately changing, hegemonic narratives in and about German and European film—for example, by alluding to Rwandan, German, and Belgian colonial histories, as Umuhire does, or by exploring current and historical Turkish inquiries, as do Akın and Çatak. Ultimately, I hope to have exposed that these directors and their films actually transform Germany's and Europe's film industries and that one component of this transformative contribution is their filmic sound.

The lives and works of Akın, Çatak, and Umuhire delineate interventions into German film through their active diversification of sound, as much as subject matter, and image. More precisely, this means that their filmic soundtrack testifies to a normalization of sonic heterogeneity—multilingualism, variety of accents, and musical mixes from around the globe—in the new Europe. Ultimately this sound helps diversify both our understanding of Europe and the public image of European film and its soundtrack. This not only is an aesthetic quality but also has political implications. Through the staging of European diversity within their filmmaking, Akın, Çatak, and Umuhire intervene in the discourse of what Europe and European film was, is, and could be. They do so by helping to disseminate this vibrancy and diversity of German film and its soundtrack globally via festivals and the internet.

The German films discussed here, together with the Europe-wide examples provided at the beginning of this chapter, demonstrate that the diversification of the European sound in European cinema is a larger project that has been noticeably in progress since the early post–Cold War years and is becoming more prominent in the new millennium. At a time when the xenophobic rhetoric of right-wing and populist nationalists reaches new heights, such impulses are all the more relevant. They help by providing audiovisual examples that normalize contemporary sights and sounds of urban metropolitan areas in Europe, and they also help by creating fictional narrative accounts that normalize new protagonists—the urban, diverse, nonwhite, polyglot navigators of a new Europe.

Berna Gueneli is associate professor of German in the Department of Germanic and Slavic Studies at the University of Georgia, Athens. In addition to her book *Fatih Akın's Cinema and the New Sound of Europe* (Indiana University Press, 2019), she has published articles and coedited two special issues on Turkish German studies. Her second book-length study explores orientalism's impact on film and visual culture in the Weimar Republic.

Notes

1. Pegida is the acronym for "Patriotische Europäer gegen die Islamisierung des Abendlandes," which translates to "Patriotic Europeans against the Islamisation of the Occident."
2. In 2017, the AFD emerged as the third strongest party in the German parliament elections, the Front National claimed the second highest number of votes in the French presidential elections of that year, and the FPÖ formed a government coalition with the conservative ÖVP (Österreichische Volkspartei [Austrian People's Party]) in Austria.
3. Such discourse is not limited to the ultraconservative and the right-wing movements. More generally, according to Fatima El-Tayeb, racist discourse in Germany (and in Europe for that matter, too) is not in fact new but is recreated, repeatedly over time, in order to construct a German national (and also European) identity. Those who have been typically excluded as "others" despite German residency or citizenship, for example, have been people of Jewish, Polish, Turkish, or Arab background, depending on the historical context. This process of creating German identity via the foil of the other has repeated itself throughout history and continues to do so today. See, for example,

Fatima El-Tayeb, *Undeutsch: Die Konstruktion des Anderen in der postmigrantischen Gesellschaft* (Bielefeld: transcript, 2016), 8–11, 14, 149, 157.
4. For a discussion of the concept of "fortress Europe" and the cinematic portrayal of immigrants and refugees in this context, see, for example, Yosefa Loshitzky's persuasive discussion of the topic in Loshitzky, *Screening Strangers: Migration and Diaspora in Contemporary European Cinema* (Bloomington: Indiana University Press, 2010). Regarding notions of race, El-Tayeb states that Germany (and Europe) avoid a discussion on racism by substituting the term "racism" with "xenophobia." For further discussion and a differentiation between the terms *racism* and *xenophobia*, see, El-Tayeb, *Undeutsch*, e.g., 14–15.
5. Such fortified edges are also actively paid for, if we consider Merkel's endeavors to make payments to Turkey to keep Syrian refugees from continuing their journey to central Europe. Merkel called on EU member states in summer 2018 "to allocate an additional 3 billion euros in assistance for Syrian refugees in Turkey." She phrased this monetary deal with Turkey as "helping Turkey in overcoming the challenges of having over 3 million Syrian refugees." Berlin, Anadolu Agency, "Merkel Praises Turkey, Pushes for More Support for Refugees," *Hürriyet Daily News*, 28 June 2018, retrieved 4 September 2018 from http://www.hurriyetdailynews.com/merkel-praises-turkey-pushes-more-support-for-refugees-133914.
6. Between the completion of my work and the publication of it, some publications have appeared in the meantime that also address Amelia Umuhire's fine work. One such piece is an interview: Gabi Kathöfer and Beverly Weber, "Heimat, Sustainability, Community: A Conversation with Karina Griffith and Peggy Piesche," *Seminar* 54, no. 4 (November 2018): 418–27.
7. For a detailed discussion of the diversification of European cinema sound and several of the filmmakers mentioned here, see chapter 4 in Berna Gueneli, *Fatih Akın's Cinema and the New Sound of Europe* (Bloomington: Indiana University Press, 2019).
8. The use of Romani musicians and their music in such films has been criticized by some scholars as orientalizing or Balkanizing. Ioana Szeman, "'Gypsy Music' and Deejays: Orientalism, Balkanism, and Romani Musicians," *TDR: The Drama Review* 53, no. 3 (2009): 98–116.
9. Will Higbee, "Hope and Indignation in Fortress Europe: Immigration and Neoliberal Globalization in Contemporary French Cinema," *SubStance* 43, no. 1 (2014): 26–43; Isabelle McNeill, "Virtual Homes: Space and Memory in the Work of Yamina Benguigui," *L'Esprit Créateur* 51, no. 1 (2011): 12–25.
10. Higbee, "Hope and Indignation." In the case of Benguigui's film *Inch'Allah Dimanche* (*Inch'Allah Sunday*, 2001), for example, set in 1974, the diversification even goes beyond the contemporary and helps to retroactively diversify the acoustic memory of France of the 1970s, as the soundtrack employs diegetic French and Arabic music popular during that time.
11. It is not only films but also film festivals that help construct the new sound of Europe in European film and cinema. They do so by helping to distribute new diversified European sounds. The Sarajevo Film Festival, for example, diversifies sounds and sights of European cinema by offering a platform for Southeastern and Central European films, especially Balkan, Turkish, and Greek films. For more discussions on the Sarajevo Film Festival, see Kristine Kotecki, "Europeanizing the Balkans at the Sarajevo Film Festival," *Journal of Narrative Theory* 44, no. 3 (2014): 344–66.

12. For an in-depth discussion of the diversification of German and European cinema through Fatih Akın's work, see Gueneli, *Fatih Akın's Cinema*.
13. The NSU murders have been previously thematized within different genres and artistic disciplines. Esther Dischereit, for example, wrote an opera reworking the traumata of the victims. For this project, Dischereit collaborated with two Turkish German musicians: Sinem Altan and İpek İpekçioğlu (DJ Ipek). Roman Kern and Ann Kathrin Thüringer, "Klagelieder für die Opfer der NSU-Mordserie," *Kontur*, 1 September 2013, retrieved 3 October 2018 from http://kontur-medien.de/project/klagelieder-fur-die-opfer-der-nsu-mordserie/; for a discussion of the "Klagelieder," see Ela Gezen, "Poetic Empathy, Political Criticism, and Public Mourning: Esther Dischereit's *Klagelieder*," *Gegenwartsliteratur: Ein germanistisches Jahrbuch* 17 (2018): 313–30.
14. Selmin Kara, "Reassembling the Nation: *Iraq in Fragments* and the Acoustics of Occupation," *Studies in Documentary Film* 3, no. 3 (2009): 259–74, doi:10.1386/sdf3.3.259/1.
15. Tania Gentic, "Beyond the Visual City: The Sound of Space in Fernando Pérez's Suite Habana," *Hispanic Review* 82, no. 2 (2018): 199–220; Amanda Holmes, "Backstage Pass to the City: The Soundscape of *Suite Habana*," *Studies in Spanish & Latin American Cinemas* 12, no. 2 (2015): 123–37.
16. Holmes, "Backstage Pass," 125–26.
17. Andrew Czink, "Sound Reasons: Auditory Experience and the Environment," *International Journal of the Humanities* 7, no. 6 (2009): 59–60.
18. Anahid Kassabian, *Hearing Film: Tracking Identification in Contemporary Hollywood Film Music* (New York: Routledge, 2001), 4.
19. Kassabian, *Hearing Film*, 4.
20. For the purposes of my chapter and the spatial limitation imposed by the format of a chapter, I will not differentiate between production and postproduction sounds (onsite sounds versus the sound effects added later), both of which are used in the films I discuss. However, I will acknowledge Emily Yu's scholarship that states that due to technical limitations of onsite recording, it is often postproduction sounds and sound effects, rather than the production sounds themselves, that create a more "realistic" experience for the viewer. Emily Yu, "Sounds of Cinema: What Do We Really Hear?" *Journal of Popular Film & Television* 31, no. 2 (2003): 93–96, 93.
21. Additionally, Naficy describes the "accented cinema" of Turkish directors as "a Turkish cinema in exile," which further suggests a distinction from other European cinema and film, while I maintain the "Europeanness" of the films I discuss, as I especially regard the migratory and transnational background of their directors and producers as integrated to European cultural practices. Hamid Naficy, "Phobic Spaces and Liminal Panics: Independent Transnational Film Genre," in *Multiculturalism, Postcoloniality, and Transnational Media*, ed. Ella Shohat and Robert Stam, 203–26 (New Brunswick, NJ: Rutgers University Press, 2003), 215–16. For Naficy's introduction of the category of "accented cinema" see, Hamid Naficy, *An Accented Cinema* (Princeton, NJ: Princeton University Press, 2001). Additionally, the films discussed in this chapter also differ from Naficy's newer concept of the "multiplex cinema" that highlights the more commercialized form of films, in which mass media merges with multiethnic content. Hamid Naficy, "From Accented Cinema to Multiplex Cinema," in *Convergence Media History*, ed. Janet Staiger and Sabine Hake (New York: Routledge, 2009), 3–13.
22. Deniz Göktürk, "World Cinema Goes Digital: Looking at Europe from the Other Shore," in *Turkish German Cinema in the New Millennium*, ed. Sabine Hake and Bar-

bara Mennel (Oxford: Berghahn Books, 2012), 198–211; Berna Gueneli, "The Sound of Fatih Akın's Cinema: Polyphony and the Aesthetics of Heterogeneity in *The Edge of Heaven*," *German Studies Review* 37, no. 2 (2014): 337–56; Roger Hillman and Vivien Silvey, "Remixing Hamburg: Transnationalism in Fatih Akın's Soul Kitchen," in Hake and Mennel, *Turkish German Cinema*, 186–97; Barbara Kosta, "Transnational Space and Music: Fatih Akın's *Crossing the Bridge: The Sound of Istanbul* (2005)," in *Spatial Turns: Space, Place, and Mobility in German Literary and Visual Culture*, ed. Jaimey Fisher and Barbara Mennel (New York: Rodopi, 2010), 343–60; Senta Siewert, "Soundtracks of Double Occupancy: Sampling Sounds and Cultures in Fatih Akin's Head On," in *Mind the Screen: Media Concepts According to Thomas Elsaesser*, ed. Jaap Kooijman, Patricia Pisters, and Wanda Strauven (Amsterdam: Amsterdam University Press, 2008), 198–208.
23. Gueneli, "The Sound."
24. In Akın's 2005 music documentary *The Sound of Istanbul*, for example, the languages Romani as well as Kurdish are performed in songs. In *In July*, spoken languages include Serbo-Croatian and Hungarian. For a discussion of spoken and sung languages and dialects in Akın's *The Edge of Heaven*, see, for example, Gueneli, "The Sound," 349–51; Barbara Mennel, "Überkreuzungen in globaler Zeit und globalem Raum in Fatih Akın's *Auf der anderen Seite*," in *Kultur als Ereignis: Fatih Akıns Film Auf der anderen Seite als transkulturelle Narration*, ed. Özkan Ezli (Bielefeld: transcript, 2010), 98. For a discussion of the use of different languages in Akın's films, see also David Gramling, "On the Other Side of Monolingualism: Fatih Akın's Linguistic Turn," *The German Quarterly* 83, no. 3 (2010): 353–72.
25. Gueneli, "The Sound," 346–48.
26. For a discussion of Kazim Koyuncu and his music in *The Edge of Heaven* see, Göktürk, "World Cinema Goes Digital," 199–202.
27. For further discussions of various forms of exoticism in several of these films, see, for example, Berna Gueneli, "Mehmet Kurtuluş and Birol Ünel: Sexualized Masculinities, Normalized Ethnicities," in Hake and Mennel, *Turkish German Cinema*, 136–48; Al LaValley, "The Gay Liberation of Rainer Werner Fassbinder: Male Subjectivity, Male Bodies, Male Lovers," in "Rainer Werner Fassbinder," special issue, *New German Critique* 63 (1994): 108–37; Katie Trumpener, "Puerto Rico Fever: Douglas Sirk, La Habanera (1937) and the Epistemology of Exoticism," in *"Neue Welt" / "Dritte Welt": Interkulturelle Beziehungen Deutschlands zu Lateinamerika und der Karibik*, ed. Sigrid Bauschinger and Susan Cocalis (Tübingen and Basel: Francke, 1994), 115–39; Cynthia Walk, "Anna May Wong and Weimar Cinema: Orientalism in Postcolonial Germany," in *Beyond Alterity: German Encounters with Modern East Asia*, ed. Qinna Shen and Martin Rosenstock (New York: Berghahn Books, 2014), 137–67.
28. In this context, Priscilla Layne's book *White Rebels in Black* is of interest. In her work, Layne traces the history of postwar German appropriation of Black culture in literature and film. These become a place for rebellion for white German masculinities. That is, the white Germans' otherness (rebellion against hegemonic, heteronormative, "Western" postwar culture) is housed in the space stereotypically reserved for Black others (jazz, jazz club). *White Rebels in Black: German Appropriation of Black Popular Culture* (Ann Arbor: University of Michigan Press, 2018), 8, 12, 61.
29. For a discussion on İlker Çatak and his work, see also the introduction and interview between Gueneli and Çatak, Berna Gueneli, "'Ja, dann mach doch was mit Film. Werd' doch Filmemacher': Eine Einleitung von Berna Gueneli und ein Interview mit İlker

Çatak," in *Deutsch-Türkische Filmkultur im Migrationskontext*, ed. Ömer Alkın (Wiesbaden: Springer VS Verlag, 2017), 404–23.

30. For further discussions of media and cinematic depictions of Turkish women in the context of violence and victimhood, see, for example, Ipek Çelik's chapter on *Head-On*, "Ethnicity and Melodrama in the German Media and Fatih Akın's *Head-On*," in *In Permanent Crisis: Ethnicity in Contemporary European Media and Cinema* (Ann Arbor: University of Michigan Press, 2015), 102–26.
31. Rachel Donadio mentions in a *New York Times* article the different criticisms that were raised early on about *Mustang*. Donadio, "With 'Mustang,' a Director Breaks Free of Cultural Confines," *New York Times*, 18 November 2015, retrieved 1 August 2018 from https://www.nytimes.com/2015/11/22/movies/with-mustang-a-director-breaks-free-of-cultural-confines.html.
32. Information about biographical details on Amelia Umuhire, "Amelia Umuhire," Tribeca Film, n.d., retrieved 15 August 2016 from https://tribecafilm.com/festival/tribecanow/amelia-umuhire; also see Akua Agyen "Talking Film with Director and Filmmaker Amelia Umuhire," *Ayiba Magazine*, 9 May 2016, retrieved 8 May 2018 from http://ayibamagazine.com/talking-film-director-filmmaker-amelia-umuhire/
33. Amelia Umuhire, email message to the author, 9 September 2018.
34. Quoted in Jennifer Sefa-Boakye, "'Polyglot,' A New Web Series on Young Creatives of Color in Berlin," *Okayafrica*, 30 June 2015, retrieved 19 March 2018 from http://www.okayafrica.com/polyglot-webseries-amelia-umuhire/.
35. Kurt Scheffler, quoted in Harald Neumeyer, *Der Flaneur: Konzeptionen der Moderne* (Würzburg: Königshausen & Neumann: 1999), 299.
36. "DJ Zhao—Part 1—NGOMA 4 Generation Bass," YouTube, 4 July 2011, retrieved 9 May 2018 from https://www.youtube.com/watch?v=v4pdKBHfbM0.
37. Quoted in Julius Bizimungu, "Rwandan Music in Exile," 8 March 2016, *Music Africa*, retrieved 3 October 2018 from https://www.musicinafrica.net/magazine/rwandan-music-exile.
38. Rwanda Podium, "RWANDA: Cecile Kayirebwa, Guardian of Rwanda's Traditional Music," 2018, retrieved 2 October 2018 from http://www.rwanda-podium.org/index.php/actualites/education/478-rwanda-cecile-kayirebwa-guardian-of-rwanda-s-traditional-music; for more information on Kayirebwa, see also, "Cécile Kayirebwa," African Musicians Profiles, retrieved 3 October 2018 from http://www.africanmusiciansprofiles.com/CecileKayirebwa.htm.
39. For a wide-reaching discussion of appropriations of Black culture in German literature and film, see Priscilla Layne's discussions in her book *White Rebels in Black: German Appropriation of Black Popular Culture* (Ann Arbor: University of Michigan Press, 2018).
40. NPR Berlin, "Interview with Amelia Umuhire," retrieved 15 February 2016 from http://www.nprberlin.de/post/life-berlin-exploring-identity-language-and-race-polyglot#stream/0.
41. Such cinematic transnationalism, including its production methods, has been discussed at length, for example, in the scholarship of Randall Halle, Anna Jäckel, Katrin Sieg, and Mike Wayne. Randall Halle, *German Film After Germany: Toward a Transnational Aesthetic* (Urbana: University of Illinois Press, 2008); Anne Jäckel, *European Film Industries* (London: British Film Institute, 2003); Katrin Sieg, *Choreographing the Global in European Cinema and Theater* (New York: Palgrave Macmillan, 2008); Mike Wayne, *The Politics of Contemporary European Cinema: Histories, Borders, Diasporas* (Bristol: Intellect, 2002).

Bibliography

Agyen, Akua. "Talking Film with Director and Filmmaker Amelia Umuhire." *Ayiba Magazine*, 9 May 2016. Retrieved 8 May 2018 from http://ayibamagazine.com/talking-film-director-filmmaker-amelia-umuhire/.
"Amelia Umuhire." Tribeca Film. N.d. Retrieved 15 August 2016 from https://tribecafilm.com/festival/tribecanow/amelia-umuhire.
Berlin, Anadolu Agency. "Merkel Praises Turkey, Pushes for More Support for Refugees." *Hürriyet Daily News*, 28 June 2018. Retrieved 4 September 2018 from http://www.hurriyetdailynews.com/merkel-praises-turkey-pushes-more-support-for-refugees-133914.
Bizimungu, Julius. "Rwandan Music in Exile." *Music Africa*, 8 March 2016. Retrieved 3 October 2018 from https://www.musicinafrica.net/magazine/rwandan-music-exile.
"Cécile Kayirebwa," African Musicians Profiles. Retrieved 3 October 2018 from http://www.africanmusiciansprofiles.com/CecileKayirebwa.htm.
Çelik, Ipek. "Ethnicity and Melodrama in the German Media and Fatih Akın's *Head-On*." In *In Permanent Crisis: Ethnicity in Contemporary European Media and Cinema*, 102–26. Ann Arbor: University of Michigan Press, 2015.
Czink, Andrew. "Sound Reasons: Auditory Experience and the Environment." *International Journal of the Humanities* 7, no. 6 (2009): 59–71.
"DJ Zhao—Part 1—NGOMA 4 Generation Bass." YouTube, 4 July 2011. Retrieved 9 May 2018 from https://www.youtube.com/watch?v=v4pdKBHfbM0.
Donadio, Rachel. "With 'Mustang,' a Director Breaks Free of Cultural Confines." *New York Times*, 18 November 2015. Retrieved 1 August 2018 from https://www.nytimes.com/2015/11/22/movies/with-mustang-a-director-breaks-free-of-cultural-confines.html.
El-Tayeb, Fatima. *Undeutsch: Die Konstruktion des Anderen in der postmigrantischen Gesellschaft*. Bielefeld: transcript, 2016.
Gentic, Tania. "Beyond the Visual City: The Sound of Space in Fernando Pérez's Suite Habana." *Hispanic Review* 82, no. 2 (2018): 199–220.
Gezen, Ela. "Poetic Empathy, Political Criticism, and Public Mourning: Esther Dischereit's Klagelieder." *Jahrbuch Gegenwartsliteratur* 17 (2018): 313–30.
Göktürk, Deniz. "World Cinema Goes Digital: Looking at Europe from the Other Shore." In *Turkish German Cinema in the New Millennium*, edited by Sabine Hake and Barbara Mennel, 198–211. Oxford: Berghahn Books, 2012.
Gramling, David. "On the Other Side of Monolingualism: Fatih Akın's Linguistic Turn." *The German Quarterly* 83, no. 3 (2010): 353–72.
Gueneli, Berna. *Fatih Akın's Cinema and the New Sound of Europe*. Bloomington: Indiana University Press, 2019.
———. "'Ja, dann mach doch was mit Film. Werd' doch Filmemacher': Eine Einleitung von Berna Gueneli und ein Interview mit İlker Çatak." In *Deutsch-Türkische Filmkultur im Migrationskontext*, edited by Ömer Alkın, 404–23. Wiesbaden: Springer VS Verlag, 2017.
———. "Mehmet Kurtuluş and Birol Ünel: Sexualized Masculinities, Normalized Ethnicities." In *Turkish German Cinema in the New Millennium*, edited by Sabine Hake and Barbara Mennel, 136–48. Oxford: Berghahn Books, 2012.
———. "The Sound of Fatih Akın's Cinema: Polyphony and the Aesthetics of Heterogeneity in *The Edge of Heaven*." *German Studies Review* 37, no. 2 (2014): 337–56.

Halle, Randall. *German Film after Germany: Toward a Transnational Aesthetic.* Urbana: University of Illinois Press, 2008.

Higbee, Will. "Hope and Indignation in Fortress Europe: Immigration and Neoliberal Globalization in Contemporary French Cinema." *SubStance* 43, no. 1 (2014): 26–43.

Hillman, Roger, and Vivien Silvey. "Remixing Hamburg: Transnationalism in Fatih Akın's *Soul Kitchen.*" In *Turkish German Cinema in the New Millennium,* edited by Sabine Hake and Barbara Mennel, 186–97. Oxford: Berghahn Books, 2012.

Holmes, Amanda. "Backstage Pass to the City: The Soundscape of *Suite Habana.*" *Studies in Spanish & Latin American Cinemas* 12, no. 2 (2015): 123–37.

Jäckel, Anne. *European Film Industries.* London: British Film Institute, 2003.

Kara, Selmin. "Reassembling the Nation: *Iraq in Fragments* and the Acoustics of Occupation." *Studies in Documentary Film* 3, no. 3 (2009): 259–74, doi:10.1386/sdf3.3.259/1.

Kassabian, Anahid. *Hearing Film: Tracking Identification in Contemporary Hollywood Film Music.* New York: Routledge, 2001.

Kathöfer, Gabi, and Beverly Weber. "Heimat, Sustainability, Community: A Conversation with Karina Griffith and Peggy Piesche." *Seminar* 54, no. 4 (November 2018): 418–27.

Kern, Roman, and Ann Kathrin Thüringer. "Klagelieder für die Opfer der NSU-Mordserie." *Kontur,* 1 September 2013. Retrieved 3 October 2018 from http://kontur-medien.de/project/klagelieder-fur-die-opfer-der-nsu-mordserie/.

Kosta, Barbara. "Transnational Space and Music: Fatih Akın's *Crossing the Bridge: The Sound of Istanbul* (2005)." In *Spatial Turns: Space, Place, and Mobility in German Literary and Visual Culture,* edited by Jaimey Fisher and Barbara Mennel, 343–60. New York: Rodopi, 2010.

Kotecki, Kristine. "Europeanizing the Balkans at the Sarajevo Film Festival." *Journal of Narrative Theory* 44, no. 3 (2014): 344–66.

LaValley, Al. "The Gay Liberation of Rainer Werner Fassbinder: Male Subjectivity, Male Bodies, Male Lovers." In "Rainer Werner Fassbinder," special issue, *New German Critique* 63 (1994): 108–37.

Layne, Priscilla. *White Rebels in Black: German Appropriation of Black Popular Culture.* Ann Arbor: University of Michigan Press, 2018.

Loshitzky, Yosefa. *Screening Strangers: Migration and Diaspora in Contemporary European Cinema.* Bloomington: Indiana University Press, 2010.

McNeill, Isabelle. "Virtual Homes: Space and Memory in the Work of Yamina Benguigui." *L'Esprit Créateur* 51, no. 1 (2011): 12–25.

Mennel, Barbara. "Überkreuzungen in globaler Zeit und globalem Raum in Fatih Akın's *Auf der anderen Seite.*" In *Kultur als Ereignis: Fatih Akıns Film* Auf der anderen Seite *als transkulturelle Narration,* edited by Özkan Ezli, 95–118. Bielefeld: transcript, 2010.

Naficy, Hamid. *An Accented Cinema.* Princeton, NJ: Princeton University Press, 2001.

———. "From Accented Cinema to Multiplex Cinema." In *Convergence Media History,* edited by Janet Staiger and Sabine Hake, 3–13. New York: Routledge, 2009.

———. "Phobic Spaces and Liminal Panics: Independent Transnational Film Genre." In *Multiculturalism, Postcoloniality, and Transnational Media,* edited by Ella Shohat and Robert Stam, 203–26. New Brunswick, NJ: Rutgers University Press, 2003.

NPR Berlin. "Interview with Amelia Umuhire." Retrieved 15 February 2016 from http://www.nprberlin.de/post/life-berlin-exploring-identity-language-and-race-polyglot#stream/0.

Rwanda Podium. "RWANDA: Cecile Kayirebwa, Guardian of Rwanda's Traditional Music." 2018. Retrieved 2 October 2018 from http://www.rwanda-podium.org/index

.php/actualites/education/478-rwanda-cecile-kayirebwa-guardian-of-rwanda-s-traditional-music.

Scheffler, Kurt, quoted in Harald Neumeyer. *Der Flaneur: Konzeptionen der Moderne*. Würzburg: Königshausen & Neumann, 1999.

Sefa-Boakye, Jennifer. "'Polyglot,' a New Web Series on Young Creatives of Color in Berlin." *Okayafrica*, 30 June 2015. Retrieved 19 March 2018 from http://www.okayafrica.com/polyglot-webseries-amelia-umuhire/.

Sieg, Katrin. *Choreographing the Global in European Cinema and Theater*. New York: Palgrave Macmillan, 2008.

Siewert, Senta. "Soundtracks of Double Occupancy: Sampling Sounds and Cultures in Fatih Akin's *Head On*." In *Mind the Screen: Media Concepts According to Thomas Elsaesser*, edited by Jaap Kooijman, Patricia Pisters, and Wanda Strauven, 198–208. Amsterdam: Amsterdam University Press, 2008.

Szeman, Ioana. "'Gypsy Music' and Deejays: Orientalism, Balkanism, and Romani Musicians." *TDR: The Drama Review* 53, no. 3 (2009): 98–116.

Trumpener, Katie. "Puerto Rico Fever: Douglas Sirk, La Habanera (1937) and the Epistemology of Exoticism." In *"Neue Welt" / "Dritte Welt": Interkulturelle Beziehungen Deutschlands zu Lateinamerika und der Karibik*, edited by Sigrid Bauschinger and Susan Cocalis, 115–39. Tübingen and Basel: Francke, 1994.

Walk, Cynthia. "Anna May Wong and Weimar Cinema: Orientalism in Postcolonial Germany." In *Beyond Alterity: German Encounters with Modern East Asia*, edited by Qinna Shen and Martin Rosenstock, 137–67. New York: Berghahn Books, 2014.

Wayne, Mike. *The Politics of Contemporary European Cinema: Histories, Borders, Diasporas*. Bristol: Intellect, 2002.

Yu, Emily. "Sounds of Cinema: What Do We Really Hear?" *Journal of Popular Film & Television* 31, no. 2 (2003): 93–96.

CHAPTER 8

Subjunctive Remembering; Contingent Resistance
Katja Petrowskaja's Vielleicht Esther

MAYA CASPARI

Looking back ... keeps open the possibility of going astray.
—Sara Ahmed, "Orientations: Toward a Queer Phenomenology"

Introduction: Grammars of Memory

In 1882, at a time when many European countries were anxious to establish their identities, French historian Ernest Renan famously commented:

> Forgetting ... is an essential element in the creation of a nation ... unity is always brutally established.[1]

Arguing that nations should be defined on the basis of a "rich legacy of memories" and a shared "heroic past," Renan depicted the nation as a discursive construct, a symbolic archive that necessarily "forgets" elements that might threaten its unity. In recent years, numerous scholars have shown how this exclusionary framing process has indeed been key to the formation of hegemonic national identities, with hugely violent effects.[2] Yet, the idea of the nation as a kind of archive has also opened space for important critical interventions. Some scholars have uncovered the memories and lives that have been forgotten in narratives of homogenous nationhood, highlighting how nations are in fact shaped through diverse cultural histories and movements of peoples. Others have sought new models for theorizing identity beyond nineteenth-century notions of the "coherent and bounded nation," invoking the concept of diaspora as an alternative paradigm through which to characterize identity as multiple, unstable, or hybrid.[3] In the increasingly globalized world of the twenty-first century, the demand for transnational forms of identification is also often tempered by an awareness of the particularity of different lived experiences of border crossing. Yet some have pointed out that naively celebratory readings of migration and/or diaspora may enact further erasures, reducing varied histories to a single redemptive metaphor and even repeating the flattening effects of globalization.[4] As Anna Guttman among others, has argued, this has particularly problematic implications in the context of Jewish history: noting that the Jewish diaspora is often implicitly the "theoretical antecedent" to postmodern celebrations of the cosmopolitan subject, she suggests that contemporary articulations of cosmopolitan identity can constitute an abstraction that suppresses the difference and plurality of Jewishness.[5]

Such discussions have set the tone for the critical reception of literatures of migration, which are often read for their potential to resist both—in David Damrosch's formulation—"narrowly bounded nationalism and a boundless, breathless globalism."[6] In Germany, this tension is further complicated by sometimes competing political demands to, on the one hand, recall traumatic legacies and accept *German* responsibility for past crimes and to, on the other, depart from binary-based, ethnicized understandings of national identity.[7] Along these lines, some scholars have recently read migration literatures as counterhegemonic by virtue of their representations (or even supposed embodiment) of the cosmopolitan and/or postcolonial nature of the nation, disrupting its illusory unity through positioning apparently foreign memories *within* the national space.[8] Others, meanwhile, have explored writers' representations of the particular, at times traumatic, histories of minoritarian subjects, highlighting how these may draw attention to the limitations of flat, celebratory narratives of transnational memory.[9] Indeed, at a time when the humanities are facing renewed demands to prove their worth, there can be a redemptive strain in the critical desire to read migrant writing for the strength of its political interventions as countermemory.

This is important work. Yet, along with reading texts through the lens of these contemporary debates, it is also important to ask how texts might more radically reimagine the possibilities of what literature's political intervention could be at the contemporary moment. For, I would tentatively suggest, despite the differences between these varied critical readings, texts' political potential is often understood as *making visible* that which has been erased or hidden, waiting to be discerned by insightful readers. This approach relies on a limiting opposition between the static *reality* of experiences of migration and the *artifice* of a hegemonic framework, whether this hegemony is defined as the nation-state or as abstract theorizations of diaspora. Such readings abound: Simon Gikandi, for example, invokes the lived experience of refugees as the potentially disruptive "mote in the eye" of liberal cosmopolitanism, which is characterized as a "discursive pose" based on a fantasy of free movement.[10]

From a different angle, in his work on multidirectional memory, Michael Rothberg writes that he reveals examples of memories that have *"persistently broken the frame* of the nation-state" and thus *"make . . . visible* a [multidirectional] counter-tradition," an alternative archive.[11] His argument seeks to depart from "dominant" competitive and binary-based understandings of memory, suggesting instead that the memory of one group's suffering can open up—rather than erase—another. Yet interestingly, even as they seek to disrupt the inside/outside oppositions of dominant frameworks, readings such as this paradoxically often draw on binary logic to articulate their own interventions—an approach that locates politics in the *vision* of the critic: when read in opposition to that which is defined as hegemonic, the experience of displacement is instrumentalized, metaphorically, as a pre-given reality, a source of illegible alterity that might disrupt the artifice of a dominant (trans)national narrative.[12] This is not to suggest that critics affirm the notion of an authentic or original experience of migration but rather that these arguments rely on affording it a fixed rhetorical function as a disruptive real.[13] As such, I want to ask: Is it possible to imagine literary political interventions beyond the binary terms still implied by the familiar critical trope of *the frame*? In what other ways might texts address and reimagine the archive of nationhood?

Through a close reading of Katja Petrowskaja's text *Vielleicht Esther*, this chapter explores whether a narrative strategy of "subjunctive remembering" might open up new approaches to these questions.[14] Published to critical acclaim in Germany in 2014, *Vielleicht Esther* appeared in Shelley Frisch's English translation as *Maybe Esther* in 2018.[15] The book follows its first-person Jewish-Ukrainian narrator's process of tracing her family history across several generations and European countries. Written in six chapters that loosely follow the autobiographical narrator's research process, the text enacts the material, emotional, and tactile process of uncovering traumatic twentieth-century stories in the digital and globalized twenty-first-century present. The text opens in Berlin and follows the narrator in her search for family history across several countries, including present-day Poland, Russia, Austria, and Ukraine, the country in which she grew up while it was still part of the Soviet Union. Some responses to Petrowskaja's text categorized it as a "family story" (the subtitle to the US edition) or "Holocaust memoir."[16] As such, they seem to position it within a familiar, and perhaps easily consumable, tradition of testimonial writing, emphasizing its autobiographical aspect over its formal experimentations. Yet, as the majority of reviewers noted, while it may be described as "life-writing" in its blend of autobiography, fiction, myth, and history, the text in fact refuses traditional genre categories.[17] Throughout, Petrowskaja employs multiple modes and registers of representation, including historical citation, theoretical reflection, childhood memories, photographs, mythology, and fragmented dream narratives. Though awarded the 2013 Ingeborg Bachmann prize for literature, Petrowskaja prefers to describe her work with the more ambiguous and plural term *Geschichten*, which means both "stories" and "histories."[18]

This generic hybridity is in part symptomatic of the belated twenty-first-century moment in which the earlier twentieth-century past is increasingly only accessible through material traces, secondhand memories, and the uncanny connectivities of the digital. As Marianne Hirsch observes, imaginative work is perhaps a necessary aspect of later generations' attempts to remember and work through the increasingly distant traumatic pasts of the twentieth century.[19] Yet, recent critical work has drawn attention to the ways in which Petrowskaja's work also extends the conventions of postmemorial writing.[20] As Maria Roca Lizarazu notes, the text simultaneously, and quite cannily, taps into multiple contemporary literary trends. It not only evokes tropes from the postmemorial Holocaust narrative, including metacommentary on the ethics writing about traumas one has not oneself experienced, but also relates to what Brigid Haines, referring to the increase in German-language texts by authors from former Soviet countries, termed the "eastern turn" in contemporary German-language writing.[21] As such, Lizarazu argues that the text also works beyond the tradition of the postmemorial family book, drawing on "textile imagery" to establish horizontal, often transnational webs of connection beyond the linearity of a conventional inheritance narrative.[22]

Along these lines, as in the theoretical discussions cited above, other critics have frequently focused on how Petrowskaja's work interrogates hegemonic narratives of national identity and history in its transnational approach to memory. As Katja Garloff and Agnes Mueller argue, German-language work by Jewish authors from the former Soviet Union frequently "establishes connections between oppression and violence in different locations, including eastern Europe."[23] In these terms, Andree Michaelis-König suggests that Petrowskaja departs from the work of an earlier generation of German Jewish writers.[24] Jessica Ortner, meanwhile, emphasizes the way in which Petrowskaja's perspective, as a Jewish Eastern European woman in Germany, also interrogates dominant readings of European history, "broadening" Germany's cultural memory by "supplementing it with 'new' memories," including "lesser-known aspects of the Holocaust" and Soviet and Stalinist atrocities.[25] Certainly, as the narrator relates her experiences of online searches as well as trips to archives and memorial sites, including Babi Yar, Mauthausen, and Auschwitz, she also engages with how the past is archived, institutionalized and marketed in the present, often finding that her own memory work troubles the framings of history that she encounters in state memorials and public institutions. As Dora Osborne argues, the text thus consistently draws attention to the political nature of the archive, interrogating varied past and present hegemonies, from the Soviet state's repressive mechanisms to the Berlin Republic's *Erinnerungskultur*.[26]

Here, I similarly illustrate that Petrowskaja is concerned with finding a mode of remembering the past that interrogates fixed national and cultural borders, while simultaneously attending to the particularity and sometimes unknowability of others' experiences of loss and trauma. However, I suggest that Petrowskaja also moves beyond these critical expectations of her work through her engagement with the politics of touch and, concurrently, contingency. As will become clear, my understanding of contingency draws on recent work by theorists of affect such as Sara Ahmed, who reads contingency not only in temporal terms—as related to condition, coincidence—but also materially, as a form of touch. As Ahmed observes, to suggest that what comes into being is necessarily contingent upon other past and present encounters is to recognize its relational and also its material nature: it is shaped and reshaped through *contact* with others.[27] To focus on the contingency of what happens— as well as our memories of what happened—is therefore also to recognize the fragility of these processes, how at each encounter there are other possibilities for what *might be* or *might have been*. Here, scales that are sometimes opposed coincide: the particularity of any point of contact is formed not in opposition to but because of its *relation* to past, present, and potential future others: "other encounters that are part of the horizon which allows that encounter to happen in the first place."[28] The concrete locatedness of each encounter also implies the possible, the potential. In this chapter, I will suggest that this approach fruitfully opens up new ways of thinking about the politics of memory in literatures of migration, departing from the temporal fixities of a normative critical opposition between hegemonic abstraction and the disruptive real of migration: for, as Ahmed also suggests elsewhere, thought of in these material terms, normative archives and narratives of identity do not—as is often assumed—simply establish mastery over the varieties of lived reality through their abstraction from, and masking of, alterity.[29] Rather, they can be understood as the "sedimented" effect of lived patterns of repetition. As such, the role of political intervention may not simply be to reveal the artifice of hegemonic frameworks—what is missing or outside them—but rather to locate them materially, and trace alternative possible webs of thought, which may in turn affect, reshape, and shift the normative.[30]

Drawing on the work of scholars like Ahmed, I argue that rather than creating an opposition between a supposedly abstracted or metaphorical *discursive* framework and a grounded awareness of the difference of *real* experiences and histories, Petrowskaja foregrounds the materiality of social and linguistic structures, as well as the contingency and movement of the material histories of "what happened."[31] Petrowskaja posits and performs memory as a tactile act of translation—or an act of tactile translation: an intimate, embodied process of physically and emotionally relating to—touching—past others in a way that both disrupts and extends beyond the boundaries of present subjectivity to open space for connection to past and present others while also moving—translating—and mediating the past through this very process.[32] As such, *Maybe Esther* defers the possibility of fully connecting to others, except through the provisional, subjunctive mode of "as if." This constitutes what I term "subjunctive remembering."

In what follows, I first discuss how Petrowskaja's text thus both acknowledges the reality and inaccessibility of the pain of past others and at the same time gestures toward the possibility of other stories and other potential pasts and futures. Petrowskaja's work prompts us to rethink our relations to others and to ourselves through the precarities and potentialities of "perhaps." After illustrating this dynamic in *Maybe Esther*, I will explore how Petrowskaja's narrative strategy is thus self-consciously positioned as a mode of countermemory. Rather than simply establishing or even deferring connections to the past, I suggest that Petrowskaja's approach opens up a register of *provisional*, possible moments of contact to imagine other possible pasts, and potential future forms of relatedness. This narrative strategy is necessarily risky.[33] Its status "countermemory" is, paradoxically, dependent upon the fact that it does not function in a predetermined way.

Tactile Translations

Opening in a Berlin train station, *Maybe Esther* follows its autobiographical narrator as she travels across Europe in search of her family history. Though intertwined, each of the book's six sections has a subtly different focus: the first, "An Exemplary Story," begins with the narrator's initial attempts to address her history from fragments (such as an old recipe on a scrap of paper) and her own memories. The second, "Rosa and the Mute Children," focuses on the narrator's nineteenth-century relative Simon Geller and his descendants, who taught deaf-mute children in schools across Europe. In the third section, "My Beautiful Poland," she travels to present-day Poland, the birthplace of her grandmother Rosa, where she remembers family members, including their lives in the prewar period, murdered in the Holocaust. The fourth section, "In the World of Unstructured Matter," focuses on Judas Stern, the relative who attempted to shoot the German ambassador in Moscow in 1932. In section five, "Babi Yar," the narrator travels to her birthplace of Kiev, recounting the story of how her grandmother—the eponymous Maybe Esther—was killed. The final section, "Deduska," follows the narrator as she travels to Mauthausen concentration camp where her grandfather, who was not Jewish, was a Soviet prisoner of war.

At the outset, the narrator characterizes history in terms of absence: "History begins when there are no more people to ask, only sources."[34] This is not only a general condition for how the past is mediated but also a specific characteristic of the trauma of the narrator's own family history and the politics of how it has been recorded. The majority of her relatives were Jewish, and she is confronted by the murder of family members and the subsequent systematic erasure of their stories. Her great-grandmother and great-aunt were killed at Babi Yar.[35] Her grandfather's son from his first marriage was murdered at Treblinka.[36] While many of her relatives escaped Kiev in 1941, they were forced to leave behind the eponymous great-grandmother "Esther." But Esther's very name is uncertain, as are the details of her death at the hands of German soldiers. At first, the narrator's awareness of absence engenders a desire to give voice to and "recover" lost histories through the work of her narrative: "a . . . restitution of vanished things."[37] She positions this desire for restitution as part of her inheritance, both in literary terms—as part of the "generation of postmemory"—and in relation to her family history specifically.[38] For generations, her family taught deaf-mute children to speak, and she implies that her work is a metaphorical continuation of this "battle against muteness."[39]

Yet, as the text continues, the narrator highlights the impossibility of recovering what has been lost and expresses a need to read her family history beyond a melancholic lens, through which her representation would be predicated only upon absence. The assumption that Jewish history is inevitably associated with loss, she suggests, risks a dangerous normalization of atrocity, an acting-out of a totalitarian logic: "as though this disappearance or this nothingness was natural or self-evident."[40] Moreover, while she claims that she at one point envisaged the possibility of a "complete return" to a stable point of origin, the text consistently demonstrates that this is not possible; the notion of return is itself a fiction that is continuously frustrated.[41] "I wanted a complete return, like [a] . . . fairy tale" she tells us, at one point.[42] Instead, she finds, "the past betrayed my expectations."[43] When researching Simon Geller—the relative who first started the family profession of teaching deaf-mute children—for example, the narrator finds that his story can only be traced through a Russian translation of a newspaper article that was first published in Hebrew. The original text can no longer be found. As she therefore concludes, "At the beginning of the history of my family stood a translation."[44] Here, as throughout the text, remembering is metaphorically associated not with the linearity of returning but with translation—depicted as a *relational* and generative process of transformation, which changes both past and present contexts.[45]

The metaphor of remembering as translation is not presented as an abstract process only but is, crucially, developed in tactile terms throughout. This relates both to the way in which the text's remembering process is anchored in the narrator's specific encounters with material and affective traces of the past in different contexts and also concurrently to the metaphorical vocabulary of touch the narrator invokes to reflect on her own memory and writing work. Throughout, the narrator's encounters with the past are presented as moments of touch that offer points of potential connection—extending the narrator's experience and perspective beyond the bounds of her location in the present—and yet also defer this possibility. At one moment, for example, as the narrator is reading through an archive to find out about another relative, Judas Stern, the paper she is reading begins to fall apart in her hands. On her father's side of the family, Stern is a great-uncle who was executed for attempting to assassinate the German ambassador in Moscow in 1932. The attempt to trace his story takes her to Moscow's archive of secret service files, where she finds piles of deteriorating newspaper reports. On their pages, Stern's voice is both physically and symbolically occluded.[46] The history, she tells us, becomes increasingly "ungraspable."[47] In one sense, the tactility of this moment stresses her connection to the past: she is quite literally touching—as well as touched by—it. At the same time, it also once again highlights the way in which the past is both physically and metaphorically slipping from her grasp; it is unstable, vulnerable, and affected by her reading in the present—to touch is also to move, to further translate.

Through foregrounding the ambivalent tactility of these encounters, the narrator draws attention to the fragility of the particular histories she is exploring, as well as the contingent nature of any attempt to remember the past. This fragility is both material and temporal; as well as being shaped by her access to whatever material traces are available, the narrator's understanding of the past is often formed through coincidence. During an episode titled "Magen David" (*Mogendovid*), the narrator recalls how she returned to Kiev to visit her grandmother Rosa with a record of Yiddish songs that she bought in Warsaw in 1989, a moment that prompts an unexpected encounter with Rosa's past. Adopting a tone that is both playful and melancholic, the narrator characterizes the time itself as one of both possibility and loss. As the Cold War comes to an end, the narrator finds she has new opportunities for traveling and connecting to histories across borders. Yet, the potential that the narrator finds in the supposed openness of this ostensibly newly cosmopolitan context is mediated by her awareness of the traumatic histories through which it has been created and by the imbalances of the freedoms that are on offer perhaps only for those who can afford to buy them. Tellingly, it is thus while imagining that she is "floating" (*schweifen*) through the city with the superficiality of a cosmopolitan flaneur—"I strolled in the reconstructed historical center"—that the narrator is taken by surprise at seeing the Star of David on a record cover.[48] The initial discovery of the record is characterized as a fleeting, chance encounter with a strand of her family history that she is in the process of learning about. On seeing the record, she tells us that she had only recently heard the word *Mogendovid* (*Magen David*), and, as she runs her hand over the image, imagines that it could at any moment change or move away:

> I examined it the way I might watch an unknown animal that was on the verge of moving; I felt each of the six points, every corner, every angle.[49]

The moment not only attests to new possibilities for touching her family's past but also to this past's fragility. The contingency of this encounter is symptomatic of a context in which Jewish history has been erased during the Holocaust and by the Soviet state and in which her family have often repressed their memories.

Playing the record for her grandmother on her return to Kiev is similarly ambivalent. Her grandmother has never been able to remember the Yiddish that she spoke as a child when she lived in Poland. Yet, she suddenly begins singing along. The encounter is characterized as a moment of physical and affective touch, in which the narrator and her grandmother are "reached" by the past, taken beyond the bounds of their present:

> As though she was caught in the act of recollection, her time stretched out and took hold of Rosa, and the record made it reach out to me.[50]

Here, the past and present are quite literally coinciding. In light of her grandmother's story, the narrator finds this particularly moving. As she argues, without this moment she and her grandmother would possibly have never recalled a history and a language that had been erased and perhaps also repressed:

> if this record had not existed, this sealed window of her early childhood would never have opened up to us, and I would never have been able to understand that my babushka came from a Warsaw that no longer exists.[51]

As a coincidence, however, it is double-edged. In foregrounding the contingent nature of this encounter, the narrator not only draws attention to its vulnerability to change but also highlights how it continues to translate and mediate the past itself. It enables the past to resonate in the present yet also engenders distance and movement. Soon after describing playing the songs to her grandmother, she introduces another record as a metaphor:

> Then I, too, skipped . . . like a needle on a worn record, skipped over the whole war . . . and wound up in the 1970s setting of my childhood, which my parents would have been able to leave. But they stayed to protect actions and objects that are long since obsolescent and no longer on the market.[52]

Invoking the image of a "worn record," the narrator again connects the process of touching—and being touched by—the past with further mediating and changing it. A vinyl record is an analog form, it plays through a process of physical contact, changing subtly—becoming more worn—each time. Not only is it vulnerable to physical change itself but it also actively translates what it plays in the process, making the songs harder to access. As she draws on this image, the narrator also demonstrates what she describes: not only does this moment add new resonance to the song—connecting it to the narrator's own childhood as well as to her grandmother's—it also reminds the narrator of the distance of her own past and her family within it. Reflecting on her memories of her parents in the 1970s, she characterizes them in terms of distance rather than connection. They do not seem to be able to reach her present but have stayed in the 1970s of her memories, in a world that is obsolete, literally no longer "in use."

The metaphor of the broken record also further extends, to borrow Hirsch's evocative phrase, the "potential resonances" of the particular, original recording in this episode.[53] It is positioned both as the object of a *specific* encounter—which engenders a provisional point of material and affective connection to a traumatic past—*and* as a metaphor for the instability of remembering. As such, it destabilizes the difference between the material and the metaphorical. On the one hand, the very tactile fragility of this moment resists translation. Paradoxically, its openness to change with each new touch suggests that "what happened" cannot ever be fully accessed or perceived with a fixed content or meaning. At the same time, however, this sense of the moment's material precarity is exactly what enables it to function as a metaphor. In using the episode to emphasize the provisional nature of her own understanding of her grandmother's past, the narrator is able to gesture toward the other chance encounters and singular instances of contact that shaped—and might have shaped—the course of history. As she celebrates in negative terms the unexpected encounter with a past she hadn't had access to ("not ... never ... in no way"), she also recalls the ghost of the stories, lives, and words that she might never have heard—or that might indeed never have happened were it not for similar coincidences and meetings. She therefore finds herself reflecting on "the endless possible variations of our fate that could have chimed through entirely different songs."[54] The very articulation and performance of the translation engendered by the tactile also evokes potential other stories within her family history. Touching the past is a movement that engenders change but, in the process, also plays on the flip side of this: in drawing attention to the inaccessibility of what happened—the impossibility of ever fully making contact—the text is also able to evoke it in the subjunctive mode.

In this sense, the narrator's remembering process is not only retrospective but also generative. The very process of drawing attention to the past's material fragility evokes textual possibility, performing a mode of remembering that draws attention to its own contingencies. Throughout, the text also thematizes the way in which this doubleness is generated by the tactility of its remembering strategy, often invoking the metaphor of vulnerability to link textual possibility and material instability. As she walks through Warsaw, for example, the narrator describes the half-destroyed houses that she sees as standing like "open books, naked, facing outward."[55] On a metaphorical level, read as open books, the houses offer her new and intimate insights into a history she has not previously encountered; at the same time, they are testament to the pain of Warsaw's wartime destruction. Emphasizing the "nakedness" of the houses, the narrator connects the process of reading them in this way with the exploitative gaze of a voyeur, self-reflexively drawing attention to the potential complicity of her own representation.[56] Yet, through this very acknowledgment of the houses' material vulnerability she also performs a mode of remembering that also unsettles this voyeuristic perspective, rendering itself metaphorically "vulnerable" by drawing attention to its own potential implication.

Similarly, in an episode titled "Ariadne's Thread," the narrator discovers memoirs written by Rosa shortly before her death. Almost blind, Rosa has written lines of text over each other rather than starting a new page. Although the narrator initially considers finding a way to decipher them, she comes to realize that

> Rosa's writings were not intended for reading, *but rather for holding on to*, a thickly woven, unbreakable Ariadne's thread.[57]

As in "Magen David," the tactility of this moment both draws attention to the inaccessibility of her grandmother's past and also evokes new possibilities. It not only represents a specific point of connection to a fragile past but also is performed as an alternative mode of remembering, which relates to the past through a focus on materiality rather than legibility. In deciding to "hold" and not "read" her grandmother's memoirs, the narrator also performatively draws attention to the illegible archives of emotional moments and coincidental connections that (might) have shaped past lives—uncertain tactile connections that are perhaps lost in historical narratives, even while they may have changed the shape of history. At the same time, here—as throughout—the tactility of the encounter is itself also *already* a form of mediation, an encounter with a boundary, and a translation. Not only is her grandmother's story already "unbreakable" (*unzereissbar*) but the past it describes is further rendered inaccessible by its fragility and vulnerability to change. The tactile here, in other words, is not simply a cipher for that which has been excluded from official historical archives—that which is buried, or there to be found—but rather a site through which the *possibility of* alternative pasts is both imagined and deferred.

Abstract Thinking

Petrowskaja consistently characterizes this generative process of "touching" the past as a form of resistance to the binary-based, utilitarian logic that she associates with totalitarian thinking and also finds continuing through present-day readings of history and organizations of geographical space. Throughout, she invokes a connection between binary-based identifications and totalitarianism, characterizing this logic in terms of stasis, frictionlessness and a drive towards abstraction. She often develops this characterization through mathematical metaphors. Early in the text, for instance, she describes how her uncle Wil is determined to understand the world as if it is a "question of mechanics" through "abstract thinking."[58] She relates this desire to his Soviet upbringing and his experience of conflict in World War II. In the Soviet context, the narrator suggests, "everything human was regarded as friction loss," including "questions of proximity, warmth, doubt, and possibly even kinship. . . ."[59] This totalitarian opposition between functional abstraction and friction is racialized. The narrator explains that while Soviet citizenship is associated with abstraction and "optimizing . . . efficiency," Jewishness is characterized as "weight" and "a superfluous add-on that was better left unmentioned."[60] For this reason, although he has Jewish parents, Wil is keen to "shed the weight of his Jewish background."[61] Here, totalitarianism not only rests on an opposition between self and other but also, relatedly, on a racialized opposition between abstraction and materiality. The alterity of Jewishness is produced in opposition to the presumed neutrality and lightness of the citizen-subject.

An association between the frictionlessness of mathematical calculation and totalitarianism continues throughout. After the massacre at Babi Yar during the Holocaust, the *Sonderkommando* reports that the operation has gone "smoothly"—in literal translation, "without friction."[62] When visiting Mauthausen concentration camp toward the end of the text, meanwhile, the narrator comments:

> We are indulged and spoiled through numbers, violated by presentations of violence; to understand these numbers is to accept the violence.[63]

Here, as elsewhere, she implies that totalitarian ideology rested upon the abstraction of individuals into numbers and categories in order to justify its violence. It is this mode of extreme rationality, she suggests, that enabled friends and neighbors to be designated as others and that legitimized the violence against them.

The narrator finds a similarly oppositional logic replicated in many of the historical sites that she visits, despite their different cultural and national locations. Drawing attention to the way in which different memorials have been constructed for different groups of victims at Babi Yar, she argues, for example, "Even in commemoration, there was no end to *selection*."[64] In this way, the memorials risk emphasizing the otherness of the victims—always representing "the misfortune of others"—and thus perpetuating fascist ideology.[65] Indeed, as Ortner notes, selection becomes a recurrent metaphor for the "segmentation of cultural memory" throughout the text.[66] Again, Petrowskaja suggests that this hegemonic mode of memorialization reinforces binary-based, essentialist definitions of national history. When returning to Warsaw a second time, she finds for example that, as a tourist, one can either go on a tour of the ghetto or of the locations important to the Warsaw resistance—a division that risks once again positioning Jews as others in Poland: "There were always the others . . . Poles and Jews, Jews and Poles."[67] Once again, Jewishness is positioned as modernity's ghettoized other, as though fulfilling an abstract mathematical equation: "Warsaw plus Jews equals ghetto."[68]

It is in this context that *Maybe Esther*'s emphasis on the translations—and frictions—engendered by moments of tactile encounter becomes politically significant. As Petrowskaja suggests in an interview, to read history in terms of static categories and abstract orders is to in some way replicate or "accept" the violence:

> Labels suggest predetermination, as if these divisions and categories were natural. They feed into a reading of history as if it were always linear—as if there is fixed causality. That's exactly what I don't accept here.[69]

As well as evoking the objectifying gaze of the spectator, the distance of this form of writing emerges from its temporality. The abstraction of labels is connected to "predetermination," writing in the past tense: the stasis of the already written. In contrast, as we will see, Petrowskaja's emphasis on the changes engendered by tactile encounter highlights the continuous presence of alternative possibilities at each moment: what might happen as well as what might have happened.

Though emerging from a different context, Ahmed's work on queer phenomenology sheds further light on how this approach might work as a political intervention.[70] Drawing on the work of Edmund Husserl and Maurice Merleau-Ponty, Ahmed argues that "bodies as well as objects take shape" through their tactile relations with, and orientations to, each other.[71] Rather than inhabiting a fixed identity position, in other words, we are shaped, and reshaped, through relations and contact with others. This is both a horizontal and a vertical relationality. As Ahmed explains in a 2013 interview:

> I've always liked this word "contact" anyway. And obviously it has an etymological relation to "contingency," to touch, to come into contact. And to think about that coming into contact, one body with another, or a body with an object, how in that encounter there's already at stake other encounters that are part of the horizon which allows that encounter to happen in the first place.[72]

Ahmed's evocative remarks here suggest that—as with Petrowskaja's description of Rosa's worn record—each instance of touch is in some sense *archival*, adding new layers to a "sedimented history" of "other encounters" that shapes the present.[73] However, as she points out elsewhere, the path of "other encounters" that have allowed a present encounter to happen—that which it is contingent on—is not neutral or natural but has emerged through "the repetition of norms and conventions."[74] In other words, those objects or others that we come into contact with, or toward whom we are orientated, are determined by cultural norms—"how spaces are already orientated"—which are both followed and reinforced by new points of contact and use. This approach denaturalizes the dominant ways in which spaces are "orientated" *through* emphasizing their materiality and contingent nature rather than their artifice or abstraction: as she writes, lines of thought and motion are "both created by being followed and are followed by being created." This also opens up the possibility of finding (non-oppositional) "queer moments of deviation":

> If orientations point us to the future, to what we are moving toward, then they also keep open the possibility of changing directions, of finding other paths, perhaps those that do not find a common ground, where we can find hope in what goes astray. Looking back is what keeps open the possibility of going astray.[75]

Significantly, rather than situating these "other paths" as new fictionalized possibilities that emerge in opposition to the prescribed material realities of the past, Ahmed's focus on contingency highlights the *imbrication* of the real and the possible, the imperfect and the subjunctive, what has happened—looking back—and what is "open" to going astray. To be contingent on something, in other words, implies coming into being through a web of past and present encounters, as well as the fragility of this process—the other directions that could have been or could be taken.

Contingent Resistances

Petrowskaja continues to develop a strategy of evoking other potential pasts throughout the text, foregrounding the ambivalent tactility of her remembering process. Significantly, her emphasis on tactility not only relates to her encounters with archival material but is also associated with the process of narrative representation. As Lizarazu has observed, like Rosa's memoirs, the narrator characterizes her writing as a texture or network.[76] Throughout, the narrator invokes the metaphor of weaving to self-reflexively highlight the materiality and fabrication of the process of representing the past as well as a sense of its plurality—being woven from multiple threads. Rather than forming any single linear narrative, her family history appears to her, for example, as a moving, material web, in which she searches for "lost threads":

> The history of the Krzewins did not form a taut thread; it circled and circled and got torn away like Kalisz lace.[77]

As well as evoking a specific material history, the metaphor of Kalisz lace describes the ways in which words, histories and languages, slip, shift, and *change*—are "torn away"—as they are brought into material and symbolic proximity with each other.[78] This is enacted as well as described by the text. Metaphors such as "Ariadne's thread" are performative, recalling—and translating—past texts such as the Greek myths referenced by the narrator, as well as the digital networks that she often finds herself navigating, into the context of the present narrative. The text not only describes the tactility of the narrator's encounters with past traces but also includes images of archival documents. As Hirsch explains, in a different context, reframing archival images in this way grants them "multiple afterlives in which they continue to develop," not only renewing attention to past atrocities but also carrying the potential for future change in encounters with new readers.[79]

One manifestation of this narrative strategy is Petrowskaja's interweaving of languages. Although German is not her mother tongue, it is the language she writes in. Meanwhile, Russian, Yiddish, English, and French words also make their way into the narrative, "touching" German on a symbolic and material level. Given that normalization of "monolingualism" in literature emerges from the history of constructing discrete national identities and proper individual subjects, especially in the German context, the use of multiple languages has been read as an interrogation of the perceived homogeneity of national discourses.[80] Certainly, the text engages this on one level. In interviews, Petrowskaja asserts that her use of language complicates the relationship between "German" history and that of her family:

> If I write my history in Russian, it's clear where the history is located . . . in a sense, my role as a victim is always already implied by [the use of] Russian. If I write the same in German, it isn't clear who I am. There's a certain estrangement.[81]

The implication is that to use a different language can, to some extent, unmoor it from any single history or context. Rather than maintaining binary identifications, the strategy reimagines identity in cosmopolitan terms as productive "estrangement" from fixed attachments.

To some extent, this idea of remembering as productive displacement—a kind of translation—evokes the work of critics such as Rothberg. As in Rothberg's "multidirectional memory," the narrator's multilingualism illustrates how national pasts speak to, and are imbricated in, each other. However, Petrowskaja also extends the scope of theoretical models such as Rothberg's through her engagement with contingency and touch. Rothberg's emphasis on "multidirectionality" usefully stresses the reciprocal nature of interconnected memories—the sense that both are translated and changed in the process of contact with each other. Yet, this to some extent occludes the material and affective differences between varied moments and forms of contact between pasts; the sometimes uneven and unpredictable effects of these meetings. In contrast, Petrowskaja's text also pays close attention to the contingencies and frictions of language: exploring how each word's effect and significance also highlight the unevenness of such meetings.

Throughout, the text illustrates how moments of material and symbolic touch between words can entail friction, loss, and even violence. This is evident firstly through Petrowskaja's attention to historical location. If every moment of contact implies a form of translation, that is not to say that each form of translation or touch has the same effects in each context. They attest to different languages' potential relatability and changeability—unsettling fixed national divisions—yet at the same time recall particular, painful histories. For instance, the text traces how the names of places and characters shift. On one level, this attests to the ephemerality of tracing history and to the text's destabilization of "proper" identities: the name Geller is a translation of Krzewin; Gutek Krzewin becomes Gustaw. Gustaw becomes Anthony Gorbutt. Yet, the text makes clear that such shifts are not simply a mode of textual play; they are the result of histories of persecution. Anthony Gorbutt changed his name on moving to London after the war, having escaped from Warsaw. His decision to adopt a new identity is a symptom of his desire to repress his memories: he tells no one about his past names, the ghetto, or his parents.

Secondly, the text performs the ambivalence of multilingual "touch" through its emphasis on the material locatedness of words: how their significance is formed through material and symbolic relations to those around them. Petrowskaja's awareness of the material, affective, and embodied nature of language informs her use of German. In interviews, Petrowskaja describes how she wants readers to experience the difficulty of her use of German as a Jewish author: the writing process entailed a "struggle with [the] language" and an experience of loss.[82] She characterizes her encounter with history as a process of "stumbling over" fragments.[83] Interestingly her use of German incorporates the ambiguities of stumbling over something: it is an encounter with an obstacle, which may have adverse effects, but which also opens up the potential for finding something new, for changing direction.

At various points, the narrator highlights the "stumbling" of language in moments where the narrator uses nonstandard grammar and syntax. For example, in the episode "Gorgon Medusa," she describes the torture of her great-uncle Judas Stern, who attempted to shoot the German ambassador. She characterizes the Soviet system of the time in terms of mechanical violence to bodies: "The grinding of the machines, aortic rupture, bones, machines that crush consciousness into powder."[84] Yet, she does so in nonstandard grammar. She largely abandons capital letters. Her lines run without full stops. This approach foregrounds the form of the language she uses: it forces readers to notice, perhaps to even "stumble over" the sentences they are reading.

On one level, this strategy resists the mechanical typification and abstraction of the totalitarian system. The speaker refuses to be fixed by the spectator's gaze: "i will not turn to stone."[85] The words perform the resistance to petrification that they describe, refusing to adhere to any single grammatical system. Meanwhile, the narrator's use of German to describe her uncle's torture in the Soviet Union also unsettles her identity position: it complicates what Petrowskaja describes—cited above—as her inherent "role as a victim" in Russian as a Ukrainian-Jewish-German speaker. Here, German is not only the perpetrator's language but also is mobilized to resist the mechanisms of totalitarianism. As such, the narrator performs the movement—the changing significance—of German as she deploys it in the new context of the book. At the same time, the narrator's knotted use of syntax simultaneously enacts how this is part of painful struggle and traumatic history—"aortic rupture"—rather than a smooth celebration of translatability. The use of nonstandard grammar also evokes the grammatical system it departs from: to foreground the changed nature of present usage also makes readers aware of the words' standard form. Tellingly, the episode ends without a full stop—as if it is open to further movement. But the final words remind us that language's changeability does not mean an escape from material or historical location—"there is no place left where there is no corruption or crime. . . ."[86] To move does not mean freedom from location or embodiment: it is also to acknowledge the impossibility of finding a nonimplicated, stable position from which to write.

In this way, Petrowskaja illustrates how symbolic and material touch between languages engenders the possibility of changing hegemonic modes of thought, yet she simultaneously attests to the history and continuing realities of hegemony—the existing archives of articulation from which she writes. Like other moments of "touch" in the text, Petrowskaja's use of German is contingent in a double sense: its significance is dependent on an existing chain of relations and events (what has already happened), yet it is also open to change in new relations and encounters.

This encapsulates Petrowskaja's complex understanding of the relationship between writing and political resistance. The use of German generates frictions that resist the mechanical abstractions of totalitarian systems as well as official present-day representations of this history. However, importantly, Petrowskaja does not simply oppose the contingencies or proximities of the "tactile" to the abstractions of dominant readings of history. For, an emphasis on the deterritorializing and multidirectional nature of memory—in implied opposition to the artifice of the nation-state—can risk once again universalizing its displacements as part of the performance of an ethical critical stance. Petrowskaja's work does something different. As she comments in another interview:

> [That's] what I am trying to do in my book—staging this co-existence of different modes of thinking and possibilities. That's what freedom means for me—to

see that there is a moment of bifurcation, a moment of decision, a moment of non-acceptance. There is a moment when you can change something.[87]

The doubleness of the term "non-acceptance" is interesting here, implying as it does the preexistence of certain hegemonic "modes of thinking," which she must try to circumnavigate but cannot entirely depart from. Paradoxically, for Petrowskaja, it would seem that if the narrative is to resist subsuming the particularities of different possible encounters into a totalizing ethical frame, it must also take the risk of leaving open the implications of its own strategies. Indeed, it is surely no coincidence that the text's central metaphor of weaving—*spinnen*—is part of a play on words in itself. In German, *spinnen* of course means not only to spin or fabricate but also, colloquially, to be mad—a concept that Petrowskaja also plays with throughout. The connection between fabrication and madness necessarily evokes not only the possibilities but also the potential dangers (and perhaps absurdity) of the narrator's desire to imagine an identity that is somehow beyond the proprieties and determinations of normative structures; the risk that this will not function, or be read, as a form of resistance at all. In this sense, the word performs what it describes, pointing back to its own "spinning" strategies to highlight the potential otherness within them.

Changing Direction

The ambivalence of contingency is key to how Petrowskaja's "subjunctive remembering" might work as a form of non-oppositional countermemory, a kind of contingent—in Eve K. Sedgwick's terms, "weak"—resistance.[88] Rather than simply opposing contingency to abstract frameworks, the very process of "changing direction[s]" necessitates an unsettling of abstraction. In this sense, while Petrowskaja's strategy disrupts the notion of a single, static identity position, it does not simply represent a kind of imaginative or fictional release into an entirely open world of deterritorialised possibility. If—as discussed in the first section—the text's depiction of material fragility opens up textual possibilities for "changing directions" and potential new readings of the past, the opposite is also true: the potentialities explored by the text also necessarily evoke the (hegemonically formed and understood) realities of what did happen, the paths that were taken. The narrator draws attention to the fact that the other possible paths she identifies are not only abstract, indifferent metaphors that might simply be exchanged for "what happened" or for each other but also, in reality, paths that meant the difference between who survived and who did not. As she comments when discussing her grandfather: "If my grandfather survived, it means that someone died in his place."[89]

The mixed genre of *Maybe Esther* further enacts this double-edged approach to the past. In an episode titled "The Train," for instance, the narrator tries to piece together the story of how her grandmother and mother left Kiev in 1941—a story that involves the family boarding a crowded cattle train and spending days without enough food or water. The narrator's mother was five at the time and—based on her fragmented recollections—the narrator tells us how Rosa almost missed getting back on the train when she went to fetch water at a short stop-off. Confronted by uncertain traces and her own mother's memories of stories about Rosa, she thus begins to tell a story that is self-conscious about its own fabricated quality. As she recounts it, the narrator characterizes the memory as appearing to her in dreams like a "film cut," in which her grandmother runs after the train in slow motion, water spilling from the container she is carrying.[90] The tale not only emphasizes the contingency of its retelling, based as it is on fragments of inherited memory. It also draws attention to the "what ifs" of the moment itself: if Rosa had missed the train, she is told, her daughter (the narrator's mother) might have died.

On the one hand, the narrator plays with the fabricated nature of her narrative. Rather than inhabiting a position that is abstracted from her grandmother's story, and thus running the risk of representing it from the perspective of a voyeuristic onlooker, she imagines herself into this dream version: "I run for her."[91] In foregrounding the fabrications—the as ifs—of this encounter, the narrator also sets up her perspective on the past as only a provisional—a version of what might have happened. She cannot of course actually exchange herself "for" her grandmother in this way. As such, she is able to unsettle her own relation to her grandmother's past, complicating her position, so as to once again be simultaneously connected to and distanced from the scene: "I am the one above, no, wait, my Rosa is."[92]

At the same time, the account of what might have happened also evokes the fragile, contingent reality of what *did* happen: the fact that Rosa's survival depended on everything that could have happened not happening. Here, as elsewhere, the very process of imagining—"as if"—engendered by the past's precarity is also recognition of its actual and often painful effects. In this sense, paradoxically, in the very process of apparently emphasizing its possible distance from "reality," the subjunctive also necessarily evokes it. Rather than being some kind of abstract fiction that is somehow cut off from material reality and where everything is open to interpretation, the narrative is itself positioned and performed as a mode of tactile translation, generated from material traces and memories, which continue to move the narrator and the past. As Petrowskaja also comments in an interview:

> I think throughout, there are things that are *almost* metaphors, but they are never really complete because *they're always also concrete*. I think using names like "Maybe Esther" is almost the same.[93]

The modality of "maybe" or "perhaps" to some extent unmoors what is described from its particular roots, allowing for it to be potentially relatable to—to stand in for—others as a metaphor. However, this is, as Petrowskaja argues, in itself necessarily only "almost" possible. Metaphors here are never purely abstract but always also "concrete." Neither unbound nor prescribed, fictional nor real, her subjunctive remembering reimagines history as a texture of imbrications and coincidences, through which certain paths are sedimented but others might be imagined.

Conclusion: Subjunctive Remembering

Early in the text, the narrator visits a German museum with her young daughter. When they reach an exhibit on the Nuremberg trials, her daughter looks at the display and asks, "Where are we here?" Though the question is in the present tense, the narrator argues that it should have been in the more distanced, mediated form of the imperfect or the subjunctive: where would we have been if we had been there? To do otherwise, she suggests, would be to imagine that one could somehow fully inhabit the position of another in a way that is neither possible nor perhaps ethically desirable:

> Because avoidance of the subjunctive turns imagination into recognition or even statement, you take another's place, catapult yourself there . . . and thus I try out every role on myself as though there was no past without an *if, as though*, or *in that case*.[94]

In their emphasis on "place," these comments at first appear to evoke the oppositional logic that the narrator critiques. The narrator once again finds this framework echoed in the institutional structure of the museum itself: with its chronological displays and a tour guide taking visitors on appropriate routes through history, it also rests on an implied connection between the organization of space and ethical propriety, between where you stand (*stehen*) and the path of your understanding (*Verständnis*). Yet, even as she draws on this logic to reflect on the problematics of representation, the narrator also complicates it. Indeed, formulated in the double negative—"no past without an [as] if"—the narrator's reflections on representing the past are highly ambivalent. Here, she implies both that there *is* a past without the retrospective conjecture of an "as if"—in the imperfect, it happened—and yet also that it is not directly accessible; even to draw attention to this point paradoxically requires an act of imaginative construction ("*as though* there were no past . . ."). This acknowledgment of the distance of the past is, however, also what enables the narrator's sense of possible connection to it: through foregrounding the constructed and problematic nature of any attempt to position herself within the past, she is able to evoke an imagined "as if" scenario where this *might* be potentially possible, a form of negative yet also anticipatory conjecture—"thus I try out every role on myself."⁹⁵ In other words, she imagines inhabiting others' "roles" through articulating the performative, problematic, and impossible nature of this process. Stating that something is impossible here paradoxically relies on the fantasy that it could be possible, even as this avenue is apparently being closed down. Unlike the binary-based lines of remembering and identification that shaped the past and present, here and throughout she enacts a mode of remembering that engenders provisional, potential networks of connection to others.

There is no space here to fully detail the complexity of *Maybe Esther's* narrative processes. As I have begun to show, however, here and throughout, Petrowskaja's text performs a mode of subjunctive remembering that both plays with the textual possibilities of past and present uncertainty and draws attention to the material realities of what happened in doing so. In this process, it also attempts to enact a mode of tactile resistance that does not destabilize abstract representational frames through drawing attention to their gaps—their difference from material reality—but rather through destabilizing the difference between tactile presence and symbolic abstraction via a thread of shared contingency. As such, she gestures toward the possibility of political intervention through a practice of remembering based on contingency, which enables provisional connections beyond the fixities of abstract positions, while also drawing attention to the difference between them. This strategy is, however, in itself necessarily provisional and raises further questions: If it is a political strategy to interrogate the abstract, how can it *always* function politically? Or, put more simply, what can be the value of a mode of contingent resistance? Petrowskaja's *Maybe Esther* might offer a new way to approach this dilemma, which nonetheless risks leaving her text radically open to question, including leaving open the possibility of her own implication in the structures she critiques. This imagines a mode of resistance to abstraction located in subjunctive remembering, which, however necessarily and riskily, also opens the possibility that the text may not (all) work in this way. As throughout, however, this is a paradox that forms the very condition of her ethics.

Maya Caspari is postdoctoral research and engagement fellow at the University of Leeds and associate curator at the German Historical Institute in London.

Notes

1. Ernest Renan, *Qu'est-Ce Qu'une Nation?* trans. Ethan Rundell (Paris: Presses-Pocket, 1992).
2. See, for example, Judith Butler, *Frames of War: When Is Life Grievable?* (New York: Verso, 2009). See also Andreas Huyssen, *Present Pasts: Urban Palimpsests and the*

Politics of Memory (Stanford, CA: Standford University Press, 2003). For a focus on the European context, see also Aleida Assmann, "Transnational Memories," *European Review* 22 (2014): 546–56; Aleida Assmann, *Der Lange Schatten Der Vergangenheit: Erinnerungskultur und Geschichts-Politik* (Munich: C. H. Beck, 2008).
3. Aleida Assmann claims that transnationalism has become a normative stance in the humanities, "often underpinned by a cosmopolitan ethos that betrays a general dissatisfaction with the dated nineteenth century ideal of the autonomous, free, coherent and bounded nation." Assmann, "Transnational Memories," 547. On notions of diasporic identity, see, for example, Salman Rushdie, "Imaginary Homelands," in *Imaginary Homelands: Essays and Criticism 1981–1991* (London: Granta Books, 1992), 9–21. See also James Clifford, "Diasporas," *Cultural Anthropology* 9, no. 3 (1994): 302–38.
4. See, for example, Simon Gikandi, "Between Routes and Roots: Cosmopolitanism and the Claims of Locality," in *Rerouting the Postcolonial: New Directions for the New Millennium*, ed. Janet Wilson, Cristina Şandru, and Sarah Lawson Welsh (New York: Routledge, 2010), 22–35. See also Pheng Cheah, "Given Culture: Rethinking Cosmopolitical Freedom in Transnationalism," in *Cosmopolitics: Thinking and Feeling beyond the Nation*, ed. Pheng Cheah and Bruce Robbins (Minneapolis: University of Minnesota Press, 1998), 290–38.
5. As Guttman comments thus, "The Jewish subject may be an exemplary cosmopolitan—and thus the basis for further globalized imaginings, both in theory and in literature—but only if that Jewishness is at least partially suppressed and carefully delimited." See Anna Guttman, "The Jew in the Archive: Textualizations of (Jewish?) History in Contemporary South Asian Literature," *Contemporary Literature* 51, no. 3 (2010): 65, 528. See also Aamir R. Mufti and Ato Quayson, "The Predicaments of Postcolonial Thinking," *Cambridge Journal of Postcolonial Literary Inquiry* 3, no. 1 (2016): 143–56, http://dx.doi.org/10.1017/pli.2015.28.
6. David Damrosch, "Toward a History of World Literature," *New Literary History* 39, no. 3, Literary History in the Global Age (Summer 2008): 481–95, 490. The term *literatures of migration* is drawn from Leslie Adelson. Unlike "migrant writing" or migrants' literature, the term aims to avoid defining a text through the (normative) framing of the author's biography. See Leslie A. Adelson, *The Turkish Turn in Contemporary German Literature: Toward a New Critical Grammar of Migration* (New York: Palgrave Macmillan, 2005).
7. For further discussion of this topic, see, for example, Michael Rothberg and Yasemin Yildiz, "Memory Citizenship: Migrant Archives of Holocaust Remembrance in Contemporary Germany," *Parallax* 17, no. 4 (November 2011): 32–48.
8. On Petrowskaja, see, for example, Jessica Ortner, "The Reconfiguration of the European Archive in Contemporary German-Jewish Migrant-Literature: Katja Petrowskaja's Novel *Vielleicht Esther*," *Nordisk Judaistik: Scandinavian Jewish Studies* 28, no. 1 (2017): 38–54. For further discussion of the topic, see, for example, Moray McGowan, "Turkish-German Fiction since the Mid-1990s," in *Contemporary German Fiction: Writing in the Berlin Republic*, ed. Stuart Taberner (Cambridge: Cambridge University Press, 2007), 196–214. See also Margaret Littler, "Cultural Memory and Identity Formation in the Berlin Republic," in *Contemporary German Fiction: Writing in the Berlin Republic*, ed. Stuart Taberner (Cambridge: Cambridge University Press, 2007), 177–95.
9. See, for example, Stuart Taberner, "The Possibilities and Pitfalls of a Jewish Cosmopolitanism: Reading Natan Sznaider through Russian-Jewish Writer Olga Grjasnowa's German-Language Novel *Der Russe Ist Einer, Der Birken Liebt* (All Russians Love

Birch Trees)," *European Review of History: Revue Européenne d'histoire* 23, nos. 5–6 (November 2016): 912–30 See also Jonathan Skolnik, "Memory without Borders? Migrant Identity and the Legacy of the Holocaust in Olga Grjasnowa's *Der Russe Ist Einer, Der Birken Liebt*," in *German Jewish Literature after 1990*, ed. Katja Garloff and Agnes Mueller (Rochester, NY: Camden House, 2018).

10. Gikandi, "Between Routes and Roots."
11. Michael Rothberg, *Multidirectional Memory: Remembering the Holocaust in the Age of Decolonization* (Stanford, CA: Stanford University Press, 2009), 20, emphasis mine. Here, Rothberg draws on the work of Nancy Fraser. See Nancy Fraser, "Reframing Justice in a Globalizing World," ed. Nancy Fraser, *Lua Nova—Revista de Cultura e Política* 77 (2009): 11–39.
12. This argument draws on feminist critiques that understand twentieth-century theoretical work as problematically reliant on "surface/depth" oppositions as a means of producing knowledge about a text. See Eve Kosofsky Sedgwick, *Touching Feeling* (Durham, NC: Duke University Press, 2003). On the perils of understanding a critical object "waiting to be found" in another context, see also Sara Ahmed, "Open Forum Imaginary Prohibitions: Some Preliminary Remarks on the Founding Gestures of the 'New Materialism,'" *European Journal of Women's Studies* 15, no. 1 (2008): 23–39, https://doi.org/10.1177/1350506807084854. See also Wendy Brown, "Resisting Left Melancholy," *Boundary 2* 26, no. 3 (1999): 19–27.
13. Rothberg is clearly attempting to move beyond a reductive opposition between cosmopolitan translatability and a politics of singularity. However, I would suggest that the trope of "breaking the frame" to some extent retains an opposition between the artifice of hegemonic frameworks and the reality of that which is concealed or excluded by them. This risks limiting the scope of texts' political interventions to locating that which hegemonic frameworks have concealed.
14. Osborne also refers to Petrowskaja's attention to the "contingency of history"; however, here I am focusing on this in *material* terms.
15. Katja Petrowskaja, *Maybe Esther: A Family Story*, trans. Shelley Frisch (New York: Harper, 2018). All page numbers in text refer to this edition. Katja Petrowskaja, *Vielleicht Esther* (Berlin: Suhrkamp, 2015). All subsequent translations in notes refer to this edition.
16. Consider for example the titles of the following articles: Marina Benjamin, "Holocaust Memoir Maybe Esther Is a Mesmerising Work of Reconstruction and Reflection," New Statesman, updated 28 June 2021, retrieved 8 August 2018 from https://www.newstatesman.com/culture/books/2018/02/holocaust-memoir-maybe-esther-mesmerising-work-reconstruction-and-reflection; Lara Feigel, "*Maybe Esther* by Katja Petrowskaja Review—a Family Story of 20th-Century Europe," *The Guardian*, 1 February 2018, sec. Books, retrieved 8 August 2018 from http://www.theguardian.com/books/2018/feb/01/maybe-esther-katja-petrowskaja-review. See also Sebastian Hammelehle, "Familiengeschichte 'Vielleicht Esther': Nächster Halt Holocaust," *Spiegel Online*, 11 March 2014, sec. Kultur, retrieved 8 August 2018 from http://www.spiegel.de/kultur/literatur/katja-petrowskaja-vielleicht-esther-a-957065.html.
17. See for example: Samuel Moser, "Auf der Schwelle von Mauthausen | NZZ," *Neue Zürcher Zeitung*, 5 April 2014, sec. Bücher, retrieved 8 August 2018 from https://www.nzz.ch/feuilleton/buecher/auf-der-schwelle-von-mauthausen-1.18277615. See also Catherine Taylor, "*Maybe Esther* by Katja Petrowskaja—'When There Are No More People to Ask,'" *Financial Times*, 26 January 2018, retrieved 8 August 2018

from https://www.ft.com/content/35f6ea88-004e-11e8-9e12-af73e8db3c71. See also Holger Heimann, "Deutsche Sprache kam einer Befreiung gleich," *Deutsche Welle*, 10 July 2013, sec. Kultur, retrieved 31 August 2017 from http://www.dw.com/de/deutsche-sprache-kam-einer-befreiung-gleich/a-16935579.

18. In an interview, Petrowskaja comments: "I used the word 'Geschichten' because small stories reflect the 'big history'. Moreover, the idea of a 'novel' still implies an attempt to depict something as a whole. I recall, restore, or experience only the fragments of a lost epic, as if the world is broken and you can find only pieces." See Helmut Böttiger, "Katja Petrowskaja: 'Wir sind die letzten Europäer!'" Zeit Online, 13 March 2014, retrieved 8 August 2018 from https://www.zeit.de/2014/12/katja-petrowskaja-vielleicht-esther.

19. Marianne Hirsch, *The Generation of Postmemory: Writing and Visual Culture after the Holocaust* (New York: Columbia University Press, 2012).

20. There has been much critical discussion of Petrowskaja's work, including, in addition to those cited in the text, Gabrielle Eckhart, "The Functions of Multilingual Language Use in Katja Petrowskaja's *Vielleicht Esther*," *Glossen: German Literature and Culture after 1945* (June 2015), retrieved 8 August 2018 from http://blogs.dickinson.edu/glossen/archive/most-recent-issue-glossen-402015/gabriele-eckart-glossen40-2015/; Ulrich Gutmair, "'Würdigt Die Katastrophe in Angemessener Weise': Die Erzähldebüts von Katja Petrowskaja Und Per Leo," *Merkur* 68 (2014): 1026–32; Elin Nesje Vestli, "'Mein Fremdes Deutsch': Grenzüberschreitungen in Der Deutschsprachigen Gegenwartsliteratur: Katja Petrowskajas Vielleicht Esther," in *Language and Nation: Crossroads and Connections*, ed. Guri Ellen Barstad et al. (New York: Waxmann, 2016), 143–60.

21. Brigid Haines, "The Eastern Turn in Contemporary German, Swiss and Austrian Literature," *Debatte: Journal of Contemporary Central and Eastern Europe* 16, no. 2 (August 2008).

22. Maria Roca Lizarazu, "The Family Tree, the Web, and the Palimpsest: Figures of Postmemory in Katja Petrowskaja's *Vielleicht Esther* (2014)," *Modern Language Review* 113, no. 1 (2018): 171.

23. Katja Garloff and Agnes Mueller, "Introduction," in *German Jewish Literature after 1990*, ed. Katja Garloff and Agnes Mueller (Rochester, NY: Camden House, 2018), 8.

24. Andree Michaelis-König, "Multilingualism and Jewishness in Katja Petrowskaja's *Vielleicht Esther*," in *German Jewish Literature after 1990*, ed. Katja Garloff and Agnes Mueller (Rochester, NY: Camden House, 2018).

25. Ortner, "Reconfiguration," 51.

26. Dora Osborne, "Encountering the Archive in Katja Petrowskaja's *Vielleicht Esther*," *Seminar: A Journal of Germanic Studies* 52, no. 3 (September 2016): 255–72, https://doi.org/10.3138/seminar.52.3.01.

27. Sara Ahmed, "'NOT WITHOUT AMBIVALENCE': An Interview with Sara Ahmed on Postcolonial Intimacies," interview by Phanuel Antwi, Sarah Brophy, Helene Strauss, and Y-Dang Troeung, McMaster University, Canada, 3 March 2011, http://www.tandfonline.com/doi/abs/10.1080/1369801X.2013.771011, 110–26.

28. Ahmed, "NOT WITHOUT AMBIVALENCE," 120.

29. Ahmed, "Orientations."

30. As Ahmed explains "Phenomenology helps us explore how bodies are shaped by histories, which they perform in their comportment, their posture, and their gestures. Both Husserl and Merleau-Ponty, after all, describe bodily horizons as "sedimented histories." This model of history as bodily sedimentation has been taken up by social

theorists as well as philosophers.... For Judith Butler, it is precisely how phenomenology exposes the sedimentation of history in the repetition of bodily action that makes it a useful resource for feminism. What bodies 'tend to do' are effects of histories rather than being originary." See Ahmed, "Orientations," 552–53.
31. This also speaks to the work of feminist new materialists. As Karen Barad argues, "Materiality is discursive (i.e., material phenomena are inseparable from the apparatuses of bodily production: matter emerges out of and includes as part of its being the ongoing reconfiguring of boundaries), just as discursive practices are always already material (i.e., they are ongoing material (re)configurings of the world)." See Karen Barad, "Posthumanist Performativity: Toward an Understanding of How Matter Comes to Matter," *Signs: Journal of Women in Culture and Society* 28, no. 3 (2003): 801–31.
32. The notion of "touch" as a means of conceptualizing the affective and material relationships between histories has been previously invoked in similar contexts. Most notably, Leslie Adelson's work on "touching tales" productively explores the proximities between different histories, particularly in relation Turkish/German/Jewish relations. See Leslie A. Adelson, "Touching Tales of Turks, Germans, and Jews: Cultural Alterity, Historical Narrative, and Literary Riddles for the 1990s," *New German Critique* 80 (2000): 93–124. Here, however, my focus is on the contingencies and distance engendered by moments of physical and metaphorical touch, as well as the proximity. This in part relates to Derrida's reading of touch, in which—contesting Husserl's idea that touch generates self-presence—he argues, there can be no "pure, immediate experience of the continuous, nor of closeness, nor of absolute proximity, nor of pure indifferentiation." See Jacques Derrida, *On Touching—Jean-Luc Nancy*, trans. Christine Irizarry (Stanford, CA: Stanford University Press, 2005), 125. See also Edmund Husserl, *Ideas: General Introduction to Pure Phenomenology*, trans. W. R. Boyce Gibson (London: Routledge, 2012). However, rather than invoking the inherently spatial metaphor of absence, Petrowskaja reads the "difference" within presence not as a stable point or space of disruption, but—rather more riskily—in terms of contingency.
33. See also Hannah Tzschentke, "Motive Der Verschränkung von Gegenwart und Vergangenheit in Katja Petrowskaja's Vielleicht Esther," in *Erschriebene Erinnerung: Die Mehrdimensionalität Literarischer Inszenierung*, ed. Sanna Schulte (Cologne: Böhlau, 2015), 270–86.
34. Katja Petrowskaja, *Maybe Esther: A Family Story*, trans. Shelley Frisch (New York: Harper, 2018), 22–23. All page references refer to this edition unless otherwise stated. In German original: "Geschichte ist, wenn es plötzlich keine Menschen mehr gibt, die man fragen kann, sondern nur Quellen," in Petrowskaja, *Vielleicht Esther*, 30. All following quotations from original text refer to this edition unless otherwise stated.
35. Babi Yar is a ravine located in northwest Kiev that was the site of mass killings by German forces during World War II. On 29–30 September 1941, over thirty-three thousand Jewish civilians were murdered. In the months following this, thousands more Jews and non-Jews, including Roma, communists, and Soviet prisoners, were murdered. It is estimated that some 100,000 people were killed at Babi Yar. See Karel C. Berkhoff, "'The Corpses in the Ravine Were Women, Men, and Children': Written Testimonies from 1941 on the Babi Yar Massacre," *Holocaust and Genocide Studies* 29, no. 2 (13 August 2015): 251–74.
36. The name Treblinka refers to the site of a penal labor camp (Treblinka I) and a death camp (Treblinka II) in Poland. For further information, see Chris Webb and Michal

Chocholatý, *The Treblinka Death Camp: History, Biographies, Remembrance* (Stuttgart: ibidem Verlag, 2014).
37. Petrowskaja, *Maybe Esther*, 118. In German original: "... eine fragwürdige Restitution von verschwundenen Dingen" (136).
38. See, Hirsch, *Generation of Postmemory*.
39. Petrowskaja, *Maybe Esther*, 68. In German original: "der Kampf gegen die Stummheit" (79).
40. Petrowskaja, *Maybe Esther*, 4. In German original: "... als ob dieses Verschwinden oder dieses Nichts natürlich oder auch selbstsverständlich sei" (10).
41. Osborne, "Encountering the Archive."
42. Petrowskaja, *Maybe Esther*, 112. In German original: "Ich wollte eine totale Rückkehr *wie im Märchen*" (128, italics mine).
43. Petrowskaja, *Maybe Esther*, 133. In German original: "die Vergangenheit betrog meine Erwartungen" (133).
44. Petrowskaja, *Maybe Esther*, 44. In German original: "so gründet die Herkunft unsere Familie in einer fragwürdigen Übersetzung ohne Original" (53).
45. This sense of translation as transformation has been most articulated in poststructuralist readings of translation such as Jacques Derrida's, which draws on and rereads Walter Benjamin's famous "The Task of the Translator." Dora Osborne draws this link between Petrowskaja's depiction of remembering and Derrida's reading of translation, which she characterizes as always exposing "the gap between origin and trace." While in agreement with this reading in some ways, I aim to develop it further through focusing on the tactility of Petrowskaja's translations. Osborne, "Encountering the Archive." See also Jacques Derrida, "Des Tours de Babel," in Jacques Derrida, *Acts of Religion*, ed. Gil Anidjar (New York: Routledge, 2002), 102–34. See also Walter Benjamin, "The Task of the Translator," in *Illuminations*, ed. Hannah Arendt, trans. Harry Zorn (London: The Bodley Head, 2015), 70–82.
46. Also cited in Osborne, "Encountering the Archive." 264.
47. In the 2018 English translation, this appears as "more and more unfathomable." I use the word *grasp* here to retain the sense of tactility that the original German implies.
48. Petrowskaja, *Maybe Esther*, 63. In German original: "ich flanierte in der wiederaufgebauten Altstadt" (74).
49. Petrowskaja, *Maybe Esther*, 65. In German original: "Ich beobachtete ihn, als wäre er ein unbekanntes Tier, das sich im nächsten Moment bewegen könnte, ich tastete jede der sechs Spitzen ab, jede Drehung, jeden Winkel" (75).
50. Petrowskaja, *Maybe Esther*, 66. In German original: "Als wäre sie beim Erinnern ertappt worden, streckte sich die Zeit aus und griff nach Rosa, durch die Schallplatte erreichte sie mich" (77).
51. Petrowskaja, *Maybe Esther*, 66. In German original: "... wäre diese Schallplatte nicht gewesen, so hätte ich das versiegelte Fenster ihrer frühen Kindheit nie mehr für uns geöffnet, und ich hätte niemals verstehen können, dass meine Babuschka aus einem Warschau kommt, das es nicht mehr gibt" (76).
52. Petrowskaja, *Maybe Esther*, 66. In German original: "dann hüpfte ich.wie eine Nadel auf einer abgespielten Platte, übersprang den ganzen Krieg ... und landete in den siebziger Jahren meiner Kindheit, aus denen meine Eltern schon hätten wegfahren können. Aber sie blieben, um Bewegungen und Gegenstände aufzubewahren, die längst außer Gebrauch sind und nicht mehr im Handel" (77).

53. Hirsch, *Generation of Postmemory*, 212.
54. My translation; in German: "die unendlichen Varianten unseres Schicksals ... die in ganz anderen Liedern hätten erklingen können" (77). In the English translation: "I've been spending all my time mulling over the infinite variants of our lot in life, which could have been expressed in very different songs" (66). I have chosen to translate this slightly differently, shifting the focus of "erklingen" from *expressed* into *chimed*, as I understand the point here as not so much only how lives might have been represented or expressed but also how they might have been lived.
55. Petrowskaja, *Maybe Esther*, 64. In German original: "Sie standen dort wie aufgeschlagene Bücher, nackt, das Innere nach aussen gewendet" (74).
56. Petrowskaja, *Maybe Esther*, 75.
57. Petrowskaja, *Maybe Esther*, 53. In German original: "Rosas Schriften [waren] nicht zum lesen gedacht, *sondern zum Festhalten*, ein dick gedrehter, unzerreissbarer Ariadnefaden" (62, italics mine).
58. "... als ginge es auch hier nur um Mechanik" (30); "Abstraktes Denken" (39, capitalization in original).
59. Petrowskaja, *Maybe Esther*, 31. In German original: "denn in Wils Aufgaben galt alles Menchliche als Reibungsverlust, als Hindernis für die ewige Bewegung der geheimen Energien, dem raum meines Onkels" (39).
60. Petrowskaja, *Maybe Esther*, 28. In German original: "[er] optimierte ... seinen Wirkungsgrad" (36); "Die wahre Herkunft war ein Detail, eine unnötige Zugabe, an die man sich lieber nicht erinnerte" (36).
61. Petrowskaja, *Maybe Esther*, 28.
62. Petrowskaja, *Maybe Esther*, 165. The German word used here is *reibungslos* (186), literally translated "without friction."
63. Petrowskaja, *Maybe Esther*, 239. In German original: "Durch Zahlen sind wir verwöhnt und verdorben, von der Vorstellung der Gewalt Vergewaltigt, wenn man diese Zahlen versteht, akzeptiert man auch die Gewalt" (269).
64. Petrowskaja, *Maybe Esther*, 171. In German original: "sogar im Gedenken setzt die Selektion sich fort" (191).
65. Petrowskaja, *Maybe Esther*, 165. In German original: "immer das Unglück der Anderen" (185).
66. Ortner, "Reconfiguration," 44.
67. Petrowskaja, *Maybe Esther*, 92. In German original: "immer gab es die anderen ... Polen und Juden, Juden und Polen" (105).
68. Petrowskaja, *Maybe Esther*, 88. In German original: "Warschau plus Juden gleich Ghetto" (100).
69. Maya Caspari, "There Are No 'Other' People": A Conversation with Katja Petrowskaja, *Los Angeles Review of Books*, 7 March 2018, retrieved 8 August 2018 from https://lareviewofbooks.org/article/there-are-no-other-people-a-conversation-with-katja-petrowskaja/.
70. Ahmed's work here relates to queering phenomenology, taking as a starting point the concept of "orientation" and attending to the way in which these function as "straightening devices," making some bodies appear "in line." While my focus here differs somewhat, there are interesting resonances between this (re)reading of the tactile and the normative and Petrowskaja's approach to history, particularly so-called minority history. Ahmed, "Orientations," 562.
71. Ahmed, "Orientations," 552.
72. Ahmed, "NOT WITHOUT AMBIVALENCE."

73. See note 30 above and Ahmed, "Orientations," 552–53.
74. Ahmed, "Orientations," 555.
75. Ahmed, "Orientations," 569–70.
76. Lizarazu, "Family Tree."
77. Petrowskaja, *Maybe Esther*, 117. In German original: "Die Geschichten der Krzewins ergaben keine gerade Linie, sie kreisten und kreisten, rissen ab" (34).
78. Located in Poland, the city of Kalisz was home to a large Jewish population from approximately the end of the twelfth century until the late nineteenth century. The city was renowned for its textile industry. See: United States Holocaust Memorial Museum, "Jewish Community of Kalisz: Youth, Culture, Religion," retrieved 5 March 2020 from https://encyclopedia.ushmm.org/content/en/article/jewish-community-of-kalisz-youth-culture-religion. For more recent history, see: Lukasz Krzyzanowski, "An Ordinary Polish Town: The Homecoming of Holocaust Survivors to Kalisz in the Immediate Aftermath of the War," *European History Quarterly* 48, no. 1 (1 January 2018): 92–112, https://doi.org/10.1177/0265691417742017. One of the distant relatives that Petrowskaja discovers during her research is Mira Kimmelman, who is living in the United States. Kimmelman published a book in which she describes how her father was the owner of a lace factory in Kalisz before it burned down when the German army entered the city at the outbreak of World War I. See Mira Ryczke Kimmelman, *Life Beyond the Holocaust: Memories and Realities* (Knoxville: University of Tennessee Press, 2005).
79. Marianne Hirsch, "Connective Histories in Vulnerable Times: Presidential Address 2014," *PMLA* 129, no. 3 (2014): 342. See also Ariella Azoulay, "Potential History: Thinking through Violence," *Critical Inquiry* 39, no. 3 (March 2013): 548–74. Drawing on Ariella Azoulay's fruitful notion of "potential history," Hirsch develops a link between tactility and potentiality by explicitly invoking "vulnerability" as a metaphor for radical openness. This clearly resonates with Petrowskaja's work, yet I would suggest here and elsewhere that Hirsch still tends to invoke tactile metaphors—"the wounding look"—as kind of disruptive blind spot. Petrowskaja extends this by emphasizing both the unstable and the already mediated nature of tactility, and she alludes to the negative flipside of radical openness—the potential for failure to work in a disruptive way.
80. Yasemin Yildiz, *Beyond the Mother Tongue: The Postmonolingual Condition* (New York: Fordham University Press, 2012).
81. My translation of Katja Petrowskaja, "Es gibt keine Grenze zwischen Literaturen": Katja Petrowskaja im Gespräch mit Ulrike Timm, interview by Ulrike Timm, 8 July 2013, retrieved 8 August 2018 from http://www.deutschlandradiokultur.de/es-gibt-keine-grenze-zwischen-literaturen.954.de.html?dram:article_id=252300. The original quotation reads: "Also wenn ich meine Geschichte auf Russisch schreibe, es ist klar, wo man eine Geschichte platziert, das ist irgendwelche Geschichte wieder aus diesem Raum, wieder zum Thema, sozusagen meine Opferrolle ist in russischer Sprache impliziert. Wenn ich aber dasselbe auf Deutsch schreibe, ist es nicht ganz klar, wer ich bin, und es ist eine gewisse Entfremdung."
82. Heimann, "Deutsche Sprache kam einer Befreiung gleich." In the German original: "es ist ein Kampf mit dieser Sprache. Doch gerade diese Schwierigkeit impliziert eine Gewisse Qualität."
83. Maya Caspari, "Writing Violence: In Conversation with Katja Petrowskaja," *Wasafiri* 34, no. 3 (2019): 71–74. https://doi.org/10.1080/02690055.2019.1613021. On the significance of "stumbling," see also Osborne, "Encountering the Archive."

84. Petrowskaja, *Maybe Esther*, 157. In German original: "das knirschen der maschinen, aorta rupture, knochen, maschinen, die das bewusstsein zu pulver mahlen ..." (178, capitalization in original).
85. Petrowskaja, *Maybe Esther*, 156. In German original: "ich werde nicht versteinern" (177).
86. Petrowskaja, *Maybe Esther*, 157. In German original: "... es gibt keienen Ort mehr, wo es kein verderben und kein verbrechen gibt ..." (178).
87. Caspari, "Writing Violence," 74.
88. Eve Kosofsky Sedgwick, *Touching Feeling* (Durham, NC: Duke University Press, 2003).
89. Petrowskaja, *Maybe Esther*, 244. In German original: "Wenn mein Grossvater überlebt hat, bedeutet es, dass jemand an seiner Stelle sterben musste" (275).
90. Petrowskaja, *Maybe Esther*, 71.
91. Petrowskaja, *Maybe Esther*, 72.
92. Petrowskaja, *Maybe Esther*, 72. In German original: "ich bin oben, oder nein, oben ist meine Rosa" (83).
93. Caspari, "Writing Violence" (my italics), 73
94. Petrowskaja, *Maybe Esther*, 35. In German original: "Denn die Vermeidung des Konjunktivs macht aus einer Vorstellung eine Erkenntnis oder sogar einen Bericht, man nimmt die Stelle eines anderen ein, katapultiert sich dorthin, und so erprobe ich jede Rolle an mir selbst, als gäbe es keine Vergangenheit ohne irgendein Als-ob, Wenn oder Falls" (45).
95. Petrowskaja, *Maybe Esther*, 36.

Bibliography

Adelson, Leslie A. "Touching Tales of Turks, Germans, and Jews: Cultural Alterity, Historical Narrative, and Literary Riddles for the 1990s." *New German Critique* 80 (2000): 93–124. https://doi.org/10.2307/488635.

Ahmed, Sara. "'NOT WITHOUT AMBIVALENCE': An Interview with Sara Ahmed on Postcolonial Intimacies." Interview by Phanuel Antwi, Sarah Brophy, Helene Strauss, and Y-Dang Troeung, McMaster University, Canada, 3 March 2011. http://www.tandfonline.com/doi/abs/10.1080/1369801X.2013.771011.

———. "Open Forum Imaginary Prohibitions: Some Preliminary Remarks on the Founding Gestures of the 'New Materialism.'" *European Journal of Women's Studies* 15 (February 2008): 23–39. https://doi.org/10.1177/1350506807084854.

———. "Orientations: Toward a Queer Phenomenology." *GLQ: A Journal of Lesbian and Gay Studies* 12, no. 4 (14 September 2006): 543–74.

Assmann, Aleida. *Der Lange Schatten Der Vergangenheit: Erinnerungskultur Und Geschichts-Politik*. Munich: C. H. Beck, 2008.

———. "Transnational Memories." *European Review* 22 (2014): 546–56.

Azoulay, Ariella. "Potential History: Thinking through Violence." *Critical Inquiry* 39, no. 3 (March 2013): 548–74. https://doi.org/10.1086/670045.

Barad, Karen. "Posthumanist Performativity: Toward an Understanding of How Matter Comes to Matter." *Signs: Journal of Women in Culture and Society* 28, no. 3 (2003): 801–31.

Benjamin, Marina. "Holocaust Memoir Maybe Esther Is a Mesmerising Work of Reconstruction and Reflection." New Statesman, updated 28 June 2021. Retrieved 8 Au-

gust 2018 from https://www.newstatesman.com/culture/books/2018/02/holocaust-memoir-maybe-esther-mesmerising-work-reconstruction-and-reflection.
Benjamin, Walter. "The Task of the Translator." In *Illuminations*, edited by Hannah Arendt, translated by Harry Zorn, 70–82. London: The Bodley Head, 2015.
Berkhoff, Karel C. "'The Corpses in the Ravine Were Women, Men, and Children': Written Testimonies from 1941 on the Babi Yar Massacre." *Holocaust and Genocide Studies* 29, no. 2 (13 August 2015): 251–74.
Böttiger, Von Helmut. "Katja Petrowskaja: 'Wir sind die letzten Europäer!'" Zeit Online, 13 March 2014. Retrieved 8 August 2018 from https://www.zeit.de/2014/12/katja-petrowskaja-vielleicht-esther.
Brown, Wendy. "Resisting Left Melancholy." *Boundary 2* 26, no. 3 (1999): 19–27.
Butler, Judith. *Frames of War: When Is Life Grievable?* New York: Verso, 2009.
Caspari, Maya. "There Are No 'Other' People": A Conversation with Katja Petrowskaja. *Los Angeles Review of Books*, 7 March 2018. Retrieved 8 August 2018 from https://lareviewofbooks.org/article/there-are-no-other-people-a-conversation-with-katja-petrowskaja/.
———. "Writing Violence: In Conversation with Katja Petrowskaja." *Wasafiri* 34, no. 3 (2019): 71–74. https://doi.org/10.1080/02690055.2019.1613021.
Cheah, Pheng. "Given Culture: Rethinking Cosmopolitical Freedom in Transnationalism." In *Cosmopolitics: Thinking and Feeling beyond the Nation*, edited by Pheng Cheah and Bruce Robbins, 290–38. Minneapolis: University of Minnesota Press, 1998.
Clifford, James. "Diasporas." *Cultural Anthropology* 9, no. 3 (1994): 302–38.
Damrosch, David. "Toward a History of World Literature." *New Literary History* 39, no. 3 (Summer 2008): 481–95.
Derrida, Jacques. "Des Tours de Babel." In *Acts of Religion*, edited by Gil Anidjar, 102–34. New York: Routledge, 2002.
———. *On Touching—Jean-Luc Nancy*. Translated by Christine Irizarry. Stanford, CA: Stanford University Press, 2005.
Eckhart, Gabrielle. "The Functions of Multilingual Language Use in Katja Petrowskaja's Vielleicht Esther." *Glossen: German Literature and Culture after 1945*, June 2015. Retrieved 8 August 2018 from http://blogs.dickinson.edu/glossen/archive/most-recent-issue-glossen-402015/gabriele-eckart-glossen40-2015/.
Feigel, Lara. "Maybe Esther by Katja Petrowskaja Review—A Family Story of 20th-Century Europe." *The Guardian*, 1 February 2018, sec. Books. Retrieved 8 August 2018 from http://www.theguardian.com/books/2018/feb/01/maybe-esther-katja-petrowskaja-review.
Fraser, Nancy. "Reframing Justice in a Globalizing World." Edited by Nancy Fraser. *Lua Nova—Revista de Cultura e Politica* 77 (2009): 11–39.
Garloff, Katja, and Agnes Mueller, eds. *German Jewish Literature after 1990*. Rochester, NY: Camden House, 2018.
———. "Introduction." In *German Jewish Literature after 1990*, edited by Katja Garloff and Agnes Mueller, 123–45. Rochester, NY: Camden House, 2018.
Gikandi, Simon. "Between Routes and Roots: Cosmopolitanism and the Claims of Locality." In *Rerouting the Postcolonial: New Directions for the New Millennium*, edited by Janet Wilson, Cristina Şandru, and Sarah Lawson Welsh, 22–35. New York: Routledge, 2010.
Gutmair, Ulrich. "'Würdigt Die Katastrophe in Angemessener Weise': Die Erzähldebüts von Katja Petrowskaja Und Per Leo." *Merkur* 68 (2014): 1026–32.

Guttman, Anna. "The Jew in the Archive: Textualizations of (Jewish?) History in Contemporary South Asian Literature." *Contemporary Literature* 51, no. 3 (2010): 503–31.

Haines, Brigid. "The Eastern Turn in Contemporary German, Swiss and Austrian Literature." *Debatte: Journal of Contemporary Central and Eastern Europe* 16, no. 2 (August 2008): 135–49. https://doi.org/10.1080/09651560802316899.

Hammelehle, Sebastian. "Familiengeschichte 'Vielleicht Esther': Nächster Halt Holocaust." *Spiegel Online*, 11 March 2014, sec. Kultur. Retrieved 8 August 2018 from http://www.spiegel.de/kultur/literatur/katja-petrowskaja-vielleicht-esther-a-957065.html.

Heimann, Holger. "Deutsche Sprache kam einer Befreiung gleich." *Deutsche Welle*, 10 July 2013, sec. Kultur. Retrieved 31 August 2017 from http://www.dw.com/de/deutsche-sprache-kam-einer-befreiung-gleich/a-16935579.

Hirsch, Marianne. "Connective Histories in Vulnerable Times: Presidential Address 2014." *PMLA* 129, no. 3 (2014): 330–48.

———. *The Generation of Postmemory: Writing and Visual Culture after the Holocaust*. New York: Columbia University Press, 2012.

Husserl, Edmund. *Ideas: General Introduction to Pure Phenomenology*. Translated by W. R. Boyce Gibson. London: Routledge, 2012.

Huyssen, Andreas. *Present Pasts: Urban Palimpsests and the Politics of Memory*. Stanford, CA: Standford University Press, 2003.

Kimmelman, Mira Ryczke. *Life beyond the Holocaust: Memories and Realities*. Knoxville: University of Tennessee Press, 2005.

Krzyzanowski, Lukasz. "An Ordinary Polish Town: The Homecoming of Holocaust Survivors to Kalisz in the Immediate Aftermath of the War." *European History Quarterly* 48, no. 1 (1 January 2018): 92–112. https://doi.org/10.1177/0265691417742017.

Littler, Margaret. "Cultural Memory and Identity Formation in the Berlin Republic." In *Contemporary German Fiction: Writing in the Berlin Republic*, edited by Stuart Taberner, 177–95. Cambridge: Cambridge University Press, 2007.

Lizarazu, Maria Roca. "The Family Tree, the Web, and the Palimpsest: Figures of Postmemory in Katja Petrowskaja's Vielleicht Esther (2014)." *Modern Language Review* 113, no. 1 (2018): 168–89.

McGowan, Moray. "Turkish-German Fiction since the Mid-1990s." In *Contemporary German Fiction: Writing in the Berlin Republic*, edited by Stuart Taberner, 196–214. Cambridge: Cambridge University Press, 2007.

Michaelis-König, Andree. "Multilingualism and Jewishness in Katja Petrowskaja's Vielleicht Esther." In *German Jewish Literature after 1990*, edited by Katja Garloff and Agnes Mueller, 146–68. Rochester, NY: Camden House, 2018.

Moser, Samuel. "Auf der Schwelle von Mauthausen | NZZ." *Neue Zürcher Zeitung*, 5 April 2014, sec. Bücher. Retrieved 8 August 2018 from https://www.nzz.ch/feuilleton/buecher/auf-der-schwelle-von-mauthausen-1.18277615.

Mufti, Aamir R., and Ato Quayson. "The Predicaments of Postcolonial Thinking." *Cambridge Journal of Postcolonial Literary Inquiry* 3, no. 1 (2016): 143–56. http://dx.doi.org/10.1017/pli.2015.28.

Ortner, Jessica. "The Reconfiguration of the European Archive in Contemporary German-Jewish Migrant-Literature: Katja Petrowskaja's Novel Vielleicht Esther." *Nordisk Judaistik: Scandinavian Jewish Studies* 28, no. 1 (2017): 38–54.

Osborne, Dora. "Encountering the Archive in Katja Petrowskaja's Vielleicht Esther." *Seminar: A Journal of Germanic Studies* 52, no. 3 (September 2016): 255–72. https://doi.org/10.3138/seminar.52.3.01.

Petrowskaja, Katja. "Es gibt keine Grenze zwischen Literaturen." Interview by Ulrike Timm, 7 August 2013. Retrieved 8 August 2018 from http://www.deutschlandradiokultur .de/es-gibt-keine-grenze-zwischen-literaturen.954.de.html?dram:article_id=252300.
———. *Vielleicht Esther*. 1st ed. Berlin: Suhrkamp, 2015.
———. *Maybe Esther: A Family Story*. Translated by Shelley Frisch. New York: Harper, 2018.
Renan, Ernest. *Qu'est-Ce Qu'une Nation?* Translated by Ethan Rundell. Paris: Presses-Pocket, 1992.
Rothberg, Michael. *Multidirectional Memory: Remembering the Holocaust in the Age of Decolonization*. Stanford, CA: Stanford University Press, 2009.
———. "From Gaza to Warsaw: Mapping Multidirectional Memory." *Criticism* 53, no. 4 (2011): 523–48. https://doi.org/10.1353/crt.2011.0032.
Rothberg, Michael, and Yasemin Yildiz. "Memory Citizenship: Migrant Archives of Holocaust Remembrance in Contemporary Germany." *Parallax* 17, no. 4 (November 2011): 32–48. https://doi.org/10.1080/13534645.2011.605576.
Rushdie, Salman. "Imaginary Homelands." In *Imaginary Homelands: Essays and Criticism 1981–1991*, 9–21. London: Granta Books, 1992.
Sedgwick, Eve Kosofsky. *Touching Feeling*. Durham, NC: Duke University Press, 2003.
Skolnik, Jonathan. "Memory without Borders? Migrant Identity and the Legacy of the Holocaust in Olga Grjasnowa's Der Russe Ist Einer, Der Birken Liebt." In *German Jewish Literature after 1990*, edited by Katja Garloff and Agnes Mueller, 123–45. Rochester, NY: Camden House, 2018.
Taberner, Stuart. "The Possibilities and Pitfalls of a Jewish Cosmopolitanism: Reading Natan Sznaider through Russian-Jewish Writer Olga Grjasnowa's German-Language Novel *Der Russe Ist Einer, Der Birken Liebt* (All Russians Love Birch Trees)." *European Review of History: Revue Européenne d'histoire* 23, nos. 5–6 (November 2016): 912–30. https://doi.org/10.1080/13507486.2016.1203872.
Taylor, Catherine. "Maybe Esther by Katja Petrowskaja—'When There Are No More People to Ask.'" *Financial Times*, 26 January 2018. Retrieved 8 August 2018 from https://www.ft.com/content/35f6ea88-004e-11e8-9e12-af73e8db3c71.
Tzschentke, Hannah. "Motive Der Verschränkung von Gegenwart Und Vergangenheit in Katja Petrowskajas Vielleicht Esther." In *Erschreibene Errinerung: Die Mehrdimensionalität Literarischer Inszenierung*, edited by Sanna Schulte, 270–86. Cologne: Böhlau, 2015.
United States Holocaust Memorial Museum. "Jewish Community of Kalisz: Youth, Culture, Religion." Retrieved from 5 March 2020 from https://encyclopedia.ushmm.org/content/en/article/jewish-community-of-kalisz-youth-culture-religion.
———. "Kiev and Babi Yar." 3 January 2007. Retrieved 8 August 2018 from https://web.archive.org/web/20070103133722/http://www.ushmm.org/wlc/article.php?lang=en&ModuleId=10005421.
Vestli, Elin Nesje. "'Mein Fremdes Deutsch': Grenzüberschreitungen in Der Deutschsprachigen Gegenwartsliteratur; Katja Petrowskaja's Vielleicht Esther.'" In *Language and Nation: Crossroads and Connections*, edited by Guri Ellen Barstad, Arnstein Hjelde, Sigmund Kvam, Anastasia Parianou, and John Todd, 143–60. New York: Waxmann, 2016.
Webb, Chris, and Michal Chocholatý. *The Treblinka Death Camp: History, Biographies, Remembrance*. Stuttgart: ibidem Verlag, 2014.

CHAPTER 9

Posthumanism and Object-Oriented Ontology in Sharon Dodua Otoo's *Synchronicity* and "Herr Gröttrup setzt sich hin"

EVAN TORNER

Posthumanism is a much-debated[1] paradigm that prioritizes the subjective and intersubjective positions of objects excluded from the category of "human." This chapter applies it to works by Sharon Dodua Otoo, an Afrofuturist author within the contemporary Afro-German literary movement. Ushered into being by a 1977 lecture by Ihab Hassan[2] and then transformed by Donna Haraway, N. Katherine Hayles, and Athena Athanasiou[3] into a feminist critique of modern subjecthood, posthumanism contends that whatever we define as the "human" is simply a question of what is useful to technologies and logics of control.[4] Giorgio Agamben's *homo sacer* framework of "exclusionary inclusion"[5] describes posthumanism well: certain subjects, be they robots or human slaves or asylum seekers or prisoners, are seen as objects to be managed but excluded from humanity and basic human rights, and thus from subjecthood, as a result of specific configurations of political power. Athanasiou connects this state of (non)being with the "biopolitical technology of the concentration camp,"[6] demonstrating how interrelated the modern discourse on machine intelligence, racial categories of exclusion, and the still-extant horrors of the Holocaust are. Problems of definitions *themselves* are therefore central to the discourse.

Posthumanism as an intellectual movement, to put it bluntly, reconfers subjecthood onto those whom society would consider objects. Afro-Europeans find their subjecthood under constant question by the white-dominated institutions that surround them. Such pressure fuels efforts to create new, open futures in Europe that include them as fully recognized subjects. Fatima El-Tayeb speculates, for example, that white constructions of Europeanness create a "queerness in time and space, which is epistemologically imposed rather than agentially chosen," and those displaced individuals capable of manipulating this queerness "[open] up the possibility of yet undefined futures, which is to say: futures that are themselves open rather than closed."[7] Priscilla Layne echoes this queer positioning of the Afrofuturist movement discussed below, reminding us that "Afrofuturists are highly appreciative of the past" and that "Afrofuturist work seeks to contribute to the liberation of black people."[8] The literature analyzed in this chapter explores white Eurocentrism and the act of fiction as a map toward queer Afrofuturist liberation, which stands very much in dialogue with the intersectional liberation and subjecthood of other groups such as Muslim and Jewish Europeans.

An Afro-German movement in narrative fiction has emerged within the past several decades, helping other nonwhite literary movements such as Turkish German, Jewish German, and Eastern European German literature refigure the white-dominated German literary canon.[9] Narratives of Otherness, of racist community norms, survival, and bittersweet humor, characterize this vibrant body of work.[10] Within the movement taken as a whole, however, two exemplary authors transcend their cultural moment: May Ayim[11] and Sharon Dodua Otoo.[12] Ayim's history of Afro-Germans in Germany from the groundbreaking 1986 work *Farbe bekennen* (*Showing Our Colors*)[13] continues to be the lodestar for all writing on the topic over three decades later. Her poetry in *Blues in Black and White*[14] is taught in classrooms around the globe. Otoo's writings, on the other hand, express not only humorous insight on identity and politics but also the weighty philosophical ramifications of imagining alternative identities and politics. Ayim's influence lives on in Otoo's parallel literary fiction, nonfiction, and activism. An Afro-British citizen of Berlin who describes herself as "Mother, Activist, Author, and Editor" (in that order), Otoo is known for her 2012 book *the things I'm thinking while smiling politely*, a meditation on everyday German racism and the frustrating conversations one has with oneself in confronting an irritating social order, as well as her 2014 novella *Synchronicity*, a science fiction work about a woman who undergoes a startling transformation over the course of a month. She stands at the forefront of the Afro-German literary and dramaturgical establishment, having won the prestigious Ingeborg-Bachmann-Preis for her 2016 short story "Herr Gröttrup setzt sich hin" (Herr Gröttrup sits down). The award marks her acceptance as a fiction writer, parallel to her activism. This chapter concerns the content of both her prize-winning short story as well as *Synchronicity*, since both pieces are object lessons in the refiguration of the German present. In dialogue with other contemporary authors,[15] her fiction is suffused with resistance to white German oppression as well as quiet contemplation of everyday future-making by Afro-German creators. She asks uncomfortable questions about definitions of race, nation, and personhood; about the material relations that shape contemporary Europe and strategies to model and resist them. Rather than simply regarding a singular Afro-German or white German experience in the present, Otoo extends her interest to intersectional identities of the past and the future, of subject and object, seeking in posthumanism a means of binding together the blind spots of white society, a political economy critique of modern-day Germany, and the way for marginalized populations to re-enchant the world in their own image.[16]

I argue that Otoo's resolute literary journeys into fragmented social realities and their objects make her a poetic posthumanist. Her work is not so much interested in observing and describing humanity as demarcating our limits and potential, especially given dynamics of exclusionary inclusion in our often suffocating social and cultural spheres. Race and identity are therefore just a few variables among many in her work. She makes social niceties and daily routines seem somehow as immutable as skin color or heritage, even as the rules of reality bend and break around her protagonists. Otoo is thus also a contributor to the philosophical archipelago known as speculative realism or object-oriented ontology.[17] Objects and objectified beings, according to these schools of thought, push back against those deemed "subjects" by society and the stories told to legitimate their power. "Otoo's books," writes one reviewer, "are brilliantly aware of traditions and contexts, of how assumptions and narratives intersect."[18] I contend that both *Synchronicity* and "Herr Gröttrup setzt sich hin" frame the bewildered interiority of many of us as we experience the intersections of time, culture, race politics, neoliberal economics, and biology, but both works also serve as blueprints for how one comports oneself in the face of change, signposts for navigating the fraught circumstances of the everyday from an Afro-European perspective.

Afrofuturism and Afro-German Temporality

Otoo's biography and work relate to broader Afro-European efforts to reframe the "future" and the "human," such that Afrofuturism, the African-diasporic multimedia science fiction movement including Samuel R. Delany, is one framework for understanding Otoo's work. Afrofuturism, however, is also perfectly complementary to other discourses Otoo invokes.

The future, contrasted with the present, is often articulated through a language of dystopia rather than a language of hope. We see bleak futures of increased control and precarity, as our everyday lives are characterized by repetition and small crises. The incredible atrocities of the twentieth century—the Holocaust, the bombings of Hiroshima and Nagasaki, the Belgian Congo, the Great Leap Forward, among others—not only weigh heavily in the past but also appear to foreclose possible futures, especially ones that demand drastic shifts in human behavior patterns. Hope appears naïve in this context. Immanuel Kant's metaphysics hinged on the question "What may we hope for?" and Ernst Bloch describes how much of the Western philosophy of hope, even those raceless, classless utopias offered by Marxism, is built on the foundations of Christianity. Bloch writes: "The rigid divisions between future and past thus themselves collapse, unbecome future becomes visible in the past, avenged and inherited, mediated and fulfilled past in the future."[19] Which is to say: hope is a construct—and a result—of time and temporality, of conceiving our horizons of expectation differently. The present becomes a struggle over the future by way of unfulfilled hopes from the past. Sociopolitical subjecthood within the public sphere for People of Color, women, queer folx, religious minorities, and other marginalized groups is either negated or under constant threat of negation. Both the costs and aspirations of this struggle are passed on from generation to generation, as exploitation, appropriation, and exclusion cannot be resisted without active, long-term effort.[20] Thus every marginalized population inherits a Blochian *Noch-Nicht* (not yet), a promise of full societal support and recognition despite continuous setbacks and disappointment in the present. Hope binds past, present, and future together into a temporality that yields "future-making" activity insistent on the viability of past promises. Hope is also a sensory experience, connected with specific sensations, tropes, and aesthetic practices.[21] Artists lay out narratives that critique the present by chronicling its brutalities and permitting protagonists to engage in meaningful activities toward a better future. Temporality itself must be wrested from the grasp of dominant narratives of success and failure, hope and despair.

Demarcating a temporality for one's own self and one's diaspora community therefore forces a sensuous reckoning with history—a hallmark of Otoo's work.[22] "History" in the Afro-German context means both the dominant white German historical discourse and the Afro-European history that El-Tayeb sees as a corrective to ongoing white supremacist processes of racialization and marginalization.[23] History not only becomes a contested site but also is continuously reinvented through actions in the present. Giorgio Agamben has a provisional answer as to *how* this reinvention occurs. In his essay "In Playland: Reflections on History and Play," Agamben writes how *play* and *ritual* demarcate the synchronic and diachronic moments in cultures, respectively. Play creates a kind of eternal present, dissolving our very sense of time itself in a vertiginous moment or state of flow. Rites and rituals, by contrast, demarcate historical time. In Agamben's system, "history is nothing other than the result of the relation between diachronic signifiers and synchronic signifiers produced incessantly by ritual and play."[24] Philipp Khabo Koepsell describes Afrofuturism in the German context as "having nothing to do with space travel" but rather "telling a progressive and self-determined narrative" against a white German narrative rather than seeing Afro-Germans "described as a footnote of German postwar and migration history."[25] To this end, Koepsell and Otoo are both engaged in the German master narrative of history: Koepsell by way of recapturing the present through the lens of a progressive futurity for Afro-Germans; Otoo by way of (ritualistically) reclaiming the December period of advent through her protagonist's journey in *Synchronicity*.

Common white European paradigms for over two centuries have classified the world into societies *with* and *without* history. Such formulations with a specifically racist cast are found in the work of Hegel. In both his appendix to *Vorlesungen über die Philosophie der Geschichte* (*Lectures on the Philosphy of History*, 1837) and *Enzyklopädie der philosophischen Wissenschaften im Grundrisse* (*Encyclopedia of the Philosophical Sciences*, 1817), Hegel positions Africa, and to a lesser extent Asia, *outside* of history, and therefore outside of a system for attaining the European standard of self-consciousness.[26] When one *hopes* for a better society in the white Western philosophical paradigm, a white Christian European worldview centers itself and the "proper" relationship between play and ritual structures what we may hope for. Unconscious white-supremacist bias reigns.

Afrofuturism[27] intervenes in the discourse by disrupting a white European view of time, with its smug progress narrative that excludes People of Color. "Science fiction," Alondra Nelson says, "... was an apt metaphor for black life and history."[28] Afrofuturism posits that the very notion of "race," itself a modern invention, is also a kind of technology. Race and systems of racial control not only seek to dominate their subjects but also—as with robots and automata—instrumentalize them,[29] denying these subjects of subjectivity itself. There is no "natural" order that would confer management positions to white people or manual-labor-oriented positions to Black people. Afrofuturism appropriates this conception of Black Africans as tools or assets, using imaginative leaps of African-culture-inspired robots, vast Egyptian spacefaring societies and Rastafarian utopias to convey this "audacity of hope, the bold declaration to believe ... the expectation for transformative change,"[30] as Ytasha Womack puts it. The movement parallels the inversion of subject and object in continental philosophy—called *speculative realism* or *object-oriented ontology*—in which the anthropocentrism of Kant and René Descartes is rejected in favor of a flat ontology that considers all things equal. Graham Harman, one of the movement's primary theorists, postulates the following:

If all relations are on the same footing, and all relations are equally inept at exhausting the depths of their terms, then an intermediate form of contact between things must be possible. This contact can only take a *sensual* form, since it can only encounter translated or distorted versions of other objects.[31]

Objects withhold their existence from each other, and all beings are forced into radical, sensual contact with those objects within their immediate vicinity. Science fiction and surreal realities of robots and aliens are able to grapple with the strangeness of this relation, whereas humanist drama cannot. Alexander Weheliye articulates the stakes of Afrofuturist aesthetics:

> This is a battle to supplant the current instantiation of the human as synonymous with the objective existence of white, western Man and his various damned counterparts, especially black subjects, offering in its stead new styles of human subjectivity and community that are no longer based on the glaring rift between the folk as the nonhuman other and *ein Volk* as the most extreme version of the immaculately homogenous political subject.[32]

Afrofuturistic works often mean an emphasis on *boldness* and *exteriority*—of openly showing this audacity of a Black future through the music of Sun Ra or the films of Marlon Riggs—over a sort of Blochian quiet hope found in the everyday and our continuous action made toward a future of any kind. But it would be a mistake to exclude precisely *this* kind of hope from the contributions of African diasporic writers such as Otoo.

Afro-Germans and Writing

Otoo innovates in continuity with Afro-German writings from Anton Wilhelm Amo to May Ayim (all of whom share heritage in Ghana, a trajectory that merits further research).[33] This body of work is primarily written by women[34] and constitutes a way to heal from and resist against past oppressions.[35] "By telling their own story," Leroy Hopkins argues, "Afro-Germans have attempted to liberate themselves from the strictures and barriers erected against them by a society whose ultimate control over their destiny was visible in the very process of naming."[36] Due to the predominance of white bigotry and systems of domination, Afro-Germans were seen as an anomaly—"a (violent) disruption of normalcy"[37]—and due to Germany's comparatively abbreviated colonial history between 1885 and 1918, a lack of former colonial subjects "writing back" produced collective amnesia about the colonies and crimes committed there.[38] Of particular importance are also Afro-German perspectives on the peculiarities of whiteness, because white-dominated German culture, language, and traditions constitute the underexamined core of German society with which Afro-Germans reckon in daily life.[39] Afro-Germans seek not to be labeled as "Afro-German poets" but simply "poets," refusing categorical identity determination.[40]

Writers in the Afro-German tradition appropriate power for themselves through two verbs: *to name* (*selbst benennen*)[41] and *to become* (*werden*). Naming is significant for Afro-German writers both in the selection of a pen name and in the neologisms they create. For example, Ayim's birth name is Sylvia Andler, a name that helped with integration into white society, but was changed to the name of a city in Ghana. In *Synchronicity*, Otoo invents the new German word "Polysinn," which implies a permanent synesthetic experience of the world. As Maisha Eggers argues, becoming (*werden*) is a framework that lets Afro-Germans dignify their unique life experiences—the sensations and cultural dissonance one feels on a daily basis—in a longer narrative of self-liberation.[42] *Becoming* is more important than *being*,[43] sensing and intuition more important than the capitalist instrumental reason encouraged by the white, Western European world. *Werden* as a verb lets the Afro-German populace affirm its diversity as a community, already understood as a diaspora and amalgam of people of many different backgrounds (but with a shared experience of anti-Black racism). De-essentializing what it means to be Afro-German through new language and a new framing of life experiences is a rhetorical move against *Black negation*, an erosive force that actively erases Black subjectivities and contributions to society. In the words of Keguro Macharia, Black negation "makes one unrecognizable to oneself... [make us] unknown to ourselves and to each other."[44] The Afro-German movement recognizes the multiplicity of identities and knowledges that form its foundation, and its artists give them a sensual shape.

Ayim's work in *Farbe bekennen* created a master narrative of the Afro-German movement from a strict rereading of Central European history. She pulled together multiple centuries, from the Black presence in Germanic lands during the Middle Ages to the scholarship of Anton Wilhelm Amo to the Audre Lorde–inspired movement of her time in the mid-1980s. The message is clear: we have always been here, and we deserve equal recognition as subjects in history. But what Ayim does not cover in her history (but *does* cover in her poetry) is how she feels to be accepted and Othered at the same time,[45] of how this turmoil impacts someone such as Ayim. Otoo understands this lack of clarity all too well, and she parses the ambiguities of race and German-ness at the foundation of Afro-German identity. There are objects as well as social and symbolic acts that have effects on one's body and psyche, and she explores the peculiarity of those interactions. She is not preoccupied with suffering or oppression but with subtly crafting a political literature that operates through humor, self-confident characters, and the *play* (in Agamben's sense)[46] that being/becoming an Afro-German in this period of time has to offer. Her personal stories suit the collective temporality of the Afro-German poets. Impatient for the change to come, Sheila Mysorekar has, for example, adapted Amiri Baraka's 1970 poem "It's Nation Time!" to the German context: "It's Nation Time! . . . / Schwarze Stimmen in Berlin und Köln / . . . und geballte Fäuste / wie spät ist es / spät ist es / what's the time / now . . . / Und jetzt / Jetzt ist Zeit / Jetzt ist die Zeit / Gekommen."[47] Otoo's work reminds the reader that this nation period is long overdue and that white Germans simply do not have the sensory capacity to perceive the Black voices and bodies around them, voices and bodies that testify to a non-white-dominated future already in creation. What reigns instead, as Otoo has recently asserted, is silence (*Schweigen*).[48] My purpose here is to convey Otoo's counternarrative against such silence: a posthumanist meditation on being Black in Germany in *Synchronicity* and a corresponding estrangement of German whiteness in "Herr Gröttrup setzt sich hin."

Synchronicity

Synchronicity (2014) is a novella that describes the startling transformation of Charlie Mensah ("Cee"), a Black British graphic designer living in Berlin, during *Adventzeit* (the twenty-four days before Christmas) in 2013. It involves both her diachronic progression through daily diary entries as well as her synchronic transformation from a marginalized black-skinned human into a fantastical, multisensory alien being. Her text captures the banal and the fantastic to portray Afro-German experiences of the world as multilayered, ambiguous interior struggles.

Each day, Cee loses the ability to see a specific color on the spectrum—yellow, light blue, red, and so on—but then still has to go about her day: finding work, dealing with an eviction notice, doing the laundry. The synchronic events of losing one's sense of color soon become an expected diachronic reality. By day 11, she can see only a gray world around her, which dramatically affects her work as a graphic designer. But on that day, in between an HTML crash course and meditating on the white hipster-ness of the latte macchiato versus the *Milchkaffee*, Cee somehow begins to absorb the aura of a police officer:

> There was a fraction of a moment, as thin as paper, as I walked by "my" police officer and took his aura into me . . . Yes. I did it.[49]

Both she and the police officer recognize that she is, like a psychic vampire, somehow capturing part of his essence. She does so anyway, flexing her newfound powers against a figure of the white establishment. On her subsequent days, her body begins to tickle, itch, and hurt.

Otoo fashions a character whose narrative arc includes undergoing daily painful transformation and acquiring fantastical psychic and biological capabilities while still experiencing the perpetual, dull drumbeat of everyday pressures that cannot be ignored. Cee receives an awkward big-money design contract from Herr Welker, her ruthless landlord who wishes to evict her. At the same time, as she experiences the return of all the colors around her, she becomes overwhelmed with the hum, smell, and taste of the process. She faints one day due to sensory overload and is then chastised by her distant mother, who reminds Cee that she is an *Ejis*: one of a unique, alien species of parthenogenetic women from Africa who possess "Polysinn." Parthenogenesis means that the Ejis can asexually reproduce—Cee has an estranged daughter named Sam who came into the world in exactly this way—and then at some point their world becomes a synesthetic muddle compared to those designated as "human."[50] Cee's colors return to her in the final third of the book in a full synesthetic onslaught. She contemplates suicide but decides to persist. Despite her tumultuous sensory experience, Cee manages her ruthless everyday life as an intellectual worker in the twenty-first-century digital labor economy, and there is no promised salvation for her. She turns down Herr Welker's big design contract because it turns out that she would have to create a webpage for a brothel—the exploitative underbelly of wealthy white society is exposed. The story ends with Cee heading to the post office with its vibrant yellow signs, at least satisfied that she still has a roof over her head, money in her bank account, and groceries in the fridge.

The story is written in a daily diary format, and Otoo has remarked that she wrote it as a commentary on the lives of so many contingent workers who have to spend Christmas alone. The work is punctuated by Sita Ngoumou's watercolor illustrations, which emote the loss of color in an everyday world full of images. Cee and much of the everyday world are portrayed as gray and indistinct, but each picture contains colorful accents: a sign, a hoodie, wallpaper, and so forth. Ngoumou foregrounds the role of color distinction in the narrative and social milieus of the book. On first glance, Otoo's text appears to be a metaphorization of (Afro-German) experience: drudgery and discrimination disenchant the everyday, whereas a turn to one's unique heritage and gifts at the end offer respite and the "capacity to aspire."[51]

Otoo's uncanny writing also enshrines specific hypertexts that address the uncanniness of everyday structures, namely Franz Kafka's *Die Verwandlung* (*The Metamorphosis*, 1915) and Ralph Ellison's *Invisible Man* (1952), as well as Advanced Chemistry's "Fremd im eigenen Land" (Stranger in my own country, 1992) and Nadia Brönimann's *Seelentanz* (Soul dance, 2006). Hypertexts in the literary theory of Gerard Genette relate to earlier texts by way of adaptation, imitation, or parody.[52] By confronting uncanniness in her own forthright manner, Otoo reckons with a multigenerational conversation on the general alienation of modern life. Kafka demonstrates that the synchronic event of Gregor Samsa turning into a cockroach must necessarily balance out with the oppressive, diachronic everyday bourgeois structures that also weigh upon him, much as Cee must balance between being a graphic designer and undergoing a bodily and sensory metamorphosis at the same time. Ellison's tome refers to the social invisibility of Blackness in America, just as Cee's daily experiences reveal the microaggressions and transactional negotiations that allow one to exist as an Afro-British German citizen. Advanced Chemistry highlights one's constant negotiation as an "alien" in one's own country, whereas Brönimann's description of gender dysphoria fits with the bodily discomfort Cee experiences over the course of the narrative: there is no home in one's own country or in one's own skin. Otoo's *literary* Afrofuturism therefore differs from the flamboyant and commercially oriented audiovisual Afrofuturism normally associated with Monáe or Beyoncé. Rather, Otoo refers to a larger literary history and marks diachronic progression into the future with an undiluted mixture of vertiginous (synchronic) bodily developments: stubbing one's foot in the morning, reading between the lines on a rental agreement, making moral and ethical choices, and dealing with a broken family situation. In other words, there is hope for the future, but the psychic realities of bewildering and Othering day-to-day interactions must be accounted for. Rather than simply regarding a singular Afro-German experience in the present, Otoo reaches out to intersectional identities of various voices of the past and future, seeking in posthumanism—the implicit critique of the category of the "human" through those considered borderline figures possessing humanity—a means of binding together the blind spots of white society. She performs a political economy assessment of the "hustle" in modern-day Germany and advocates for marginalized populations to re-enchant the world in their own image. The Ejis species to which Cee belongs grants her lineage special dimensions, while Otoo consistently reminds the reader that her specialness does not exempt her from stubbing her toe or having to go to work and earn a paycheck.

Arjun Appadurai has posited the future as "cultural fact" and frames it as a tectonic struggle between the "ethics of possibility," or the utopian visions of a better world and programs to match, and the "ethics of probability," or the cost-benefit analyses of predictions and the market.[53] He posits that intellectuals should be "mediators, facilitators and promoters of the ethics of possibility against the ethics of probability."[54] Audre Lorde's oft-recited aphorism "The Master's tools will never dismantle the Master's house" applies to Otoo's vision of futurity, which demands not a collective revolution or destruction of an old order but the nursing of a quiet but firm discontentment with the present. The subtitle of the final chapter is "Heute denke ich überwiegend an die Gegenwart" (Today I primarily think of the present),[55] and the last line is "Ich werde es einfach langsam angehen lassen—Tag für Tag" ("I will just let it go on—day after day").[56] Appadurai's "ethics of possibility" begins, in Otoo's protagonist's estimation, with a personal and private struggle against one's own social conditioning, one's own body and senses, and ultimately one's own acceptance of subject-object binaries that ever position various masters "in control" of us, be they bureaucracy, work demands, racism, or violence. The first battlegrounds against neoliberalism are in one's own thoughts and vision of the world, in which one must undergo a painful transformation from Monosinn, or a colorless and straightforward perception of the world, to Polysinn, or the synesthetic and colorful reordering of the cosmos from one's own viewpoint. By focusing on even just describing the day-to-day moments of our lives and our sensual observations of the systems and objects that surround us, we can begin to enchant the substance that exists between the gray and monotonous processes that care only for financial exchange value and little else. Otoo's Afrofuturism speaks through *interiority*, through ritually marking diachronic time *in one's own way*, thus setting the clock to one's own history. Thus one can then manage overwhelming sensation and geopolitical events with a firm conviction that, like so many before us, we are all lonely aliens with ethical responsibilities in a strange and overwhelming world that also leaves room for our own enchantment of it.

Herr Gröttrup's Shock

Whereas *Synchronicity* functions well as introspective Afrofuturism, "Herr Gröttrup setzt sich hin" is a posthumanist meditation on German whiteness. The short story begins with instructions to the reader as to how to read the story, including how pleasant the temperature needs to be and that one needs to print out the story and read it aloud with one eye closed and one's left hand raised in the air. The year is 1994, just after Helmut Kohl had been elected for a fourth term in West Germany. The narrated story concerns an elderly white German couple, Herr Helmut and Frau Irmi Gröttrup, as they sit down to have breakfast. The narrator explicitly mentions their whiteness: "And if someone were to call [Herr Gröttrup] 'white,' then he would have regarded this as synonymous with 'German' or asked whether or not this was meant as an insult. Or both."[57] Otoo describes the scene with operational precision: the inventory and arrangement of the breakfast, Herr Gröttrup's expectations, the rhythms of the routine. White German breakfast deserves anthropological study, just like any other human instance. But then Herr Gröttrup discovers that his egg, which had been cooked exactly seven minutes as he liked it, was still soft somehow. Frau Gröttrup leaves the room to make a new egg, and "so the both of them were now alone in the dining room: Herr Gröttrup and the egg which had dared to remain soft. As though this object had its own ideas and preferences . . ."[58] In that moment, Otoo's narration is interrupted with another set of instructions for the reader: to close the open eye and open the closed one and to lower the left hand and raise the right before continuing to read. "Sometimes

I wake up," begins the next section, "and I think: today I'm an egg." She then speaks from the first-person perspective of an omniscient "German" egg that has decided not to become hard when boiled. Behind the decision lies the egg's engagement with Irmi's past lives, as someone present at the 1862 earthquake in Ghana or meeting the Russian engineer Boris Chertok during the Third Reich. The egg confesses that remaining soft is not a difficult act, one not nearly as difficult as getting used to the fact that, say, the living beings around them communicate via "this prison named language."[59] The story stops again with more instructions, and then resumes focus on Herr Gröttrup. The maid Ada, whom Gröttrup himself had hitherto not met, comes into the apartment and shows him overt familiarity (as she is involved with some conspiracy with the egg), and the story ends with her cleaning the toilet.

In her own edited volume *The Little Book of Big Visions: How to Be an Artist and Revolutionize the World* (2012), Otoo published pieces that posit an Afro-European understanding of—and guide to survival in—a white-dominated art world. Such strategies—Appadurai's "future-making" activities—also show how strategic essentialism[60] helps Black African artists adopt a *double consciousness* of being both positioned as "outsiders" to that art world and having an intimate, firsthand insider knowledge of all its racialized contradictions. Black writing possesses an outsider-as-insider position toward white behavior and consciousness, knowledge that Otoo herself expresses in her work. Otoo offers a satisfyingly playful (i.e., synchronic) description of an ordinary diachronic event—elderly white Germans having breakfast—from the perspective of one of their eggs. Otoo's short story reminds us of the object-oriented modernism of Alfred Döblin and the larger literary tradition of conferring objects consciousness, but it also brings to mind comparable moves in Afro-European and African American art. Creators such as Ralph Ellison, AiRich, Nyra Bakiga, and Daniel Kojo Schrade, as with Otoo, are also deeply concerned with the melding of subject and object, of exploring modernist play combined with Black subversion of white epistemology. My initial response to the story, in written correspondence with Otoo, was that the scenario felt like a cross between *Pleasantville* (1998) and the work of R. W. Fassbinder: the white Germans have established an *Ordnung* that highlights its own pathological qualities to the reader. The eggs function as outside commentators on a normalized white European society that refuses to see alternate perspectives or accept different modes of European being (or *becoming*). The modernist interruptions via the "set of instructions" focuses on strategies the readers themselves might adopt to achieve this raised consciousness, where the Gröttrups fail. The surreptitious entrance of the cleaning lady reminds us of the sociomaterial relations that underwrite the Gröttrups' perceived reality, mocking their marital and philosophical crisis over an egg that refused to harden while invisible labor by women of color keeps them afloat.

The white pathological sense of order—one that obscures obvious material relations—is precisely what Afrofuturism aspires to supplant. But while white authors can lay claim to national relevance and poetic universality, Otoo had been consigned to only being able to comment on the Black experience in Germany rather than *also* being able to comment on class, precarity, and posthumanism. This is a tragic oversight and must be remedied. Class, as interpreted by Otoo, cannot be separated from older racial and ethnic divisions in society. In the case of "Herr Gröttrup setzt sich hin," Russians and African migrants are brought into the picture, groups that offer both different views of white Germany as well as their own paradigms of refusal. Precarity is embodied in the presumed transience of the egg, the presumed presence of the cleaning maid. The European economy revolves around the comfort of white men, but a quiet, synchronic intervention into that space reminds us of how absurd (and diachronic—historically specific) that dynamic is.

Conclusion

Otoo's work refuses to position black-skinned Germans as victims or white Germans as dominant. Rather, it takes for granted the forthright, self-determined existence of Afro-Germans (*Synchronicity*) who must somehow thrive within the strange world of the white Germans, with their self-conscious eggs and cleaning maids ("Herr Gröttrup"). Otoo's subjects not only put up with racism but also constitute the future of Europe—one in which all people from all cultures can intermingle on equal footing. Object-oriented ontology assists us in understanding *how* she makes this argument: through objects and objectified peoples that have their own withheld being, that resist domination and submission through sheer stubborn perseverance.

Literature, a medium centered on characters' internal worlds, makes possible the cognitive estrangement necessary to see the alienness of past, present, and future, as well as the subjectivities we construct to deal with time itself. Furthermore, Afro-Europeans such as Otoo are not *just now* entering the discourse but have always been present, and have had to refigure white European senses of time and subject-object relations in order to be recognized.

In a time when the bold and expressive Afrofuturism of megastar Janelle Monáe or Ryan Coogler's Disney-produced *Black Panther* (2018) have become readily consumable objects, the quieter, literary forms of Afrofuturism do not readily play into normative narratives of capitalist progress but rather frame spaces hospitable to nonwhite thinking and social life. Racialized minorities, as El-Tayeb points out, have the opportunity now to reformulate what it means to be European. But new words and sensoria (e.g., *Polysinn*) are needed to make this reformulation possible. Otoo's characters do more than just live, work, eat breakfast, and have medical problems, albeit in surrealist circumstances. They also demonstrate that the quiet objects, demure subjects, racialized Others, and normalized white populace are not what they seem: they offer us a way of upending our present temporal and power relations, one Eji or egg at a time.

Evan Torner is associate professor of German studies at the University of Cincinnati, where he serves as undergraduate director of German studies and director of the UC Game Lab.

Notes

1. For a summary of this debate, see Alex Hogue, "I, (Post)Human: Being and Subjectivity in the Quest to Build Artificial People" (PhD diss, University of Cincinnati, 2016).
2. Ihab Hassan, "Prometheus as Performer: Toward a Posthumanist Culture?" *Georgia Review* 31, no. 4 (1977): 830–50.
3. Donna Jeanne Haraway, *Simians, Cyborgs, and Women: The Reinvention of Nature* (New York: Routledge, 1991); N. Katherine Hayles, *How We Became Posthuman: Virtual Bodies in Cybernetics, Literature, and Informatics* (Chicago: University of Chicago Press, 1999). Athena Athanasiou, "Technologies of Humanness, Aporias of Biopolitics, and the Cut Body of Humanity," in *differences: A Journal of Feminist Cultural Studies* 14, no. 1 (Spring 2003): 125–62.
4. To quote Athanasiou: "[There] is no human. There is only the dizzying multiplicity of the cut human, the human body as interminably cut, fractured" ("Technologies of Humanness," 125).
5. Giorgio Agamben, *Homo Sacer: Sovereign Power and Bare Life* (Stanford, CA: Stanford University Press, 1998).
6. Athanasiou, "Technologies of Humanness," 130.
7. Fatima El-Tayeb, "Time Travelers and Queer Heterotopias: Narratives from the Muslim Underground," *Germanic Review* 88, no. 3 (2013): 319.
8. Priscilla Layne, "Space Is the Place: Afrofuturism in Olivia Wenzel's *Mais in Deutschland und anderen Galaxien* (2015)," *German Life and Letters* 71, no. 4 (October 2018): 512–28.
9. Besides the poetry and writings of May Ayim, figures such as Natasha A. Kelly and Philipp Khabo Koepsell are part of a movement creating fiction and nonfiction from an openly politicized Afro-German perspective. For other good examples, see Kelly's film *Millis Erwachen* (*Milli's Awakening*, 2018) and Koepsell's coedited anthology: Asoka Esuruoso and Philipp Khabo Koepsell, eds., *Arriving in the Future: Stories of Home and Exile* (Berlin: epubli Gmbh, 2014).
10. Noah Sow's well-regarded book *Deutschland Schwarz Weiß* is one pole of the movement, in that Afro-Germans specifically articulate racist norms and histories found in white-dominated Germany. The other pole can be seen in the work of Victoria B. Robinson, in that it articulates an optimistic new social location for Afro-Germans to inhabit in contemporary and future Germany. Noah Sow, *Deutschland Schwarz Weiß: Der alltägliche Rassismus* (Norderstedt: BoD-Books on Demand, 2018).
11. On Ayim, see Tiffany Florvil, "Distant Ties: May Ayim's Transnational Solidarity and Activism," in *To Turn This Whole World Over: Black Women's Internationalism during*

the *Twentieth Century*, ed. Tiffany M. Gill and N. Keisha Blain (Urbana: University of Illinois Press, 2019): 74–100.
12. Helga Goehring-Schneider, "Synchronicity" (bachelor's thesis, Vrije Universiteit Brussel, Brussels, 2017).
13. Katharina Oguntoye, May Opitz (Ayim), and Dagmar Schultz, *Farbe bekennen: Afro-Deutsche Frauen auf den Spuren ihrer Geschichte* (Frankfurt am Main: S. Fischer Verlag, 1986).
14. May Ayim, *Blues in Black and White* (Trenton, NJ: Africa World Press, 2003).
15. See Esuruoso and Koepsell, *Arriving in the Future*.
16. Olivia Wenzel's play *Mais in Deutschland und andere Galaxien* (2015) also fits as an Afrofuturist contribution to the Afro-German canon, but there is not enough space to discuss that here.
17. Philosophers working in this vein follow the actor-network theory of Bruno Latour and the phenomenology of Martin Heidegger, and include Graham Harman, Ray Brassier, Quentin Meillassoux, and Katherine Behar.
18. Shigekuni. "Sharon Dodua Otoo: Synchronicity." 2016. https://shigekuni.wordpress.com/tag/edition-assemblage/
19. Ernst Bloch, *The Principle of Hope*, trans. Neville Plaice, Stephen Plaice, and Paul Knight (Cambridge, MA: MIT Press, 1996), 1:8–9.
20. Cheryl Higashida, *Black Internationalist Feminism* (Urbana: University of Illinois Press, 2011), 173.
21. Here I point to the work of Mich Nyawalo and Christopher Castiglia for recent examples of hope aesthetics in action.
22. More recently, Otoo delivered a damning talk, "Droste-Hülshoffs gesammeltes Schweigen," in which she criticizes the historical foundations of the German literary canon and documents her own lived experience of encountering Droste-Hülshoff in a sleepy Monday-morning Germanistik seminar.
23. See Fatima El-Tayeb, *Undeutsch: Die Konstruktion des Anderen in der postmigrantischen Gesellschaft* (Münster: Unrast Verlag, 2016).
24. Giorgio Agamben, *Infancy and History / On the Destruction of Experience*, trans. Liz Heron (New York: Verso, 2007), 85.
25. Philipp Khabo Koepsell, ed, *The Afropean Contemporary: Literatur- und Gesellschaftsmagazin* (Berlin: epubli Gmbh, 2015), 6–7.
26. Paul Gilroy, "Exterritorialität: Die Entfremdung der Entfremdung," in *Loving the Alien: Science Fiction, Diaspora, Multikultur*, ed. Diedrich Diedrichsen (Berlin, ID Verlag: 1998), 32.
27. Afrofuturism was popularized in musical movements of the 1970s and seen as a substratum unifying both the genre fiction of Charles Chesnutt and the future projections of W. E. B. Du Bois.
28. Alondra Nelson, "Afrofuturism: Definition," quoted in Griffith Rollefson, "The 'Robot Voodoo Power' Thesis: Afrofuturism and Anti-anti-essentialism from Sun Ra to Kool Keith," *Black Music Research Journal* 28, no. 1 (2008): 83.
29. This concept of tool-being I borrow from Martin Heidegger by way of Graham Harman's famous 2002 interpretation. Here, I mean something akin to "use value," but always with a metaphysical dimension layered on top of it.
30. Ytasha Womack, *Afrofuturism: The World of Black Sci-Fi and Fantasy Culture* (Chicago: Chicago Review Press, 2013), 42.
31. Graham Harman, *The Quadruple Object* (Washington, DC: Zero Books, 2011), 120.

32. Alexander Weheliye, "My Volk to Come: Peoplehood in Recent Diaspora Discourse and Afro-German Popular Music," in *Black Europe and the African Diaspora*, ed. Darlene Clark Hine, Trica Danielle Keaton, and Stephen Small (Urbana: University of Illinois Press, 2009), 174.
33. Aija Poikane-Daumke, *African Diasporas: Afro-German Literature in the Context of the African American Experience* (Berlin: LIT Verlag, 2006), 91.
34. Leroy Hopkins, "Writing Diasporic Identity: Afro-German Literature since 1985," in *Not so Plain as Black and White*, ed. Patricia Mazón and Reinhild Steingröver (Rochester, NY: University of Rochester Press, 2005), 183.
35. Poikane-Daumke, *African Diasporas*, 85.
36. Hopkins, "Writing Diasporic Identity," 186.
37. Fatima El-Tayeb, "Dangerous Liaisons: Race, Nation, and German Identity," in *Not so Plain as Black and White*, ed. Patricia Mazón and Reinhild Steingröver (Rochester, NY: University of Rochester Press, 2005), 53.
38. Sara Friedrichsmayer, Sara Lennox, and Susanne Zantop, eds, *The Imperialist Imagination: German Colonialism and Its Legacy* (Ann Arbor: University of Michigan Press, 1999), 23.
39. Poikane-Daumke, *African Diasporas*, 110.
40. Poikane-Daumke, *African Diasporas*, 86.
41. Here I refer to the "self-naming" (*Selbstbennenung*) advocated by Der Braune Mob. https://www.derbraunemob.de/faq/#f02.
42. Maureen Maisha Eggers, "Knowledges of (Un-)Belonging: Epistemic Change as a Defining Mode for Black Women's Activism in Germany," in *Remapping Black Germany*, ed. Sara Lennox (Amherst: University of Massachusetts Press, 2016), 43–44.
43. Goehring-Schneider, "Synchronicity," 3. See also Tobias van Veen, "Robot Love Is Queer: Afrofuturism and Alien Love," *Liquid Blackness* 3, no. 6 (2017): 92–106.
44. Keguro Macharia, "black (beyond negation)," *New Inquiry*, 26 May 2018, retrieved 7 December 2019 from http://bit.ly/2swHMdP
45. This connection between W. E. B. DuBois's idea of a double consciousness—of dually experiencing acceptedness and Otherness—and May Ayim's work has been pointed out and discussed in detail in Natasha Kelly's 2016 monograph *Afrokultur*.
46. In *In Playland*, again, Agamben sees historical narrative as a product of specific forms of ritual and play.
47. Sheila Mysorekar, quoted in Hopkins, "Writing Diasporic Identity," 191–92.
48. Sharon Dodua Otoo, "Droste-Hülshoffs gesammeltes Schweigen," *Hundertviertzehn*, 2019, retrieved 29 November 2020 from https://www.hundertvierzehn.de/artikel/droste-huelshoffs-gesammeltes- schweigen_2724.html.
49. "Da war das Bruchstück eines Moments, wirklich, es war dünn wie Papier, als ich an 'meinen' Polizisten vorbeiging und seine Aura in mich aufnahm.... Ja. Ich tat es." Sharon Dodua Otoo, *Synchronicity* (Berlin: Edition Assemblage, 2014), 30.
50. If this reminds the reader of similar plot devices in the Wachowskis' *Sense8* (2017–18), the resemblances are telling.
51. Arjun Appadurai, as quoted in Leslie Adelson, "Futurity Now: An Introduction," *The Germanic Review: Literature, Culture, Theory* 88, no. 3 (2013): 213.
52. Gerard Genette, *Palimpsests: Literature in the Second Degree* (Lincoln: University of Nebraska Press, 1997), 5.
53. Arjun Appadurai, *The Future as Cultural Fact: Essays on the Global Condition* (New York: Verso, 2013), 419.

54. Appadurai, *Future as Cultural Fact*, 425.
55. Otoo, "Synchronicity," 90.
56. Otoo, "Synchronicity," 92.
57. "Und wenn jemensch ihn als 'weiß' bezeichnet hätte, hätte er dies entweder als synonym für 'deutsch' aufgefasst oder sich gefragt, ob dies als Beleidigung zu verstehen war. Oder beides." Sharon Dodua Otoo, "Herr Gröttrup setzt sich hin" (Vienna: Bachmannpreis, 2014), https://files.orf.at/ vietnam2/files/bachmannpreis/201619/ herr_grttrup_setzt_sich_ hin_sharon_dodua_otoo_439620.pdf. The file is no longer accessible. Translation by the author.
58. "Also waren die Beiden nun alleine im Esszimmer: Herr Gröttrup und das Ei, das sich traute, noch weich zu sein. Als hätte dieses Objekt eigene Ideen und Präferenzen...," Otoo, "Herr Gröttrup."
59. "dieses Gefängnisses namens Sprache," Otoo, "Herr Gröttrup."
60. Gayatri C. Spivak, "Subaltern Studies: Deconstructing Historiography," *Selected Subaltern Studies*, ed. Ranajit Guha and Gayatri C. Spivak (New York: Oxford University Press, 1988): 4.

Bibliography

Adelson, Leslie A. "Futurity Now: An Introduction." *The Germanic Review: Literature, Culture, Theory* 88, no. 3 (2013): 213–18.

Agamben, Giorgio. *Infancy and History / On the Destruction of Experience*. Translated by Liz Heron. New York: Verso, 2007.

———. *Homo Sacer: Sovereign Power and Bare Life*. Translated by Daniel Heller Roazen. Stanford, CA: Stanford University Press, 1998.

Appadurai, Arjun. *The Future as Cultural Fact: Essays on the Global Condition*. New York: Verso, 2013.

Athanasiou, Athena. "Technologies of Humanness, Aporias of Biopolitics, and the Cut Body of Humanity." *differences: A Journal of Feminist Cultural Studies* 14, no. 1 (Spring 2003): 125–62.

Ayim, May. *Blues in Black and White*. Trenton, NJ: Africa World Press, 2003.

Bloch, Ernst. *The Principle of Hope*. Vol. 1. Translated by Neville Plaice, Stephen Plaice, and Paul Knight. Cambridge, MA: MIT Press, 1996.

Castiglia, Christopher. *The Practices of Hope: Literary Criticism in Disenchanted Times*. New York: NYU Press, 2017.

Eggers, Maureen Maisha. "Knowledges of (Un-)Belonging: Epistemic Change as a Defining Mode for Black Women's Activism in Germany." In *Remapping Black Germany*, edited by Sara Lennox, 33–45. Amherst: University of Massachusetts Press, 2016.

El-Tayeb, Fatima. "Dangerous Liaisons: Race, Nation, and German Identity." In *Not so Plain as Black and White*, edited by Patricia Mazón and Reinhild Steingröver, 27–60. Rochester, NY: University of Rochester Press, 2005.

———. "Time Travelers and Queer Heterotopias: Narratives from the Muslim Underground." *The Germanic Review* 88, no. 3 (2013): 305–19.

———. *Undeutsch: Die Konstruktion des Anderen in der postmigrantischen Gesellschaft*. Münster: Unrast Verlag, 2016.

Esuruoso, Asoka, and Philipp Khabo Koepsell, eds. *Arriving in the Future: Stories of Home and Exile*. Berlin: epubli Gmbh, 2014.

Florvil, Tiffany. "Distant Ties: May Ayim's Transnational Solidarity and Activism." In *To Turn This Whole World Over: Black Women's Internationalism during the Twentieth Century*, edited by Tiffany M. Gill and N. Keisha Blain, 74–100. Urbana: University of Illinois Press, 2019: 74–100.
Friedrichsmeyer, Sara, Sara Lennox, and Susanne Zantop, eds. *The Imperialist Imagination: German Colonialism and Its Legacy*. Ann Arbor: University of Michigan Press, 1999.
Genette, Gerard. *Palimpsests: Literature in the Second Degree*. Lincoln: University of Nebraska Press, 1997.
Gilroy, Paul. "Exterritorialität: Die Entfremdung der Entfremdung." In *Loving the Alien: Science Fiction, Diaspora, Multikultur*, edited by Diedrich Diedrichsen, 31–47. Berlin: ID Verlag, 1998.
Goehring-Schneider, Helga. "Synchronicity." Bachelor's thesis, Vrije Universiteit Brussel, Brussels, 2017.
Harman, Graham. *The Quadruple Object*. Washington, DC: Zero Books, 2011.
Hassan, Ihab. "Prometheus as Performer: Toward a Posthumanist Culture?" *Georgia Review* 31, no. 4 (1977): 830–50.
Hegel, G. W. F. *Enzyklopädie der philosophischen Wissenschaften im Grundrisse*, 1830.
———. *Vorlesungen über die Philosophie der Geschichte*, 1837.
Higashida, Cheryl. *Black Internationalist Feminism*. Urbana: University of Illinois Press, 2011.
Hogue, Alex. "I, (Post)Human: Being and Subjectivity in the Quest to Build Artificial People." PhD diss., University of Cincinnati, 2016.
Hopkins, Leroy. "Writing Diasporic Identity: Afro-German Literature since 1985." In *Not so Plain as Black and White*, edited by Patricia Mazón and Reinhild Steingröver, 183–208. Rochester, NY: University of Rochester Press, 2005.
Kelly, Natasha A. *Afrokultur: >>der raum zwischen gestern und morgen<<*. Münster: Unrast Verlag, 2016.
Koepsell, Philipp Khabo, ed. *The Afropean Contemporary: Literatur- und Gesellschaftsmagazin*. Berlin: epubli GmbH, 2015.
Layne, Priscilla. "Space Is the Place: Afrofuturism in Olivia Wenzel's *Mais in Deutschland und anderen Galaxien* (2015)." *German Life and Letters* 71, no. 4 (October 2018): 512–28.
Macharia, Keguro. "black (beyond negation)." *The New Inquiry*, 26 May 2018. Retrieved 7 December 2019 from http://bit.ly/2swHMdP.
Nelson, Alondra. "Afrofuturism definition." Retrieved 1 October 2003 from http://afrofuturism.com/text/about.html.
Nyawalo, Mich. "Afro-futurism and the Aesthetics of Hope in Bekolo's *Les Saignantes* and Kahiu's *Pumzi*." *Journal of the African Literature Association* 10, no. 2 (2017): 209–21.
Oguntoye, Katharina, May Opitz (Ayim), and Dagmar Schultz. *Farbe bekennen: Afro-Deutsche Frauen auf den Spuren ihrer Geschichte*. Frankfurt am Main: S. Fischer Verlag, 1986.
Otoo, Sharon Dodua. *the things I am thinking while smiling politely*. Berlin: Edition Assemblage, 2012.
———. *Synchronicity*. Berlin: Edition Assemblage, 2014.
———. "Herr Gröttrup setzt sich hin." Vienna: Bachmannpreis, 2014. https://files.orf.at/vietnam2/files/bachmannpreis/201619/herr_grttrup_setzt_sich_hin_sharon_dodua_otoo_439620.pdf.

———. "Droste-Hülshoffs gesammeltes Schweigen." *Hundertviertzehn*, 2019. Retrieved 29 November 2020 from https://www.hundertvierzehn.de/artikel/droste-huelshoffs-gesammeltes-schweigen_2724.html.

Poikane-Daumke, Aija. *African Diasporas: Afro-German Literature in the Context of the African American Experience*. Berlin: LIT Verlag, 2006.

Rollefson, Griffith. "The 'Robot Voodoo Power' Thesis: Afrofuturism and Anti-anti-essentialism from Sun Ra to Kool Keith," *Black Music Research Journal* 28, no. 1 (2008): 83–109.

Shigekuni. "Sharon Dodua Otoo: Synchronicity." 2016. https://shigekuni.wordpress.com/tag/edition-assemblage/.

Sow, Noah. *Deutschland Schwarz Weiß: Der alltägliche Rassismus*. Munich: Bertelsmann, 2008.

Spivak, Gayatri C. "Subaltern Studies: Deconstructing Historiography." In *Selected Subaltern Studies*, edited by Ranajit Guha and Gayatri C. Spivak, 3–32. New York: Oxford University Press, 1988.

Tautz, Birgit. *Reading and Seeing Ethnic Differences in the Enlightenment: From China to Africa*. New York: Palgrave Macmillan, 2007.

van Veen, Tobias C. "Robot Love Is Queer: Afrofuturism and Alien Love." *Liquid Blackness* 3, no. 6 (2017): 92–106.

Weheliye, Alexander G. "My Volk to Come: Peoplehood in Recent Diaspora Discourse and Afro-German Popular Music." In *Black Europe and the African Diaspora*, edited by Darlene Clark Hine, Trica Danielle Keaton, and Stephen Small, 161–179. Urbana: University of Illinois Press, 2009.

Womack, Ytasha. *Afrofuturism: The World of Black Sci-Fi and Fantasy Culture*. Chicago: Chicago Review Press, 2013.

CHAPTER 10

Future Narrative as Contested Ground

Emine Sevgi Özdamar's "On the Train" and Michael Götting's Contrapunctus

LESLIE A. ADELSON

Written in exile from Nazi Germany in 1945, part 2 of Theodor W. Adorno's *Minima Moralia: Reflections from Damaged Life* opens with a literary miniature about writing. "Memento"—as E. F. N. Jephcott titles this piece in the English translation—includes an especially captivating description of well-crafted prose.

> Properly written texts are like spiders' webs: tight, concentric, transparent, well-spun and firm. They draw into themselves all the creatures of the air. Metaphors flitting hastily through them become their nourishing prey. Subject matter comes winging towards them. The soundness of a conception can be judged by whether it causes one quotation to summon another. Where thought has opened up one cell of reality, it should, without violence by the subject, penetrate the next. It proves its relation to the object as soon as other objects crystallize around it. In the light that it casts on its chosen substance, others begin to glow.[1]

This well-spun web of Adorno's own making—an ostensible homage to coherence, connectivity, and sequence—is immediately followed by this miniature's finale, in which "disorder" explicitly proliferates in thought and nothing at all seems to glow. Here Adorno likens text to a locale in which "the writer sets up house," before the housekeeping metaphor is tightened and simultaneously begins to disintegrate when we read that, for a person "who no longer has a homeland, writing becomes a place to live."[2] Writing becomes a mark of displacement in this rhetorical shift, and for the generic writer Adorno appears to describe, the "danger" of "filling his pages" with unruly "left-overs" stems not only from the literal lack of a "store-room" (*Speicher*) but also and even more so from the idle allure of seeming continuity in the things and habits one tends to accumulate, including habits of thought. "In the end," Adorno writes with self-admonition in the final sentence of this text, "the writer is not even allowed to live in his writing," and readers are left, like flies in a web, with a sticky paradox in which writing is both the only "place to live" and a displacement from living at the same time.³

For all its spatial metaphors, Adorno's "Memento" is also an exilic reflection "from damaged life" on writing as a break in time. It serves here as a springboard for contemporary reflections on migration literature and minoritarian writing in twenty-first-century German culture, not with a predictable focus on what is carried over from the past but with curious attention to narrative forms of future-making in the breach instead.⁴ This crucial distinction in the present chapter is especially important in light of the narratological concept of "future narratives" as defined by Christoph Bode and Rainer Dietrich, who speak in pointedly formal terms of narratives organized around "nodal" situations rather than past events. According to Bode and Dietrich, the nodal situations that characterize future narrative as a generic form allow readers to experience "situations that fork into different branches" and to literally experience the future as "unrealized potentiality."⁵ Albrecht Koschorke's theory of narrative speaks in a related vein of "future fictions,"⁶ one modern subset of which cultivates temporal consciousness of futurity as emphatically "pliable."⁷ This chapter on twenty-first-century writing by Emine Sevgi Özdamar and Michael Götting asks in probing detail what it would mean to consider the formal and social implications of these authors' non-generic nodal narratives as radical experiments in future narrative, experiments that pivot not on radical suturing of past, present, and future but on radical breaks in time. The analysis undertaken here may thus also be understood against the contemporary backdrop of what Aleida Assmann has more generally termed "transformations of the modern time regime" in the age of globalization.⁸

From the vantage of postcolonial anthropologies of globalization, Arjun Appadurai argues in *The Future as Cultural Fact* that cultural forms of future-making must be understood as unevenly distributed social goods in the world today.⁹ I would underscore that futurity designates first and foremost a temporal structure rather than a substantive vision of future life. Yet futurity also connotes affective orientation to time as what Niklas Luhmann defines as an "interpretation of reality."¹⁰ To what extent, then, and how does a minoritarian narrative poetics pertaining to migration and race help us grasp the social parameters of futurity that literature itself helps engender in "other Europes" today?¹¹ The second section of this chapter will focus on a little-known fictional narrative by Emine Sevgi Özdamar, a prize-winning novelist who holds emblematic status on German culture's path from Turkish labor migration in the

1960s to a transcultural poetics of migration in twenty-first-century Europe. However, in this first section of the chapter I will lay the foundation for my discussion of this Turkish-German writing, not with Özdamar but with Hannah Arendt, a German Jewish political theorist whose 1943 English-language essay "We Refugees" famously indicted Jewish forgetting in terms of an "insane optimism which is next door to despair" (113).[12] Without explicitly referencing futurity, Arendt foregrounds competing affective relationships to the future in rhetorical terms that stress a spatial configuration: optimism lives "next door to despair." Eighteen years later, Arendt published a collection of essays in English on what she called "exercises in political thought." Collectively titled *Between Past and Future* (or in its German translation of 1994, *Zwischen Vergangenheit und Zukunft*), these essays begin with a preface that helps us understand, however indirectly, why her spatial configuration of optimism and despair signals a temporal problematic in Arendt's thinking about futurity. For Arendt, this temporal problematic is by no means confined to any aggregate community of Jews or any other peoples, for it affects us all.[13] Consideration of Arendt's approach to a core break in time will, I suggest, help us parse Özdamar's formal experiments with future narrative in one gem of a story about migration and Europe. In the third and final section of my analysis, I shall consider whether writing in the breach by Özdamar and Arendt helps us understand narrative forms of future-making in Michael Götting's novel of 2015, *Contrapunctus*, which might be regarded as a kind of German Afrofuturism without the science fiction, though it does involve social time travel in its narrative orientation to futurity.[14]

Writing in 1961 and alluding to her earlier work on "the human condition" from 1958, Arendt saw a "loss of world" as a political feature of the human condition that becomes acutely intensified in the middle of the twentieth century. She cast this feature philosophically as a temporal "gap between past and future."[15] She did not call this gap the present, because "the gap between past and future" was for Arendt a real gap in time, in which embodied human agents struggle to establish the meaning of lived time when such meaning is not pre-scripted by unbroken temporal succession from pastness into futurity. For Arendt, the modern relationship between past and future is necessarily and increasingly antagonistic because the future is authorized less and less by any lived past. A meaningful relationship to the future must instead be wrested from the present, which is however understood only *as* a blank spot or open question in time ("gap in time" in the English rendition [11] or "Lücke in der Zeit" in the German [14]). For Arendt (aided and inspired by a parable from Kafka's diaries), such relationships can only be hard won; the gap between past and future is what she calls "a battlefield and not a home" (*ein Schlachtfeld und kein Zuhause*).[16] Two aspects are striking in Arendt's formulations about time, and these aspects help open up some new questions about the futurity of "other Europes" under the transnational sign of multidimensional minorities and migrations some fifty years later. First, from Arendt's political and philosophical perspectives, tradition as a putative source of meaning is not given (or even invented) but always already lost, temporally broken—acutely so from the mid-twentieth century on—and as she says, "for all,"[17] that is to say in my terms, for society at large and not only for the migrants, minorities, and refugees among us. This is not to say that the temporal gap between past and future is uniformly constituted or socially uncontested, but it does mean that the minoritarian experience of time has something fundamental to teach us about social time, and not only for selected groups. Second, for Arendt, if the future is not authorized or pre-scripted by the pastness of tradition, the meaning of futurity must be scribed in struggle anew without unbroken recourse to the past. I take this to indicate that, for Arendt, the most important thing about memory as a "mode of thinking" (rendered in English as "only one, though one of the most important, modes of thought" [6]; in German as "nur eine, wenn auch die wichtigste Art des Denkens" [9]) is not its rootedness in historical experience or even any constructed continuity in the present but its fundamentally broken relationship to futurity as a social structure in time.[18] This futurity is never temporally continuous with the past but temporally in search of its own grounding, so to speak. Yet Arendt is quick to point out that any such grounding has no ground other than the indexicality of social futurity for which thought allows. "Auf diesen kleinen Nicht-Zeit-Raum im eigentlichen Herzen der Zeit kann nur hingewiesen werden, er kann nicht wie die Welt und die Kultur, in die wir hineingeboren werden, von der Vergangenheit ererbt und kann auch nicht überliefert werden."[19] In English the relevant quote reads: "This small non-time-space in the very heart of time, unlike the world and the culture into which we are born, can only be indicated, but cannot be inherited and handed down from the past."[20] Orientations in thought and feeling to this structural temporal gap are what I call future affects. These affects will constitute in turn the textual nodes on which the narrative radicality of "On the Train" and *Contrapunctus* as future narratives will rest.

On the Train

At first glance, Emine Sevgi Özdamar's short prose piece "On the Train" appears to have little to do with future affects in this sense of a structural gap in time. However, this largely overlooked piece of writing by Özdamar has much to teach us about futurity and the "heart of time" in the twenty-first-century story of so-called other Europes. First published in German in the weekly *Die Zeit* in October 2008 and republished in English translation in *Transit* in 2014, the text recounts the teleological trajectory of a train traveling from "the

Turkish border town of Edirne" to immigration destinations in Europe, beginning with the Austrian town of Villach, which lies "really close" to Ingeborg Bachmann's birthplace of Klagenfurt, and from which all the train's passengers will "continue on," by train or by car, "in the direction of Holland, France, and Germany" to preassigned work sites. "'It's all Europe,'" we read. The text also alludes in retrospective fashion to the teleological chronology of both transnational labor migration to Germany in the latter part of the twentieth century, on the one hand, and the expanding supranational institutionalization of the European Union in the early part of the twenty-first century, on the other. The pseudo-autobiographical narrative voice of the text belongs to a Turkish woman with some experience traveling repeatedly in both directions between Germany and Turkey, and she too is now on the train to Villach. As she observes in one longer passage in the voice of recollection, "years ago" she had been riding the train to Istanbul together "with a Turkish laborer from Frankfurt, a Greek laborer from Düsseldorf, and two Yugoslav laborers from Augsburg." As she explains: "At that time, there was no Serbia, no Croatia, everything was Yugoslavia." The only language these accidental travel companions in the train compartment shared was German, and they proceeded to translate their "songs" and "images" of "longing and love" into "their broken German" for each other. This scene of directional affect and multilingual translation into a shared "broken" language is compounded by something just outside the scene, where "two old men in the aisle" appear, "uninterruptedly (*ununterbrochen*) offering each other cigarettes and crying." As the narrative voice elaborates, these old men are Turkish fathers who "had traveled to Yugoslavia with empty coffins" to retrieve the corpses of their adult children, victims of traffic accidents in Yugoslavia while en route from Germany to Turkey. This prompts the Turkish narrator to reflect in the present: "On every train, death is a passenger too." Emotional affects of love and grief are strongly in evidence here, and the directional storytelling motifs of death, loss, and even a "broken" language of translation initially seem to serve a narrative continuity of temporal translation from past to present to future. A thematic motif of futurity is underscored in the text's many supranational allusions to EU expansion in pointedly categorical, chronological, and also affective terms:

> When Carl and I boarded this train yesterday in Edirne, we didn't know that our passports would be inspected six times on the way to Villach. First by Not-EU-Turks, then by EU-Bulgarians, then by Not-EU-Serbians, then by Soon-to-Be-EU-Croatians, then by EU-Slovenians, and at the end by EU-Austrians. In Bulgaria, freshly admitted to the EU, the young border guard winked at me when I showed him my German passport. He smiled and said: "A Turkish lady with a German passport." He savored the sounds of our first names as he pronounced them, Carl, Sevgi. I think he was happy that Bulgaria belongs to the EU, and that now he was meeting his European friends on this old train. How

lovely, I thought, how lovely, that the Bulgarians aren't mad at the Turks any more for the Ottoman occupation, which had lasted for centuries. Now the Bulgarians are in the EU, and the Turks are still begging to get in. That's some small comfort, you have to grant them that. Years ago, for the same reason, I had been happy for the Greeks when they got into the EU.[21]

The affective tenor of EU references here tends to be light and witty in contrast to the intense longing of singing workers and the profound sorrow of grieving parents and children.[22] Yet the teleological trajectories of both labor migration and EU expansion in "On the Train" on one level activate an affective presumption of temporal continuity from past to future, for anthropomorphic characters and the narrative persona, even if that continuity takes the form of loss. While Özdamar's original title for her German text was "Bahnfahrt," as she later reported in private communication to her translator, *Die Zeit* insisted on publishing it under the heading "Leben im Dazwischen," which the author vehemently rejected in 2014, for purposes of English translation, in favor of "Im Zug" or "On the Train." "Im Zug" can also mean "in the draft" though, and I now turn to the drafty scenes of narration to explain how "On the Train," on another level, undermines any thematic presumption of temporal continuity in favor of narrative activation of future affects, as defined above, in textual form instead.

The text's overriding macronarratives of transnational labor migration and Europeanization from above in the form of the EU are accompanied on the train by a persistent micromotif of pesky mosquitoes. These irritants, which will not leave the train even when beleaguered passengers open opposing windows when the train is in motion to create a powerful draft and rid themselves of them, signal a kind of miniaturized Europeanization from below, underlying even that Europeanization from below represented by the working songsters of labor migration.[23] This already hints that the formal function of the mosquito motif entails something other than merely comical relief or thematic critique of EU integration policies. The text's rendition of these traveling mosquitoes both mimics the story's macronarrative of EU expansion in amusing ways *and* indicates that the mosquitoes are there to disturb any sense of temporal, narrative, or figural continuity in orientation. When we first encounter the mosquitoes on the train, we read:

> Since the train hadn't stopped at any station during the night, I didn't know whether we were still in Not-EU-Serbia or already in Croatia, which is going to belong to the EU very soon. But I didn't care where we were, Soon-to-Be Europe, Croatia, or Not-Europe, Serbia. A mosquito had woken me up and was still biting my legs.

The narrator does launch into witty reflections on whether the mosquitoes will ever be able "to travel back" to their original points of departure and on how the mixed blood of these internationally minded mosquitoes might be properly categorized, since they effectively combine "Europe and Not-Europe in their blood." Ultimately the narrator pokes fun at herself though for "becoming a blood expert on this train." More precisely, the narrative voice pokes fun at or unsettles the narrative figure of her self in pre-scripted relation to discourses of Europeanization. This links her in important ways to the mosquitoes as a figure of narration. For when she goes into the washroom, she discovers a "cracked" mirror and a mosquito "flying in front of it." As we then read, the narrating persona "saw the mosquito doubled in the mirror and killed it," leaving a "spot of blood" behind.[24] While we might interpret this to mean that the "I" of the tale simply kills the irritating insect as such, Özdamar is doing much more than this, since her narrator kills the very image of the mosquito, that is to say, its mimetic double in representation. This suggests in turn that the figure of the mosquitoes on the train is an indexical decoy for something else on the move in the structure of Özdamar's thinking narration. The killing of the mosquito is narrated as an event, but it also functions formally as a node, one that will have consequences for ways in which another story can unfold as future narrative in Özdamar's diction, as we shall see.

The primary affect associated with Özdamar's mosquitoes is that of intense irritation tied to deictic disorientation. But the thematic emphasis on affective motifs shifts at another juncture or node from humans to landscapes outside the train, which the narrator's traveling companion wishes to "to paint ... as if they were living creatures.'"[25] This again conjures the image of representation, and the motifs of death and loss are close at hand when we read paratactically: "The cemeteries, the gravestones." This could suggest a broken temporal relationship to the past waiting to be narratively restored. I argue instead that we should pay keener attention to the narrator's assertion that "what we were seeing from the window of the train was telling us something." But the text's own narrative structure stresses a broken temporal relationship to the future of telling "something" rather than to the past, even if the ostensible landscape reference is to past events such as deaths, burials, and loss. An irritating mosquito plays an important role at this storytelling node too as an indexical figure of narration, for the "something" that "On the Train" has yet to tell is not inscribed in any landscape at all. While the train is standing still and other passengers are sleeping, the narrator steps into the aisle, described as "lonely," hears a mosquito buzzing her "loud as a dive bomber," and experiences a sudden temporal shift in thought. This temporal shift appears recursive at first, as a linear account of gendered atrocities in the past context of the Balkan Wars of the early 1990s:

> I slapped at my ear, at my face, hoping to hit it. I hurt myself and suddenly thought of Safiye, a woman from Yugoslavia who was now living in Berlin and

working as a cleaning woman. When Yugoslavia still existed, Safiye was living in Sarajevo and working as a teacher. Then the war broke out. One morning she was sitting at the table with her husband and her brother. While they were having breakfast, the Serbian militia suddenly came into the house, killed her husband and her brother before her eyes, and dragged her along with other women in a truck to a camp. Men there raped Safiye and the other women for two days. Safiye lost consciousness. When she came to again, the first thing she did was to reach for her hair, her long braid, which reached to her thighs, it was gone. Cut off. Safiye's first thought was: "Where is my braid?" She didn't ask herself where her husband or her brother was, she asked: "Where is my braid?" The German Red Cross brought Safiye to Berlin.

The mosquito as indexical irritant was in narrative terms only a nodal means to get us here. To be sure, the Turkish persona who narrates "On the Train" might be read in anthropomorphic terms as a kind of "secondary witness"[26] or "co-witness,"[27] except that Özdamar's narrator neither sees the reported events nor hears anyone reporting them.[28] All she hears is a mosquito buzzing her ear like a "dive bomber" at a sudden nodal shift in the temporal relationship between past and future that she experiences, in Arendtian terms, as "a battlefield and not a home." The story she is there to tell is not Safiye's past experience in any proper sense but her own future relationship to it, and this future-oriented telling proceeds in emphatically paratactic terms of indeterminate reference: "The braid. A braid. A woman's braid. Many men, a knife. A night, like this one here. The braid was lying somewhere but where?"[29] Despite repeated stresses on the "where" of things in this passage, the narrator's core social dilemma is how to parse the temporality of future telling in relation to past events. This is why she both likens the "night" of Safiye's rape to "this [night] here" and also apostrophically addresses the night as a temporal structure that is an open question, in Arendt's terminology, "in the very heart of time." "What can I ask of you with your stars, which have their fixed place every night, and the moon, which also has its fixed place? How shall I ask you where Safiye's braid is?" The question as to *how to ask the question* is not merely a question that could be answered by filling in gaps in knowledge about the past, for it is also—in Arendtian terms— an open political question about the authorization of futurity in other Europes and twenty-first-century literatures of transformation.[30] Özdamar's narrative irritation of future affects in "On the Train" goes beyond isomorphic precepts of intercultural dialogue in the 1980s and 1990s and beyond the more differentiated heteromorphic models of inter- and transcultural critique that have since displaced them.[31] Yet Özdamar's narrative irritation of future affects also pushes us beyond key "heteromorphic" insights of transcultural memory studies,[32] for the nodal radicality of her future narrative subtly questions not only the future of memory as a reflection of past experience but also the temporal structure of European futures too.

Michael Götting: *Contrapunctus*

Shifting an Arendtian focus on a "gap in time" to Michael Götting's approach to literary fiction and social reality in *Contrapunctus*, published by Unrast Verlag in 2015 and featuring multifaceted Black German experience in contemporary Berlin, immediately raises what would seem to be an intractable question. For isn't the widespread lack of historical recognition for racist and antiracist continuities over time one crucial factor that political activists, cultural critics, historical archivists, and social theorists have been working so hard to counter since at least the 1980s, when the book *Farbe bekennen (Showing Our Colors: Afro-German Women Speak Out)*[33] and the networks Initiative Schwarze Deutsche, ADEFRA, and other related collectivities first took public shape?[34] As Fatima El-Tayeb and others have critically underscored, for example in 2016 at the Black European studies roundtable celebrating the tenth anniversary of the transatlantic organization's founding at the annual convention of the German Studies Association, today "the European form of racialization is to claim that European racialization does not exist," with this denial blocking—in the guise of historical cognition—full recognition and effective countermanding of those contemporary racisms that have existed and do exist, particularly in Germany since 1945.[35] Black German studies scholars such as Peggy Piesche, Priscilla Layne, Kimberly Singletary, Sara Lennox, Fatima El-Tayeb, Damani Partridge, Tina Campt, Michelle Wright, and others have also noted that, for all the importance of transnational interlocutions informing Black German experience and culture over time, a fixation on African American frameworks for understanding racialized experience, even from an antiracist perspective, runs the risk of obscuring Black German life and contemporary European racisms alike.[36]

Götting's novel approach to historical continuity and temporal rupture in the narrative form of *Contrapunctus* therefore warrants keen attention. Can the "gap in time" that we encountered in Arendt—a constitutive gap in the structure of time as "a battlefield and not a home"—be said to operate in this literary narrative set in contemporary Berlin, and if so, how? The key to engaging this question is Indigo, one of five main characters activating the social time-space at the novel's core but one whose relationship to time is narratively related to sudden fainting spells that the text overtly describes as intensely disturbing "Ohnmachtsanfälle," or in literal English translation: "attacks of powerlessness" (7). The five-person constellation, in which she figures so critically in this tale of Black German life in early twenty-first-century Berlin, includes Rutha-Pong, a commercially sought-after and politically feisty fashion model with a drinking problem, whose transnational childhood experiences include many years in Ghana, the American South (Georgia), and Germany respectively; Rutha-Pong's loving boyfriend Habibi, a hospital nurse who grew up as a lonely and neglected ward of the state in former East Germany and to whom Rutha-Pong frequently entrusts her young son Malik, who considers Habibi to be his only father; and Olaudah, whom Rutha-Pong considers Malik's authentic father but whom the boy has never seen because Olaudah has spent the last six years in a local prison for a crime that the novel never names. Readers learn, shortly after the novel begins, that Olaudah is on the verge of release, though in narrative terms his release from prison is repeatedly deferred. (I shall come back to this point.) The only frequent fainter in this social landscape, Indigo comes from a German family with multigenerational ties to coffee production, now works in a bar called Café Dizzy, and is good friends with Rutha-Pong, with close but unspecified ties to Olaudah. This accurate description of the novel's primary social landscape is misleading though, for two reasons. First, only Indigo, Habibi, and Rutha-Pong are allowed to speak in the voice of first-person narration in *Contrapunctus*, the actions and perceptions of which are consistently recounted in multiperspectival form through individual lenses of internal focalization. By contrast, Olaudah and Malik speak only as objects of someone else's first-person narration, and neither of these two characters speaks very much at all, though both play important roles in the novel's narrative work on time, as I will demonstrate. The second reason why I call my own description of the novel's social landscape both accurate and misleading has to do with the noncontinuous indexical futurity of what Arendt termed the "small non-time-space in the very heart of time."[37] This structural "gap in time" can never be filled in with continuous or accumulated historical knowledge—as if the future or the past were merely inert constants in time—though historical experience clearly does matter for social time as contested ground "between past and future," as Arendt would say. The question is how.

Götting's novel wrestles with precisely this question in relation to the life-and-death stakes of Black German time, and to grasp how the text does this, we will need to look more closely at Indigo's textual functions as a nodal figure in narrative form. We will eventually have to come back to the storytelling function of Olaudah too, who is an especially difficult figure to read in time. The novel literally begins with Indigo's voice and perspective though, and so the analysis turns to her. She is introduced in a liminal state that she characterizes with words such as "Dunkelheit" (darkness), "Finsternis" (gloom), and "Panik" (panic) in terms of atmospheric darkness and extreme fear (7). Her first-person voice narrates this segment in a way that both signals her fainting as she loses control over her body, her speech, and her environment and, at the same time, bespeaks conscious if fearful commentary on what is happening to her without her bidding or will. The passage this fainting entails is initially described in ways that underscore a spatial transition from one world into another. "I would like to explain everything, cannot speak, not when this condition seizes me this way and tears me out of the world" (7). She experiences these attacks of powerlessness as a kind of falling into an entirely "inner world," from which she fears "there is no return." "Somewhere someone is turning the dial of an old radio and I am receiving indistinct and shrill news from a world that is apparently far and yet completely close, because I carry it inside me." This opening segment of the novel then concludes, without explanation, with the briefest and first textual reference to Olaudah: "I am waiting for Olaudah, my demon, who accompanies me through my night" (8). This temporal register is more than merely metaphorical, and Indigo's allusion to Olaudah as "my demon"—in the ancient Greek etymological sense of god, devil, spirit, or fate—is an early clue that Olaudah figures in the novel as far more than an empirical character in this Berlin landscape.

Subsequent first-person accounts of Indigo's fainting spells and liminal states are rendered in increasingly graphic and disturbingly extended narrative detail, so much so that they bespeak not a "gap" or loss of consciousness but a painful intensification and psychic condensation of historical consciousness instead. Indigo's episodes do not connote Freudian condensation however, it should be noted, for this character is neither dreaming nor repressing lived histories of modern racism. Despite significant spatial settings ascribed to each supposed loss of consciousness—a public museum, the "Dizzy" storage cellar, or the urban park of Berlin's Tiergarten, for example—Indigo's agitated sojourns in her liminal zones of internal awareness mainly constitute travel in time. I mean this in two senses. First, the author has Indigo's character not merely recall but also viscerally experience racist attacks in stylistically surreal stretches invoking Black German and Black European histories from the nineteenth and early twentieth centuries, including allusions to the transatlantic African slave trade and racist forms of modern commodification, commercialism, and knowledge production. Second, as I will argue more fully later, a key formal shift in narrative time in *Contrapunctus* pivots on synchronic rather than diachronic social transformations in Indigo's temporal relationship to other Black German characters. Both types of time travel involving Indigo—one primarily diachronic and the other primarily synchronic—also concern Olaudah, albeit in a range of ways. When Indigo discovers herself physically stuck and in excruciating distress "in a large glass showcase" (17), she sees Olaudah trapped in another glass "cage" (18) in an ethnographic museum's exhibit hall. As they silently inspire each other to move beyond exoticized reification, Olaudah shatters the walls of his glass cage with a decorative stone and frees Indigo from her entrapment too as alarms scream and museum security guards appear as "slave catchers." Mountains of skulls line the museum walls in this scene, as Indigo's visual, aural, and olfactory perception registers the living dead of her inner world (19). A fear unlike any other makes itself known to her in this fainting episode, and Olaudah literally liberates her from both the museum and this dark "night" that befalls her.

Another extended fainting episode narrated by Indigo demands nearly twice as much readerly attention as the unsettling museum piece and thus accentuates one of narrative theory's most basic registers of narrative time: textual duration.[38] This writing segment in fact feels interminable, in part because the sexual violence and affective humiliation Indigo and a beloved uncle are forced to undergo are depicted in such graphic physical detail and in part because Indigo's first-person narration recounts this racialized violation with so many sensory cues linking embodied experience and heightened emotions of terror, rage, and felt powerlessness that attentive readers are bound to feel trapped in this narrative time zone of Indigo's "inner world" too. Here historical dimensions of the transatlantic slave trade are evoked by plot elements involving metal chains and iron branding, and cultural legacies of racist commodification come forcefully into view when commercial icons of a popular chocolate brand dating back to the German loss of African colonies in 1918 figure literally as perpetrators and orchestrators of abuse.[39] Large arcs and intimate perceptions of historical as well as cultural continuity are made to feel ever-present here, and not even fainting allows for sensory release from the temporality of assault. As Indigo puts it, "I want to die and also seem slowly to be reaching my goal; my senses are fading and I come to myself again only when one of the turban wearers beats me in the face hard a few times" (44). Indigo explicitly identifies the relentless ringleader of these hostile "turban wearers" as a so-called "Sarotti M***" (39), with Götting's spelled-out term invoking an invented racist advertising icon of German chocolate sweets, one whose power and violence are compounded by four others who join him in this scene of willful degradation, in which Indigo is crudely maltreated and made to degrade her chained uncle as well.[40] This narrative use of an iconic feature from German advertising in colonialist mode highlights a persistent commingling of personalized and depersonalized agency and victimization, and Götting's stylistic mix of realist and surreal effects further contributes to a readerly sense of Indigo's temporal imprisonment in what the text calls her "inner world." This is underlined by her own sense perception near the end of this episode when she asserts, "Everything tastes like contempt" (45). With this line Götting both recalls and radicalizes Helga Emde's pronouncement in 1986 that, for her as an Afro-German child growing up in postwar Germany, Sarotti terminology and other German names for chocolate confections were humiliating, "sweet tasting insults" (102). For Indigo, especially in this "attack of powerlessness," we read instead: "Everything tastes like contempt." On the basis of the two fainting episodes discussed, we might therefore conclude that Indigo's primary narrative purpose is to function as a kind of internalized archive or human "store-room" (to recall Adorno on writing), a conjoined historical, cultural, and affective archive in which temporal continuity—however troubling—is pointedly preserved.

I suggest however that the relationship between Indigo and Olaudah troubles this reading of Indigo's temporal function and key importance in formal narrative terms. The surreal "Sarotti" episode, which literally takes place in the storage cellar of Café Dizzy, begins with Indigo's description of how this "darkness" envelops her and "devours" her voice, "like a toad capturing a fly with its sticky tongue" (37). Here we may be reminded of the sticky paradox in which Adorno's readers are left, like flies in a web, in which writing is both the only place to live and a displacement from living at the same time. Yet how does Indigo's textual relationship to Olaudah inflect her own temporal function? Can we read her not only as an anthropomorphic character but also as a narrative node in time? Unlike the museum piece, Olaudah never appears in the Sarotti scene, though he does play an important role here in two striking ways, both of which are negatively linked to continuity. First, just as Indigo is about to transition from her upstairs self at Café Dizzy to her fainted self in the storage cellar, she feels "the open hatch" staring at her "uninterruptedly" (*unentwegt*) (38). At this juncture, which can be seen not only as event-based plot development but also as a narrative node in the text's changing orientation to futurity, we read: "I looked down onto the old wooden ladder, at the lower end of which Olaudah had been standing when I had climbed up the last time" (38). This is an analeptic allusion to the ending of the museum episode, when Olaudah had helped Indigo escape their tormenters in pursuit by pushing her up the ladder without climbing it himself (20). By recalling for readers the ladder detail—where Olaudah had been standing when she last saw him—Indigo implicitly stresses a temporal principle of continued narration. Even though other events have been recounted in the interim, Indigo now signals that she is picking up a story line that readers too are meant to experience as continued narration. This expectation is formally disappointed though, for Olaudah is not there, and this ties in to the second negative link between Olaudah and continuity in the Sarotti segment. For as things go from bad to worse, Indigo calls out for Olaudah "as loud as I can" (43) and repeatedly asks herself why he does not come to help her, "now," "when I need him" (44–45). If Indigo represents an internalized archive of violent oppression and agential liberation, we might think of Olaudah's curiously missing status as a kind of archive trouble, but I think it will make more sense to read Olaudah as a textual link to future-making in the breach rather than to collective memory, even if collective memory is a selective form of social consciousness that can create the impression of a temporal continuum.[41]

Linking Olaudah to future-making in the breach seems counterintuitive, to put it mildly, when we consider that Olaudah does appear mysteriously in a later scene involving Indigo, who attempts to kill herself in the urban park of Berlin's Tiergarten, noting—just after having passed Berlin's iconic "Memorial Church"—that she feels "infinitely lonely" (77). Here Olaudah neither saves nor abandons her, as he does in her two main fainting episodes, but in Indigo's first-person narration, in what would now seem to be a realist register, Olaudah appears to slice open Indigo's wrists with a silver blade (79), leaving her, as we will later learn from Rutha-Pong's first-person narration, "half dead" in the snow (86). Several things do not cohere in textual terms here, and that is why Olaudah's appearance and behavior in the Tiergarten appear especially mysterious. For one thing, Indigo and Rutha-Pong are the main characters who repeatedly invoke Olaudah's name or bring him to mind, and this figure is always cast in such invocations as a powerful helper. Why should he wish to harm Indigo in any way? Rutha-Pong will be the one to find the seriously injured Indigo in the park and to sound the alarm that gets her to the hospital, and as we learn retroactively from Rutha-Pong's narration, Olaudah himself interrupts the fashion model's sexual dalliance with a male designer in order to insist that Rutha-Pong follow Olaudah to where Indigo lies bleeding. Olaudah in this sense makes it possible for Rutha-Pong to save her. Another mystery-heightening factor is that the Tiergarten episode shifts the life-or-death stakes of Indigo's inner world from fainting spells into empirical time—or at least so it would seem—which alters the temporal function of Indigo's story line too. A third complication comes into view when we realize that Olaudah's function pivots on an entirely different temporal plane, since there is no evidence whatsoever to indicate that he has been released from prison yet, even though the novel's opening pages establish release as a future-oriented expectation.

One possible way to read the rhetorical figure of Olaudah is as a literal invocation of the eighteenth-century historical figure known alternately as Olaudah Equiano or Gustavus Vassa, about whose presumed West African origins there is some scholarly debate but whose published and widely read autobiography of 1789, *The Interesting Narrative of the Life of Olaudah Equiano*, is often credited with originating the abolitionist "slave narrative because of [the author's] first-hand literary testimony against the slave trade" (Encyclopedia Britannica).[42] This association is certainly warranted, and the link does support the archival motif of historical continuity in recollecting and combating racism that circulates in Götting's *Contrapunctus*. More to the point though, this thematic link is not enough to explain Olaudah's function in articulating the sociotemporal structure of the novel, in which Indigo remains key as the figure on which the narrative literally turns in time. Götting in effect introduces his Olaudah twice at the beginning of the novel, first when Indigo invokes him in a surreal register as her "demon," who accompanies her through a "night" that emphatically belongs to her, and again when Rutha-Pong describes at length and in realistic tones her visit to the Berlin prison, which repeatedly disappoints a promise for Olaudah's release (8–13). Rutha-Pong's ambivalence vis-à-vis the father of her child is well in evidence here. She never visits with Olaudah in prison, and she confesses to being relieved, even "glad," that his release has been delayed yet again: "I wanted to use the time that they had given me, to my surprise, in order to move, with my life, towards Olaudah's release" (9). This double introduction points to Olaudah's dual function throughout the novel in indexing both an empirical reality shaped in significant part by racist and antiracist histories and a battle-weary but nonetheless lived relationship to future time as contested, virtual ground in the making.

Olaudah's role as a prisoner echoes in the museum piece, where we see him housed in a "cage." Yet he frees himself and Indigo in that episode, set in her ostensibly inner world, and in those subsequent passages where his virtual self mysteriously shows up in real time to say or do something with life-or-death consequences for Indigo and Rutha-Pong, we see Olaudah's virtual-real self effectively urging others toward freedom from the time that binds them to oppression, even as the empirical person that *Contrapunctus* ascribes to Olaudah remains in prison.[43] In this sense Olaudah is a relational cipher for the "indelible" indexicality of what social theorist Avery Gordon calls the "social death" associated with "racial capitalism."[44] Drawing on Orlando Patterson's earlier work,[45] Gordon views social death as "not a singular biographical condition but a relational idiom of power," one that entails a markedly privative "relationship to futurity" and a constant challenge for imprisoned persons to remake their relationship to future time while doing time.[46] According to Gordon, the social death that imprisonment brings "refers to the process by which a person is socially negated or made a human non-person as the terms of their incorporation into a society: living they nonetheless appear as if and are treated as if they were dead" (10). This is where Gordon's usefulness for understanding Olaudah falters though, for Olaudah is not "socially negated" but activated in Götting's German novel, and Olaudah never appears in the novel as if he were dead. By contrast, this descriptive detail applies to Indigo from an external perspective when she faints and when Rutha-Pong finds her "half dead" in the park.

Avery Gordon is known in Black German studies, largely for her sociotheoretical work in *Ghostly Matters* on "haunting" in relation to historical and contemporary experiences of the violent indignities of "racial capitalism."[47] Can we say that Götting's novel contrapuntally maps social death and racial haunting onto a relational field shared by Olaudah and Indigo? We have already seen that the figure of Olaudah both indexes and undercuts social death, which also explains the cut to Indigo's wrists by Olaudah's virtual hand, a symbolic cut with simultaneously real stakes and surreal effect. By contrast, Indigo herself carries the narrative weight of racial haunting in the novel in two discrete senses while moving away from some aspects of racial haunting in others. Gordon's core definition of haunting is especially apt for capturing core aspects of Indigo's fainting spells but not her real-time episodes. For the sociologist, haunting is first of all "an animated state in which a repressed or unresolved social violence is making itself known, sometimes very directly, sometimes more obliquely," and haunting figures for her in "those singular and yet repetitive instances when home becomes unfamiliar, when your bearings on the world lose direction, when the over-and-done-with comes alive, when what's been in your blind field comes into view."[48] Second, by Gordon's account, haunting is decisively "unlike trauma" because haunting actively produces an unsettling "something-to-be-done" (2), which is to say, and Gordon does say this, "a contest over the future, over what's to come next or later" (3).[49] Even more than this though, as Gordon stresses, "The something-to-be-done is not ever given in advance, but it can be cultivated towards more just and peaceful ends" (5). This sounds quite like Arendt, but for Arendt, the gap in time between past and future is always a discontinuous "battlefield and not a home." Ghosts also figure at several junctures in Götting's account of Black German life in contemporary Berlin, for example, when Olaudah is described as Indigo's companion "demon" or in Rutha-Pong's narration as a "spirit" (one "who is always vagabonding around somewhere in the ether of our being") or in starkly dire terms when Indigo encounters emaciated slaves "groaning in the corner" in her museum spell (8, 24, 19).

Götting has Indigo tip the scales of racial haunting decisively toward the future-making of something-to-be-done though, and away from social violence and social death as ever-present states. This is her pivotal function in formal narrative terms, and the careful parsing of temporal relations in *Contrapunctus* has prepared us for this counterintuitive realization. Readers who conclude that the novel ends with Indigo's death, or that she would be doomed to one fainting spell or "attack of powerlessness" after another if she lived, are likely to find little ground for hope or future-making in the figure of Indigo. Linking the novel's acoustic motifs to anti-imperialist "historical excavation," Michelle Eley for example draws on Edward Said's concept of "contrapuntal reading" (*Culture and Imperialism*) to illuminate "expanded perspectives" and critical connectivity to the past in *Contrapunctus*. In her reading, the character of Indigo definitively dies as a victim of German racism. In my conclusion I would like to make a case for a more hopeful reading that pivots precisely on Indigo, whose future life beyond inner torment and the urban park scene is indexed by the temporal structure of Götting's future narrative.

To explain this, I need to recall that the time travel involving Indigo takes both diachronic and synchronic forms. The temporality of her main fainting spells is powerfully diachronic but also strongly internalized. Her inability to bridge the gap between her "inner world" and the synchronic time of her social world in contemporary Berlin leads her to desperate measures, not in a storage cellar but in a public park. One scene reveals the depth of frustration she feels at not being able to bridge this temporal split. This scene takes place among her extended family members, who witness her fainting spells but whose response reveals "silent lack of understanding" and dismissive lack of interest (70). Indigo reflects on this state of affairs in the present:

For years this has tormented me! This eternally nagging question: Is the world that I fall into when I faint somehow connected with the world in which I am with my mother here, with Aunt Bertha, Uncle Hans, and all the others, or is that only my entirely private cosmos, through which I then race in fear when I fall out of this world? Another galaxy, the door to which opens up in my mind alone? (70)

Indigo takes action in her synchronic world to uncover an otherwise hidden "sign" of her inner world, "the incontrovertible proof of its existence" (70), but this too fails to achieve the desired social result in her family setting. This scenario nonetheless marks a temporal crux because Indigo at this point tries to build a bridge in time as a social act. According to Arendt, this can never succeed on the basis of any temporal continuity—analeptic or otherwise—but only through active struggle with a persistent split or "gap in time" between past and future.[50] This is how I would read the novel's formal deployment of future narrative and Olaudah's symbolic cut, which frees Indigo for more social future-making in what we in colloquial terms habitually call the present. There is to be sure no substantive vision of the future here, but it is highly significant that Rutha-Pong is awakened from her own self-destructive habits, by Olaudah, for the urgent purpose of saving Indigo and Rutha-Pong herself for future life. The synchronic social quality of this profound shift derives, in Bode and Dietrich's terms, from narrative nodes rather than past events, and Indigo's formal function in this nodal sense is to activate future affect as enlivening orientation to "unrealized potentiality" in the breach. This has a wider ripple effect, subtly reflected in the novel's final segment featuring Habibi and Malik playing in another snow-filled park. This is the only entry that begins with first-person "we" narration, and the novel ends with "children's laughter" that "cuts through" (*durchschneidet*) the cold winter air (89). Let us not lose sight of Indigo though, whose complex relationship to narrative time is what allows this contemporary story to turn by formal means in social time too. Indigo is not merely a key character in *Contrapunctus*. She also inhabits, in her own particular textual ways, what Arendt once called the "small non-time-space in the very heart of time." This gap in the broken heart of time has an indexical function in relation to futurity. And Indigo's indexicality points us in turn to the literary contribution to both future narrative and social future-making that Götting's innovative novel makes in a Black German key.[51]

Leslie A. Adelson is the Jacob Gould Schurman Professor of German Studies at Cornell University. Former director of the Institute for German Cultural Studies and former chair of the Department of German Studies, she teaches modern German literature, with an emphasis on literature since 1945, and transnational theories of culture, difference, migration, and futurity. Monographs include *Crisis of Subjectivity* (1984), *Making Bodies, Making History*

(1993), *The Turkish Turn in Contemporary German Literature: Toward a New Critical Grammar of Migration* (2005), and *Cosmic Miniatures and the Future Sense: Alexander Kluge's 21st-Century Literary Experiments in German Culture and Narrative Form* (2017). First published in *Gegenwartsliteratur: Ein germanistisches Jahrbuch* 17 (2018): 41–67, this chapter appears here with the kind permission of journal editor Paul Michael Lützeler and Stauffenburg Verlag under the direction of Brigitte Narr.

Notes

1. Theodor W. Adorno, "Memento," in *Minima Moralia: Reflections from Damaged Life*, trans. E. F. N. Jephcott (London: Verso, 2005), 87.
2. Adorno, "Memento," 87.
3. Adorno, "Memento," 87. See also Andreas Huyssen on the exilic dimensions of *Minima Moralia*, which pivot on the structural role of Los Angeles as "an absent presence" in Adorno, *Minima Moralia*, 276.
4. On ways in which contemporary minorities are often presumed to belong outside Europe in space and time, see Fatima El-Tayeb, "Time Travelers and Queer Heterotopias: Narratives from the Muslim Underground," in "Futurity Now," ed. Leslie A. Adelson and Devin Fore, special issue, *The Germanic Review* 88, no. 3 (2013): 305–19. On related matters in minoritarian art and activism in contemporary Germany and Europe, see El-Tayeb's monographs, *European Others: Queering Ethnicity in Postnational Europe* (Minneapolis: University of Minnesota Press, 2011), and *Undeutsch: Die Konstruktion des Anderen in der postmigrantischen Gesellschaft* [Un-German: The construction of the other in postmigrant society] (Bielefeld: transcript, 2016). Unless otherwise indicated, all translations provided in the chapter are by Leslie A. Adelson.
5. Christoph Bode and Rainer Dietrich, *Future Narratives: Theory, Poetics, and Media-Historical Moment* (Berlin: De Gruyter, 2013), 1.
6. Albrecht Koschorke, *Wahrheit und Erfindung: Grundzüge einer Allgemeinen Erzähltheorie*, 2nd ed. (Frankfurt am Main: Fischer, 2012), 229–36.
7. Koschorke, *Wahrheit und Erfindung*, 230.
8. For a range of newer approaches to temporality in German literary studies, see Birgit R. Erdle, *Literarische Epistemologie der Zeit: Lektüren zu Kant, Kleist, Heine und Kafka* (Paderborn: Fink, 2015), as well as Anne Fuchs and J. J. Long, eds., *Time in German Literature and Culture, 1900–2015: Between Acceleration and Slowness* (Houndmills: Palgrave Macmillan, 2016). On futurity, see Amir Eshel, *Futurity: Contemporary Literature and the Quest for the Past* (Chicago: University of Chicago Press, 2012); Leslie A. Adelson and Devin Fore, eds., "Futurity Now," special issue, *The Germanic Review* 88, no. 3 (2013); Benjamin Bühler and Stefan Willer, eds., *Futurologien: Ordnungen des Zukunftswissens* (Munich: Wilhelm Fink, 2016). Critical approaches to temporal reckonings have proliferated widely across the disciplines since Marxist geographer David Harvey introduced his influential and problematic presentist concept of time-space "compression" in *The Condition of Postmodernity: An Enquiry into the Conditions of Cultural Change* (Cambridge, MA: Blackwell, 1990), 240.
9. Arjun Appadurai, *The Future as Cultural Fact: Essays on the Global Condition* (London: Verso, 2013), 289.

10. Niklas Luhmann, "The Future Cannot Begin: Temporal Structures in Modern Society," *Social Research* 43, no. 1 (Spring 1976): 135.
11. For its first convention outside North America, held in Düsseldorf in June 2016, the Modern Language Association chose the overarching title "Other Europes: Migrations, Translations, Transformations."
12. In this chapter, for ease of reading, references to the two primary literary texts discussed, Emine Sevgi Özdamar's "On the Train" and Michael Götting's *Contrapunctus*, will be included as parenthetical citations including the page numbers. Full references for these texts can be found in the bibliography.
13. Arendt's exact phrasing in 1943 reads: "For the first time Jewish history is not separate but tied up with that of all other nations." Hannah Arendt, "We Refugees," in *Altogether Elsewhere: Writers on Exile*, ed. Marc Robinson (Boston: Faber and Faber, 1994), 119. She accounts more rigorously for the temporal problematic in evidence even here in her 1961 preface to *Between Past and Future: Six Exercises in Political Thought* (New York: Viking, 1961). My discussion of Arendt's preface will also provide key quotations from the later German publication of 1994, "Vorwort: Die Lücke zwischen Vergangenheit und Zukunft," in *Zwischen Vergangenheit und Zukunft: Übungen im politischen Denken I* (Munich: Piper, 1994), 7–19.
14. See also Peggy Piesche's insights on the general categorical deployment of "Afrofuturism," as cited by Jochen Dreier for *Deutschlandfunk Kultur* in January 2017, retrieved 17 March 2018 from http://www.deutschlandfunkkultur.de/afrofuturismus-widerst and-gegen-eine-weisse-zukunft.976.de.html?dram:article_id=376520. For additional remarks on Black German Studies and futurity, see also Peggy Piesche, "Inscribing the Past, Anticipating the Future," in *Audre Lorde's Transnational Legacies*, ed. Stella Bolaki and Sabine Broeck, (Amherst: University of Massachusetts Press, 2015); "Towards a Future African Diasporic Theory: Black Collective Narratives Changing the Epistemic Map," *Frauen*solidarität* 1 (2016): 22–24; and "Deposits of the Future through Times and Spaces," in *Deposits of Future: Future African Visions in Time, An Exhibition by the Bayreuth Academy of Advanced African Studies* (Bayreuth: Bayreuth Academy of Advanced African Studies, 2016), 7–11.
15. Arendt, *Between Past and Future*, 3–15. A later edition of *Between Past and Future* includes eight rather than six such "exercises." For Arendt's extended consideration of the "loss of world," see *The Human Condition*, 2nd ed. (Chicago: University of Chicago Press, 2013), 115 et passim.
16. Arendt, *Between Past and Present*, 13; Arendt, "Vorwort," 16.
17. Arendt, *Between Past and Present*, 14; Arendt, "Vorwort," 17.
18. Arendt writes in German: "Denn die Erinnerung, die nur eine, wenn auch die wichtigste Art des Denkens ist, ist außerhalb eines vor-errichteten Bezugsrahmens hilflos, und das menschliche Gedächtnis ist nur bei den wenigsten Gelegenheiten fähig, etwas gänzlich Unverbundenes zu behalten" (9–10). As Arendt argues, a meaningful relationship to the "Schatz" or "treasure" of time is not lost "aufgrund historischer Umstände und der Widerwärtigkeit der Wirklichkeit . . . , sondern weil keine Tradition sein Erscheinen oder seine Wirklichkeit vorausgesehen hatte, weil kein Testament über ihn eine Verfügung für die Zukunft getroffen hatte" (9).
19. Arendt, "Vorwort," 17.
20. Arendt, *Between Past and Present*, 13.
21. Reference to a Bulgaria "freshly admitted to the EU" situates the time of narration after January 2007, while the post-Yugoslavian states of Croatia and Serbia become

in Özdamar's phrasing "Soon-to-Be Europe" and "Not-Europe." Croatia was formally admitted to the EU in 2013, and Serbia became a candidate for admission in 2012, four years after Özdamar's story was published. Heated controversies about Turkey's eligibility have been ongoing to varying degrees since 1997.

22. Children who mourn the loss of beloved mothers include the narrator herself and three young women who seek, in the Turkish woman recounting the story of the train ride, "'a woman whose company can warm them up some.'"
23. For analysis of additional forms of antiracist Europeanization in minoritarian art and activism, see El-Tayeb, *European Others*. Arendt details her philosophical distinctions among labor, work, and action in *The Human Condition*, originally published in 1958.
24. For additional analyses of "mirror" functions in other works by Özdamar, see my discussion of Özdamar's "The Courtyard in the Mirror" (*Der Hof im Spiegel*) in Leslie A. Adelson, *The Turkish Turn in Contemporary German Literature: Toward a New Critical Grammar of Migration* (New York: Palgrave Macmillan, 2005), 39–77, and Angela Weber, *Im Spiegel der Migration: Transkulturelles Erzählen und Sprachpolitik bei Emine Sevgi Özdamar* (Bielefeld: transcript, 2009), which is entirely devoted to Özdamar's mirror motifs from a transcultural perspective.
25. Contrast Özdamar's approach to affective landscapes with Bettina Stoetzer's insightful analysis of a 2005 film documentary set "almost entirely in the claustrophobic environment of a gloomy forest in which refugees live" (n.p.). Stoetzer refers here to the film *Forst*, directed by Ascan Breuer, Ursula Hansbauer, and Wolfgang Konrad, together with African refugees associated with the activist group The Voice.
26. Aleida Assmann, "The Empathetic Listener and the Ethics of Storytelling," in *Storytelling and Ethics: Literature, Visual Arts and the Power of Narrative*, ed. Hanna Meretoja and Colin Davis (London: Routledge, 2017), 203–18.
27. Irene Kacandes, *Talk Fiction: Literature and the Talk Explosion* (Lincoln: University of Nebraska Press, 2001).
28. On German-language literature addressing gendered atrocities in the Balkan Wars, see Jill Suzanne Smith, "Sounds of Silence: Rape and Representation in Julie Zeh's Bosnian Travelogue," in *German Women's Writing in the Twenty-First Century*, ed. Hester Baer and Alexandra Merley Hill (Rochester, NY: Camden House, 2015), 175–96. The Zeh text Smith analyzes is *Die Stille ist ein Geräusch* (Silence is a noise), which Smith contrasts with Peter Handke's literary treatment of the Balkan Wars.
29. See also Shlomith Rimmon-Kenan's elaboration of distinctions between syntagmatic and paradigmatic structures of narration in *Narrative Fiction: Contemporary Poetics*, 2nd ed. (London: Routledge, 2002), 10.
30. The openness of this "gap in time" between past and future should therefore not be confused with the structural undecidability that Luhmann ascribes to the future as a modern temporal concept in "The Future Cannot Begin," 131.
31. See especially Ortrud Gutjahr, "Von der Nationalkultur zur Interkulturalität: Zur literarischen Semantisierung und Differenzbestimmung kollektiver Identitätskonstrukte," in *Interkulturalität und Nationalkultur in der deutschsprachigen Literatur*, ed. Maja Razbojnikova-Frateva and Hans-Gerd Winter (Dresden: Thelem, 2006), 91–122, and Wolfgang Welsch, "Was ist eigentlich Transkulturalität?" In *Kulturen in Bewegung: Beiträge zur Theorie und Praxis der Transkulturalität*, ed. Dorothee Kimmich and Schamma Schahadat (Bielefeld: transcript, 2012), 25–40. See also the special issue of *text + kritik* devoted to Özdamar in 2016, Yasemin Dayıoğlu-Yücel and Ortrud Gutjahr, eds., "Emine Sevgi Özdamar," special issue, *text + kritik* 211 (July 2016),

and Julia Boog's monograph comparing difference in the works of Özdamar, Felicitas Hoppe, and Yoko Tawada in a book series on "intercultural modernity," *Anderssprechen: Vom Witz der Differenz in den Werken von Emine Sevgi Özdamar, Felicitas Hoppe und Yoko Tawada*, Interkulturelle Moderne 6 (Würzburg: Königshausen & Neumann, 2017).

32. See Michael Rothberg's seminal monograph *Multidirectional Memory: Remembering the Holocaust in the Age of Decolonization* (Stanford, CA: Stanford University Press, 2009), and the anthology *The Transcultural Turn: Interrogating Memory Between and Beyond Borders*, ed. Lucy Bond and Jessica Rapson (Berlin: De Gruyter, 2014), which includes A. Dirk Moses and Michael Rothberg, "A Dialogue on the Ethics and Politics of Transcultural Memory," 29–38. In this dialogue, Rothberg draws attention to transculturality as "a valuable methodological intervention—directing us toward heteromorphic constellations instead of isomorphic territories of memory" (32). See also Astrid Erll's essay, "Traveling Memory," *parallax* 17, no. 4 (2011): 4–18, in which she stresses, together with Paul Gilroy, "*routes*" rather than "*roots*" of memory (11). Erll pointedly asks about the future of memory studies as a field of research (4). Her essay is reprinted and included with relevant conceptual reflections by others in the anthology Rick Crownshaw, ed., *Transcultural Memory* (London: Routledge, 2014).

33. May Opitz, Katharina Oguntoye, and Dagmar Schultz, eds., *Showing Our Colors: Afro-German Women Speak Out*, trans. Anne V. Adams (Amherst: University of Massachusetts Press, 1992).

34. These developments took place in West Germany. For related commentary on Black German experience in East Germany, see Peggy Piesche, "Black and German? East German Adolescents before 1989: A Retrospective View of a 'Non-existent Issue' in the GDR," in *The Cultural After-Life of East Germany: New Transnational Perspectives*, ed, Leslie A. Adelson, Harry & Helen Gray Humanities Program Series 13 (Washington, DC: American Institute for Contemporary German Studies, 2002), 37–59.

35. Here I cite El-Tayeb from memory based on conference notes. For related arguments in print, see El-Tayeb, "Time Travelers and Queer Heterotopias," *European Others*, and *Undeutsch*. See also a range of contributions to *Remapping Black Germany*, edited by Sara Lennox. The year 2017 marked the tenth anniversary of the transnational research network known as BEST (Black European Studies); a formal research center for studies of "Black Europe" was established in 2004 at the Johannes Gutenberg University of Mainz.

36. Stressing "the intersectionality of poetic diasporas," Arina Rotaru illuminates links between May Ayim's poetics and "Afro-French" poetics of postcolonial critique. See also Haus der Kulturen der Welt, Tina Campt and Paul Gilroy, eds., *Der Black Atlantic* (Berlin: Haus der Kulturen der Welt, 2004).

37. Arendt, *Between Past and Future*, 13.

38. Postclassical narratologist David Herman calls this "a ratio between how long events take to unfold in the world of the story and how much text is devoted to their narration"; David Herman, *Basic Elements of Narrative* (West Sussex: Wiley-Blackwell, 2009), 130.

39. For a detailed cultural-historical account of the Sarotti Company's favored icon for selling chocolate to Germans from 1918 on, see Silke Hackenesch, "Der Sarotti-M*** (1918/1922), oder: Was hat Konsum mit Rassismus zu tun?" in *Race & Sex: Eine Geschichte der Neuzeit*, ed. Jürgen Martschukat and Olaf Stieglitz (Berlin: Neofelis Verlag, 2016), 217–25.

40. Hackenesch explains that the Sarotti Company originally used multiple such images before settling on one in 1922. However, Götting does not seem to be alluding to historically verifiable quantity here, since the Sarotti Company began with only three images (see Hackenesch, "Der Sarotti-M***"). I suggest that Götting is indexing a multiplication factor that exceeds quantification.
41. See Maurice Halbwachs, *On Collective Memory*, trans. and ed. Lewis A. Coser (Chicago: University of Chicago Press, 1992). For an especially interesting reading of sound motifs and "contrapuntal" collective consciousness in *Contrapunctus*, see Michelle Eley, who discusses the novel in terms of both "historical excavation" and Black diasporic "self-making" in contemporary Germany. Michelle Eley, "Excavation, Curation, and the Sounds of Self-Making," German Studies Association Annual Convention, San Diego, California, 2 October 2016.
42. For a sampling of both Equiano's narrative and the scholarly debate it has generated, see the Werner Sollors edition of Equiano's widely read autobiography. Olaudah Equiano, *The Interesting Narrative of the Life of Olaudah Equiano, or Gustavus Vassa, the African: An Authoritative Text, Written by Himself*, ed. Werner Sollors (1789; New York: Norton, 2001).
43. Olaudah's multiple functions would be interesting to consider in relation to Nahum Dimitri Chandler's brilliant analysis of Du Boisian "double consciousness" between empirical history and future possibility.
44. Avery F. Gordon, "Some Thoughts on Haunting and Futurity," *borderlands* 10, no. 2 (2011): 2, 9, 10, retrieved 27 March 2017 from averygordon.net/files/GordonHauntingFuturity.pdf.
45. See Orlando Patterson, *Slavery and Social Death: A Comparative Study* (Cambridge, MA: Harvard University Press, 1982).
46. Gordon, "Some Thoughts," 13, 15.
47. Avery Gordon, *Ghostly Matters: Haunting and the Sociological Imagination* (Minneapolis: University of Minnesota Press, 2008), 194. For a discussion of Gordon's work in Black German studies, see, for example, Kimberly Singletary's critical discussions of "racial haunting" in relation to *Leroy räumt auf* (dir. Armin Völckers), a German comedy and prize-winning short film about an Afro-German teenager's efforts to defeat German racism on the extreme right. The film was later made into a feature-length film titled *Leroy*. Kimberly Singletary, "Everyday Matters: Haunting and the Black Diasporic Experience," *Rethinking Black German Studies: Approaches, Interventions, and Histories*, ed. Tiffany N. Florvil and Vanessa D. Plumly (Oxford: Peter Lang, 2018), 137–67. See also Gordon, "Some Thoughts."
48. Gordon, "Some Thoughts," 2.
49. Not all trauma studies scholars would agree with Gordon's sharp distinction between haunting and trauma. See for example Gert Buelens, Sam Durrant, and Robert Eaglestone, eds., *The Future of Trauma Theory: Contemporary Literary and Cultural Criticism* (London: Routledge, 2014).
50. For this reason I would also differentiate Götting's approach to Black German temporality from the literary approaches to traumatic history and "African American collective postmemory" that Maria Rice Bellamy analyzes in *Bridges to Memory: Postmemory in Contemporary Ethnic American Women's Fiction* (Charlottesville: University of Virginia Press, 2015), 45–75.
51. One might thus read Götting's approach to a break, cut, or "gap" in Black German time as akin to what Peggy Piesche discussed, at the BEST anniversary roundtable

in San Diego in 2016, in terms of "actualizing futures" (Audre Lorde) through an "epistemology of disruptions." Götting's use of narrative time resists even oppositional traditions of temporal continuity though, and in this sense the novel would not lend itself well to any claims of merely alternative or radically other time. *Contrapunctus* uses a narrative poetics of time to unsettle both a "contemporary condition" of Black German experience (El-Tayeb, *European Others*, xxxv) and historical hauntings of European racism.

Bibliography

Adelson, Leslie A. *The Turkish Turn in Contemporary German Literature: Toward a New Critical Grammar of Migration*. New York: Palgrave Macmillan, 2005.

Adelson, Leslie A., and Devin Fore, eds. "Futurity Now." Special issue, *The Germanic Review* 88, no. 3 (2013).

Adorno, Theodor W. "Memento." *Minima Moralia: Reflections from Damaged Life*. Translated by E. F. N. Jephcott. London: Verso, 2005. 85–87.

Appadurai, Arjun. *The Future as Cultural Fact: Essays on the Global Condition*. London: Verso, 2013.

Arendt, Hannah. *Between Past and Future: Six Exercises in Political Thought*. New York: Viking, 1961.

———. *The Human Condition*. 2nd ed. Chicago: University of Chicago Press, 2013.

———. "Vorwort: Die Lücke zwischen Vergangenheit und Zukunft." *Zwischen Vergangenheit und Zukunft: Übungen im politischen Denken I*. Munich: Piper, 1994, 7–19.

———. "We Refugees." In *Altogether Elsewhere: Writers on Exile*, edited by Marc Robinson, 110–19. Boston: Faber and Faber, 1994.

Assmann, Aleida. "The Empathetic Listener and the Ethics of Storytelling." In *Storytelling and Ethics: Literature, Visual Arts and the Power of Narrative*, edited by Hanna Meretoja and Colin Davis, 203–18. London: Routledge, 2017.

———. "Transformations of the Modern Time Regime." In *Breaking Up Time: Negotiating the Borders between Past, Present, and Future*, edited by Chris Lorenz and Berber Bevernage, 39–56. Göttingen: Vandenhoeck & Ruprecht, 2013.

Bellamy, Maria Rice. *Bridges to Memory: Postmemory in Contemporary Ethnic American Women's Fiction*. Charlottesville: University of Virginia Press, 2015.

Bode, Christoph, and Rainer Dietrich. *Future Narratives: Theory, Poetics, and Media-Historical Moment*. Berlin: De Gruyter, 2013.

Bond, Lucy, and Jessica Rapson, eds. *The Transcultural Turn: Interrogating Memory Between and Beyond Borders*. Berlin: De Gruyter, 2014.

Boog, Julia. *Anderssprechen: Vom Witz der Differenz in den Werken von Emine Sevgi Özdamar, Felicitas Hoppe und Yoko Tawada*. Interkulturelle Moderne 6. Würzburg: Königshausen & Neumann, 2017.

Buelens, Gert, Sam Durrant, and Robert Eaglestone, eds. *The Future of Trauma Theory: Contemporary Literary and Cultural Criticism*. London: Routledge, 2014.

Bühler, Benjamin, and Stefan Willer, eds. *Futurologien: Ordnungen des Zukunftswissens*. Munich: Wilhelm Fink, 2016.

Chandler, Nahum Dimitri. *Toward an African Future—of the Limit of World*. London: Living Commons Collective, 2013.

Crownshaw, Rick, ed. *Transcultural Memory*. London: Routledge, 2014.

Dayıoğlu-Yücel, Yasemin, and Ortrud Gutjahr, eds. "Emine Sevgi Özdamar." Special issue, *text + kritik* 211 (July 2016).
Dreier, Jochen. "Afrofuturismus: Widerstand gegen eine weiße Zukunft." *Deutschlandfunk Kultur*, 25 January 2017. Retrieved 17 March 2018 from http://www.deutsch landfunkkultur.de/afrofuturismus-widerstand-gegen-eine-weisse-zukunft.976.de .html?dram:article_id=376520.
Eley, Michelle. "Excavation, Curation, and the Sounds of Self-Making." German Studies Association Annual Convention, San Diego, California, 2 October 2016.
El-Tayeb, Fatima. *European Others: Queering Ethnicity in Postnational Europe*. Minneapolis: University of Minnesota Press, 2011.
———. "Time Travelers and Queer Heterotopias: Narratives from the Muslim Underground." In "Futurity Now," edited by Leslie A. Adelson and Devin Fore. Special issue, *The Germanic Review* 88, no. 3 (2013): 305–19.
———. *Undeutsch: Die Konstruktion des Anderen in der postmigrantischen Gesellschaft*. Bielefeld: transcript, 2016.
Emde, Helga. "An 'Occupation Baby' in Postwar Germany." In *Showing Our Colors: Afro-German Women Speak Out*, edited May Opitz, Katharina Oguntoye, and Dagmar Schultz, translated by Anne V. Adams, 101–12. Amherst: University of Massachusetts Press, 1992.
Encyclopedia Britannica, eds. "Olaudah Equiano: Abolitionist and Writer." *Encyclopedia Britannica*, 3 December 2004. Retrieved 26 February 2017 from https://www.britan nica.com/biography/Olaudah-Equiano.
Equiano, Olaudah. *The Interesting Narrative of the Life of Olaudah Equiano, or Gustavus Vassa, the African: An Authoritative Text, Written by Himself*. 1789. Edited by Werner Sollors. New York: Norton, 2001.
Erdle, Birgit R. *Literarische Epistemologie der Zeit: Lektüren zu Kant, Kleist, Heine und Kafka*. Paderborn: Fink, 2015.
Erll, Astrid. "Traveling Memory." *parallax* 17, no. 4 (2011): 4–18.
Eshel, Amir. *Futurity: Contemporary Literature and the Quest for the Past*. Chicago: University of Chicago Press, 2012.
Fuchs, Anne, and J. J. Long, eds. *Time in German Literature and Culture, 1900–2015: Between Acceleration and Slowness*. Houndmills: Palgrave Macmillan, 2016.
Götting, Michael. *Contrapunctus: Roman*. Münster: Unrast, 2015.
Gordon, Avery F. *Ghostly Matters: Haunting and the Sociological Imagination*. Minneapolis: University of Minnesota Press, 2008.
———. "Some Thoughts on Haunting and Futurity." *borderlands* 10, no. 2 (2011): 1–21. Academic OneFile. Retrieved 27 March 2017 from averygordon.net/files/Gordon-HauntingFuturity.pdf.
Gutjahr, Ortrud. "Von der Nationalkultur zur Interkulturalität: Zur literarischen Semantisierung und Differenzbestimmung kollektiver Identitätskonstrukte." In *Interkulturalität und Nationalkultur in der deutschsprachigen Literatur*, edited by Maja Razbojnikova-Frateva and Hans-Gerd Winter, 91–122. Dresden: Thelem, 2006.
Hackenesch, Silke. "Der Sarotti-M*** (1918/1922), oder: Was hat Konsum mit Rassismus zu tun?" In *Race & Sex: Eine Geschichte der Neuzeit*, edited by Jürgen Martschukat and Olaf Stieglitz. 217–25. Berlin: Neofelis Verlag, 2016.
Halbwachs, Maurice. *On Collective Memory*. Translated and edited by Lewis A. Coser. Chicago: University of Chicago Press, 1992.

Harvey, David. *The Condition of Postmodernity: An Enquiry into the Conditions of Cultural Change.* Cambridge, MA: Blackwell, 1990.
Haus der Kulturen der Welt, Tina Campt, and Paul Gilroy, eds. *Der Black Atlantic.* Berlin: Haus der Kulturen der Welt, 2004.
Herman, David. *Basic Elements of Narrative.* West Sussex: Wiley-Blackwell, 2009.
Huyssen, Andreas. *Miniature Metropolis: Literature in an Age of Photography and Film.* Cambridge, MA: Harvard University Press, 2015.
Kacandes, Irene. *Talk Fiction: Literature and the Talk Explosion.* Lincoln: University of Nebraska Press, 2001.
Koschorke, Albrecht. *Wahrheit und Erfindung: Grundzüge einer Allgemeinen Erzähltheorie.* 2nd ed. Frankfurt am Main: Fischer, 2012.
Layne, Priscilla. *White Rebels in Black: German Appropriation of Black Popular Culture.* Ann Arbor: University of Michigan Press, 2018.
Lennox, Sara, ed. *Remapping Black Germany: New Perspectives on Afro-German Politics, History, and Culture.* Amherst: University of Massachusetts Press, 2016.
Luhmann, Niklas. "The Future Cannot Begin: Temporal Structures in Modern Society." *Social Research* 43, no. 1 (Spring 1976): 130–52.
Özdamar, Emine Sevgi. "Bahnfahrt." *Die Zeit* Nr. 42 (9 October 2008): 91.
———. "On the Train." Translated by Leslie A. Adelson. In *Transit: A Journal of Travel, Migration, and Multiculturalism in the German-Speaking World* 9, no. 2 (2014). http://transit.berkeley.edu/2014/adelson-2/.
Oguntoye, Katharina, May Opitz, and Dagmar Schultz, eds. *Farbe bekennen: Afro-deutsche Frauen auf den Spuren ihrer Geschichte.* Berlin: Orlanda Frauenverlag, 1986.
Partridge, Damani. *Hypersexuality and Headscarves: Race, Sex, and Citizenship in the New Germany.* Bloomington: Indiana University Press, 2012.
Patterson, Orlando. *Slavery and Social Death: A Comparative Study.* Cambridge, MA: Harvard University Press, 1982.
Piesche, Peggy. "Black and German? East German Adolescents before 1989: A Retrospective View of a 'Non-existent Issue' in the GDR." In *The Cultural After-Life of East Germany: New Transnational Perspectives*, edited by Leslie A. Adelson, 37–59. Harry & Helen Gray Humanities Program Series 13. Washington, DC: American Institute for Contemporary German Studies, 2002.
———. "Deposits of the Future through Times and Spaces: African/Diasporic Safe Knowledge." In *Deposits of Future: Future African Visions in Time, An Exhibition by the Bayreuth Academy of Advanced African Studies*, 7–11. Bayreuth: Bayreuth Academy of Advanced African Studies, 2016. Retrieved 30 March 2017 from https://bayreuthacademyexhibition.files.wordpress.com/2016/01/booklet-deposits-of-future.pdf.
———. "Inscribing the Past, Anticipating the Future: Audre Lorde and the Black Women's Movement in Germany." In *Audre Lorde's Transnational Legacies*, edited by Stella Bolaki and Sabine Broeck, 222–25. Amherst, MA: University of Massachusetts Press, 2015.
———. "Towards a Future African Diasporic Theory: Black Collective Narratives Changing the Epistemic Map." *Frauen*solidarität* 1 (2016): 22–24.
Piesche, Peggy, ed. *"Euer Schweigen schützt Euch nicht": Audre Lorde und die Schwarze Frauenbewegung in Deutschland.* Berlin: Orlanda Frauenverlag, 2012.
Rimmon-Kenan, Shlomith. *Narrative Fiction: Contemporary Poetics.* 2nd ed. London: Routledge, 2002.

Rotaru, Arina. "May Ayim and Diasporic Poetics." *The Germanic Review* 92, no. 1 (2017): 86–107.

Rothberg, Michael. *Multidirectional Memory: Remembering the Holocaust in the Age of Decolonization*. Stanford, CA: Stanford University Press, 2009.

Singletary, Kimberly. "Everyday Matters: Haunting and the Black Diasporic Experience." In *Rethinking Black German Studies: Approaches, Interventions, and Histories*, edited by Tiffany N. Florvil and Vanessa D. Plumly, 137–67. Oxford: Peter Lang, 2018.

———. "Haunting and the Black Diasporic Experience." German Studies Association Annual Convention, San Diego, California, 1 October 2016.

Smith, Jill Suzanne. "Sounds of Silence: Rape and Representation in Julie Zeh's Bosnian Travelogue." In *German Women's Writing in the Twenty-First Century*, edited by Hester Baer and Alexandra Merley Hill, 175–96. Rochester, NY: Camden House, 2015.

Stoetzer, Bettina. "A Path Through the Woods: Remediating Affective Landscapes in Documentary Asylum Worlds," *Transit* 9, no. 2 (2014). https://escholarship.org/uc/item/4qk4p516.

Weber, Angela. *Im Spiegel der Migration: Transkulturelles Erzählen und Sprachpolitik bei Emine Sevgi Özdamar*. Bielefeld: transcript, 2009.

Welsch, Wolfgang. "Was ist eigentlich Transkulturalität?" In *Kulturen in Bewegung: Beiträge zur Theorie und Praxis der Transkulturalität*, edited by Dorothee Kimmich and Schamma Schahadat, 25–40. Bielefeld: transcript, 2012.

INDEX

Note: Page numbers in italics refer to figures.

Abdel-Samad, Hamed, 21, 159–61
ableism, 132–33, 141
acculturation, 17
Achinger, Christine, 19, 31n90
ADEFRA, 255
Adelson, Leslie, 11, 16–17, 22, 61, 72n33, 137, 217n6, 220n32
Adelson, Leslie A., 23
Adorno, Theodor W., 247–48, 258–59
Advanced Chemistry, 3, 236–37
AfD (Alternative for Germany), 5, 19, 140, 172, 188n2
Afghanistan, refugees from, 2, 42–43. *See also* refugees
African Americans, 7, 16–17, 107–8, 110–11, 113n5. *See also* Black Lives Matter movement
African immigrants, 12–14, 134–36
Afrikanischer Hilfsverein (AH, African Welfare Association), 13
Afro-Europeans, 173, 182, 185, 228–31, 239–40
Afrofuturism, 101–2, 228–41, 242n27, 249
Afro-Germans: use of term, 146n57. *See also* Black Germans
Afro-German temporality, 230–33
Agamben, Giorgio, 228, 231–32, 243n46
Aggadot (Jewish legends), 78–93
Ahmed, Sara, 22, 196, 199, 208–9, 219n30, 222n70
AiRich, 239
Aitken, Robbie, 15
Akgün, Hatice, 8
Akın, Fatih, 12, 173–81, 187–88, 191n24
Aksu, Sezen, 176
Aktaş, Gülşen, 7

Alahmadi, Galal, 9
Al-Asheq, Ramy, 9
Alter, Robert, 94n7
Alternative für Deutschland (Alternative for Germany). *See* AfD
Amo, Anton Wilhelm, 233–34
Angst Essen Seele auf (*Ali: Fear Eats the Soul*, 1974), 177
anti-Blackness, 7, 10, 16. *See also* racism
anti-colonialism, 13
antifascism, 160
anti-immigration discourse, 30n84, 45, 48–49, 120. *See also* xenophobia
anti-Muslim racism, 31n90, 48, 91. *See also* Islamophobia
antiracism: Black Lives Matter movement, 7, 134; in comedy, 119–41; in film industry, 172–88; slave narratives, 260–61
antisemitism, 1, 18–20, 22, 30n84, 144n35; Holocaust memory and, 160, 165–66; in Oberammergau, 94n12, 95n21; postcolonialism and, 19, 31n87, 31n89; protests against Israel and, 160; public attitudes toward, 91; stereotypes, 156
Appadurai, Arjun, 237, 239, 248
Arab immigrants, 8, 45, 51
Arab Spring, 41, 50
archive: family history and, 209–11; knowledge production and, 70n3; language and, 68–70; literary studies and archival turn, 55; of migration, 57–60, 70; nation as, 196–97; theorization of, 54–57
Arendt, Hannah, 249–50, 254–56, 262–63, 265n13, 265n18
Arndt, Susan, 124–25
Arslan, Gizem, 59
assimilation, 17, 93n2, 122
Assmann, Aleida, 217n3, 248

asylum seekers, 5, 7, 39–53. See also refugees
Atfah, Lina, 9
Athanasiou, Athena, 228, 241n4
AufBrüche (Departures), 8
Auschwitz concentration camp, 49, 152, 158, 160, 167, 199
Aus dem nichts (*In the Fade*, 2017), 174
Austria: migration and, 251; Petrowskaja and, 198; refugees and, 40–41, 46–48; xenophobia in, 140, 172
Austrian Jews, 51, 93n2
authorial agency, 83–87
Ayim, May, 7, 13, 15, 104, 135–36, 229, 233–34, 243n45, 267n36; *Blues in Black and White*, 229; "blues in schwarz weiss" (blues in black and white), 3; *Farbe bekennen* (*Showing Our Colors*), 13, 229, 234, 255

Babi Yar massacre, 199, 202, 207, 220n35
Baghdad, 64–66, 175
Bahrain, 50
Bakiga, Nyra, 239
Balkan Wars, 39, 42, 44, 253–54
Ballhaus Naunynstraße Theater, 3, 10, 16; *Schwarz tragen* (Carrying/Wearing Black), 99–113
Barad, Karen, 220n31
Baraka, Amiri, 235
Barreca, Gina, 127
BDS movement (boycott of Israel), 19
become (*werden*), 234
Behar, Katherine, 242n17
"being-in-difference," 101, 103, 112
Beisenherz, Micky, 132
Belgian colonial past, 186–87
Bellamy, Maria Rice, 268n50
belonging, 3, 119–20, 122, 135, 141
Benguigui, Yamina, 174, 189n10
Benjamin, Walter, 61–62, 66, 70n3, 221n45
Benn, Gottfried, 69
Berlin: Black German life in, 99–107, 182–86, 255–63; East-West crossings, 58, 66–67 (see also East Berlin; West Berlin); Holocaust memorials in, 152–67, 169n39; Tiergarten, 154, 162, 259–60
Berlin Friedrichshain-Kreuzberg, 140–41

Berlin-Kreuzberg, 10, 39–40, 53, 99
Berlin Wall Memorial, 152, 154, 162–63
Berlin-Wilmersdorf, 44
Bernauer Straße, 152, 162–63
Besson, Benno, 54–55
Beyoncé, 237
Bhabha, Homi, 126
Bialik, Hayim, 88
Bible: Hebrew, 92; Luther and, 85–87, 91
Biller, Maxim, 2, 160–61, 166
binaries, 9, 17, 21, 131, 197–98, 206–7, 210, 216, 238
Biondi, Franco, 7
Black diaspora. See diaspora
blackface, 10, 100, 107–9
Black German literature, 15–17, 101, 136, 228–30, 233–35, 255–63. See also Afrofuturism
Black Germans, 2–4, 12–17; in Berlin, 99–107, 182–86, 255–63; comedians, 134–37; filmmakers, 22, 173–75, 181–88; temporality, 230–33; terms for, 146n57. See also Blackness; People of Color; race/racialization
Black German studies, 2, 12–17, 255
Black German theater, 10, 21, 99–113
Black German women, 181–86, 233
Black Lives Matter movement, 7, 134
Black Lux festival, 99–100, 102
Black Mountain College, 45, 53
Black negation, 234
Blackness: German language and, 135–36; hypervisibility of, 104; relationality of, 100, 103–6; utopian discourse and, 103–4. See also anti-Blackness; Black Germans
Black Panther (2018), 240
Bloch, Ernst, 231, 233
Block, Nick, 20–21, 120, 129–30
Blonzen, Elizabeth, 103, 105–6, 109–10; *Schwarz tragen* (Carrying/Wearing Black), 21, 99–113
blood lineage (*jus sanguinis*), 120, 128
Blues in Black and White (Ayim), 229
Bode, Christoph, 248, 263
Bodemann, Y. Michal, 9, 18
Böhmermann, Jan, 127, 137, 140, 144n35

Boran, Erol, 137
Bosnia, 51
Bower, Kathrin, 139
Brahm, Felix, 15
Brandenburg, Ulla von, 155
Brandenburg Gate, 160–61
Brandt, Bettina, 4
Brassier, Ray, 242n17
Brecht, Bertolt, 12, 15, 54
Broder, Henryk, 21, 159–61, 165–67
Brönimann, Nadia, 236–37
Brooks, Daphne, 104, 111
brothels, 63, 65, 73n47
Bruce, Lenny, 129
Buabeng, Thelma, 101
Bubis, Ignatz, 165
Busch, Wilhelm, 156–57
Buß, Christian, 138
Butler, Judith, 105, 220n30

Çağlar, Ayşe, 11
Cameroon, migrants from, 12–14
Campt, Tina, 14, 255
cartoons, 127, 144nn33–34, 156–57, 167
Carvalho, Wagner, 10, 99–100, 103
Caspari, Maya, 21–22
Çatak, Ilker, 22, 173–75, 187–88
censorship, 127, 138, 144n34
Central Council of Jews in Germany, 31n89
Ceylan, Bülent, 136
Chappelle, Dave, 136
Charlie Hebdo, 127, 172
Chauvin, Derek, 7
Cheesman, Tom, 11
Chesnutt, Charles, 242n27
children as utopian trope, 101
Chin, Rita, 4, 11
Christianity, 92, 231
citizenship, 2–3
class, 1, 240
Cologne, 44, 58, 128, 134–35, 160
colonialism, 1, 10, 16; Belgian, 186–87; blackface and, 108–9; German, 12–13, 233, 258; racism and discrimination, 121, 133–34, 141. *See also* decolonization; postcolonial studies

colorblindness, 108–9
comedians, 21, 119–41; Black German, 134–37; Jewish German, 129–34; Turkish German, 137–41. *See also* humor
Constantinople, 64–66. *See also* Istanbul
constellation, concept of, 60–70
contingency, 22, 199, 208–16, 220n32
Contrapunctus (Götting), 23, 249, 255–63, 268n40, 268nn50–51
Coogan, Tom, 133
Coogler, Ryan, 240
Cooper, Davina, 102
cosmopolitan identities, 2, 10, 18, 21; Jewish, 197, 217n5; languages and, 186, 210; memory and, 164, 167; migration and, 172, 182–86, 197; refugees and, 197; transnationalism and, 217n3; traumatic histories and, 203
countermemory, 61, 71n19, 72n33, 159, 197, 201, 213
critical race theory, 1, 18. *See also* race/racialization
critical whiteness studies, 1, 124. *See also* whiteness
cultural studies, 1, 15, 18; archival turn, 55. *See also* archive
Cunningham, Merce, 45
Czink, Andrew, 175
Czollek, Max, 8–9, 120, 145n44

Damrosch, David, 197
Das Herz verlässt keinen Ort, an dem es hängt (The heart never leaves a place it is attached to), 9
Das Lachen der Anderen (The laughing of others, TV show), 132–33
Davis, Dave, 21, 119–22, 124–28, 130, 134–37, 141
death, 14, 44–45, 48, 100, 103, 106, 159–60, 202, 251–54
death threats, 137, 144n33
decolonization, 16, 71n11, 134. *See also* postcolonial studies
de Faria, Yara-Collette Lemke Muniz, 14
Dekel, Irit, 161
Delany, Samuel R., 230

Demnig, Gunter, 152–59, 162–63
Derrida, Jacques, 55, 220n32, 221n45
Der Weg zur Schande (*The Road to Dishonour*, 1930), 177
Descartes, René, 232
diaspora, 2, 22; Black, 14–16; identity and, 196–97; Jewish, 197
Dickinson, Kristin, 12, 20
Die Linke, 19
Die Partei (The Party), 140
Dietrich, Rainer, 248, 263
Diner, Dan, 18
Dirty Pretty Things (2002), 174
Dischereit, Esther, 3, 6, 8, 20, 39–53, 157–58, 161, 165, 190n13
discrimination: ageism, 132–33; against Black Germans, 236 (see also anti-Blackness); comedy as tool against, 119–41; in education system, 51; against immigrants, 120; against People of Color, 121. See also anti-immigration discourse; racism
dissimilation, 17
diversity: in activism, 7; among Jews in Germany, 9; filmic depictions of urban European sounds, 172–88; in Germany, 1–4; in Istanbul, 186; theater and, 10
Döblin, Alfred, 239
Documentation Center and Museum of Migration (DOMiD), 58
Doron, Lizzi, 43
double consciousness, 104, 239, 243n45, 268n43
Dragset, Ingar, 162
Du Bois, W.E.B., 15, 104, 242n27, 243n45
Dückers, Tanja, 9
dystopia, 231

East Berlin, 54, 72n19. See also Berlin
Eastern European German literature, 229
East Germany. See German Democratic Republic
East-West divide, 55, 64–67, 128
Ecevit, Mustafa Bülent, 67
Edelman, Lee, 101
Edge of Heaven (*Auf der Anderen Seite*, 2007), 173, 175–81

education system: decolonization in, 134; discrimination in, 51
Eggers, Maisha, 234
Eichberg, Richard, 177
Eichhorn, Kate, 55
Einmal Hans mit Scharfer Soße (*Spiced Up Jack*, 2013), 180
Einstein, Albert, 45
Eisenman, Peter, 154, 159–62, 165–66, 169n39
Eley, Michelle, 262, 268n41
El Hissy, Maha, 137–38
Ellison, Ralph, 236–37, 239
Elmgreen, Michael, 162
El-Tayeb, Fatima, 4–6, 108, 121–22, 188n3, 189n4, 229, 231, 240, 255, 269n51; *Schwarze Deutsche* (Black Germans), 13; *Undeutsch* (Ungerman), 8–9
embourgeoisement, 17
Emde, Helga, 258
English language, 182
Entfernte Verbindungen (Distant connections), 7
Entweder Broder (TV show), 159
Equiano, Olaudah, 260
Erdoğan, Recep Tayyip, 91, 127, 137, 140
Ergüven, Deniz Gamze, 180–81
Erll, Astrid, 267n32
essentialism, strategic, 125–26, 239
"ethnic comedy," 124; "ethno-comedy," 125. See also humor
European Union: borders, 172–73, 187, 189n5; expansion of, 251–54, 265n21
exclusion, 4–5; from subjecthood, 228–29, 231–34, 238–40; utopia and, 103
exiles, 4, 12, 20, 59, 61, 69, 72n20, 186, 190n21, 247–48
Exodus, 94n6
exoticism, 126, 176–77, 180–81, 257
Ezli, Özkan, 122

family history, 198–216
Fanon, Frantz, 21, 104–5, 108
Farbe bekennen (*Showing Our Colors*, 1986), 13, 229, 234, 255
far right. See right-wing groups

fascism, 138, 160. *See also* Nazi Germany; neo-Nazis
Fassbinder, R. W., 177, 239
Federal Commissioner for Jewish Life in Germany and the Fight against Antisemitism, 31n89
Federal Republic of Germany (FRG): postwar migration, 57–58. *See also* West Berlin
Fehrenbach, Heide, 4, 14
feminism: Black German movement and, 13; intersectional, 7–8; new materialists, 220n31
Fidelity (Sadakat, 2014), 173, 175–81
film festivals, 189n11
films, 22; urban sounds of Europe in, 172–88
film sound scholarship, 175
Fine, Robert, 31n90
Fittko, Lisa, 48
Florvil, Tiffany, 15
Floyd, George, 7
foreigner policy, 7. *See also* asylum seekers; immigration; migration; refugees
Foroutan, Naika, 8
"Fortress Europe," 172
40 qm Deutschland (40 Square Meters of Germany, 1986), 180
Foucault, Michel, 70n3
FPO (Freedom Party of Austria), 140, 172, 188n2
France, 189n10
Fraser, Nancy, 218n11
FRD. *See* Federal Republic of Germany
Frears, Stephen, 174
Freire, Paulo, 16
French language, 186
Freud, Sigmund, 123, 257
Frisch, Shelley, 198
Front National (France), 172, 188n2
Füchtner, Veronika, 1
futurity, 16–17, 23, 247–63; affective relationships to, 248–54; Afro-German temporality and, 230–33; Arendt on "gap between past and future," 249–50, 255–56, 266n30; utopian postmigrant theater and, 101–3, 112–13. *See also* Afrofuturism

gallows humor, 126–27
Garden of Exile, 165, 169n39
Gardner, Herb, 107
Garloff, Katja, 199
Gatlif, Tony, 174
GDR. *See* German Democratic Republic
Gelbin, Cathy, 8
Geller, Simon, 201–2, 211
Genette, Gerard, 236
Geneva Refugee Convention, 42
Gentic, Tania, 175
German colonies, 12–13, 233, 258. *See also* colonialism
German Democratic Republic (GDR), 66; memorials to refugees from, 152–54, 162–64
German identity, 3–4, 21; blood lineage (*jus sanguinis*), 120, 128; comedians on, 119–20; construction of, 128; racism and, 188n3; whiteness and, 119–20, 125, 143n15, 233–34, 238–40
German Jewish studies, 2, 17–19; Turkish German studies and, 12, 20, 55, 59, 68–69, 72n20. *See also* Jews in Germany
German language, 84–85, 135–36, 210–12, 251
German literary canon, 242n22
German Quarterly, 4
German reunification, 3–4, 7, 18
German Studies Association, 2, 11, 255
German victimhood, 152–54, 162–63
Gezen, Ela, 12, 59–60
Ghana, 233
Gikandi, Simon, 197
Gilbert, Joanne, 123
Gilman, Sander, 18, 108
Gilroy, Paul, 267n32
Ginzberg, Louis, 86–88, 90
Goethe, Johann Wolfgang von, 55–57
Göktürk, Deniz, 4, 11–12, 122
Goldstein, Bluma, 93n2
Gorbutt, Anthony, 211
Gordon, Avery, 21, 101, 103, 112, 261–62, 268n49
Gorki Theater, 9–10, 16, 99
Göth, Amon, 24n5

Götting, Michael, 16, 248–50; *Contrapunctus*, 23, 249, 255–63, 268n40, 268nn50–51
Gramling, David, 4, 11
grammar, 211–12
Grjasnowa, Olga, 1, 9–10
Grünbaum, Max, 90
Gueneli, Berna, 12, 22
guest workers. *See* labor migration
Gümüşay, Kübra, 6
Guttman, Anna, 197, 217n5

Hackenesch, Silke, 268n40
Hafez, Farid, 19–20
Hagen, Sheri, 104
Haider, Jörg, 140
Haines, Brigid, 199
Halle, Randall, 11–12
Hallervorden, Dieter, 107
Haraway, Donna, 228
harem, 64–65, 74n51
Harman, Graham, 232–33, 242n17, 242n29
Harvey, David, 264n8
Hassan, Ihab, 228
hate speech, 50–51, 133
Hauck, Hans, 14
haunting, 261–62, 268n49
Hausmann, Ernest Allan, 106
Haw, Daniel, 156–57, 166
Hayles, N. Katherine, 228
Hegel, G.W.F., 104, 232
hegemonic narratives, 10, 212–13, 218n13; in German and European film, 187; of memorialization, 207; of national identity, 122, 196–200; rebellion against, 191n28; of whiteness, 125
Heidegger, Martin, 242n17, 242n29
Heimat, 8–9, 16, 67, 187
Herdeanu, Clara, 6
Herman, David, 267n38
"Herr Gröttrup setzt sich hin" (Herr Gröttrup sits down, Otoo), 22–23, 229–30, 238–41
Heschel, Susannah, 20
Higbee, Will, 174
Hillig, Daniel, 5

Hirsch, Marianne, 199, 205, 223n79
historical consciousness, 257
history, 2–3; archival turn and, 55–57; contingency and, 201–4; temporality and, 231–32
Hitler, Adolf, 140; *Mein Kampf*, 137, 141
Hoffmann, Thomas B., 103
Höhn, Maria, 14
Holmes, Amanda, 175
Holocaust Memorial Day (Israel), 164
Holocaust memory, 1–2, 9, 20–22; antisemitism and, 160, 165–66; contingency and, 208–16; as dialogic, 154, 161–67, 169n39; German Jewish studies and, 17–19; globalism and, 167; humor and, 129–31, 137, 141, 166–67; in Israel, 164; Jewish critiques of public memorials, 152–67; memoirs, 198–216; otherness and, 207–8; Özdamar and, 72n20; postmemorial, 199; refugees and, 49; state violence in Turkey and, 58–59; stumbling blocks project, 152–59, 161–63. *See also* Nazi Germany
home, 184–87. *See also Heimat*
Homo-Mahnmal. *See* Monument to the Gays and Lesbians Persecuted under the Nazi Regime
homophobia, 140–41
homo sacer, 228
homosexuals, Holocaust memorials for, 154–55, 161–62
Honeck, Mischa, 14
hope, 231
Hopkins, Leroy, 15, 233
Huddart, David, 126
Hügel-Marshall, Ika, 7, 26n27
Hughes, David, 140
humor: anti-racist, 119–41; "ethnic," 124–25; gallows humor, 126–27; Holocaust memory and, 129–31, 137, 141, 166–67; Jewish humor, 123–24, 128–34; marginal humor, 119–28; politically incorrect, 133–35; as rhetorical tool, 142n10; self-deprecatory, 123; women's use of, 127. *See also* comedians
Hund, Wulf, 125

Hussein, Atif, 101–2
Husserl, Edmund, 208, 219n30, 220n32

identities: formed by trauma, 2; intersectional, 161–67, 229–30, 237; theater and, 100
immigration, 2–3, 5. *See also* anti-immigration discourse; asylum seekers; labor migration; migration; refugees
Inch'Allah Dimanche (*Inch'Allah Sunday*, 2001), 189n10
Initiative Schwarze Menschen in Deutschland (ISD, Initiative of Black People in Germany), 5, 255
In July, 191n24
integration, 8, 21; critiques of, 122, 139; ethnicity and, 143n16; Jewish, 17; of Turkish Germans, 8–9, 69
Interesting Narrative of the Life of Olaudah Equiano, The (1789), 260
interiority, 230, 235, 238
interracial relationships, 14
intersectional feminism, 7–8
intersectional identities, 161–67, 229–30, 237
intersectional liberation, 229–30
Ipek, DJ, 3, 6
Iraq, refugees from, 2, 46, 52. *See also* refugees
Iraq in Fragments (2006), 175
Islamophobia, 6, 19–20, 31n90, 135, 172. *See also* anti-Muslim racism
Israel: Holocaust memorials, 164; migration and, 43; protests against, 19, 160; radical jihadist-Islamists and, 22
Isra'iliyyat, 89–90
Istanbul, 20; diversity in, 186; in Özdamar, 54–56, 58–61, 64–67; sonic landscape of, 173, 177–81
Italy, 41

Jaima, Felicita, 15
Jansen, Fasia, 14
Jephcott, E.F.N., 247
Jerusalem, 66–67
Jesus, 96n26
Jewish diaspora. *See* diaspora
Jewish German literature, 229
Jewish humor, 123–24, 128–34

Jewish identity: alterity of, 207–8; cosmopolitan, 197, 217n5; difference and, 18; fragility of Jewish positionality, 22; religion and, 145n44
Jewish-Muslim relations, 78–93, 129–30
Jewish traditions, 78–83, 85–93
Jewish-Turkish relations, 12, 20, 55, 59, 68–69, 72n20, 129–30
Jewish victimhood, 152–54, 202. *See also* antisemitism; Holocaust memory
Jews in Germany, 2–4; essentialist role of, 9; from former Soviet Union, 18, 199; integration, 17; numbers of, 130; Syrian refugees and, 48–49. *See also* Jewish identity
"Jim Crow" minstrelsy, 107. *See also* blackface
Johnson, E. Patrick, 104–5

Kaddisch für einen Freund (2012), 18–19
Kafka, Franz, 236–37, 249
Kalisz, Poland, 209–10, 223n78
Kallin, Britta, 21
Kanak Attack (activist network), 3
Kant, Immanuel, 231–32
Kara, Selmin, 175
Karaböcek, Neşe, 176
Kassabian, Anahid, 175
Kayirebwa, Cécile, 184
Kelly, Natasha A., 15, 17, 241n9, 243n45
Kermani, Navid, 8
Khasin, Leo, 18
Kiev, 201–4, 214
Kimmelman, Mira, 223n78
King, Kevina, 16, 28n60
Klahn, Andrej, 125
Kleffner, Heike, 45
Klein, Felix, 31n89
Klimke, Martin, 14
Knobloch, Charlotte, 155–57, 165
Koch, Lars, 126
Koepsell, Philipp Khabo, 16, 232, 241n9
Konstellationsforschung, 61
Konuk, Kader, 8, 11–12, 59, 71n17, 72n20, 157–58
Koran, 86, 89
Koray, Erkin, 176
Koschorke, Albrecht, 248

Koyuncu, Kazım, 176
Kuhlmann-Smirnov, Anne, 14
Kulaoğlu, Tunçay, 99
Kurdish language, 191n24
Kureishi, Hanif, 174
Kuria, Emily Ngubia, 17
Kuruyazıcı, Nilüfer, 11
Kusturica, Emir, 174

labor migration, 120; guest workers, 57–58, 72n33; transnational, 251–54. *See also* immigration; migration
La Habanera (1937), 177
Landry, Olivia, 10, 17, 21
Langhoff, Shermin, 10, 99
language: authority and, 79–83, 90–92; cosmopolitan identities and, 186, 210; cultural archives and, 68–70; diversity of accents and languages in films, 174–88; grammar and, 211–12; migration and, 67–70; mother tongue, 67, 210; national identity and, 210–12. *See also* hate speech; multilingualism; speech acts; translation; *specific languages*
Lasker-Schüler, Else, 20, 59–70, 73n48, 75n71; "Black Stars," 63; "Full Moon," 66–67; *The Nights of Tino from Bagdad*, 64; *The Prince of Thebes*, 64; "Senna Hoy," 63; "Stars of Fate," 60–62
Latour, Bruno, 242n17
Layne, Priscilla, 15, 17, 101–2, 191n28, 229, 255
Lefcourt, Herbert, 124
Lemmle, Julia, 108–9
Lennox, Sara, 255
Lesbian and Gay Union in Germany (LSDV), 162
Lessing, Gotthold Ephraim, 21, 83, 92
Levinas, Emmanuel, 49
Levy, Daniel, 163–64, 167
Libeskind, Daniel, 165, 169n39
Libyan refugees, 41
Link, Caroline, 177
Lioret, Philippe, 174
literatures of migration, 22, 196–216, 217n6, 248

Little Book of Big Visions, The (ed. Otoo), 239
Littler, Margaret, 11
Lizarazu, Maria Roca, 199, 209
Loher, Dea, 107–8
Longley, James, 175
Lorde, Audre, 7, 13, 15–16, 234, 237, 269n51
Lornsen, Karin, 73n47
loss, 186, 199, 202–4, 211, 251–54, 266n22
Lübcke, Walter, 6
Luft, Else, 152
Luhmann, Niklas, 248, 266n30
Luther, Martin, 85, 91

Macharia, Keguro, 234
Mahnmal (warning memorial), 155, 165. *See also* Holocaust memory
Mandel, Ruth, 11
Mandela, Nelson, 136
Mani, B. Venkat, 4, 11, 57, 72n27
Manifest der Vielen (Manifest of the many), 8
Marcuse, Herbert, 103
"Marebe" (Kayirebwa), 184–86
marginal humor, 119–28
marginalization, 4–5. *See also* minoritized groups; Other/othering
Martin, Peter, 14
Marxism, 231
Masuhr, Lilian, 133
materiality, 220n31, 240
Mauthausen concentration camp, 199, 207
Mayer, Hans, 17–18
Mbembe, Achille, 19, 21, 31n89, 99, 104–5
McGowan, Moray, 11
Mediendienst Integration, 5
Meillassoux, Quentin, 242n17
Mein Kampf (Hitler), 137, 141
Memorial to Homosexuals Persecuted under Nazism, 154–55, 161–62
Memorial to Sinti and Roma, 161
Memorial to the Murdered Jews of Europe, 154–55, 159–62, 165–66, 169n39
memory, 2–3; competitive, 163–64; cosmopolitan, 164, 167; countermemory, 71n19; in literatures of migration, 196–216; memorials and, 163–64;

multidirectional, 71n10, 164, 198, 210; national identity and, 196–216; subjunctive remembering, 215–16; transcultural memory work, 68. See also countermemory; Holocaust memory
Merkel, Angela, 49–50, 189n5
Merleau-Ponty, Maurice, 208, 219n30
Meyer, Michael, 127–28
Michaelis, Walter, 152–53
Michaelis-König, Andree, 199
Middle Ages, 14–15
MiGAZIN (online platform), 6
migration, 1–3, 9–10, 22; archive of, 57–60, 70; homesickness and, 184–86; of Jews from former Soviet Union, 18, 199; literatures of, 22, 197, 200, 217n6; national identity and, 196–97; refugees and asylum seekers, 39–53. See also anti-immigration discourse; immigration; labor migration; literatures of migration
Migrationshintergrund, 143n16
migration studies, 2
Milagro, Lara-Sophie, 109
Miller, Jennifer, 11
mimicry, 126
"Minorities and Minority Discourses in Germany since 1990," (University of Massachusetts Amherst conference), 1–2, 19–20
minoritized groups: dialogue between, 2–11; Jewish-Muslim relations, 78–93, 129–30; Jewish-Turkish relations, 12, 20, 55, 59, 68–69, 72n20, 129–30. See also Black Germans; diversity; Jews in Germany; Muslims; race/racialization; Turkish Germans
minstrelsy, 107. See also blackface
misogyny, 138, 140–41
Mittelmann, Hanni, 123
Monáe, Janelle, 237, 240
Monument to the Gays and Lesbians Persecuted under the Nazi Regime, 155
Moses (Zaimoğlu and Senkel), 21, 78–93
Moten, Fred, 21, 104–5
mother tongue, 67, 210
mourning, 6, 106, 167, 266n22

Mueller, Agnes, 199
Muhammad, 86
Mukasonga, Amanda, 182, *183*, *185*
Müller, Heiner, 58
multilingualism, 175, 186–88, 210–11, 251
Munich, Holocaust memorials in, 155, 165
Muñoz, José Esteban, 101–2, 112
music, 15, 22, 138, 174–86
Muslims, 4, 8, 21–22, 161, 229; Jewish-Muslim relations, 78–93, 129–30. See also anti-Muslim racism; Islamophobia
Muslim traditions of Moses, 86–93
Mustang (2015), 180–81
My Beautiful Launderette (1985), 174
Mysorekar, Sheila, 235

Naficy, Hamid, 176, 190n21
Nakba Day, 164
name *(selbst benennen)*, 234
Naremore, James, 106
Nathan the Wise (Lessing), 21, 83, 92
national identity: memory and, 196–216. See also German identity
nationalism, 4, 128, 164, 197
National Theatre (London), 109
NATO, 48
Nazi Germany, 14; banned literature, 68–69; refugees from, 41; survivors of, 51–52. See also Holocaust memory; neo-Nazis
Ndione, Abasse, 47
Nelson, Alondra, 232
neoliberalism, 238
neo-Nazis, 5–6, 141, 160
Ngoumou, Sita, 236
Nirgendwo in Afrika (*Nowhere in Africa*, 2001), 177
"No Border Academy" initiative, 45
Noch-Nicht (not yet), 231
nostalgia, 187
NPD (National Democratic Party of Germany), 5
Nsengiyumva, Roger Jean, 182
NSU (National Socialist Underground), 6, 45, 135, 174, 190n13
Nuremberg trials, 215
Nyong'o, Tavia, 105

Oberammergau, 21, 78–93, 94n12, 95n21
object-oriented modernism, 239
object-oriented ontology, 230, 232–33, 240
Obrdlik, Antonin, 126
Oguntoye, Katharina, 13
Okpako, Branwen, 100, 105, 113
"On the Train" (Özdamar), 23, 250–54
Orbán, Viktor, 48
Orich, Annika, 131–32
orientalism, 64–66, 68–69, 75n71
Orlanda Frauenverlag (publisher), 7, 13
Ortner, Jessica, 199, 207
Osborne, Dora, 199, 218n14, 221n45
Other/othering, 4, 121, 128, 176–77, 180–81, 186, 188n3, 207–8, 237. See also marginalization
Otoo, Sharon Dodua, 9, 15, 228–41; "Herr Gröttrup setzt sich hin" (Herr Gröttrup sits down), 22–23, 229–30, 238–41; *Synchronicity*, 22–23, 229–30, 232, 234–38, 240–41; *the things I'm thinking while smiling politely*, 229
ÖVP (Österreichische Volkspartei [Austrian People's Party]), 188n2
Özdamar, Emine Sevgi, 2, 12, 16, 54–55, 59–70, 70n1, 248–54; "Bahnfahrt" ("On the Train"), 23, 250–54; *Bridge of the Golden Horn*, 58, 67–70, 73n47, 75n76; *Caravanserai*, 58, 63, 68–69, 75n76; *Mother Tongue*, 75n76; *Seltsame Sterne starren zur Erde (Strage Stars Stare to Earth)*, 20, 54–70, 71n19, 72n20, 75n78; *Sun Halfway* trilogy, 58, 69–70
Özoğuz, Aydan, 42
Özyürek, Esra, 11

Palestine and Palestinians, 43, 67, 164
parody, 122, 141. See also satire
Partridge, Damani, 20, 255
Patterson, Orlando, 261
Paul (apostle), 88
Peña, Rosemarie, 15
People of Color: antiracist activism, 7 (*see also* antiracism); migration to Germany, 3; right-wing violence against, 5–6 (*see also* racist violence); subjecthood, 228–29, 231–34, 238–40; use of term, 121. See also Black Germans
people smuggling, 47–48
people with disabilities, 132–33
Pérez, Fernando, 175
performance artists, 138, 140
performer-spectator relationship, 100, 110–12
Petrowskaja, Katja, 219n18, 220n32, 221n45; *Vielleicht Esther (Maybe Esther)*, 22, 198–216
phenomenology, 219n30, 242n17; queer phenomenology, 208–9, 222n70
Piesche, Peggy, 8, 16, 255, 268n51
Pizer, John, 71n19, 75n78
Plasberg, Frank, 138, 147n67
play (in Agamben's sense), 231–32, 234
Pleasantville (1998), 239
Plumly, Vanessa, 16
Poikane-Daumke, Aija, 15
Polak, Oliver, 21, 119–21, 123–34, 136, 140–41, 144n35, 156–57, 166
polemics, 122
political dissidents, 68
politics, 1, 9; antisemitism and, 19, 30n84, 160; Holocaust memorials and, 166 (*see also* Holocaust memory); satire and, 127–28, 140–41, 144nn33–34 (*see also* cartoons). See also right-wing groups; *specific political parties*
Polyglot (2015), 173, 175–76, 181–86
Polynationaler Literatur- und Kunstverein, 7
Popoola, Olumide, 8, 107
populist politics, 5, 22, 48, 120, 127, 135, 137, 141; xenophobia in, 172–74, 188. See also right-wing groups
Porzelt, Benedikt, 128
postcolonial studies, 19, 31n87, 55. See also decolonization
PostHeimat (After Heimat), 9–10
posthumanism, 22–23; in Afro-German literature, 235–38; defined, 228–29; German whiteness and, 238–40; intersectional liberation and, 229–30
postmigrant theater, 10, 99–103, 112–13
precarity, 109, 201, 205, 214, 231, 240
priests, 84–85, 88–89

prophets, 84–85, 88–89
prostitutes, 63–64, 73n47
Pryor, Richard, 129
Putin, Vladimir, 43

queerness, 8, 112, 229
queer phenomenology, 208–9, 222n70

Ra, Sun, 233
race/racialization, 3–5; German identity and (*see* German identity); German Jewish studies and, 19; German Jews and, 131–32, 142n3 (*see also* Jews in Germany); in postwar era of 1940s and 1950s, 14; strategic essentialism and, 125–26; technology and, 232. *See also* critical race theory; whiteness
racial haunting, 261–62
racism, 1–9, 19, 22, 257–58, 260–62; colonialism and, 121, 133–34, 141; resistance to, 240 (*see also* antiracism); in theater, 100, 107–9; in US history, 107–8; xenophobia and, 189n4 (*see also* xenophobia). *See also* anti-Blackness; anti-Muslim racism; antisemitism; hate speech; Islamophobia; orientalism; racist violence
racist violence, 5–7, 18–19, 45, 106, 134, 174, 190n13
rape. *See* sexual violence
Rappoport, Angelo S., 88, 90
Ravnitzky, Yehoshua, 88
refugees, 2, 39–53, 197
Reisoğlu, Mert Bahadır, 12
religion, 19; German identity and, 119–20; Jewish-Muslim dialogue, 78–93. *See also* Christianity; Jewish traditions; Muslim traditions
Renan, Ernest, 196
Rice, Thomas Dartmouth, 107
Ricketts, Tyron, 112
Riggs, Marlon, 233
right-wing groups: anti-immigrant discourse, 45, 48–49; critiqued by comedians, 127–28, 137–38, 140–41; far right, 19, 22; xenophobia in, 172, 188. *See also* neo-Nazis; populist politics; racist violence

ritual, 231–32
Robinson, Victoria B., 241n10
Romani voices and sounds, 174, 189n8, 191n24
Ronen, Yael, 10
Rosenhaft, Eve, 15
Rotaru, Arina, 267n36
Rothberg, Michael, 20, 22, 71n10, 163–64, 198, 210, 218n11, 218n13, 267n32
Royal Shakespeare Company, 109
Russian language, 210
Rwandan migrants, 181–87

Said, Edward, 262
Sälter, Gerhard, 162–63
Salzmann, Sasha Marianna, 9, 101, 145n44
Sammy and Rosie Get Laid (1987), 174
Sarajevo Film Festival, 189n11
Sarrazin, Thilo, 8
Sarotti Company, 258–59, 268n40
satire, 122; politics and, 127–28, 140–41, 144nn33–34
Schami, Rafik, 7
Schechner, Richard, 110
Scheffler, Karl, 184
Schengen agreement, 47
Schlingensief, Christoph, 138, 140, 147n67
Scholem, Gershom, 167
Schrade, Daniel Kojo, 239
Schrott, Raoul, 47–48
Schultz, Dagmar, 7, 13
Schuster-Craig, Johanna, 4
Schwarzsein (Blackness), 100
Schwarz tragen (Carrying/Wearing Black), 21, 99–113
science fiction, 232. *See also* Afrofuturism
Sedgwick, Eve K., 213
Seltsame Sterne starren zur Erde (*Strange Stars Stare to Earth*, Özdamar), 20, 54–70, 71n19, 72n20, 75n78
Senkel, Günter, 21, 78, 86–87, 93n3
Şenocak, Zafer, 2, 128
Sense8 (2017–18), 243n50
sexuality studies, 18
sexual violence, 44–45, 106, 258
Seyhan, Azade, 11, 61, 72n33

Sezen, Beldan, 8
Shantel, DJ, 176
Shapira, Shahak, 165–66, 170n46
Sharifi, Azadeh, 121
Shelly, Joshua, 20–21
Shoah, 95n21
Sieg, Katrin, 108
silence (*Schweigen*), 235
Singletary, Kimberly, 255, 268n47
Sirk, Douglas, 177
slavery and slave trade, 16, 134, 257–58, 260, 262
social death, 261–62
social media, 165–66, 170n46
Somuncu, Serdar, 21, 119–21, 125–28, 130, 137–41
Sonneborn, Martin, 140–41
Sound of Istanbul, The (2005), 191n24
Soviet bloc, Holocaust memorials in, 164–65
Soviet Union: atrocities, 199, 211–12; Jewish history in, 204, 207–8
Sow, Noah, 16, 241n10
Soysal, Levent, 11
speculative realism, 230, 232
speech acts: authority and, 79–83, 90–92. *See also* hate speech; language
Spiller, Hortense, 101, 114n5
Spivak, Gayatri Chakravorty, 62, 126
StandUpMigranten (TV show), 130–31
Stanišić, Saša, 9
States, Bert O., 111
Stauss, Kilian, 155
Steinmeier, Frank-Walter, 43
Stemmle, Robert, 177
Steppat, Timo, 140
stereotypes: about Germans, 120; of African migrants, 134–36; antisemitic, 156; comedy and, 123, 126, 128, 134–36, 141; of Jews, 136; of Turkish Germans, 180
Stern, Judas, 201, 203, 211
Stoetzer, Bettina, 266n25
Stoler, Ann, 55
strategic essentialism, 125–26, 239
Stückl, Christian, 78, 83, 94n12
stumbling blocks (*Stolpersteine*), 152–59, 161
subjecthood, 228–29, 231–34, 238–40

subjunctive remembering, 215–16
Suite Habana (2003), 175
Sweden, 47
Synchronicity (Otoo), 22–23, 229–30, 232, 234–38, 240–41
Syrian refugees, 2, 9, 39–53, 189n5
Sznaider, Nathan, 163–64, 167

al-Tabari, 90
tactility, 200–211, 214, 221n45, 223n79
Talking Home (1999), 8
Tatort (TV show), 180
Taufiq, Suleman, 7
Tawada, Yoko, 4
Teege, Jennifer, 24n5
temporality: Arendt on "gap between past and future," 249–50, 255–56, 266n30; history and, 231–32. *See also* futurity; memory
terror and terrorism, 6, 45, 49, 91, 134–35, 161, 172, 174, 258
Thalheimer, Michael, 107–8
theater, 3, 9–10, 21; Black German theater, 10, 21, 99–113; identities and, 100; in Özdamar, 54–57, 59–60; postmigrant theater, 10, 99–103, 112–13; self-expressive mode and, 109–12. *See also* performer-spectator relationship
Thompson, Peter, 20
300 Worte Deutsch (300 German words, 2013), 180
Thurman, Kira, 15
Tiergarten (Berlin), 154, 162, 259–60
time travel, 249, 257, 262–63
Torner, Evan, 15, 17, 22
totalitarianism, 202, 206–7, 212
touch, politics of, 200, 202–5, 208–12, 220n32
Toxi (1952), 177
transcendence, 61–62
translation, 56–57; multilingual, 251 (*see also* multilingualism); tactile, 200–211, 214, 221n45
transnationalism: archive and, 11, 61; Black Germans and, 255; cinematic, 22, 173–75, 187, 190n21; comedy and, 139; cosmopolitan ethos and, 217n3; memory

and, 199; migration and, 58, 120–21, 197, 250–54; theater and, 10, 99
trauma: absence and, 202; cosmopolitan identities and, 203; haunting and, 268n49; identities formed by, 2; unknowability of, 199–200
Treblinka (death camp), 202, 220n36
Trojanow, Ilija, 8
Turkish German literature, 11–12, 54–57, 61, 72n33, 75n76, 229, 250–54
Turkish Germans, 1–4; comedians, 137–41; education of, 51; filmmakers, 173–81, 190n21; integration of, 8–9, 69; Muslim minority and, 21 (see also Muslims); stereotypes of, 180
Turkish German studies, 2, 11–12; German Jewish studies and, 12, 20, 55, 59, 68–69, 72n20
Turkish-Jewish relations, 12, 20, 55, 59, 68–69, 72n20, 129–30
Turkish language, 67–70, 177–81
Turkish military coup (1971), 56–59, 67
Turkish women, 178–81
Twitter, 165–66, 170n46

Umuhire, Amelia, 22, 173–75, 181–88
United States: Holocaust memorialization, 164; racist traditions in, 107–8. See also African Americans
Universal Declaration on Human Rights, 51
Utlu, Deniz, 9, 57–58
utopian discourse, 101–4, 110, 112–13

Vergangenheitsbewältigung (working through the past), 154, 164
victimhood: equivalency of, 162; German, 152–54, 162–63; Jewish, 152–54. See also Holocaust memory
Vielleicht Esther (*Maybe Esther*, Petrowskaja), 22, 198–216
violence: against asylum seekers, 45; in Soviet Union, 211–12. See also Babi Yar massacre; Holocaust memory; racist violence; sexual violence; slavery and slave trade; terror and terrorism

Völkerschauen (ethnological exhibitions), 133–34
völkisch, 120
Volksbühne (East Berlin), 54–56, 69–70
vulnerability, 22, 49, 203–6, 223n79

Wainwright, Rob, 40
Warsaw, 205–6, 208
Watkins, Jamele, 15, 101, 136
Weber, Beverly, 11
Weg sein—hier sein (*Being away—being here*), 9
Weheliye, Alexander, 233
Weimar period, 13–14
Weiter Schreiben, 9
Weltliteratur, 56–57
Wenzel, Olivia, 101–2, 242n16
West Berlin, 58, 63–64. See also Berlin
West Germany. See Federal Republic of Germany
Wheeler, Brannon, 89–90
white Eurocentrism, 229
whiteness, 1, 9, 21; as absent Other, 100; Afro-German perspectives on, 233; critical whiteness studies, 1, 124; cultural appropriation and, 191n28; German identity and, 119–20, 125, 143n15, 233–34, 238–40; posthumanism and, 238–40; privilege and, 124–25; relationality of Blackness and, 104–5; as unmarked, 124. See also race/racialization
White Rebels in Black (Layne), 191n28
white supremacy, 16, 232
Wiesel, Elie, 166
Will, Anne, 138, 147n67
Williams, Raymond, 103
"Wilmersdorf Helps," 44, 48
Wipplinger, Jonathan, 108
Wirth, Uwe, 122
Womack, Ytasha, 232
women: in archive, 55; Black German, 181–86, 233; Black motherhood, 101–2, 113n5; humor and, 127; Turkish, 178–81. See also misogyny; sexual violence
women's movement, 7–8. See also feminism
Wong, Anna May, 177

Wright, Michelle, 15, 255

xenophobia, 2, 140, 172–74, 188, 189n4. See also anti-immigration discourse

Yasemin (1988), 180
Yeşilada, Karin, 11–12
Yeşilçam (Turkish film genre), 12, 176
Yildiz, Yasemin, 8, 11–12, 20
#YOLOCAUST, 166
Young, James, 164, 167

Young, Paul David, 138
Yu, Emily, 190n20
Yugoslavia, 251–54
Yurdakul, Gökçe, 11

Zaimoğlu, Feridun, 2, 8, 21, 78–93, 131; *Kanak Sprak*, 84–85, 91; *Moses* (with Senkel), 78–93
Zhao, DJ, 184
Zwagerman, Sean, 142n10

www.ingramcontent.com/pod-product-compliance
Lightning Source LLC
Chambersburg PA
CBHW051530020426
42333CB00016B/1860